Rogov's Guide to Israeli Wines
2006

Daniel Rogov

ROGOV'S GUIDE TO ISRAELI WINES

2006

The Toby Press

First Edition 2005
The Toby Press LLC

POB 8531, New Milford, CT 06776-8531, USA
& POB 2455, London W1A 5WY, England

www.tobypress.com

ISBN 1 59264 128 8, *hardcover*

A CIP catalogue record for this title is
available from the British Library

Typeset in Chaparral by Jerusalem Typesetting

Printed in Israel

Table of Contents

FOREWORD vii

How to Use the Guide viii
    Key to Symbols and Scores viii

INTRODUCTION 1

The History of Wine in Israel 1
    Ancient Times 1
    Modern Times 4
    The Israeli Wine Revolution 6

The Current and Future State of Wine Production in
Israel 7

The Phenomenon of the Boutique Wineries 9

The Future of the Golan 9

Grape Growing Regions . . . , , , , ... 10

Grape Varieties in Israel 13
    White Wine Grapes 14
    Red Wine Grapes 16

Vintage Reports: 1976–2003 19
    The Last Five Years 20
    Somewhat Older Vintages 21

Questions of Kashrut 21
    Some Israeli Wines are Kosher, Others are Not 22
    What Makes an Israeli Wine Kosher? 22
    The Question of Wines that are *Mevushal* 23

A Few Lists 24
    The Ten Best Wine Producers 24
    Ten New or Up-and-Coming Producers 25
    The Ten Fastest Improving Producers 25

The Ten Best Wines Released in the Last Twelve Months 25

Drinking Habits 26
   Within Israel 26
   Sacramental versus "Wine Culture". 27
   Within the "Jewish World" 27
   Israel as a Potential Supplier of "Niche Wines" 28

THE WINERIES AND THEIR WINES 29

AFTERWORD 347

Sparkling wines. 347
   How to open a bottle of sparkling wine 348

A Guide to Tasting Wines 349
   Basic Rules for tasting wines 349
   Wine Appreciation 351

How I Do My Wine Tastings 354

Several Words about Scores 356

GLOSSARY OF WINE TERMINOLOGY. 359

CONTACTING THE WINERIES 367

INDEX 381

ABOUT THE AUTHOR 383

Foreword

Israeli wines from the 2004 vintage are now making their way to market, and despite a year of cold weather and heavy rains, many of those wines are proving to be of enviably high quality. No less important, 2004 and 2005 are proving to be years in which Israeli wineries continue to make unprecedented debuts and receiving glowing reviews in venues as diverse in character as Bordeaux, London, Moscow, New York and London.

The days when Israel was primarily producing sweet red wines for sacramental purposes are now long gone, and today Israel is acknowledged as a serious wine producer. Wines are being made from highly prized grape varieties at more than 140 wineries scattered all over the country, from the Upper Galilee and the Golan Heights to the Judean Hills and the Negev Desert. The construction of state-of-the-art wineries, the ongoing import and cultivation of good vine stock from California and France, experimentation with new wine varieties and blends, and the enthusiasm and knowledge of young, well-trained winemakers has enabled the production of quality wines that can compete comfortably with the finest wines of the New World.

The purpose of this book is to provide readers with extensive knowledge about the wineries and wines of Israel, and to serve as a convenient guide for selecting and storing local wines. The introduction supplies the reader with the necessary historical and geographical background, while the major part of the guide is devoted to the wines, offering tasting notes and scores for wines that are now on the shelves or scheduled to appear within the next six to nine months, as well as wines that are still stored in the cellars of wine lovers.

How to Use the Guide

Wineries are arranged in the book by alphabetical order and in the few cases where wineries may be known by more than one name, especially outside of Israel, readers will find the alternative names listed in the index. Following a brief description of the location, history and production of each winery are the reviews, from the top-level series to the lower. Each series is arrayed from red wines to whites, and then sparkling and dessert wines. These are further divided into grape varieties such as Cabernet Sauvignon, Merlot, etc. Each variety is arranged according to vintage years, from the most current release to the most mature available, and each review concludes with a score and a suggested drinking window.

Key to Symbols and Scores

THE WINERIES

***** A world-class winery, regularly producing excellent wines

**** Consistently producing high-quality wines

*** Solid and reliable producer with at least some good wines

** Adequate

* Hard to recommend

SCORES FOR INDIVIDUAL WINES

96–100	Truly great wines
90–95	Exceptional in every way
85–89	Very good to excellent and highly recommended
80–84	Recommended but without enthusiasm
70–79	Average but at least somewhat faulted
Under 70	Not recommended

Special Note about Tentative Scores:
The scores of wines tasted only from the barrel, that is to say, well before release, are scored within a range and noted as *tentative*. Wines attaining such scores will be retasted and updated in future editions.

DRINKING WINDOWS

A drinking window is the suggested period during which the wine is at its very best. The notation "best 2007–2012" indicates that the wine needs further cellaring before it comes to its peak and will then cellar comfortably through 2012. "Drink now–2012" indicates that although the wine is drinking well now it will continue to cellar nicely until 2012. "Drink now" indicates that the wine is drinking well now but can be held for a year or so, and "drink up" suggests that the wine is at or past its peak and should not be cellared any longer. "Drink from release" refers to wines that are not yet on the market but will appear within the coming nine months.

KOSHER WINES

That there is no contradiction between making fine wine and the kosher laws is made apparent in the introduction to this guide. Within the guide, the reviews of all wines that have received a kashrut certificate from a recognized rabbinic authority are followed by the symbol K.

Introduction

The History of Wine in Israel

Ancient Times

The history of wine in the land of Israel is as old as the history of the people who have inhabited that land over the centuries. As early as five thousand years ago people cultivated vines and made, stored and shipped wines. The first mention of wine in the Bible is in a reference to Noah, who is said to have planted the first vineyard and to have become intoxicated when he drank his wine (Genesis 9:20–21). Another well known reference concerns the spies sent out by Moses to explore the land of Canaan. They returned after their mission with a cluster of grapes said to have been so large and heavy that it had to be borne on a carrying frame (Numbers 13:23). The vine is also mentioned as one of the blessings of the good land promised to the children of Israel (Deuteronomy 8:8).

The Bible lists the necessary steps to care for a vineyard:

> My beloved had a vineyard in a very fruitful hill;
> And he digged it; and cleared it of stones,
> And planted it with the choicest vine,
> And built a tower in the midst of it,
> And also hewed out a vat therein;
> And he looked that it should bring forth grapes.
> He broke the ground, cleared it of stone and planted
>   it with choice vines.
> He built a watchtower inside it,
> He even hewed a wine press inside it.
>
> *(Isaiah 5: 1–2)*

Vintners in ancient times knew as we do today that locating vineyards at higher altitudes and thus in areas with greater temperature changes between night and day would cause the fruit to ripen more slowly, adding to the sweetness of the fruit and its ability to produce fine wines. Two ways of growing vines were known then; in one the vines being allowed to grow along the ground, and in the other being trained upward on trellises (Ezekiel 17:6–8). It was widely accepted then as today that vines cultivated by the second method almost always produce superior grapes.

Remains of ancient wine presses may be found today in all parts of the Land of Israel, from the Galilee to Jerusalem and the Negev Desert. In nearly every part of Israel, archeologists have discovered hundreds of jars for storing and transporting wine. Many of the amphorae uncovered indicate in detail where and by whom the wine was made, as well as the year of the vintage, this showing that even in antiquity the source of the grapes and the quality of the harvest were considered important.

It is known today that even during the Bronze age, Egyptian Pharaohs enjoyed wines that were shipped from Canaan. The growing of grapes and the production of wine was a major agricultural endeavor during the period of the first and second Temples, and the kings of Judah and Israel were said to have owned large vineyards as well as VAst stores of wine. The vineyards and stores of King David in particular were so numerous that he is said to have appointed two officials, one to be in charge of the vineyards, and the other to be charge of storage.

In biblical times the harvest was a celebratory period as well as a period of courtship. The treading of the grapes was done most often on a *gat* or an *arevah*, the *gat* being a small, generally square pressing floor that had been cut into bedrock, and the *arevah* a smaller treading surface that could be moved from vineyard to vineyard. From either of these the must (that is to say, the fresh and as yet unfermented grape juice) ran into a *yekev*, which was a vat for collecting the must as it flowed from the treading floor through a hole carved in the stone. When natural bedrock was unavailable, an earthen treading surface lined with mosaics was used.

In several areas, caves or large cisterns carved from natural bedrock have been found, which would have served two purposes—first for storing the grapes until they were pressed and then, because they were cool and dark, for storing the wine while it fermented and then aged in clay jugs.

Once fermentation had been completed, the wines were stored in pottery vessels which were sealed with wood, stone or clay stoppers. For purposes of shipping, the stoppers were wrapped in cloth and coated with clay. Since new clay vessels tend to absorb as much as 20 percent of the wines stored in them, it became common practice to store better wines in older jars. A major development, during the third century BCE was the discovery that stoppers made from cork were an effective way to seal amphorae.

As much as these wines were prized, it must be understood that they were very different from wines as we know them today. They were often so intense and coarse that they needed a fair amount of "adjustment" before they were considered drinkable. To improve the bouquet, the Romans were known to add spices and scents to their wines. To make the wine sweeter, they added a syrup made by heating grape juice in lead containers for a long period over a low flame, and to improve flavors and hide faults it was customary to add honey, pepper, chalk, gypsum, lime, resin, herbs and even sea water.

In the time of the first and second Temples, wine was widely consumed by the local populace, but the very best wines were set aside for libations in the Temple. The Bible specified the different types of offerings—a quarter of a *hin* (one *hin* was the equivalent of about 5.7 liters or 1.5 gallons) of wine when offering a sheep; a third of a *hin* for a ram; and half a *hin* for an animal from the herd such as a cow (Numbers 15:5). In addition, people were required to give tithes of new wine to the Temple (Deuteronomy 12:17). Wines were so central to the culture during the days of the first and second Temples that those who planted vineyards were exempt from military service, and illustrations of grapes, grape leaves, amphorae and drinking vessels were often used as symbols on seals and coins as well as for decorations on the friezes of buildings.

Later, after the destruction of the second Temple, wine was integrated into all religious ceremonies including *brit milah* (circumcision), weddings, the Sabbath and high holidays, and is especially central in the Passover *seder* where it is customary to drink four glasses of wine.

Through the fourth to six centuries, during the late Roman and Byzantine periods, the wine industry shifted from Judea to the southern part of the land, where the port towns Ashkelon and Gaza became centers of wine trading. Those wines were so coveted by the Romans that they shipped them to their legions throughout the Mediterranean and North Africa, and Christian pilgrims brought them back to Europe.

The Moslem conquest of the Holy Land in the seventh century put an end to this prosperous industry. The Moslem rulers banned the drinking of alcohol and as a result the flourishing local wine industry almost ceased to exist. The only wines allowed were the small amounts that Christians and Jews required for sacramental use. Attempts were made by the Crusaders in the twelfth and thirteenth centuries to revive the wine industry in the Holy Land but these were short-lived, since they realized it would be easier to ship wines from Europe. It was only with the renewal of Jewish settlement in the nineteenth century that the local wine-making industry was reestablished.

Modern Times

The Jewish philanthropist Sir Moses Montefiore, who visited the Holy Land in the nineteenth century, encouraged the Jews living there to work the land and replant vines. One person who listened to his call was Rabbi Itzhak Schorr, who founded a new winery in Jerusalem in 1848. Rabbi Abraham Teperberg founded the Efrat winery in 1870 in the old city of Jerusalem, as well as an agricultural school in Mikveh Israel, not far from Jaffa. This school was financed and run by *Alliance Israelite Universelle*, a Jewish organization based in France that aimed at training Jewish settlers in agricultural work. The school was the first to plant European grape varieties, and had a winery as well as large wine cellars. Many of its graduates became vine growers.

An important boost to the local industry came about when Baron Edmond de Rothschild, the owner of the famed Chateau Lafite in Bordeaux, agreed to come to the help of the Jewish colonies, and financed the planting of the first vineyards near Rishon Letzion in the coastal plain. Rothschild hoped that the Holy Land would serve as the source of kosher wines for Jews the world over, and that the wine industry would provide a solid economic basis for the new Jewish communities. He brought in experts from Europe and imported grape varieties from the south of France including Alicante, Bouchet, Clairette, Carignan, Grenache, Muscat and Semillon. Rothschild funded the first wineries of the Jewish settlements—in 1882 the Rishon Letzion Winery, and in 1890 the Zichron Ya'akov winery in the Mount Carmel area, thus marking the beginning of the modern wine industry in the Land of Israel. Unfortunately, not all ran smoothly. The first harvests were lost to heat and in 1890–91 the land was overrun by phylloxera, a plague of aphid-like insects that destroyed all of the vines. The vineyards were dug up, and replanted with vines grafted onto phylloxera-resistant root stocks.

In 1906 Rothschild helped to set up a cooperative of grape growers that managed the two wineries, and in 1957 sold his share to the cooperative. It took the name Carmel Mizrachi, and continued to dominate the wine industry of the country well until the early 1980s. Rothschild's dream that viticulture would provide a major source of income for the region had been shattered with the advent of three major events—the Russian revolution, the enactment of Prohibition in the United States, and the banning of imported wines to Egypt, those virtually eliminating the fledgling industry's three largest potential markets and causing many vineyards to be uprooted. Still, in the following decades several new wineries opened, including Segal, Eliaz and Stock, but for the most part they and Carmel continued to produce wines largely destined for sacramental purposes. The 1948 records testifying to the annual consumption of a mere 3.9 liters of wine per person showed that wine had not yet become part of the culture of life in Israel.

The Israeli Wine Revolution

In 1972, Professor Cornelius Ough of the Department of Viticulture and Oenology at the University of California at Davis visited Israel and suggested that the soil and climate of the Golan Heights would prove ideal for the raising of grapes. In 1976 the first vines were planted in the Golan, and in 1983 the then newly established Golan Heights Winery released its first wines. Almost overnight it became apparent that Israel was capable of producing wines of world-class quality. During the early 1980s the Israeli wine industry endured an economic crisis, but the revolution had begun and there was no turning back.

Unfettered by outdated winemaking traditions or by a large stagnant corporate structure, the young winery imported excellent vine stock from California, built a state-of-the-art winery, and added to this the enthusiasm and knowledge of young American winemakers who had been trained at the University of California at Davis. Equally important, the Golan winery began to encourage vineyard owners to improve the quality of their grapes and, in the American tradition, paid bonuses for grapes with high sugar and acid content and rejected those grapes they perceived as substandard. The winery was also the first to realize that wines made from Grenache, Semillon, Petite Sirah and Carignan grapes would not put them on the world wine map, and focused on planting and making wines from Cabernet Sauvignon, Merlot, Sauvignon Blanc, Chardonnay, white Riesling, Gewurztraminer and other such noble grape varieties.

The Golan wines were a success from the beginning not only within Israel but abroad. This success had a great impact on other Israeli wineries, which have made major steps in improving the quality of their wines. There are now five major wineries, twelve medium-sized wineries and a host of small wineries in the country, many of which are producing wines that are of high quality, and several producing wines good enough to interest connoisseurs all over the world.

The Current and Future State of Wine Production in Israel

Specific data about the local wine industry is difficult to come by due to lack of coordination between the Israeli Wine Institute, the Ministry of Agriculture, the Export Institute and the Grape Grower's Association. When wineries submit their production and export figures, for example, they make no distinction between exports of table wines, sacramental wines, grape juice and even brandy and liqueurs. It is estimated that today Israel produces about thirty-six million bottles of table wine a year, that amount representing continued growth over the last five years of five to ten percent annually. Approximately forty thousand dunams (twenty thousand acres) of land are currently under grape cultivation, an increase of fifty percent in cultivated land area since 1995. Approximately sixty percent of the table wines produced today are dry reds, while as recently as 1995 production was seventy percent whites and only thirty percent reds.

Following an extended period in which the imagination of the wine-drinking public within Israel was captured by boutique wineries and garagistes, the years between 2003–05 might be regarded as the years during which the larger wineries re-captured the imagination of wine lovers. In 2003, the Golan Heights Winery released the country's first varietal wines made from Sangiovese, Pinot Noir and Gamay grapes, as well as the country's first single-vineyard organically grown Chardonnay. Under its Yarden label, the winery also produced the country's first Semillon-botrytis wine. During that same year, Carmel released the first wines from its new boutique winery Yatir, and has continued to give us exciting single-vineyard Cabernet Sauvignon, Syrah and Chardonnay wines. Barkan introduced the country's first Pinotage wine.

During 2005, Recanati released the country's first wine made from Barbera grapes and several of the medium-sized wineries gave us the country's first Zinfandel wines.

Although the Golan Heights Winery, with its Katzrin, Yarden, Gamla and Golan series' of wines, remains the obvious quality leader among the large wineries in the country, a great deal of excitement continues to be generated by Carmel. During the three years of David Ziv's tenure as chief executive officer of the winery it became apparent that Carmel, the largest producer in the country, had made major steps forward. In addition to bringing aboard young and well-trained winemakers and modernizing its wineries at Rishon Letzion and Zichron Ya'akov, the company continues to develop new vineyards and has made progress in gaining better control over the vineyards of the many independent growers associated with the cooperative. In those vineyards, poor clones of Petite Sirah, Carignan, French Colombard and Emerald Riesling are being replaced by Syrah, Zinfandel, Sangiovese and Barbera. At the same time, in order to enhance quality, yields in vineyards producing Cabernet Sauvignon, Merlot, Chardonnay and Sauvignon Blanc have been reduced dramatically.

Despite such positive steps, the major wineries still face several potential problems. Ziv's revolution at Carmel was not appreciated by all, with many grape growers taking a short-sighted attitude and demanding that Carmel accept any grapes they produce, regardless of quality. As a result, the board of directors of Carmel, controlled by the vintners, forced Ziv to retire in May 2005 and now many fear his dismissal may indicate that Carmel will lose many of the accomplishments of recent years and regress to the days when it produced largely mediocre wines. Moreover, several years of overplanting (from 1998–2002), including grapes that held no hope for producing fine wines, led to a grape glut. To that one can add the unsettling political and economical situation following the Intifada years, resulting in a consumer attitude that is still largely motivated by value for money.

The Phenomenon of the Boutique Wineries

In recent years, the country has seen a dramatic growth in boutique wineries, garagistes, micro-wineries and artisanal producers, each striving to produce world-class wines. Such wineries, producing anywhere from under a thousand to up to one hundred thousand bottles annually, can remain highly personalized affairs, the winemakers having full control over their vineyards, knowing precisely what wine is in what barrel at any given moment and what style they want their wines to reflect. The label of a boutique winery does not, however, guarantee quality. At the top end of the range, a handful of small wineries founded by competent, well-trained professionals are producing some of the very best wines in the country. At the bottom end are numerous wineries founded by hobbyists who produce wines that are barely acceptable.

Many local boutique wineries, continuing to grow but feeling they may have peaked in their local sales, are now seeking to export their wines. In addition to the attempts of individual wineries, Carmel has taken a group of boutique wineries under its wing for foreign promotion, including Amphorae, Castel, Tzora, Bazelet Hagolan, Saslove, Hamasrek, Margalit, Flam, Yatir and Orna Chillag. This initiative, labled "Handcrafted Wines of Israel" has managed to penetrate some new markets but its economical viability has yet to be demonstrated. Several other such consortiums are now being finalized and some of the boutique wineries plan to grant distribution rights to more than one consortium.

The Future of the Golan

Although currently in a temporary stalemate, political developments in the region may mean that in the future all or part of the Golan Heights may revert to Syrian sovereignty. As a result, the Golan Heights Winery would have to give up the soil and microclimates of the Golan, which are essential for the production of fine grape varieties.

It is widely acknowledged that the volcanic basalt soil, relatively cool climate and the night–day temperature differentials of the Golan Heights are ideal for the production of premium quality wine grapes and that this region offers a diversity of microclimates broad enough to allow for the production of many different varieties of grapes. This does not, however, mean that other areas within Israel, especially the hills of the Galilee region, will not prove equally well suited to the raising of high quality grapes. Even now, for example, parts of the Upper Galilee, the Jerusalem Mountains and the Negev are producing some of the finest grapes in the country and many wineries have expanded their vineyards in those areas.

As to the future of the Golan Heights Winery itself, some continue to hope that even after a peace treaty with Syria the winery will be allowed to continue raising grapes there. Considering that Moslem law prohibits the raising of grapes for the purpose of making wine, this is a question that remains to be answered. Even if this is not the case however, it is already known that the winery currently receives some of its finest grapes from the Galilee. Moreover, the Golan Heights Winery's partnership with the Galilee Mountain winery in the Upper Galilee indicates that they are exploring alternatives for the future.

Grape Growing Regions

The ideal areas for the cultivation of wine grapes lie in the two strips between 30–50 degrees north and south of the Equator. Israel, which is located on the southern side of that strip in the Northern Hemisphere, is thus ideally situated. Considering Israel's specific climate, it is important to note that the vine can thrive in many different types of soil, and can thrive in regions that receive little rainfall.

Although the land area of Israel is a mere 7,992 square miles (which is five percent of the land area of California), like many wine-growing nations or regions that have a long north-south axis (Italy, Chile or California, for example), the country has a large variety of microclimates. In the north, snow falls in winter and conditions are comparable to those of Bordeaux and the Northern Rhone Valley of France, yet

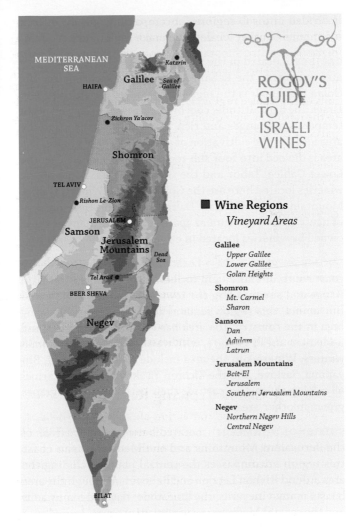

MEDITERRANEAN
SEA

Katzrin

Galilee *Sea of Galilee*

HAIFA

Zichron Ya'acov

Shomron

TEL AVIV

Rishon Le-Zion

JERUSALEM

Samson

Jerusalem
Mountains

Dead Sea

Tel Arad

BEER SHEVA

Negev

EILAT

ROGOV'S
GUIDE
TO
ISRAELI
WINES

■ **Wine Regions**
 Vineyard Areas

Galilee
 Upper Galilee
 Lower Galilee
 Golan Heights

Shomron
 Mt. Carmel
 Sharon

Samson
 Dan
 Adulam
 Latrun

Jerusalem Mountains
 Beit-El
 Jerusalem
 Southern Jerusalem Mountains

Negev
 Northern Negev Hills
 Central Negev

within a few hours' drive one arrives at the Negev Desert,
where the climate is similar to that of North Africa.

The country is divided into five vine-growing regions,
the names of which are generally accepted by the European
Community and appear on all labels of varietal wines that
are designated for sale both locally and abroad. Each region

is divided into sub-regions, encompassing specific valleys, mountains or other locales. The major regions are:

GALILEE: Located in the northern part of the country, this area extends to the Lebanese border and incorporates the Golan Heights. It is the region most suited for viticulture in Israel. The high altitude, cool breezes, marked day and night temperature changes and rich, well-drained soils make the area ideal for the cultivation of a large variety of grapes. The area is divided into four sub-regions: the Upper Galilee, the Lower Galilee, Tabor and the Golan Heights. Some of the wineries located here are the Golan Heights Winery, Galilee Mountain, Chateau Golan, Dalton and Tabor. Development of new vineyards continues apace in the area, many of these owned by wineries located in other parts of the country.

SHOMRON (SAMARIA): Located near the Mediterranean coast south of Haifa, and including the Carmel Mountain Range and surrounding the towns of Zichron Ya'akov and Binyamina, this region remains the largest grape growing area in the country. The area has medium-heavy soils and a Mediterranean climate, with warm summers and humid winters. Wineries in the area include Margalit, Tishbi, Binyamina, Saslove, and the Zichron Ya'akov branch of Carmel, all relying at least in part for their better wines on grapes grown in other areas.

SHIMSHON (SAMSON): Located between the foothills of the Jerusalem Mountains and the Mediterranean coast, this region encompasses the central plains including the area around Rishon Letzion and Rehovot. Although the area boasts many vineyards, the limestone, clay and loamy soils and the coastal Mediterranean climate of warm, humid summers and mild winters do not offer ideal conditions for the cultivation of fine varieties, and many of the wineries in the area rely on grapes from other parts of the country. Among the wineries located here are Carmel, Barkan, Karmei Yosef, Flam and Soreq.

JERUSALEM MOUNTAINS: Sometimes referred to as the

Judean Hills, this region surrounding the city of Jerusalem offers a variety of soil conditions and a cool Mediterranean climate due to its relatively high altitude. For many years the region served as home primarily to wineries that specialized in sweet sacramental wines, but about a decade ago it became clear that this area could prove excellent for raising noble varieties. The area underwent strenuous revitalization with the major planting of sophisticated vineyards and the opening of several medium-sized and an increasing number of small wineries. Among the wineries found in the area are Castel, Clos de Gat, Sea Horse, Tzora and Efrat.

NEGEV: Ten years ago, few would have thought this semi-arid desert region appropriate for growing grapes, but now, sophisticated computerized drip-irrigation systems have made it possible to grow high quality grapes here, including among others Merlot, Cabernet Sauvignon and Chardonnay. The region is divided into two sub-areas: Ramat Arad, which is situated 600–700 meters above sea level and has impressive night-day temperature changes, and where results with noble varieties has been excellent; and the Southern Negev, a lower, more arid area where sandy to loamy soils and very hot and dry summers offer a special challenge to grape growers. Carmel was the first to plant extensive vineyards at Ramat Arad. More recently, Barkan has begun extensive development of vineyards at Mitzpe Ramon in the heart of the Negev. Among the wineries found here, some rely entirely on desert-raised grapes. Others that draw as well on grapes from other areas are Yatir and Sde Boker.

Grape Varieties in Israel

The last two decades have seen a major upheaval in the vineyards of Israel. Prior to 1985 the grapes planted were largely Carignan, Petite Sirah and Grenache for red and rosé wines, and Semillon, Emerald Riesling, and Colombard for whites. The wineries focused on light, white and often sweet wines, and only a handful of noble varieties were to be found in the country. The scene shifted dramatically with the development of vineyards planted with noble varieties, first on the Golan Heights, then in the Upper Galilee. Today, from the Negev Desert to the northernmost parts of the country, the focus is on many of those varieties that have proven themselves throughout the world.

Unlike many of the wine-growing regions, especially in Europe, Israel does not have any indigenous grapes that might be considered appropriate for making wine. The closest the country came to having its own grape was the introduction of the Argaman grape, a cross between Souzao and Carignan grapes. Widely planted in the early 1980s, that experiment proved a failure; although the grape yielded wines deep in color, they lacked flavor, depth or body. In the list that follows, those grapes capable of producing quality wines in Israel are noted with an asterisk (*).

White Wine Grapes

CHARDONNAY: The grape that produces the great dry white wines of Burgundy and is indispensable to the production of Champagne. The most popular white wine grape in the world today, producing wines that can be oaked or un-oaked, and range in flavors from flinty-minerals to citrus, pineapple, tropical fruits and grapefruit, and in texture from minerally-crisp to creamy. (*)

CHENIN BLANC: Originating in France's central Loire Valley, this thin-skinned and acidic grape has a high sugar content that can give aromas and flavors of honey and damp straw. Within Israel the grape has largely produced wines best categorized as ordinary, and often semi-dry.

COLOMBARD: Known in Israel as French Colombard and producing mostly thin and acidic wines.

EMERALD RIESLING: A cross between the Muscadelle and Riesling grapes developed in California primarily for growth in warm climates, the grape produces mostly semi-dry wines of little interest.

GEWURZTRAMINER: This grape originated in Germany,

came to its glory in Alsace and has now been transplanted to many parts of the world. Capable of producing aromatic dry and sweet wines that are often typified by their softness and spiciness, as well as distinctive aromas and flavors of litchis and rose petals. (*)

MUSCAT: There are many varieties of Muscat, the two most often found in Israel being the Muscat of Alexandria and Muscat Canelli, both of which are capable of producing wines that range from the dry to the sweet and are almost always typified by their perfumed aromas.

RIESLING: Sometimes known in Israel as Johannisberg Riesling, sometimes as White Riesling and sometimes simply at Riesling, this noble German variety has the potential to produce wines that although light in body and low in alcohol are highly flavored and capable of long aging. Typified by aromas and flavors of flowers, minerals, lime, and when aged, sometimes taking on a tempting petrol-like aroma. (*)

SAUVIGNON BLANC: At its best in the Loire Valley and Bordeaux for producing dry white wines, this successful transplant to Israel is capable of producing refreshing, sophisticated and distinctively aromatic and grassy wines, often best consumed in their youth. (*)

SEMILLON: Although this native French grape was used for many years in Israel to produce largely uninteresting semi-dry white wines, its susceptibility to noble rot is now being taken advantage of to produce sweet dessert wines with the distinctive bouquet and flavors of melon, fig and citrus. (*)

TRAMINETTE: A not overly exciting hybrid, a derivative of the Gewurztraminer grape, developed primarily for use in cold weather New York State and Canadian climates.

VIOGNIER: The most recent white wine transplant to Israel, this grape produces the fascinating Condrieu wines of France's Rhone Valley. Capable of producing aromatic but crisply dry whites and full-bodied whites, some of which have long aging potential. (*)

Red Wine Grapes

ARGAMAN: An Israeli-inspired cross between Souzao and Carignan grapes. Possibly best categorized as the great local wine failure, producing wines of no interest. Many of the vineyards that were planted with Argaman continue to be uprooted to make room for more serious varieties.

BARBERA: From Italy's Piedmont region, this grape has the potential for producing wines that although light and fruity are capable of great charm. (*)

BERLINKA: A table grape imported from South Africa and used in Israel to make wines that lack interest.

CABERNET SAUVIGNON: The most noble variety of Bordeaux, capable of producing superb wines, often blended with smaller amounts of Merlot and Cabernet Franc. The best wines from this grape are rich in color and tannins, and have complex aromas and depth of flavors, those often typified by blackcurrants, spices and cedar wood. At their best, intriguing and complex wines that profit from cellaring. (*)

CABERNET FRANC: Less intense and softer than Cabernet Sauvignon, most often destined to be blended with Merlot and Cabernet Sauvignon, but even on its own capable of producing dramatically good, leafy, fruity and aromatic reds. (*)

CARIGNAN: An old-timer on the Israeli scene, this originally Spanish grape produces largely dull and charmless wines. Still commonly planted within Israel but increasingly destined for distillation in the making of brandy and liqueurs.

GAMAY: The well-known grape of France's Beaujolais region, this fairly recent introduction to Israel is capable of producing light to medium-bodied wines of fragrance and charm, intended primarily for drinking in their youth. (*)

GRENACHE: Although this grape has done well in France's Rhone Valley and Spain, it has not yielded sophisticated wines in Israel, most being somewhat pale, overripe and sweet in nature. Probably at its best for blending.

MALBEC: Well known in France's Bordeaux, the Loire and Cahors, this grape is capable of producing dense, rich, tannic and spicy wines that are remarkably dark in color. (*)

MERLOT: Softer, more supple and often less tannic than Cabernet Sauvignon, with which it is often blended, but capable of producing voluptuous, opulent, plummy wines of great interest. A grape that has proven popular on its own as it produces wines that are easier to drink and are approachable earlier than wines made from Cabernet Sauvignon. (*)

NEBBIOLO: The grape from which the Barolo and Barbaresco wines of Italy's Piedmont region are made. Still experimental in Israel but with the potential for producing perfumed, fruity and intense wines that are full-bodied, high in tannins, acidity and color, and have the potential for long-term cellaring. (*)

PETIT VERDOT: Planted only in small quantities and used in Israel as it is in Bordeaux, primarily for blending with other noble varieties to add acidity and balance. Capable on its own of producing a long lived and tannic wine when ripe. (*)

PETITE SIRAH: Related only peripherally to the great Syrah grape, this grape at its best is capable of producing dark, tannic and well-balanced wines of great appeal and sophistication, but that potential has been obtained only once or twice in Israel, the grape being used too often to produce mass-market wines that tend to be hot, tannic and without charm. A few small wineries manage to obtain excellent wines from this variety but in general it is rapidly losing its popularity as a more sophisticated drinking audience turns to more noble varieties.

PINOT NOIR: A relatively recent transplant to Israel, this grape, which is responsible for the great reds of Burgundy, is making a very good initial showing. At its best the grape is capable of producing smooth, rich and intricate wines of exquisite qualities, with flavors of cherries, wild berries and violets and, as they age, take on aromas and flavors of chocolate and game meat. Also used in Israel, as in the Champagne region of France, to blend with Chardonnay to make sparkling wines. (*)

PINOTAGE: A South African cross between Pinot Noir and Cinsault, capable of being flavorful and powerful, yet soft and full, with a pleasing sweet finish and a lightly spicy overlay. (*)

SANGIOVESE: Italy's most frequently planted variety, found in the simplest Chianti and most complex Brunello di Montalcino wines, this is another grape recently introduced to Israel, showing fine early results with wines that are lively, fruity and full of charm. (*)

SYRAH: Some believe that this grape originated in ancient Persia and was brought to France by the Romans, while others speculate that it is indigenous to France. Syrah found its first glory in France's northern Rhone Valley, and then in Australia (where it is known as Shiraz). Capable of producing deep royal purple tannic wines that are full-bodied enough to be thought of as dense and powerful, but with excellent balance and complex aromas and flavors of plums, berries, currants, black pepper and chocolate. First results from this grape have been exciting and plantings are increasing dramatically. (*)

TEMPRANILLO: The staple grape of Spain's Rioja area, with recent plantings in Israel, this is a grape with the potential for producing long-lived complex and sophisticated wines typified by aromas and flavors of black fruits, leather, tobacco and spices. (*)

ZINFANDEL: Zinfandel is not exactly new in Israel, but until recently the vines that had been planted were capable of producing only mediocre semi-dry blush wines. What is new are recently planted high-quality vines from California that offer the potential for producing full-bodied to massive wines, moderately to highly alcoholic, with generous tannins and the kind of warm berry flavors that typify these wines at their best. (*)

Vintage Reports: 1976–2003

The first formal vintage tables appeared in the 1820s and since then wine lovers have relied on them to help make their buying and drinking decisions. As popular as they are, however, it is important to remember that because all vintage tables involve generalizations, there are no firm facts to be found in them. In a sense, these charts are meant to give an overall picture and perhaps to supply clues about which wines to consider buying or drinking. In making one's decisions it is wise to remember that the quality of wines of any vintage year and in any region can vary enormously between wineries. Also worth keeping in mind is that vintage reports and tables such as those that follow are based on what most people consider "quality wines" and not those made for everyday drinking and thus not intended for aging. More than this, estimates of drinkability are based on wines that have been shipped and stored under ideal conditions.

Following are short reports on the last five vintage years, these followed by a listing of the years of interest going back to 1976. Vintage years are rated on a scale of 20–100, and these numerical values can be interpreted as follows:

100 = Extraordinary
90 = Exceptional
80 = Excellent
70 = Very Good
60 = Good But Not Exciting
50 = Average But With Many Faulted Wines
40 = Mediocre/Not Recommended
30 = Poor/Not Recommended
20 = Truly Bad/Not Recommended

The following symbols are used to indicate drinking windows (Predictions of drinking windows are based on ideal storage since the wine was released.):
C = Worthy of Cellaring
D/C = Drink or Cellar
D = Drink Now or in the Next Year or So

D– = Past Its Prime But Probably Still Drinkable
SA = Well Beyond Its Prime and Probably Undrinkable

The Last Five Years

2004 VINTAGE Rating 88

Colder than average temperatures and heavy rainfall during the winter months followed by an unusually warm and dry period during March and April caused early budbreak in warmer vineyards. Relatively cool temperatures returned in May leading to a relatively short and hectic harvest but with an overall excellent crop. A very promising year. C

2003 VINTAGE Rating 90

A cold and wet winter with precipitation about one third higher than normal was followed by unusually warm weather in May, leading to strong and rapid shoot growth and a hectic month of shoot positioning. Due to moderate and stable summer temperatures, harvest was stretched out to 17 weeks, concluding on November 18th. Overall, an excellent vintage year for both reds and whites. C

2002 VINTAGE Rating 82

In the north of the country the warm weather in February and March followed by a particularly cold spell in April and May stretched out the ripening season and resulted in an extended 15-week harvest. May rains during blooming caused a 15% reduction to yields. In the rest of the country several prolonged hot spells caused some vineyards to lose as much as 80% of their crop. Overall, only few acceptable wines and fewer appropriate for long-term cellaring. D/C

2001 VINTAGE Rating 85

This was one of the earliest harvest years in recent history. Not an exciting year, but overall, a better year for reds than whites. D

2000 VINTAGE Rating 89

Fortunately the harvest was on schedule, as torrential rains hit the area just after the picking. Had the crop been delayed, it would have been under the coldest and wettest conditions for the past quarter century. Whites and reds fared equally well during this good vintage. D/C

Somewhat Older Vintages

1999	86	D/C
1998	85	D/C
1997	90	D/C
1996	82	D–
1995	90	D–
1994	84	SA
1993	92	D/C
1992	85	SA
1991	82	SA
1990	91	D
1989	90	SA
1988	85	SA
1987	78	SA
1986	76	SA
1985	90	SA
1984	86	SA
1983	55	SA
1982	55	SA
1979	92	SA
1976	92	SA

Questions of Kashrut

For many years, wines that were kosher had a justifiably bad name, those in the United States being made largely from Concord grapes, which are far from capable of making fine wine, and many of those from Israel following the perceived need for kosher wines to be red, sweet, coarse and without any sign of sophistication. The truth is that those wines were not so much consumed by knowledgeable wine lovers as they were used for sacramental purposes. Such wines are still made but are today perceived largely as oddities, and with kosher wines now being made from the most noble grape varieties in state-of-the-art wineries by talented winemakers, composition of the wine so that it was considered unfit for pagan worship. Wines that are *mevushal* have the advantage that they can be opened and poured by non-Jews or Jews who are not Sabbath observant.

Today, *mevushal* wines are no longer boiled. After the grapes are crushed, the common practice is to rapidly raise the temperature of the liquids to 176–194 degrees Fahrenheit (80–90 Celsius) in special flash pasteurizing units, hold it there for under a minute and then return the temperature, equally rapidly, to 60 degrees Fahrenheit (15 Celsius).

There is no question but that modern technology has reduced the impact of these processes on the quality of the wine, but most winemakers and consumers remain in agreement that, with very few exceptions, wines that have been pasteurized lose many of their essential essences, often being incapable of developing in the bottle and quite often imparting a "cooked" sensation to the nose and palate.

Some wines are produced in both regular and *mevushal* versions, the *mevushal* editions destined for the export market or for the highly observant within Israel. Because it is almost impossible for anyone outside of the wineries to keep track of and taste all of those wines, no attempt is made within this book to report on such "double bottlings."

Simply stated, a wine that is *mevushal* is no more or less kosher than a wine that is not, and none of the better wines of Israel today fall into this category. Those who are concerned with such issues will find the information they require on either the front or rear labels of wines produced in the country.

A Few Lists

The Ten Best Wine Producers

1. Golan Heights Winery (Katzrin, Yarden, Gamla, Golan)
2. Castel
3. Flam
4. Margalit

5. Yatir
6. Galil Mountain
7. Saslove
8. Amphorae
9. Recanati
10. Carmel

Ten New or Up-and-Coming Producers

1. Clos de Gat
2. Chateau Golan
3. Ella Valley
4. Carmei Yosef (Bravdo)
5. Alexander
6. Gustavo & Jo
7. Bazelet ha Golan
8. Orna Chillag
9. Sea Horse Winery
10. Bustan

The Ten Fastest Improving Producers

1. Carmel
2. Barkan
3. Sea Horse
4. Tabor
5. Dalton
6. Zauberman
7. Gush Etzion
8. Segal
9. Tishbi
10. La Terra Promessa

The Ten Best Wines Released in the Last Twelve Months

Golan Heights Winery, Cabernet Sauvignon, Elrom Vineyard, Yarden, 2001

Golan Heights Winery, Merlot, Ortal Vineyard, Yarden, 2001

Carmel, Cabernet Sauvignon, Ramat Arad, 2002

Recanati, Special Reserve, 2001
Margalit, Cabernet Sauvignon, Special Reserve, 2002
Castel, Grand Vin Castel, 2001
Flam, Cabernet Sauvignon, Reserve, 2002
Yatir, Yatir Forest, 2002
Sea Horse, Elul, 2002
Amphorae, Cabernet Sauvignon, 2003

Drinking Habits

Within Israel

Since the founding of the state in 1948 and until 1997, annual Israeli wine consumption held steady at about 3.9 liters per capita. Recent years have seen a major increase, and consumption now stands at between 6.5 and 7 liters annually. This figure puts Israelis far behind the French and Italians, who consume 56 and 49 liters respectively, or even the Australians who consume 20 liters per year.

The increase in local consumption reflects of course the increasing quality of local wines, but at the same time it also reflects the fact that more and more Israelis are traveling abroad and dining in fine restaurants where wine is an integral part of the meal. Today many Israelis are touring the fine wineries of Bordeaux, Tuscany and the Napa Valley, and even though such wine appreciation is still limited to the upwardly mobile segment of the population, a vast proportion of the population will now order wine to accompany their meal in a fine restaurant.

In addition to showing a growing appreciation of wine in general, Israelis are moving in several directions that can be seen in many other countries as well. Consumption is shifting from semi-dry to dry wines, from whites to reds, from light to heavier wines and most important, there is a movement toward buying higher quality wines. Twenty-five years ago, more than eighty percent of the wines produced in the country were sweet. Today, nearly eighty percent of the wines produced are dry.

Israelis have also increased their consumption of imported

wines, and the better wine shops of the country stock wines from every region of France, Italy, Australia, New Zealand, California, Washington State, Spain, Portugal, Germany, Austria, Chile and Argentina. Some members of the local wine industry perceive the popularity of imported wines as having a negative impact on the local industry. Others, perhaps with a greater sense of foresight, realize that these imported wines pose a challenge to the local wine industry to continue to increase the quality of its products.

Sacramental versus "Wine Culture"

Within Israel, as in nearly every country with a Jewish population, some continue to drink wine entirely for sacramental purposes. An increasing number have realized that any kosher wine is appropriate for such purposes, but others hold to the perceived tradition that such wines should be red, thick and sweet. Although those wines hold no interest for sophisticated wine drinkers, several of the large wineries continue to produce "*kiddush* (the blessing over wine that begins the two main meals of the Sabbath and holidays) wines" and there are wineries that focus entirely on this audience.

Within the "Jewish World"

Nearly all of the better wine stores of the major cities of North America, the United Kingdom and France have at least a small section devoted to kosher wines, and in recent years the wines of Israel have taken a more prominent space on those shelves alongside kosher wines from California, France, Spain, Australia, Chile and Argentina. Israeli wines, both kosher and non-kosher, are receiving a warmer reception, now being reviewed more regularly in magazines devoted to wine as well as in the weekly wine columns of many critics, and also appearing on the menus of many prestigious restaurants.

Israel as a Potential Supplier of "Niche Wines"

Wine lovers enjoy few things more than hunting for previously unknown or little-known wines. So it has been in recent years, for example, with the wines of Sicily, and the Penedes region of Spain: when those wines first arrived on the shelves of wine stores in New York, London and Toronto, they filled an empty "niche." The first wines sold out quickly, those that proved to be of high quality were reordered, and those that came to be accepted as truly excellent moved out of the niche category and onto the regular shelves.

Many, including this critic, feel that Israeli wines are on the verge of being accepted, especially in North America and the United Kingdom, as niche wines. As that happens, the wines will move off those shelves limited only to kosher holdings and begin to appear in a special Israeli section. Their appeal to the broader population will come from their unique qualities, reflecting their Mediterranean and specifically Israeli source.

The Wineries and their Wines

For many years it was possible to group Israeli wine producers into one of two broad categories—large and small wineries. The last four years have seen dramatic changes, for during that time five new medium-sized producers have appeared on the local scene, several of the wineries that could be categorized as boutiques have expanded their production, and a host of small wineries continue to open. Within each category there are wineries that produce excellent and often exciting wines.

The wines reviewed in this guide include only those I have tasted. That includes wines already on the market, wines due to be released within the next several months, or those still in the cellars or homes of wine lovers. Not included in the guide are wineries whose target audience is those who drink wine only for sacramental purposes, as the vast majority of those wines hold no interest for any other than the members of that specific group. Ratings for wineries (1–5 stars) are based on current status and, especially with those that have released only one or two vintages, the ratings should be considered as tentative, being able to move up or down in the next edition of this guide.

Please note that the illustrations of wine labels in the book are representative only, and that not all the wines are illustrated.

Agur ***

Set on Moshav Agur in the Judean plains, this small winery, owned by winemaker Shuki Yashuv, has grown from releasing 1,800 bottles in the 2001 vintage to about 5,000 from 2004. The winery has its own vineyards in the Ella Valley with Cabernet Sauvignon and Merlot grapes. Grapes from each vineyard are fermented separately, some in stainless steel vats, others in new and used *barriques*.

Special Reserve

SPECIAL RESERVE, CABERNET SAUVIGNON, 2003: The best wine yet from this small winery. Dark ruby in color, medium to full-bodied, with still firm tannins that need time to integrate and reveal the generous aromas and flavors cassis, blackberries and spices waiting to unfold. Best starting in 2007. Tentative Score 87–89.

SPECIAL RESERVE, CABERNET SAUVIGNON, 2001: Deep garnet in color, this medium to full-bodied, firmly tannic and generously oaky wine offers up currant and berry fruits on a background of spices and Mediterranean herbs. Lacking in length and breadth. Drink now. Score 86.

Agur

AGUR, CABERNET SAUVIGNON, 2003: Medium to full-bodied, deep garnet in color, with near-sweet tannins, gentle wood and appealing currant, berry and herbal aromas and flavors. Drink now–2008. Score 86.

AGUR, CABERNET SAUVIGNON, 2002: A country-style wine, medium-bodied, with chunky tannins and appealing black fruit and herbal aromas and flavors. Not complex but pleasant. Drink now. Score 85.

AGUR, CABERNET SAUVIGNON, 2001: Deep ruby toward garnet in color, this medium-bodied blend of 95% Cabernet Sauvignon and 5% Merlot spent one year in new and older wood barrels. With somewhat chunky tannins, this country-style wine has a sweet herbal aroma along with currant and plum flavors. Drink up. Score 85.

AGUR, CABERNET SAUVIGNON-MERLOT, 2003: Medium-bodied, with good balance between country-style tannins, spicy wood and berry, black cherry and currant fruits. Drink now. Score 86.

AGUR, CABERNET SAUVIGNON-MERLOT, 2002: Deep ruby red, this light to medium-bodied blend of 60% Cabernet and 40% Merlot has youthful plum, berry, mineral and smoky oak aromas and flavors. Perhaps best when served lightly chilled. Drink up. Score 85.

AGUR, CABERNET-MERLOT, 2001: A perhaps too powerful toasty oak flavor imparts a chewy texture, but given a chance to open in the glass the wine yields appealing currant and berry fruits. Drink now. Score 85.

Alexander ★★★★

Founded in 1996 by Yoram Shalom and located on Moshav Beit Yitzhak in the Sharon region, the winery receives its grapes largely from several contract vineyards at Kerem Ben Zimra. Primary output to date has been of Cabernet Sauvignon, Merlot and Chardonnay, and recently the winery planted new vineyards with Shiraz and Cabernet Franc. In 2002 the winery produced about 12,000 bottles, in 2003 18,000 bottles and in 2004, 35,000. With the 2005 vintage the winery hopes to attain its capacity of 50,000 bottles annually. In addition to producing two top-of-the-line series, Alexander the Great and The Wine of Alexander, and a series of second wines, Sandro, the winery also produces a Port-style wine and several private labels for restaurants.

Alexander the Great

ALEXANDER THE GREAT, CABERNET SAUVIGNON, 2004: Youthful deep royal purple, full bodied and with firm tannins well-balanced by complex currant, herb, mineral and herbal aromas and flavors. Generous and long. Best 2007–2011. Tentative Score 88–90.

ALEXANDER THE GREAT, CABERNET SAUVIGNON, 2003: Medium to full-bodied, with chunky tannins and a touch of herbaceousness. Mocha, currant, plum, spice and cedar aromas and flavors lead to a rich, concentrated and firm wine with potential for bottle aging. Best 2007–2011. Tentative Score 89–91.

ALEXANDER THE GREAT, CABERNET SAUVIGNON, 2002: A full-bodied Cabernet Sauvignon blended with 7% of Merlot. Generous tannins and wood, the tannins integrating to reveal blackcurrant, berry and sweet cedar aromas and flavors, all leading to a long finish. Drink now–2008. Score 90.

ALEXANDER THE GREAT, CABERNET SAUVIGNON, 2001: Almost massive in structure and body, this elegant wine promises to settle down nicely with time and reveal tannins nicely balanced by black fruits, herbs and a hint of eucalyptus as well as good but not exaggerated wood. Drink now–2007. Score 92.

ALEXANDER THE GREAT, CABERNET SAUVIGNON, 2000: This firm and concentrated blend of 95% Cabernet Sauvignon and 5% Merlot boasts a dark ruby toward garnet color and a rich, almost luxurious texture, along with layers of currants, wild berries, black cherries and plums. Good toasty oak flavors and a long opulent finish. Drink now–2008. Score 92.

ALEXANDER THE GREAT, CABERNET SAUVIGNON, 1999: Deep purple, this medium to full-bodied blend of 95% Cabernet Sauvignon and 5% Merlot spent 24 months in American and French oak barrels. When young it was overpowered by vanilla and oak but those have settled down nicely now, yielding rich and concentrated aromas and flavors of currants, plums and orange peel along with chocolate, vanilla, light spicy overlays and a distinct hint of mint on the long finish. Drink now. Score 91.

The Wine of Alexander

ALEXANDER, CABERNET SAUVIGNON, 2004: Medium to full-bodied, with gripping tannins and wood needing time to settle down but inherent good balance that bodes well for the future. A fruity, mouthfilling wine. Drink from release–2009. Tentative Score 87–89.

ALEXANDER, CABERNET SAUVIGNON, 2003: Not as aromatic as earlier vintages but opening to an array of flavors including black fruits, Mediterranean herbs and licorice. Medium to full-bodied, with soft tannins and a moderately long vanilla and mint finish. Drink from release–2008. Tentative Score 87–89.

ALEXANDER, CABERNET SAUVIGNON, 2002: Deep royal purple in color, this young wine with still closing tannins shows good blackcurrant, berry and earthy-herbal aromas and flavors, but lacks somewhat in depth and length. Drink now. Score 86.

ALEXANDER, CABERNET SAUVIGNON, 2001: Spicy, earthy overlays complement rich plum and berry flavors and just a hint of vanilla. Soft tannins already integrating well in this full-bodied wine. Drink now–2007. Score 90.

ALEXANDER, CABERNET SAUVIGNON, 2000: Medium to full-bodied with well-integrated tannins, the wine shows warm blackcurrant, berry, toasty oak and vanilla flavors, all on a delicate spicy background. Mouth-filling and with a moderately long finish. Drink now–2007. Score 89.

ALEXANDER, CABERNET SAUVIGNON, 1999: Full-bodied, with generous and well-integrated tannins, the wine offers aromas and flavors of currants, berries, herbs and a light earthiness. Elegant and complex. Drink now. Score 90.

ALEXANDER, CABERNET SAUVIGNON, 1998: This round Cabernet still shows freshness and good fruits but is now taking on overtones and a finish of bitter herbs. Past its peak. Drink up. Score 86.

ALEXANDER, CABERNET SAUVIGNON, 1997: When first released the wine earned a Score of 84 and then, surprisingly, improved somewhat in the bottle. Now, although still offering rich and up-front fruits, it shows hints of oxidation. Drink up. Score 85.

ALEXANDER, MERLOT, 2004: Deep cherry red, medium-bodied, with soft tannins and promising to be round and fruity. On the nose and palate plums, black cherries and hints of pepper and nutmeg. Drink from release–2008. Tentative Score 86–88.

ALEXANDER, MERLOT, 2003: Well-balanced with ripe plum, black cherry, currant, sweet cedar and hazelnut aromas and flavors. Smooth, supple, with soft tannins and a hint of mocha on the finish. Drink from release–2008. Tentative Score 87–89.

ALEXANDER, MERLOT, 2002: Medium to full-bodied, with anise and menthol aromas and flavors backing up cherry, plum and currant fruits. As the wine opens on the palate look as well for layers of green olives, herbs and tobacco. Elegant and supple but not meant for long-term cellaring. Drink now–2007. Score 89.

ALEXANDER, MERLOT, 2001: Intense, deep and elegant, with a solid core of cherry, currant and light oak, this medium to full-bodied wine is now showing excellent depth and complexity. Drink now. Score 90.

ALEXANDER, MERLOT, 2000: Medium to full-bodied, with its tannins starting to integrate nicely, this cherry, berry and currant flavored wine continues to show good balance between oak, fruits and tannins. Look for a very appealing herbal finish. Drink now. Score 89.

ALEXANDER, MERLOT, 1999: Medium to full-bodied, with abundant soft tannins and berry, cherry and toasty oak aromas and flavors, those with appealing spicy notes, the wine offers up a generous and rich mouthful with a moderately long finish. Clearly at its peak. Drink now. Score 88.

ALEXANDER, SHIRAZ, 2002: Dark garnet red, this medium to full-bodied wine was aged in French oak *barriques* for 15 months. Made enitrely from Shiraz grapes, the wine now shows soft tannins, a wood reflected largely by spices and a hint of vanilla and ripe berry-cherry fruits. Generous and long. Drink now. Score 88.

ALEXANDER, CABERNET-MERLOT, YAMA'S WINE, 2002: Dark cherry red towards garnet, medium-bodied, with moderate soft tannins and pleasant enough black cherry and currant fruits. Drink up. Score 86.

ALEXANDER, CHARDONNAY, 2003: A blend of Chardonnay with a small amount of Sauvignon Blanc, this medium-bodied white offers up generous citrus, pineapple and tropical fruit aromas and flavors, those well balanced by natural acidity to keep it lively. Drink now. Score 86.

ALEXANDER, CHARDONNAY, 2002: Light golden straw in color, medium-bodied and with abundant oak, this buttery wine shows aromas and flavors of green apples, melons and peaches. Nicely dry and long. Drink up. Score 87.

ALEXANDER, CHARDONNAY, LIZA, 2003: Deep golden in color, this oak aged, medium to full-bodied white shows a tempting array of melon, pear and summer fruits, those backed up by moderate oak and a gentle creme brulé finish. Drink now–2007. Score 88.

ALEXANDER, CHARDONNAY, LIZA, 2002: Aged in oak for 18 months, this deep almost honeyed colored wine shows medium to full-body and aromas and flavors of pineapple, summer fruits and melon that are somewhat buried under the rather massive oak. Drink up. Score 86.

ALEXANDER, CHARDONNAY, 2001: Clear straw yellow in color, this medium to full-bodied white was oak-aged for 16 months without being subjected to malolactic fermentation. A bit more acidic and less buttery than most of the Chardonnays we see today, the wine has a sparkling and crisp sharpness and tempting green apple and white peach aromas and flavors. Somewhat past its peak. Drink up. Score 86.

Sandro

SANDRO, 2003: Medium-bodied, dark garnet in color, with soft tannins and reflecting a gentle hand with the wood, this blend of Cabernet Sauvignon and Merlot offers up currant, cranberry and red plum fruits. Soft, round and easy to drink. Drink now–2007. Score 87.

SANDRO, 2002: A medium-bodied Cabernet-Merlot blend with soft tannins, generous black fruits and appealing vanilla and smoky oak overlays. Drink now. Score 85.

SANDRO, 2001: This medium-bodied oak-aged blend of 70% Cabernet Sauvignon and 30% Merlot shows soft tannins already well integrated, just enough sweet wood and vanilla, and plenty of up-front currant, black cherry and berry fruits. Drink up. Score 87.

Aligote **

Established by Tsvika Fante and located on Moshav Gan Yo-shiya on the central Coastal Plain, the first wines released by this winery were from the 2002 harvest. Production in 2002 was 800 bottles, in 2003, 2500 and in 2004, 3,000 bottles. Plans for maximum growth are of 5,000 bottles annually.

ALIGOTE, CABERNET SAUVIGNON, 2003: Dark garnet, this full-bodied red shows good balance between soft tannins and sweet vanilla from the American oak in which it was aged. Round and mouth-filling , with blackcurrant, plum and orange peel aromas and flavors. Long and comfortable on the palate. Drink now–2007. Score 86.

ALIGOTE, CABERNET SAUVIGNON, 2002: Deep ruby red, medium to full-bodied, with chunky tannins and pronounced acidity on berry, cherry and cassis fruits. Lacking balance. Drink up. Score 83.

ALIGOTE, MERLOT, 2003: Showing better now than at an earlier tasting, this deep garnet, medium-bodied, softly tannic wine shows appealing berry, black cherry and orange peel aromas and flavors as well as light overlays of bittersweet chocolate and freshly picked tarragon on the long finish. Drink now–2007. Score 87.

ALIGOTE, MERLOT, 2002: Medium-bodied, with generous, well-integrating tannins, this oak-aged blend of 93% Merlot and 7% Shiraz offers ample plum, berry and currant aromas and flavors, those backed up by spices and vanilla as well as a rather marked oaky note. Drink now. Score 85.

ALIGOTE, SANGIOVESE, 2003: Medium deep purple in color, medium-bodied, with soft tannins and good balance between soft tannins, gentle influence of the wood and appealing raspberry, black cherry fruits, all backed up nicely by hints of Mediterranean herbs and a light spicy overlay. Drink now. Score 86.

ALIGOTE, CABERNET SAUVIGNON-MERLOT, 2002: Medium-bodied, with chunky tannins and somewhat stingy black fruits. Lacking balance or length. Drink up. Score 82.

Alon *

Located on Moshav Alonei Aba, north of Haifa, owner-winemaker Gal Segev is now producing about 3,000 bottles annually. To date the winery has released two varietal wines, Cabernet Sauvignon and Merlot. Drawing largely on grapes from the Galilee and the Jezreel Valley, the winemaker is currently experimenting with other varieties, those including Petit Verdot, Cabernet Franc, Shiraz, Sangiovese and Nebbiolo.

ALON, CABERNET SAUVIGNON, 2003: Dark ruby, medim-bodied, with a somewhat woody influence but also showing attractive cassis and berry fruits along with hints of vanilla. Firmly tannic on the finish. Drink now. Score 83.

ALON, CABERNET SAUVIGNON, 2002: Garnet toward purple, medium-bodied, with appealing currant and berry fruits, this is a simple country-style wine. Drink now. Score 80.

ALON, CABERNET SAUVIGNON, 2001: Medium-bodied, with fruits hidden under coarse tannins and the too-strong influence of wood. Drink up. Score 75.

ALON, CABERNET SAUVIGNON, 2000: Dark royal purple and medium-bodied, faulted, with aromas and flavors that are too reminiscent of concentrated fruit juice. Drink up. Score 74.

ALON, CABERNET SAUVIGNON, 1999: Medium-bodied, with perhaps overly sweet plum and cherry flavors, this rather coarse country-style wine is showing age. Score 72.

ALON, MERLOT, 2003: Dark ruby in color, a somewhat oaky and tannic country-style wine with a few black fruits and a hint of spiciness. Drink now. Score 83.

ALON, MERLOT, 2002: Ruby toward garnet in color, this simple medium-bodied, oak-aged wine has well integrated soft tannins and pleasant currant and berry fruits. Drink now. Score 82.

ALON, MERLOT, 2001: Deep ruby toward purple in color, medium-bodied, with chunky tannins that place it distinctly in the country-style, and with berry black cherry fruits. Drink now. Score 78.

ALON, MERLOT 2000: Aged in oak for one year, this dark purple, medium-bodied wine offers up unusually tough tannins for a Merlot, and subdued aromas and flavors of stewed black fruits that fail to linger. Drink up. Score 76.

Amiad *

Located on Kibbutz Amiad in the Upper Galilee, this small winery that specializes in liqueurs produced kosher wines under the Amiad label until 2002. Following the untimely death of winemaker Jeffrey Marx, no wines were made from the 2003 vintage and whether the winery will continue with wine production is not known at this time.

AMIAD, SPECIAL RESERVE, 2000: A step-up in quality for Amiad. Dark garnet toward purple in color, this deep full-bodied wine has excellent balance between oak, soft tannins and fruit. Complex flavors of vanilla, smoky oak, currant, berries and plums, all with a hint of spices on the long finish. Drink now–2007. Score 90. K

AMIAD, CABERNET SAUVIGNON, 2002: This cherry red, light to medium-bodied low tannic and somewhat watery wine has a few berry-cherry flavors and imparts a light herbal-earthy sensation to the palate. Drink up. Score 77. K

AMIAD, CABERNET SAUVIGNON, 2000: So cherry red in color that you might mistake this wine at first glance for a Beaujolais. The wine is lean, earthy and without fruit, and showing age. Score 72. K

AMIAD, MERLOT, 2002: This light to medium-bodied, unoaked and low tannic wine has tutti-frutti flavors and is already shows its age. Score 76. K

AMIAD, CHARDONNAY, 2000: The wine is dominated by overt sourness and thin, earthy and weedy aromas and flavors. Showing age. Score 70. K

Amphorae *****

Set in a green and luxuriant mouth of a long dormant volcano on the Makura Ranch, on the western slopes of Mount Carmel, and using grapes from some of the best vineyards of the Golan Heights and the Upper Galilee, the winery is headed by winemaker Gil Shatzberg, one of the young winemakers at the cutting edge of today's Israeli wine scene.

Production from the 2000 vintage was 23,000 bottles, from the 2003 vintage about 55,000 and from 2004, 70,000 bottles. In 2005 the winery moved into a new, beautiful, state-of-the-art winery and target production is 80,000–100,000 bottles annually.

The winery's top-of-the-line series is Amphorae, and their second wines are under the Rhyton label. Both of these series are age-worthy, while the most recent introduction, Med. Red, is meant for relatively early drinking. Amphorae is the Greek term for those tall, double handled jugs with narrow necks and bases, often made of clay, that were used by the Greeks and later by the Romans for storing and shipping wine. Rhyton is an ancient Greek cup, most often shaped like a drinking horn.

Amphorae

Cabernet
Sauvignon 2001 Amphorae vineyard

AMPHORAE, CABERNET SAUVIGNON, 2003: Blended with a small percentage of Petite Sirah, this full-bodied, harmonious wine shows excellent balance between still firm tannins, wood, and juicy currant and cherry fruits and spices. With intriguing raspberry, chocolate and mocha flavors on the finish, this is a complex and delicious wine. Best 2007–2011. Tentative Score 91–93.

AMPHORAE, CABERNET SAUVIGNON, 2002: A good effort from the spotty 2002 vintage year. An appealing medium to full-bodied wine with generous fruits well balanced by oak and moderate tannins but without the concentration or structure for long-term cellaring. Drink now–2007. Score 88.

AMPHORAE, CABERNET SAUVIGNON, 2001: Delicious, traditional Cabernet with a small amount of Syrah blended in, this full-bodied, deep garnet toward royal purple wine shows a tempting array of black-currant and plum fruits, those backed up nicely by generous hints of spices and mocha. Still young but with tannins well balanced by wood and fruits, and with a long and luxurious finish. Drink now–2009. Score 91.

AMPHORAE, CABERNET SAUVIGNON, SPECIAL RESERVE, 2000: This deep red, remarkably rich wine falls somewhere in style between the Mediterranean and Bordeaux. Complex, aromatic, concentrated and with excellent balance, with tiers of currant, plum, Mediterranean herbs and sweet oak, and with a long finish, this is a wine well worthy of cellaring. Drink now–2014. Score 93.

AMPHORAE, CABERNET SAUVIGNON, 2000: A full-bodied Cabernet so intense and powerful that you might be tempted to think of it as potent. Still young but with its firm tannins now integrating nicely, this dark and deep wine is now showing currant, blackberry and plum aromas and flavors, all with generous overlays of pepper and chocolate. Drink now–2008. Score 93.

AMPHORAE, MERLOT, 2003: True to its varietal characteristics, this outstanding Merlot offers cherry, currant, anise and cedar aromas and flavors, those coming together nicely with still firm tannins and the judicious use of oak. Concentrated, elegant, graceful and long, the wine needs time to come into its own. Drink now–2010. Score 90.

AMPHORAE, MERLOT, 2002: Supple, well balanced and with just enough berry and plum flavors, gentle tannins and a not exaggerated feel of the oak. Drink now. Score 87.

AMPHORAE, MERLOT, 2001: Medium to full-bodied, with its firm tannins now integrating nicely and with tempting berries, plums, herbs and light spices and more aromatic now than during earlier tastings, this is a wine that clearly reflects its Mediterranean *terroir*. Good balance and structure and a long ripe finish. Drink now–2008. Score 90.

AMPHORAE, MERLOT, 2000: Deep royal purple in color, this blend of 95% Merlot, 2% Cabernet Sauvignon and 3% Petite Sirah is well knit but not tight, firm but not muscular, and very well balanced, with dark fruits well set off by light and appealing herbal and vanilla aromas and flavors. Lingers nicely on the palate. Drink now. Score 91.

AMPHORAE, CABERNET SAUVIGNON-MERLOT, 2002: Young, tight, ripe and complex, with layers of black cherry, plum, berry and spices, and with hints of herbs and black olives that come in near the finish, this medium to full-bodied wine offers well-integrated tannins, a smooth texture and a moderately long fruity finish. Drink now. Score 90.

AMPHORAE, CABERNET FRANC, 2004: Deep garnet, with bright raspberry and plum flavors, this dark, rich and plush wine shows thick, earthy tannins and gamy currant and cedar wood aromas and flavors. With such generous firm tannins this is not destined to be an elegant wine so much as powerful and complex. Best 2007–2012. Tentative Score 90–92.

AMPHORAE, SHIRAZ, 2004: Firm and well structured, with chunky tannins and a solid core of leather, earth, currants, blackberries, anise and beef flavors that yield on the long finish to mocha and toffee. Needs time to show its elegance. Best 2007–2012. Tentative Score 89–91.

AMPHORAE, SHIRAZ, 2003: Medium to full-bodied, a deep almost inky purple in color, with tempting plums and violets from the first sip, those yielding to smoke, chocolate and earthy-herbal aromas and flavors. Long and intriguing. Drink now–2009. Score 92.

AMPHORAE, CHARDONNAY, 2003: Deep gold in color with orange reflections, this medium to full-bodied white reflects its 12 months in *barriques* with complex, rich and concentrated aromas and flavors of figs, tangerines, nectarines and hazelnuts. Light buttery-oak shadings on the finish add understated elegance. Best white to date from Amphorae. Drink now–2008. Score 91.

AMPHORAE, CHARDONNAY, 2002: Ripe, subtle and refreshing, with well-integrated pear, pineapple, butterscotch and vanilla aromas and flavors, those well matched by spices, creamy oak and a long mineral-rich finish. Drink now. Score 89.

AMPHORAE, CHARDONNAY, 2000: Lively, deep and well rounded, the wine shows rich and concentrated grapefruit, pear and fig flavors as well as a nice note of toasty oak and spices. Complex and delicious from start to finish. Drink now. Score 91.

Rhyton

Rhyton Red 2001 AmphoraeVineyard

RHYTON, 2003: A blend of 82% Cabernet Sauvignon, 10% Petite Sirah and 4% each Shiraz and Merlot, this wine reflects its nearly 24 months in used oak with a gently felt oak influence, well integrating tannins and medium-body. On the nose and palate black fruits, white chocolate and a welcome hint of spiciness. Drink now–2008. Score 89.

RHYTON, 2002: Medium-bodied, with overall good balance between soft tannins, a gentle hand with the wood and almost sweet currant and berry aromas and flavors. Soft and flavorful. Drink now–2007. Score 88.

RHYTON, 2001: This medium-bodied blend of Cabernet Sauvignon, Merlot and Petite Sirah from 25–30-year-old vines has soft, well-integrated tannins and abundant currant and berry aromas and flavors, all leading to an almost sweet fruity finish. Soft and comfortable on the palate. Drink now. Score 89.

RHYTON, 2000: A medium to full-bodied oak-aged blend of 60% Cabernet Sauvignon and 40% Merlot showing excellent balance between fruits and wood, smooth tannins and lively acidity. Drink now. Score 90.

Med.Red

MED.RED 2003: Deep garnet red in color, medium-bodied, with spicy oak balanced and soft tannins backed up nicely by blackcurrant and black cherry fruits. An oak aged blend of 97% Cabernet Sauvignon and 3% Shiraz, with appealing wild berries and spices on the moderately-long finish. Drink now 2007. Score 88.

MED.RED 2002: Dark in color, with somewhat chunky and still firm tannins, a hint of toasty oak, and a tempting array of herbal, currant and cherry aromas and flavors. Made entirely from Cabernet Sauvignon grapes aged in one-year-old oak barrels for 12 months, it has a fascinating raspberry flavor that comes in on the finish. A wine that falls between the rustic and the elegant. Drink now. Score 89.

Amram's *

Founded in 2001 on Moshav Ramot Naftali in the Upper Galilee by grape grower Amram Azulai who has vineyards of Cabernet, Merlot and Shiraz grapes in Emek Kadesh, this small winery is currently producing several hundred bottles annually and targeting for 7,000–8,000 within the next five years.

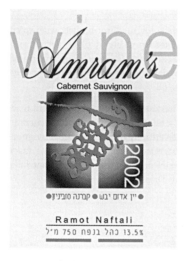

AMRAM'S WINE, CABERNET SAUVIGNON, 2002: Weedy and acidic, with aromas that call to mind a cow-shed rather than fresh country air, the wine is too tannic and its fruits are hardly felt. Drink up. Score 75.

AMRAM'S WINE, MERLOT, 2002: This musty, medium-bodied red yields an aroma of wet cement and has only the stingiest of plum and pepper flavors. Score 68.

AMRAM'S WINE, CABERNET SAUVIGNON-MERLOT, 2002: Medium-bodied, with dusty-earthy aromas and chunky tannins overshadowing rather stingy plum fruits. Score 70.

AMRAM'S WINE, CABERNET SAUVIGNON-SHIRAZ, 2002: Dark red and turning somewhat cloudy once poured, the wine is far too acidic and is dominated by earthy-mushroom flavors. Score 68.

Anatot *

Founded in 1998 by Aharon Helfgot and Arnon Erez, the winery, which is located in Anatot, a community north of Jerusalem, is currently producing 17,500 oak-aged bottles annually from Cabernet Sauvignon and Merlot grapes. The grapes come primarily from vineyards in the Lachish and Shiloh regions.

ANATOT, CABERNET SAUVIGNON, 2002: This pleasant deep ruby toward garnet medium-bodied red shows moderate tannins, a hint of spicy oak, and appealing plum, black cherry and currant fruits. Drink now. Score 81.

ANATOT, CABERNET SAUVIGNON, 2001: Dark ruby toward purple in color and medium-bodied, the wine has subdued tannins and oak and dull aromas and flavors of black fruits. It is stingy on the palate and already showing age. Score 76.

ANATOT, CABERNET SAUVIGNON, 1999: An organic wine that yields an odd mixture of bubble gum and wood aromas and flavors and a coarse alcoholic texture that seems to burn the palate and the throat. Score 65.

ANATOT, MERLOT, 2001: This somewhat cloudy deep ruby wine seems muddy on the palate with its muted fruits, far too much earthiness and a barnyard aroma that creeps in over time. Score 68.

ANATOT, MERLOT, 2000: This deep purple medium-bodied wine retains a firm, somewhat tannic texture with its black fruit flavors now showing severe signs of oxidation. Score 78.

ANATOT, NOTERA, 2001: This pleasant medium-bodied oak-aged blend of 60% Merlot and 40% Cabernet Sauvignon is a distinct step up in quality. The wine has soft tannins, appealing black fruits and just a hint of spiciness. Showing age. Score 80.

ANATOT, PETITE SIRAH, 1999: Stewed fruit and barnyard aromas and flavors with too coarse tannins yield an unappealing wine. Score 60.

ANATOT, RED, 1999: Made entirely from Carignan grapes that rarely produce good wines on their own, this flat, dull and astringent wine has far too many vegetal notes. Score 60.

Avidan **

This mini-winery set in a shed near the home of founders Tsina and Shlomo Avidan, in the town of Ra'anana in the Sharon region, relies on Chardonnay, Shiraz, Cabernet Sauvignon and Merlot grapes selected from various vineyards at Moshav Kerem Ben Zimra. The winery produced 1,300 bottles in 2002, 2,500 in 2003 and is currently producing 5,000 bottles annually. Plans for the future include building a winery in the Galilee and the eventual production of 50,000 bottles annually.

AVIDAN, CABERNET SAUVIGNON, 2003: Dark ruby towards garnet in color, this medium-bodied blend of Cabernet Sauvignon and Merlot shows generous oak and firm tannins, those matched nicely by currant, berry and black cherry fruits. Drink now–2007. Score 86.

AVIDAN, CABERNET SAUVIGNON, 2002: Deep garnet in color, this blend of 85% Cabernet Sauvignon and 15% Merlot spent 18 months in oak. Ripe and plummy, with fleshy tannins and medium body, backed up by supple cherry, berry and spice notes and a nice fruity finish. Drink now. Score 86.

AVIDAN, CABERNET SAUVIGNON, 2001: The wine yields firm tannins, aromas that are far from fresh, searing acidity and minimal fruit. Score 60.

AVIDAN, SHIRAZ, 2003: Medium-dark ruby, medium to full-bodied, with good balance between soft tannins, wood and plum, cherry and earthy aromas and flavors. On the moderately-long finish look for a hint of leather. Drink now–2007. Score 86.

AVIDAN, CHARDONNAY, 2001: Deep honey in color, the wine is also dominated by honey flavors with perhaps some hints of caramel, but minimal fruits and an odd, semi-dry finish. Score 55.

Bar **

Established in 2002 by Ilan Bar in the village of Binyamina, and drawing largely on grapes from the surrounding vineyards, this family-owned winery produces Cabernet Sauvignon, Merlot, Carignan, Sauvignon Blanc and Chardonnay wines as well as Jonathan Red, a blend of Merlot and Cabernet. The winery is currently producing about 4,500 bottles annually.

BAR, CABERNET SAUVIGNON, 2002: Soft and round, medium-bodied and with soft, well-integrated tannins, the wine offers appealing currant and berry flavors. Drink now. Score 85.

BAR, JONATHAN RED, 2002: Aged in used oak barrels for 9 months, this blend of 70% Merlot and 30% Cabernet Sauvignon shows good balance between blackberries, earthiness and spices. Medium-bodied, with chunky tannins, this is a pleasing country-style wine. Drink now, Score 85.

BAR, SAUVIGNON BLANC, 2003: Bright and lively, with citrus, earthy and grassy overtones. Not complex but a well made and enjoyable wine. Drink now. Score 85.

BAR, MERLOT, 2002: Soft and round with forward black cherry, raspberry and herbal aromas and flavors. Soft tannins and an earthy-tobacco and smoky wood finish to add charm. Drink now. Score 86.

BAR, CARIGNAN, 2002: Medium-bodied, well-balanced with smooth, almost sweet tannins and black cherry and herbal aromas and flavors. Soft and lively. Drink now. Score 85.

Barkai **

Located on Moshav Roglit in the Ella Valley, winemaker Itai Barkai relies on Cabernet Sauvignon and Merlot grapes from the winery's own vineyards. Production for 2002 and 2003 was under 1,000 bottles annually and 2004 production was 2,400 bottles. A new winery is currently being constructed with a capacity for 10,000 bottles annually.

BARKAI, CABERNET SAUVIGNON-MERLOT, 2003: Medium-bodied, with soft, near-sweet tannins and hyper-ripe, almost jammy berry and plum aromas and flavors. Drink now. Score 83.

BARKAI, CABERNET SAUVIGNON-MERLOT, 2002: Dark garnet red in color, medium-bodied, with chunky, country-style tannins and appealing blackberry and cassis fruits. A bit earthy and alcoholic, but opens nicely in the glass. Drink now. Score 85.

BARKAI, CABERNET SAUVIGNON-MERLOT, 2001: A simple but pleasant country-style wine, with generous berry and black cherry fruits backed up by earthiness and hints of Mediterranean herbs. Drink up. Score 84.

Barkan ✳✳✳

Founded in 1990 by Shmuel Boxer and Yair Lerner with the buyout of the former wine and liqueur producer "Stock", the winery was first located in the industrial area of Barkan, not far from Kfar Saba on the Trans-Samaria Highway. In 1999 Barkan started to plant vineyards in Kibbutz Hulda, on the central plain near the town of Rehovot, where it now has a state-of-the-art winery. Under the supervision of wine-makers Ed Salzberg, Yotam Sharon and Itay Lahat, the first of whom studied in California, the second in France, and the third in Australia, this is now the second largest winery in Israel, with current production of six million bottles annually and projected growth to ten million by 2010.

With an investment exceeding $20 million in the winery and adjoining vineyards (1500 dunams owned jointly by the winery and the *kibbutz*, making this the largest single vineyard in the country), and ongoing construction of a visitors' center and underground barrel room, Barkan is also now the parent company of Segal Wines. The winery releases varietal wines in three labels, Superieur, Millennium, Reserve and Classic, as well as table wines in the Lachish series and several other series, and a line of sacramental wines. The winery is currently developing a vineyard of 150 dunams (75 acres) in Mitzpe Ramon in the Negev Desert, and starting to release wines from there under the label Negev Project.

Superieur

SUPERIEUR, CABERNET SAUVIGNON, 2002: Full-bodied, with generous spicy oak and lively acidity for balance. Features a core of ripe blueberry, cassis and blackcurrant fruits, those matched nicely by overlays of spices and cocoa and, on the long finish, appealing hints of minerals and licorice. Drink now–2008. Score 89. K

SUPERIEUR, CABERNET SAUVIGNON, 2000: Made from grapes harvested on the Golan and in the Upper Galilee. Aged first in new oak and transferred later to used oak, this full-bodied and concentrated, deep royal toward purple wine offers up generous blackcurrant, blackberry and chocolate aromas, all with an appealing overlay of Mediterranean herbaceousness. Drink now. Score 89. K

SUPERIEUR, CABERNET SAUVIGNON, 1999: The best to date in this series. Medium to full-bodied, round and well balanced, with soft, well-integrated tannins and aromas and flavors of currants, berries and white chocolate. Drink now. Score 88. K

SUPERIEUR, CABERNET SAUVIGNON, 1996: Aged in new oak casks for 18 months, this medium-bodied, moderately tannic wine is a bit too simple and earthy, and from its youth has shown slightly sour flavors that tend to hide the cherry, berry and plum flavors which never fully succeeded in bursting forth. Now well past its peak and no longer scoreable. K

SUPERIEUR, CABERNET SAUVIGNON, 1995: Even after having spent 18 months in oak casks, this wine showed only modest cedar, spice and berry flavors. Lacking in balance and too tight and austere, this medium-bodied wine has rather flat tannins and a notable lack of ripe fruit flavors. Now past its peak and no longer scoreable. K

SUPERIEUR, MERLOT, 2000: Showing somewhat better now than at earlier tastings. Medium to full-bodied, with soft tannins and generous but not exaggerated smoky oak, but with still somewhat stingy currant and plum fruits. Drink up. Score 85. K

SUPERIEUR, MERLOT, 1998: After 18 months in small oak casks, this blend of 90% Merlot and 10% Cabernet Sauvignon has a deep purple color and layers of plum, currant and black cherry aromas and flavors, these matched nicely by hints of spices and cedar. With once firm tannins now well integrated, the wine has an appealing fruity finish. Somewhat past its peak. Drink up. Score 86. K

SUPERIEUR, CHARDONNAY, 2002: Complex and full-bodied, with juicy pear, spice, vanilla, hazelnut and honeyed aromas and flavors that reveal hints of earth and mineral on the long finish. A very limited edition, destined primarily for restaurants. Drink now. Score 90. K

SUPERIEUR, CHARDONNAY, 2000: Damp golden straw in color, this full-bodied wine was fermented in American oak barrels and then aged *sur lie* for an additional four months. On the nose, the strong oaky-vanilla aromas that are felt at first never quite blend into the background, thus tending to hide whatever fruits may be underneath, and on the palate, the first impressions of pears, apples and citrus fade too rapidly. One-dimensional. Somewhat past its peak. Drink up. Score 84. K

SUPERIEUR, CHARDONNAY, 1997: Simple and a bit on the watery side, the wine has only a few hints of oak, citrus and apples in its aromas and flavors, and is too light. Past its peak and no longer scoreable. K

Reserve

RESERVE, CABERNET SAUVI-GNON, 2002: Dark royal purple, medium to full-bodied and with good balance between well-proportioned wood, tannins and black fruits, this wine is now starting to show its best. Drink now–2008. Score 87. K

RESERVE, CABERNET SAUVI-GNON, 2001: Deep garnet toward purple in color, well balanced, with generous cherry and plum fruits as well as a spicy, toasty oak overlay. Soft tannins and a rich fruity finish. Drink now–2007. Score 88. K

BARKAN
RESERVE
Merlot
מרלו
DRY RED WINE יין אדום יבש
2001
GALIL
CONT. 750 ML. 13.8% ALC. BY VOL.
PRODUCED & BOTT. BY BARKAN WINE CELLARS, ISRAEL.

RESERVE, CABERNET SAUVIGNON, 2000: With its once almost searing tannins now well integrated, this deep royal purple, medium to full-bodied red opens nicely in the glass to reveal aromas and flavors of blackcurrants, berries and black cherries, along with a spicy, smoky-oak overlay. Drink now. Score 87. K

RESERVE, CABERNET SAUVIGNON, 1999: Full-bodied, with generous tannins and smoky wood balanced by blackcurrants, plums and spices. Firm, long and mouth-filling with an appealing hint of bitterness on the long finish. Somewhat past its peak. Drink up. Score 86. K

RESERVE, CABERNET SAUVIGNON, 1998: Medium to full-bodied, with tannins now nicely integrated and showing good balance between spicy oak, black fruits, vanilla and a hint of licorice. Fully mature now. Drink up. Score 88. K

RESERVE, CABERNET SAUVIGNON, 1997: Rich, generous and with abundant and mouth-filling blackcurrant, black cherry and spice overtones that linger nicely on the palate, the wine continues to show style, grace and a long finish, but is now past its peak. Drink up. Score 86. K

RESERVE, CABERNET SAUVIGNON, 1996: Dark garnet, showing signs of browning, and with somewhat chunky tannins that have never quite integrated and still work hard to hide berry, currant and plum fruits. Past its peak. Drink up. Score 84. K

RESERVE, MERLOT, 2003: Barkan's best-ever Merlot. Deep garnet in color, full-bodied and harmonious, with soft tannins, a gentle sense of spicy oak, and an array of purple plum, currant and wild berry fruits. Compact, round and with the potential for elegance. Drink now–2010. Score 89. K

RESERVE, MERLOT, 2002: Dark garnet in color, with soft, well-integrated tannins and overall good balance, the once powerful and dominating oak now receding to let the plum and berry fruits make themselves felt. Drink now–2007. Score 87. K

RESERVE, MERLOT, 2001: Medium to full-bodied and medium dark garnet in color, this wine is still showing plenty of tannins and oak, but given time to open in the glass reveals an appealing core of currant, black cherry, and herbs. Drink up. Score 86. K

RESERVE, MERLOT, 2000: Showing better now than at earlier tastings. Medium-bodied, with soft tannins and a generous core of currant, black cherry and plums, and appealing overlays of spicy oak and tea. Somewhat past its peak. Drink up. Score 86. K

RESERVE, MERLOT, 1999: Deep royal purple with clearing at the rim, this medium-bodied wine offers up soft tannins, light wood and a few currant and berry fruits. One dimensional, lacking length and somewhat past its peak. Drink up. Score 83. K

RESERVE, MERLOT, 1998: Medium to full-bodied, deep garnet in color and now showing a bit of browning. Blackcurrant and black cherry fruits matched nicely by spicy wood, vanilla, light herbal overtones and well-integrated tannins. Fully mature and a bit past its peak. Drink up. Score 87. K

RESERVE, MERLOT, 1997: In its youth this medium to full-bodied deep ruby toward purple wine offered up a generous mouthful and good balance between soft tannins, wood and black fruits, but it is now well past its peak and no longer scoreable. K

RESERVE, PINOT NOIR, NEGEV PROJECT, 2003: Subdued ruby in color, medium-bodied, with soft, well-integrated tannins and appealing berry and black cherry fruits backed up by light herbal and earthy sensations. Drink now–2007. Score 89. K

RESERVE, PINOT NOIR, 2002: Darker, more tannic, and far more representative of the Pinot Noir grape than earlier releases from the winery, this medium-bodied red spent 10 months in small oak barrels and now reflects tempting dusty plum and berry fruits, together with an appealing earthy finish. Look as well for a pleasing lightly bitter herbal sensation as the wine lingers on the palate. Drink now. Score 88. K

RESERVE, PINOTAGE, 2003: The third and best Pinotage release from Barkan. Dark and deep, full-bodied, with fine balance between generous tannins, a not-exaggerated sense of wood, and tempting plum, black cherry, blueberry and chocolate aromas and flavors all lingering nicely. Drink from release–2009. Tentative Score 90–92. K

RESERVE, PINOTAGE, 2002: Youthful royal purple in color, this medium to full-bodied red is packed with lush raspberry, blackberry, black cherry and currant fruits, those matched nicely by sweet spices, dark chocolate and, from mid-palate light hints of smoked bacon. A tantalizing hint of bitter herbs on the moderately long finish. Drink now–2007. Score 90. K

RESERVE, PINOTAGE, JUDEA, 2001: Developing nicely, showing a welcome bare hint of sweetness overlaying its blackcurrant and black cherry fruits. Medium to full-bodied, with generous but soft and well integrated tannins and dashes of smoked meat and herbs. Soft, round and appealing. Drink now. Score 90. K

RESERVE, CHARDONNAY, 2003: Medium-bodied but satisfyingly mouth-filling, with rich apple, melon and citrus fruits coming together well with light vanilla and toasted oak, all lingering nicely on the palate. Drink now. Score 88. K

RESERVE, CHARDONNAY, NEGEV PROJECT, 2003: Medium-bodied, this unoaked white shows a stony dryness that at one moment calls to mind unoaked Chablis and at the next a Loire Valley Sauvignon Blanc. Features white peaches, green apples and citrus fruits on an herbaceous background. Unusual and delicious. Drink now–2007. Score 89. **K**

RESERVE, CHARDONNAY, 2002: Light gold in color, medium-bodied and fully mature, but still showing good balance between fruits, wood and acidity. Citrus, melon and pear aromas and flavors along with spices lead to a mouthfilling finish. Drink up. Score 87. **K**

RESERVE, CHARDONNAY, 2001: Smooth and with appealing aromas and flavors of pears, figs, melon and vanilla, this medium-bodied wine maintains its creamy and spicy finish. Well past its peak and no longer scoreable. **K**

RESERVE, CHARDONNAY, 1999: Bright and lively, but a bit on the simple side, with floral notes and ripe pear and apple flavors. Well past its peak and fading quickly. No longer scoreable. **K**

RESERVE, SAUVIGNON BLANC, 2004: Bright and lively, golden-straw in color, medium-bodied, with ample acidity and tempting melon and apple fruits. Generous grassy-mineral hints throughout. Drink now–2007. Score 88. **K**

RESERVE, SAUVIGNON BLANC, 2003: Showing better now than at earlier tastings. Medium to full-bodied, light golden straw in color with green reflections and melon, gooseberry and apple fruits on a mineral-rich background. Appealing spiciness and lively acidity carry through to a moderately long finish. Drink now. Score 89. **K**

RESERVE, SAUVIGNON BLANC, 2002: Bright light straw in color, fruity, with grassy and mineral notes and flinty dryness, this aromatic wine was wisely left in oak for only two months before bottling. Fragrant and refreshing, it shows tropical fruit, citrus and fig aromas and flavors, as well as a long finish. Drink up. Score 87. **K**

RESERVE, SAUVIGNON BLANC, 2001: Aromatic, with flavors of apples and melons and nice balancing acidity, this was a simple but appealing wine in its youth. Somewhat past its peak. Drink up. Score 83. **K**

RESERVE, EMERALD RIESLING, 2004: Medium-bodied, with a light, not-offensive level of sweetness and good balancing acidity. Appealing citrus and summer fruits. Drink up. Score 84. **K**

RESERVE, EMERALD RIESLING, 2003: Medium-bodied, with a fruity nose and lacking the often cloying floral aromas of Emerald Riesling, the wine shows only a light hint of sweetness, as well as tempting citrus and peach aromas and flavors. Overall good balance although lacking a bit in liveliness. Drink up. Score 84. **K**

Classic

CLASSIC, CABERNET SAUVIGNON, 2004: Medium-bodied, with firm tannins waiting to yield and good levels of currant and black cherry fruits. A good entry-level quaffer. Drink now. Score 84. K

BARKAN

CLASSIC

DAN

SHIRAZ
DRY RED WINE
2003 שיראז

Alc. 13.5% vol. 750 ml. Prod. & Bot. by Barkan Wine Cellars, Israel

CLASSIC, CABERNET SAUVIGNON, 2003: Showing better than at earlier tastings. Deep ruby red, medium-bodied, with chunky tannins and appealing berry, cherry and currant fruits. Not complex but appealing. Drink now. Score 84. K

CLASSIC, CABERNET SAUVIGNON, 2002: Medium-bodied, with plum and berry aromas and flavors, hints of spices and a bit of chocolate that comes in near the end, this is a simple but pleasant enough little wine. Drink up. Score 84. K

CLASSIC, CABERNET SAUVIGNON, 2001: This medium-bodied deep purple wine offers up plum, currant and black cherry aromas and flavors, but is low in tannins and lacking in depth and breadth. Somewhat past its peak. Drink up. Score 81. K

CLASSIC, CABERNET SAUVIGNON, 2000: Medium-bodied, with smooth tannins and an appealing dark cherry color. Lots of up front blackcurrant, plum and wild berry flavors on a tight but appealing frame. Past its peak. Drink up. Score 83. K

CLASSIC, CABERNET SAUVIGNON, 1999: Deep ruby toward purple in color, with moderate tannins and medium body, this was an appealing little wine in its youth, showing black plum, black cherry, currant and mint notes. Well past its peak and no longer scoreable. K

CLASSIC, MERLOT, 2004: Soft, warm and round, with blackberry and plum fruits. Somewhat one dimensional but an acceptable entry-level wine. Drink now. Score 83. K

CLASSIC, MERLOT, 2003: Medium-bodied, dark ruby in color, with dark plum fruits and soft, just gripping-enough tannins to add backbone and an appealing hint of bitter herbs on the finish. Drink up. Score 84. K

CLASSIC, MERLOT, 2002: A pleasant little light to medium-bodied wine, more or less international in style but with appealing berry, plum and spice aromas and flavors. Not complex but an option for everyday drinking. Drink up. Score 84. K

CLASSIC, MERLOT, 2001: Firm and tight, this compact Merlot has warm currant, herb and earthy notes and a short, tannic finish. Look for nice peppery notes as the wine sits on the palate. Somewhat past its peak. Drink up. Score 83. K

CLASSIC, MERLOT, 1999: Medium-bodied and with soft tannins, this is a rather simple Merlot with plum, currant and berry flavors coming together in pleasant but not-at-all complex ways. Well past its peak. Drink up. Score 82. K

CLASSIC, PINOT NOIR, 2000: Made entirely from Pinot Noir grapes grown in the vineyards of Mitzpeh Ramon in the Negev Desert, this appealing little wine was aged in oak casks for 11 months. Medium-bodied and ruby colored in its youth but now showing signs of browning, the wine still maintains black cherry and berry aromas and flavors as well as hints of spices and licorice, but is now past its peak. Drink up. Score 83. K

CLASSIC, SYRAH, 2004: Light garnet red in color, light to medium-bodied, with soft tannins and some appealing plum and berry aromas and flavors backed up by a hint of spiciness. Drink now. Score 84. K

CLASSIC, SYRAH, 2003: Medium-bodied, with appealing black fruits and spices, a not-at-all complex but simple and appealing little wine. Drink now. Score 84. K

CLASSIC, SYRAH, 2002: Not much bouquet in this medium-bodied wine, but good plum and currant fruits and hints of mint and juniper berry. Drink up. Score 85. K

CLASSIC, PETITE SIRAH, 2004: Dark in color, with brooding tannins and somewhat skimpy black fruits. Somewhat flat and one dimensional. Drink up. Score 82. K

CLASSIC, PETITE SIRAH, 2003: Deep ruby in color, with chunky, country-style tannins and a few cherry-berry fruits. Drink now. Score 83. K

CLASSIC, PETITE SIRAH, 2002: Lightly earthy, firm and tight, this medium-bodied and tannic wine shows good cherry-berry fruits, and earthy-cedar notes. Not long or overly complex but a good Israeli Petite Sirah. Drink up. Score 85. K

CLASSIC, CHARDONNAY, 2003: With its golden color and forward pear, apple and summer fruit aromas and flavors, this appealing medium-bodied wine white shows good balance but lacks depth. Drink up. Score 85. K

CLASSIC, SAUVIGNON BLANC, 2004: Light to medium-bodied, with low acidity and a hint of sweetness but clean and appealing as a summertime quaffer. Drink up. Score 84. K

CLASSIC, SAUVIGNON BLANC, 2003: Light to medium-bodied, somewhat flat on the nose but with appealing citrus and summer fruits and good balancing acidity. Drink up. Score 84. K

CLASSIC, SAUVIGNON BLANC, 2002: Lacking the varietal traits of Sauvignon Blanc but with appealing aromas and flavors of citrus and summer fruits. Past its peak. Drink up. Score 80. K

CLASSIC, SAUVIGNON BLANC, 2001: Medium-bodied, with fresh floral, grassy, green apple and grapefruit aromas and flavors that linger nicely, but now past its peak. Drink up. Score 84. K

CLASSIC, EMERALD RIESLING, 2004: Semi-dry, with simple but rewarding tropical fruit and flowery aromas and flavors. Serve well chilled. Drink now. Score 84. K

CLASSIC, EMERALD RIESLING, 2003: Off dry, with its light sweetness nicely balanced by acidity and with appealing tropical and citrus fruit flavors and aromas. Drink up. Score 84. K

CLASSIC, EMERALD RIESLING, 2002: Categorized as semi-dry but with only a hint of sweetness, this is a surprisingly tempting little wine with appealing pineapple, apple and citrus flavors and aromas, and good balancing acidity. Now past its peak. Drink up. Score 82. K

Millennium

MILLENNIUM, CABERNET SAUVIGNON, 2004: Medium-bodied, with soft, almost unfelt tannins and simple but pleasant berry and cherry fruits. A pleasant quaffer. Drink now. Score 85.

MILLENNIUM, CABERNET SAUVIGNON, 1999: Bright garnet red in color, medium-bodied, with soft tannins and generous currant and berry fruits. Somewhat past its peak. Drink up. Score 85. K

MILLENNIUM, CABERNET SAUVIGNON, 1996: Dark cherry red toward garnet, medium to full-bodied, with somewhat coarse tannins and stingy berry and plum fruits. Well past its peak and no longer scoreable. K

Bazelet Hagolan ****

Founded in 1998 by Yo'av Levy on Moshav Kidmat Tsvi in the Golan Heights, the first facility of this winery was located in a cow shed and initial production from that vintage year was 1,800 bottles. Today, working with Australian trained winemaker Tal Pelter, the winery is producing about 30,000 bottles annually, all from Cabernet Sauvignon grapes grown in their own vineyards on the Golan Heights and target production is 50,000. The wines are in three series: Private Collection, Reserve and Bazelet Hagolan, the first two aged in oak for between 12–14 months, the third for 6 months. The winery, which released its first Chardonnay wine in 2005, has recently completed construction of a new underground barrel room and starting with the wines of the 2004 vintage the wines will be kosher.

Private Collection

PRIVATE COLLECTION, CABERNET SAUVIGNON, 1999: Supple, velvety, moderately tannic and with generous black cherry, currant and tobacco flavors, this is a rich and well-made wine. Drink now. Score 87.

Reserve

RESERVE, CABERNET SAUVIGNON, 2003: Full-bodied, with soft tannins well balanced by a rich array of aromas and flavors, those including berries, black cherries, orange peel, star anise and white pepper. Long, round and generous. Drink from release–2010. Tentative Score 89–91.

RESERVE, CABERNET SAUVIGNON, 2002: Inky dark purple, with still firm tannins starting to integrate now to reveal complex aromas and flavors of blackcurrant and black cherry fruits, Mediterranen herbs and, on the long finish, an appealingly light layer of earthiness. Drink now–2008. Score 90.

RESERVE, CABERNET SAUVIGNON, 2001: Not so much elegant as it is powerful, this rich and concentrated wine offers up a generous mouthful of currants and wild berries on a background of spices. Overall good balance between intense tannins, wood and fruit, but somewhat short and overly herbal on the finish. Drink now–2007. Score 87.

MILLENNIUM RESERVE, CABERNET SAUVIGNON, 2000: Medium to full-bodied, this deep ruby toward purple wine shows good balance between still firm tannins, oak, and fruits, those including generous and concentrated layers of currants and berries. Look for mint, minerals and earthy flavors on the long finish. Drink now. Score 89.

Bazelet Hagolan

BAZELET HAGOLAN, CABERNET SAUVIGNON, 2003: Ruby towards garnet in color, medium to full-bodied with aromas and flavors of cherries and Mediterranean herbs, hints of currants and chocolate that arise on the medium-long finish. Long and generous. Drink from release–2010. Tentative Score 88–90.

BAZELET HAGOLAN, CABERNET SAUVIGNON, 2002: Deep cherry-red towards garnet in color, medium to full-bodied, with concentrated currant, blackberry, spice and peppery notes. Good balance between wood and soft tannins and a moderately long finish. Drink now–2007. Score 87.

BAZELET HAGOLAN, CABERNET SAUVIGNON, 2001: Dark garnet toward ink-black in color, this full-bodied still firmly tannic wine shows rich Cabernet aromas and flavors of blackcurrants and blackberries, generous spiciness and nice earthy-olive hints, all on a broad background and with a long finish. Drink now–2007. Score 90.

BAZELET HAGOLAN, CABERNET SAUVIGNON, 2000: Royal purple in color, medium-bodied and with moderate levels of smooth tannins, the wine has tempting currant, plum, mint and earthy aromas and flavors. Drink now. Score 88.

BAZELET HAGOLAN, CABERNET SAUVIGNON, 1999: Full-bodied, with its once firm tannins now well integrated and with light overlays of spices and smoke from the oak in which it aged, the wine shows still youthful currant and plum fruits. Long and mouth-filling. Drink now. Score 89.

BAZELET HAGOLAN, CABERNET SAUVIGNON, 1998: During its youth this first release of the winery showed good balance and a moderate level of tannins. Medium to full-bodied and still showing plum and spice aromas and flavors, but with overlays of tobacco and leather rising to the fore, the wine is now past its peak. Drink up. Score 86.

Beit-El *

Established by California trained winemaker Hillel Manne in 2001 and located in the settlement of Beit-El, north of Jerusalem, this small winery has been producing Cabernet Sauvignon and Merlot wines from their own vineyards. The winery is currently producing about 3,000 bottles annually, nearly all of those destined for export to the United States.

BEIT-EL, CABERNET SAUVIGNON, 2004: Medium to full-bodied, with coarse tannins that seem not to want to integrate and, despite being categorized as dry, an unwanted touch of sweetness. Aromas and flavors of stewed plums, a foxy sensation on the palate and an alcoholic finish. Drink up. Score 72. K

BEIT-EL, MERLOT, 2004: Medium-bodied, with chunky tannins, too generous wood influence and forward aromas and flavors of ripe black fruits. Lacking complexity or sophistication. Drink up. Score 77. K

Benhaim **

Founded in 1997 by the Benhaim family on Moshav Kfar Azar in the Sharon region, the winery is currently producing about 40,000 bottles annually from Cabernet Sauvignon, Merlot, Petite Sirah, Chardonnay and Muscat Canelli grapes as well as a Port-style wine. With their own vineyards now planted on the eastern slopes of Mount Meron in the lower Galilee, those also containing Traminette and Gewurztraminer grapes, the winery is planning to expand its production to 50,000–60,000 bottles annually. Releases of Grande Reserve and regular Benhaim series have been kosher since the 2001 vintage.

Grande Reserve

BENHAIM, CABERNET SAUVIGNON, GRANDE RESERVE, 2001: Deep royal purple in color and reflecting its 26 months in oak casks with very generous vanilla-flavored wood and with rather coarse tannins that seem not to want to open. Stingy on its currant and black fruits and somewhat short. Drink now–2007. Score 85. K

BENHAIM, CABERNET SAUVIGNON, GRANDE RESERVE, 2000: Austere, tannic and with a narrow range of cedar, anise and black fruit aromas and flavors, this medium to full-bodied red spent 26 months in oak. Short on the finish, without depth and with too much wood. Drink up. Score 76.

Benhaim

BENHAIM, CABERNET SAUVIGNON, 2003: Dark garnet in color, medium to full-bodied, with generous wood and still firm tannins but those showing signs of integrating nicely with aromas and flavors of blackcurrants, blackberries, espresso and chocolate. Perhaps the best to date from the winery. Drink from release–2008. Tentative Score 87–89. K

BENHAIM, CABERNET SAUVIGNON, 2002: A blend of 85% Cabernet Sauvignon rounded out by the addition of Merlot and Petite Sirah. Medium to full-bodied, with soft tannins and generous spicy oak matched by wild berry, cassis and on the moderate finish a hint of minty-chocolate. Drink now–2007. Score 85. κ

BENHAIM, CABERNET SAUVIGNON, 2001: After 18 months in oak this medium-bodied wine has smooth tannins and appealing currant, berry and cassis flavors and an almost sweet finish. Drink now. Score 84. κ

BENHAIM, CABERNET SAUVIGNON, 2000: Beyond its attractive deep royal purple color, this wine has astringent tannins, not nearly enough fruit and imparts an odd salty taste to the palate. Showing age. Score 60.

BENHAIM, CABERNET SAUVIGNON, 1999: This medium-bodied wine has herbal and weedy overtones along with flat-edged tannins, but lacks any core of fruit flavors. Showing age. Score 70.

BENHAIM, CABERNET SAUVIGNON, 1998: Aged in oak barrels for 12 months, the wine had modest tannins along with ripe plum and wild berry flavors in its youth but now showing age. Score 70.

BENHAIM, MERLOT, 2003: Dark garnet towards purple, medium-bodied, with generous tannins and wood but those balanced nicely by aromas and flavors of cassis, black cherries and purple plums. Drink from release–2007. Tentative Score 85–87. κ

BENHAIM, MERLOT, 2002: Dark royal purple in color, medium-bodied, with soft tannins integrating nicely, this blend of 85% Merlot and 15% Cabernet Sauvignon and Petite Sirah that was oak-aged for 14 months is soft and round, with aromas and flavors of currants, purple plums and wild berries. Somewhat one-dimensional. Drink now. Score 85. κ

BENHAIM, MERLOT, 2001: This medium-bodied, not overly complex red shows moderate, well-integrated tannins along with generous plum and cassis fruits. Drink now. Score 85. κ

BENHAIM, MERLOT, 2000: Deep purple, medium-bodied, with moderate tannins and the barest hints of black fruits in its aromas and flavors, this somewhat overly earthy wine is now showing age. Score 70.

BENHAIM, PINOT NOIR, 2003: Cherry towards garnet red, medium-bodied, with soft tannins and ripe berry, cherry and plum notes. Lacks complexity, but pleasant. Drink now. Score 84. κ

BENHAIM, LE PEITE SIRAH DE BENHAIM, 2003: Garnet to royal purple in color, this medium-bodied blend of 60% Petite Sirah and 40% Merlot aged 12 months in oak shows soft tannins along with appealing currant and black cherry fruits. Not complex but pleasant. Drink now. Score 85 K

BENHAIM, LE PETITE SIRAH DE BENHAIM, 2002: This unusual and not successful blend of Petite Sirah and Merlot is somewhat musky and too earthy on the nose and palate, and has only stingy black fruits. Drink now. Score 76. K

BENHAIM, PETITE SIRAH, GRANDE RESERVE, 2000: Oak-aged for 30 months, this dark, almost chewy red offers up aromas and flavors of sweet-scented violets, cinnamon, vanilla and raspberries. A bit of unwanted coarseness on the finish. Drink now. Score 82.

BENHAIM, ROSÉ DE CABERNET, 2003: This rosé, made entirely from Cabernet Sauvignon grapes kept on the skins for only a short time and then allowed to develop in 500 liter barrels for 2 months, shows refreshing aromas and flavors of strawberries and raspberries. Drink up. Score 84. K

BENHAIM, CHARDONNAY, 2004: Medium-bodied, with pear, green apple and light spicy overtones. Drink now. Score 84. K

BENHAIM, CHARDONNAY, SINGLE VINEYARD, HAR MERON, 2003: Light golden in color, medium-bodied and with moderate wood-influence, this lightly buttery white shows melon, pineapple and summer fruits. Drink now. Score 84. K

BENHAIM, CHARDONNAY, 2003: Light to medium bodied, with refreshing acidity and pineapple, melon fruits. Drink up. Score 82. K

BENHAIM, CHARDONNAY, 2002: Medium-bodied, without much depth and somewhat on the tart side, with green apple and citrus aromas and flavors, and just a hint of minerals. Past its peak. Drink up. Score 77. K

BENHAIM, CHARDONNAY, 2001: This first kosher wine made by Benhaim is simple and fruity, with hints of pear, apple and spice aromas and flavors. Light to medium-bodied, the wine turns somewhat tart on the finish. Showing age and no longer scoreable. K

BENHAIM, MUSCAT CANELLI, DESSERT, 2003: This golden colored medium-bodied dessert wine offers up plenty of sweetness and fruity-floral aromas and flavors, those matched nicely by acidity. Drink up. Score 81. K

BENHAIM, MUSCAT, 2002: Unabashedly sweet, this light, golden medium-bodied wine has aromas and flavors of ripe white peaches and spring flowers but lacks the balancing acidity that might have kept it lively. Drink up. Score 80. K

BENHAIM, MARINA, 2000: This dark, sweet red wine, said to be made in the style of Port, imparts a coarseness that brings to mind a plum flavored cough medicine. Score 68. K

Ben-Hannah **

Located in Moshav Kfar Ruth in the central plains near the city of Modi'in, and receiving Cabernet Sauvignon, Merlot and Zinfandel grapes from the Negev and the Judean Mountains, this winery is the venture of Shlomi Zadok, who is also the winemaker at Nachshon. The winery's first release was of 2,500 bottles and plans to grow to 10,000 bottles annually.

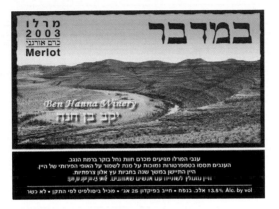

BEN-HANNAH, CABERNET SAUVIGNON, 2003: Aging in barrels originally used for Chardonnay, this dark cherry red, medium to full-bodied and still firmly tannic wine needs time, but as it develops look for currant, blueberry and mineral aromas and flavors all well balanced by lightly spicy oak. Drink from release–2007. Tentative Score 86–88.

BEN-HANNAH, CABERNET SAUVIGNON, BREISHEET, 2002: After eight months in oak, this medium-bodied light adobe brick red wine shows light tannins and a bare hint of wood along with currant and black cherry fruits and a light touch of Mediterranean herbs. Drink now. Score 84

BEN-HANNAH, MERLOT, 2004: Deep garnet in color, light to medium-bodied, this straightforward but pleasant little wine has focused cherry, vanilla and toasty oak notes. Drink from release. Tentative Score 84–86.

BEN-HANNAH, MERLOT, BAMIDBAR, 2003: Made from grapes from both the Negev and the Jerusalem Hills and aged in oak for one year, an appealing medium-bodied red, with soft tannins and aromas of plums and currants on a mineral-rich background. Drink now. Score 85.

BEN-HANNAH, CABERNET SAUVIGNON-MERLOT, SHALEM, 2003: Dark ruby towards royal purple, medium to full-bodied, with still firm tannins nicely balanced by spicy wood and already showing tempting berry, currant and black cherry fruits, those backed up nicely by light hints of earthiness and herbaceousness. The best yet from Ben-Hannah. Drink from release–2008. Tentative Score 87–89.

Binyamina ✳✳✳

First established in 1952 as Eliaz Wineries, the winery is located in the town of Binyamina at the foothills of the Carmel Mountains. In 1994 a group of investors bought out the outdated winery, replaced the existing management, and is still gradually introducing modern technology and equipment. Quality has been improving year by year, this manifested as well in the newly remodeled *chais* (barrel room), one of the most attractive in the country.

Under the supervision of winemaker Sasson Ben-Aharon, the winery is now the fourth largest in the country and produces nearly 2.8 million bottles annually from a large variety of grapes, those from vineyards in nearly every part of the country. To the winery's credit, they were the first in the country to introduce Viognier and Tempranillo varietals. Wines of interest are produced in the Special Reserve and regular Binyamina series as well as in the recently released non-vintage wines in the "Tiltan" series.

Special Reserve

SPECIAL RESERVE, CABERNET SAUVIGNON, 2003: Medium to full-bodied, dark garnet in color, with still firm tannins, but already showing ripe plum, blackberry and cherry fruits, a gentle overlay of spicy oak and an appealing herbal overtone on the finish. Drink now–2007. Score 86. K.

SPECIAL RESERVE, CABERNET SAUVIGNON, 2002: This medium to full-bodied wine continues to show firm tannins that seem not to want to integrate and a hint of sweetness that runs through. There are some dark, minty fruits here but those are a bit stingy. Drink now. Score 85. K.

SPECIAL RESERVE, CABERNET SAUVIGNON, 2001: Reflecting its 18 months in new and old *barriques*, this deep royal purple wine shows good balance between fruits, tannins and wood. It has generous but well-integrated tannins, a modicum of spicy oak and good currant and berry fruits as well as a warm herbal overlay that lingers nicely. Drink now. Score 87. K

SPECIAL RESERVE, CABERNET SAUVIGNON, 2000: Dark cherry-red toward purple, this medium to full-bodied wine spent 18 months in French oak *barriques*. Currant and black berry fruits dominate on the first sip, but let the wine open and it will reveal an appealing herbal-earthy background and a moderately long finish. Good balance between fruits, wood, acidity and tannins. Drink up. Score 88. K

SPECIAL RESERVE, CABERNET SAUVIGNON, 1999: This medium to full-bodied, not overly-oaked wine, offers up ample currant, black cherry, plum and herbal aromas and flavors, all on a well balanced frame and a relatively long finish. Past its peak. Drink up. Score 87. K

SPECIAL RESERVE, CABERNET SAUVIGNON, 1998: After spending 20 months in oak barrels, some French and some American, this smooth and moderately tannic wine had once appealing smoky, cherry and currant flavors but now well past its peak and no longer scoreable. K

SPECIAL RESERVE, CABERNET SAUVIGNON, 1996: Following a long skin contact of 12 days this medium to full-bodied wine was aged in new oak barrels for 16 months. During its youth it showed a nice overlay of spices as well as an abundance of blackberry and currant flavors, but now well past its peak and showing signs of caramelization. No longer scoreable. K.

SPECIAL RESERVE, MERLOT, 2003: This dark cherry red medium-bodied wine is not overly complex but has soft tannins and good balance between those, wood and fruits. Look for hints of licorice and chocolate on the berry-cherry fruits. Drink now. Score 87. K

SPECIAL RESERVE, MERLOT, 2002: The heavy wood once felt here has now settled down nicely and the wine now shows good balance between lightly smoky oak, soft tannins and fruits. Look for black plums, black cherries and berries here, all with a light spicy overlay. Not overly complex but appealing. Drink now. Score 85. K.

SPECIAL RESERVE, MERLOT, 2001: Reflecting its 14 months in *barriques*, this medium-bodied wine offers up sweet, smoky oak that comes together nicely with currant and almost jammy blackberry fruits. Good overlays of spices from mid-palate and then eucalyptus and Mediterranean herbs on the finish. Drink now. Score 87. K

SPECIAL RESERVE, MERLOT, 2000: This deep ruby toward garnet medium-bodied red was aged in a combination of new and one-year-old French and American oak casks, and even though it is somewhat acidic, it shows good currant, berry and black cherry aromas and flavors. Drink up. Score 86. K

SPECIAL RESERVE, MERLOT, 1999: Medium-bodied and dark garnet in color, the wine is starting to brown now, and its once appealing aromas and flavors of black fruit are fading. Somewhat past its peak. Drink up. Score 85. K

SPECIAL RESERVE, SHIRAZ, 2003: Royal purple in color, medium to full-bodied, with soft tannins, sweet cedar wood, black cherries, plums and a lightly earthy background. Well balanced, long and generous. Drink now–2007. Score 87. K

SPECIAL RESERVE, CABERNET SAUVIGNON-MERLOT SHIRAZ, 2003: Dark garnet red, full-bodied and deeply tannic at this stage but showing good balance between tannins, wood and fruits, already opening to show currant, berry and plum fruits, those intertwining nicely with hints of tobacco and chocolate. Drink now–2007. Score 88. K.

SPECIAL RESERVE, CHARDONNAY, 2004: Aged *sur lie* in French *barriques*, with a lively golden color and crisply refreshing spicy pear and apple fruits, this medium to full-bodied white shows appealing nectarine and vanilla flavors on the moderately long finish. Drink now–2007. Score 87. K

SPECIAL RESERVE, CHARDONNAY, 2003: Bright shining golden in color, with orange and green reflections, this oak-aged medium-bodied white offers up a nice mouthful of melon, peach and apple fruits. Give it time and it will reflect its aging *sur lie* with hints of toasted white bread and spicy oak. Drink now. Score 87. K

SPECIAL RESERVE, CHARDONNAY, 2002: After aging for 6 months *sur lie*, this bright golden wine shows clean apple, pineapple and melon fruits and just the right hints of wood and yeast. Moderately long on the finish. Drink up. Score 86. K

SPECIAL RESERVE, CHARDONNAY, 2001: This light straw medium-bodied wine has a stingy nose with hardly any fruit, flower or mineral flavors. On the palate it is somewhat dull, reflecting an imbalance between acidity and wood, and only bare hints of citrus and pineapple fruits. Well past its peak and no longer scoreable.K

SPECIAL RESERVE, SAUVIGNON BLANC, 2004: Unoaked, medium-bodied, with grassy, herbaceous and citrus flavors, this clean, crisp and refreshing wine opens nicely on the palate. Drink now. Score 85. K

SPECIAL RESERVE, SAUVIGNON BLANC, 2003: Light straw colored, medium-bodied and with crisp acidity, this unoaked white offers up generous pineapple, citrus and grassy flavors along with a light and appealing asphalt overlay. Drink now. Score 85. K

SPECIAL RESERVE, SAUVIGNON BLANC, 2002: This pale straw light to medium-bodied wine shows only stingy pineapple and citrus aromas and flavors. Drink up. Score 84. K

SPECIAL RESERVE, VIOGNIER, 2004: Aged *sur lie* in 80% new barrels and 20% formerly used for Chardonnay, with gentle acidity that yields to buttery-mineral nuances and with lemon and apple aromas and flavors as well as a lightly earthy note on the finish. Best Viognier from Binyamina to date. Drink now. Score 86. K

SPECIAL RESERVE, VIOGNIER, 2003: This unoaked light to medium-bodied wine shows light golden color and lively aromas of grapefruit, apricot and mint, as well as good balancing acid and a green apple note. Drink now. Score 86. K

SPECIAL RESERVE, VIOGNIER, 2002: Failing to reflect the characteristics of the Viognier grapes, this not very successful unoaked pioneering effort offers up grapefruit, orange peel and green apple flavors. Drink up. Score 82. K

SPECIAL RESERVE, GEWURZTRAMINER, HALF-DRY, 2003: A pleasant white, with fresh citrus and tropical fruits, and good balancing acidity to set off the sweetness. Drink up. Score 83. K

SPECIAL RESERVE, GEWURZTRAMINER, 2004: Golden straw in color, medium-bodied, barely off-dry and with good balancing acidity to keep it lively. Appealing spicy aromas and flavors of citrus, litchis and summer fruits. Drink now. Score 86. K

SPECIAL RESERVE, GEWURZTRAMINER, DESSERT WINE, 2003: Medium-bodied, with tropical fruits, citrus peel and floral aromas. Lacking the spiciness that should typify the variety and the acidity that might have made the wine more lively. Drink now. Score 83. K

Tiltan

TILTAN, CABERNET SAUVIGNON, N.V.: Showing better now than during earlier tastings, this medium-bodied wine made from grapes harvested in 2001, 2002 and 2003 and then blended after oak-aging shows softening but still-chunky tannins and moderate wood influence, balanced nicely by plum, blackcurrant and earthy aromas and flavors. Drink now. Score 85. K

TILTAN, MERLOT, N.V.: A blend of Merlot grapes from the Upper Galilee that were harvested in 2001, 2002 and 2003, the first batch aged in oak for fourteen months, the second for ten months and the third for three months. Soft tannins but somewhat heavily oaked and with only moderate aromas and flavors of currants, berries. Drink now. Score 85. K

Binyamina

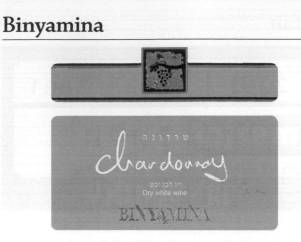

BINYAMINA, CABERNET SAUVIGNON, 2004: Light wood influences and chunky tannins give this medium-bodied wine a distinctly rustic touch. Simple but pleasant berry, cherry and cassis aromas and flavors. Drink now. Score 83. K

BINYAMINA, CABERNET SAUVIGNON, 2003: Aged partly in American and partly in French oak, this medium to full-bodied-wine shows dusty tannins that promise to integrate well, along with currant, berry and light earthy notes. Look for a hint of cinnamon on the moderately long finish. Drink now–2007. Score 86. K

BINYAMINA, CABERNET SAUVIGNON, 2002: Showing better now than it did in its youth, this bright cherry toward garnet medium-bodied wine may lack complexity but has an appealing cherry-berry personality. A simple but pleasant quaffer. Drink up. Score 84. K

BINYAMINA, CABERNET SAUVIGNON, 2001: Medium-bodied and softly tannic, this simple but pleasing wine has berry, cherry and currant fruits along with a hint of spiciness. Somewhat past its peak. Drink up. Score 85. K

BINYAMINA, MERLOT, 2003: Dark royal purple in color, this lightly oaked, medium-bodied wine shows generous but yielding tannins well balanced by wood and fruits. Good currant, raspberry and plum aromas and flavors along with a hint of cocoa on the finish. Drink now. Score 86. K

BINYAMINA, MERLOT, 2002: Blended with 10% Cabernet Sauvignon, this dark cherry-colored red has clean aromas that reflect several months in oak. Medium-bodied, with black cherry, currant and oak aromas and flavors, the wine is faulted because it is somewhat hot and has an overly earthy finish. Drink now. Score 80. K

BIYMANINA, SHIRAZ, 2003: Blended with 2% of Viognier, this medium-bodied, deep garnet wine reflects its twelve months in oak with soft tannins and a light vanilla overlay with spicy plums on a light herbal-earthy background. Drink now. Score 85. K

BINYAMINA, SHIRAZ, 2002: A wine that started well but seems to have aged prematurely and now showing somewhat stale stewed fruits and bitter herbs. Drink up. Score 73. K

BINYAMINA, TEMPRANILLO, 2002: Little here calls to mind the Tempranillo grape. Blended with 15% Cabernet Sauvignon, the wine is too light in body, lacks balance, length or breadth, and has stingy plum and blackberry fruits. Somewhat past its peak. Drink up. Score 80. K

BINYAMINA, CHARDONNAY 2004: Unoaked, youthful, fruity, fresh and friendly, not particularly strong on the nose but with tempting flavors of peaches and nectarines. Drink now. Score 85. K

BINYAMINA, CHARDONNAY, 2003: Light gold in color, this simple but pleasant white reflects its short time in oak with a spicy overlay on appealing citrus and green apple fruits. Drink now. Score 85. K

BINYAMINA, CHARDONNAY, 2002: Aged partly in American, partly in French oak, this medium-bodied white shows appealing citrus and melon fruits, those coming together nicely with light hints of oak and spring flowers. Drink up. Score 84. K

BINYAMINA, CHARDONNAY, 2001: Rustic in style, with a trace of unwanted bitterness that lingers on the palate and with a light earthy accent to citrus, pear and fig notes. Lacks focus. Past its peak. Drink up. Score 79. K

BINYAMINA, SAUVIGNON BLANC, 2004: Fresh and well balanced, unoaked and with generous acidity to keep it lively and backing up tropical fruit, green apple and light floral aromas and flavors. An unoaked good quaffing wine. Drink now. Score 84. K

BINYAMINA, SAUVIGNON BLANC, 2003: A pleasant little white showing pear, melon and citrus fruits on a lightly spicy background. Drink up. Score 85. K

BINYAMINA, SAUVIGNON BLANC, 2002: An abundance of pear and apple flavors on a background of earthy and mineral aromas and flavors in this simple white. Drink up. Score 83. K

BINYAMINA, MUSCAT, 2004: Semi-dry, not so much floral as it is herbal, with hints of mint on the citrus and summer fruits. Not overly sweet and perhaps best as an aperitif. Drink now. Score 83. K

BINYAMINA, MUSCAT, 2003: Light and bright in color, this medium-bodied white shows flavors of dried summer fruits and light pepper, its moderate sweetness offset nicely by natural acidity. Drink up. Score 83. K

BINYAMINA, MUSCAT, 2002: Pale golden in color and medium-bodied, the wine shows summer fruit aromas and flavors as well as a distinct caramel-toffee nature, but its very generous sweetness is not balanced properly by acidity. Drink up. Score. 82. K

BINYAMINA, MUSCAT, 2001: In its youth so deep gold that you might describe its color as liquid caramel, this semi-dry wine was rich in aromas but on the palate tastes somewhat like a fruit salad. Well past its peak and no longer scoreable. K

BINYAMINA, EMERALD RIESLING, 2004: Semi-dry, with floral aromas and flavors of nectarines and citrus, but a bit on the sweet side without enough balancing acidity. Drink up. Score 82. K.

BINYAMINA, EMERALD RIESLING, 2003: Half-dry but with refreshing natural acidity and citrus and tropical fruits, this is a good quaffer. Drink up. Score 83. K

Birya **

Founded by Moshe Porat in the community of Birya near the town of Sefad in the Galilee and drawing on grapes from Ramot Naftali in the Upper Galilee, the winery released its first wines from the 2003 vintage. Current production is about 4,500 bottles, two-thirds of which were released in April 2004 and the remainder given additional time in barrels.

BIRYA, CABERNET SAUVIGNON, 2004: Deep royal-purple in color, medium to full-bodied, with soft tannins integrating nicely and good balance between wood and fruits. Aromas and flavors of blackcurrants and berries on a light herbal background. Drink from release–2007. Tentative Score 84–86. K

BIRYA, CABERNET SAUVIGNON, PORAT WINE, 2003: A fair first effort, medium to full-bodied with firm but well integrating tannins and traditional Cabernet fruits of blackcurrants and berries. Look as well for hints of herbs and spices on the moderately long finish. Drink now. Score 85. K

BIRYA, MERLOT, 2004: Medium-bodied, soft and round, with forward berry, black cherry and currant fruits. A good quaffer. Drink from release. Tentative Score 84–86. K

BIRYA, MERLOT, PORAT WINE, 2003: Dark cherry-red toward garnet, this medium-bodied red offers up soft tannins and a berry-cherry-currant personality. Drink now. Score 84. K

Bustan ✳✳✳✳

Founded in 1994 by Ya'akov Fogler, this small winery situated on Moshav Sharai Tikva near Tel Aviv draws Cabernet Sauvignon and Merlot grapes from the Jerusalem and Judean Mountains, and produces about 2,000 bottles annually. The winery has earned a good name for its distinctly French-style wines, which have had a formal kashrut certificate since 1999.

BUSTAN, CABERNET SAUVIGNON, 2003: Dark ruby to garnet, medium-bodied, with soft tannins integrating well and with generous but not overwhelming spicy oak. Spicy currant and berry fruits along with chocolate and tobacco on the finish. Drink from release–2010. Tentative Score 90. K

BUSTAN, CABERNET SAUVIGNON, 2002: Medium to full-bodied, deep garnet towards royal purple, with firm tannins now integrating nicely to reveal sweet cedar wood, currants, wild berries and hints of chocolate, espresso and anise. Drink now–2008. Score 89. K

BUSTAN, CABERNET SAUVIGNON, 2000: Medium-bodied, lacking balance between too soft tannins, heavy acidity and black fruits that seem too sweet on the palate, this is the first disappointing wine from an otherwise excellent winery. Drink now–2007. Score 84. K

BUSTAN, CABERNET SAUVIGNON, 1999: An intense wine with rich and vibrant currant, black cherry and mocha aromas and flavors, these unfolding on the palate to reveal complexity and depth. After losing the rough edges of youth, the wine is now long and elegant and is starting to reveal delicious chocolate, tobacco and anise notes. Drink now–2007. Score 92. K

BUSTAN, CABERNET SAUVIGNON, 1998: Full-bodied and rich, the wine shows aromas and flavors of black cherries, currants and oak as well as spicy overtones, all sitting comfortably on the palate. Deep, long and complex, the wine opens in the glass to reveal its elegance. Drink now–2007. Score 91.

BUSTAN, CABERNET SAUVIGNON, 1997: With 21 months in small oak casks, this ripe and generous wine has distinctive mouth filling aromas and flavors of blackcurrants and black cherries as well as minty and spicy overtones that linger on and on. Well structured, stylish and graceful, and with soft, now well-integrated tannins. Drink now–2007. Score 90.

BUSTAN, CABERNET SAUVIGNON, 1996: During its youth this wine was searingly tannic but even then showed balance that boded well for its future. Now full-bodied and deep, with the tannins having taken on a softer, sweeter nature and with aromas of black and red currants, wild berries, tobacco, coffee and oak, the wine is drinking beautifully. Drink now. Score 92.

BUSTAN, CABERNET SAUVIGNON, 1995: Oak-aged for 20 months, now fully mature and showing tempting blackcurrant, plum and berry fruits, those matched nicely by aromas and flavors of toasty oak, espresso coffee and black olives on the finish. Drink now. Score 92.

BUSTAN, CABERNET SAUVIGNON, 1994: Oak-aged for 19 months, with its tannins and wood now fully integrated, this well balanced wine from a problematic vintage still shows complex aromas and flavors of currants, berries and black cherries, those matched nicely by minerals, while the finish yields spices and a hint of mint. Still delicious but not for further cellaring. Drink up. Score 89.

BUSTAN, MERLOT, 2000: Dark royal purple in color, this medium to full-bodied red shows good balance between soft tannins, sweet cedar, plum and blackberry aromas and flavors. Softening nicely on the palate, this is a round and flavorful wine. Drink now–2007. Score 89. K

BUSTAN, MERLOT, 1999: Deep, dark, rich and full-bodied, with spicy currant, mocha, nut, herbal and coffee aromas and flavors, this well-balanced wine has firm but well-integrated tannins and a long complex finish. The best Merlot from Bustan to date. Drink now. Score 93. K

BUSTAN, MERLOT, 1998: Round and soft, and with deep layers of wild berries, black cherries, mint and spices that open nicely in the glass, the wine has generous but well-integrated tannins, a good hand with the oak and a long, mouth-filling finish. Drink now. Score 91.

BUSTAN, MERLOT, 1997: Bold, ripe and delicious, with layers of rich plums, currants and black cherries along with a bare herbal accent. The wine has deep flavors that linger comfortably on the palate, good balance between fruits, acids and tannins, and a long finish. Drink now. Score 90.

BUSTAN, MERLOT, 1996: When first released, the wine was so dense and tannic that one might easily have taken it for a Rhone Syrah. The wine still shows firm tannins but those are now well integrated with smoky-spicy oak, natural acidity and appealing black cherry and wild berry fruits, all coming together in a long finish. Drink up. Score 91.

BUSTAN, MERLOT, 1995: Medium-bodied, with silky tannins and holding nicely to the caressing texture of its youth, the wine yields stewed black fruits, tobacco and chocolate, those matched well by light herbal overtones. Past its peak. Drink up. Score 90.

BUSTAN, MERLOT, 1994: Complex and delicious in its heyday, with aromas and flavors of black cherries, raisins, chocolate and spices, but now past its peak and showing age. No longer scoreable.

Bustan Hameshusheem *

Located on Moshav Had Ness on the Golan Heights, wine-maker-owner Benny Josef released his first wines to the market from the 2001 vintage. Production of 8,000 bottles annually is primarily of Cabernet Sauvignon, Merlot, Barbera and Sangiovese, and the grapes are drawn from the upper Galilee and nearby vineyards.

BUSTAN HAMESHUSHEEM, CABERNET SAUVIGNON, 2003: Deep royal purple in color, medium-bodied, with country-style chunky tannins matched nicely by smoky oak, plum and blackberry aromas and flavors. Drink now. Score 84.

BUSTAN HAMESHUSHEEM, CABERNET SAUVIGNON, 2002: Medium to full-bodied, with somewhat coarse tannins that mark it as country-style, and with ripe plum and berry fruits. Simple but pleasant. Drink now. Score 82.

BUSTAN HAMESHUSHEEM, CABERNET SAUVIGNON, 2001: Dark garnet in color, medium-bodied and with soft tannins, the wine is somewhat stingy in its fruit and vanilla aromas and flavors and a bit overly acidic. Drink up. Score 78.

BUSTAN HAMESHUSHEEM, SANGIOVESE-CABERNET SAUVIGNON-MERLOT, 2002: Medium-bodied, dark cherry red in color, and with soft tannins but somewhat diffuse aromas and flavors, the wine is quite acidic and doesn't reflect the nature of any of the varieties in the blend. Drink up. Score 78.

Carmel ✶✶✶✶

Carmel was founded as a cooperative of vintners in 1882 with funding provided by the Baron Edmond de Rothschild. Its first winery was constructed that same year in Rishon Letzion, in the central coastal region of the country, followed in 1890 by a winery in Zichron Ya'akov, in the Mount Carmel area. Carmel receives grapes from about 300 vineyards throughout the country, some owned by the winery, others by individual vintners and by *kibbutzim* and *moshavim*. Even though their share of the local wine market has dropped from over ninety percent in the early 1980s to somewhat under fifty percent today, Carmel remains the largest wine producer in the country, currently producing over 13 million bottles annually.

For many years, Carmel was in a moribund state, producing wines that while acceptable, rarely attained excellence and failed to capture the attention of more sophisticated consumers. In the last three years, under former CEO David Ziv, Carmel took dramatic steps to improve the level of their wines. Senior winemakers Lior Laxer at the Rishon Letzion winery and Philippe Lichtenstein at the Zichron Ya'akov facility are now overseeing a staff of eight talented winemakers, most of whom have trained and worked outside of Israel; the winery is developing new vineyards in choice areas of the country and gaining fuller control over contract vineyards; and major steps have already been undertaken to bring the two wineries to fully modern status. In the 1990s Carmel was the first winery to plant major vineyards in the Negev Desert, has more recently established a quasi-independent boutique arm in Zichron Ya'akov, and is also a partner in the new Yatir winery.

Current releases include the top-of-the-line varietal Single Vineyard series, the wines in the Regional series and the Private Collection series. Other wines of interest are in the Zichron Ya'akov series, the Selected series (sometimes known as Vineyards or Vineyards Selected Series outside of Israel) and the Hiluleem series.

Single Vineyard

SINGLE VINEYARD, CABERNET SAUVIGNON, KEREM BEN ZIMRA, 2002: Deep garnet-purple towards black, full-bodied, reflecting its fourteen months in new and used French oak with generous tannins and spicy oak, well balanced by berry, plum and currant fruits set off nicely by hints of vanilla and eucalyptus. On the long finish of this round and complex wine look for yields of tobacco and green olives. Drink now–2009. Score 91. **K**

SINGLE VINEYARD, CABERNET SAUVINGON, KEREM ZARIT, EMEK KADESH, 2003: Dark garnet, with firm, near sweet tannins that yield nicely in the glass to reveal an appealing touch of rustic earthiness that adds dimension to rich, ripe black fruits. Complex and concentrated. Best 2007–2011. Score 90. **K**

SINGLE VINEYARD, CABERNET SAUVIGNON, KEREM ZARIT, EMEK KADESH, 2002: Dark cherry-red, this medium to full-bodied wine shows soft tannins and generous vanilla and smoky overtones. First impressions are of berries and eucalyptus, those yielding to currants, vanilla, black tea and a light spiciness that lingers nicely on the moderately long finish. Warm, round and well balanced. Drink now- 2008. Score 90. **K**

SINGLE VINEYARD, CABERNET SAUVIGNON, KEREM ZARIT, EMEK KADESH, 2001: Made entirely from Cabernet Sauvignon grapes and aged in French oak *barriques* for 12 months, the wine has a lively cherry-ruby color. The opening impression on the nose is of eucalyptus and black fruits, and on the palate, of sweet berries. Medium-bodied and with soft tannins, the wine opens nicely in the glass and has a medium-long finish. Drink now–2009. Score 87. **K**

SINGLE VINEYARD, CABERNET SAUVIGNON, RAMAT ARAD, 2002: One of Carmel's best efforts ever. Dark garnet red, full-bodied, with abundant but soft, almost sweet and already well integrating tannins. Opens on the palate with black fruits and sweet cedar wood, those yielding to currants, berries and vanilla and finally to a tempting herbal-earthy sensation. Long and complex. Drink now–2009. Score 92. κ

SINGLE VINEYARD, CABERNET SAUVIGNON, RAMAT ARAD, 2000: Aged in French *barriques* for 14 months, this is one of Carmel's best efforts. Deep red toward garnet, this full-bodied red boasts excellent balance between abundant but soft and well-integrated tannins, just the right hints of vanilla and smoke from the wood, and tempting aromas and flavors that start off with stewed black fruits and then lead to a long earthy-spicy finish. Drink now–2008. Score 92. κ

SINGLE VINEYARD, CABERNET SAUVIGNON, KAYOUMI, 2004: Rich, ripe and well balanced, with complex and concentrated berry, plum, cassis, mineral, sage and cedar aromas and flavors that firm up to become somewhat tannic on the finish. Best 2007–2011. Tentative Score 88–90. κ

SINGLE VINEYARD, CABERNET SAUVIGNON, SCHECH, 2004: From a not yet well known vineyard on the Golan Heights, this red lives up nicely to the stereotypes of what makes a wine "feminine." Soft, round and caressing, elegant without being intense, full-bodied without being concentrated and with tempting aromas and flavors of black cherries, currants and anise. Drink from release–2012. Tentative Score 88–90. κ

SINGLE VINEYARD, MERLOT, HAR BRACHA (IN THE USA KEREM SHOMRON), 2002: Full-bodied and complex, this dark purple towards black wine shows still rather firm tannins but has balance and structure that bode well for the future. In time look for black cherry, currant and plum fruits, those on a spicy cedar-wood background. Drink now–2009. Score 92. κ

SINGLE VINEYARD, SHIRAZ, KAYOUMI, 2003: Firm and well-structured and with balance that bodes well for a soft and caressing wine. Rich tannins, vanilla, chocolate and mocha together with currant, blackberry and anise aromas and flavors that linger nicely. Drink now–2009. Score 89. κ

SINGLE VINEYARD, SYRAH, RAMAT ARAD, 2003: Oak aged for about nine months, this dark cherry red towards purple, medium to full-bodied wine shows excellent balance between soft tannins, smoke, spices, and aromas and flavors of currants, plums and chocolate. Long, smooth and generous. Drink now–2008. Score 90. κ

SINGLE VINEYARD, SYRAH, RAMAT ARAD, 2002: Made from the grapes of young vines, this fresh and lively medium-bodied wine was wisely placed in oak for only 4 months and now shows soft tannins, generous plum, currant and berry fruits as well as a nice layer of spiciness, and just the barest hint of freshly turned earth. Drink now. Score 89. K

SINGLE VINEYARD, CHARDONNAY, KAYOUMI, 2004: Bright and lively and with enough complexity to catch your attention. Developed in 300 liter barrels, this medium-bodied white shows aromas and flavors of citrus peel, vanilla pastry cream and brioche, all lingering nicely. Drink now–2007. Score 90. K

SINGLE VINEYARD, CHARDONNAY, MERON, 2003: After fermenting in stainless steel, the wine was transferred to new oak casks to develop *sur lie*. Medium to full-bodied, it already shows appealing buttery and vanilla flavors on a background of pears, spices and citrus, all with just the right level of smoky, toasty oak. Rich, mouth-filling and long. Drink now–2007. Score 90. K

SINGLE VINEYARD, CHARDONNAY, HAR TAVOR, 2002: Medium-bodied, smooth and supple, the wine offers up ripe pear, pineapple and grapefruit fruits backed up nicely by hints of oak, spices, and a wisp of honey that comes in on the finish. Look as well for light hints of vanilla and nutmeg. Drink now. Score 89. K

SINGLE VINEYARD, SAUVIGNON BLANC, RAMAT ARAD, 2004: Light golden-straw in color with a surprising tinge of pink, medium-bodied, unoaked and remarkably light on the palate. Bright, clean and crisp, with fresh citrus, tropical fruits and appealing herbal overtones leading to a moderately-long finish. Drink now. Score 88. K

SINGLE VINEYARD, SAUVIGNON BLANC, RAMAT ARAD, 2003: Bright golden straw in color, medium-bodied and with fresh nectarine, citrus and floral aromas and flavors on a mineral-rich background. Rich, clean and refreshing. Drink now. Score 89. K

Regional (Appelation)

REGIONAL, CABERNET SAUVIGNON, UPPER GALILEE AND RAMAT ARAD, 2002: Deep garnet towards purple, medium to full-bodied and reflecting generous but well integrated tannins after aging in new French oak for fourteen months. Compact and well focused, showing aromas and flavors of cedary oak, red currants, violets and dark chocolate. On the medium-long finish look for appealing hints of spices and tobacco. Drink now. Score 87. K

REGIONAL, CABERNET SAUVIGNON, UPPER GALILEE AND RAMAT ARAD, 2001: Made entirely from Cabernet Sauvignon grapes and aged for fourteen months in small oak barrels, this deep purple, medium to full-bodied red shows good balance between wood, soft tannins and fruits. On the nose and palate red and black berries, purple plums and a hint of eucalyptus on the medium-long finish. Drink now. Score 88. K

REGIONAL, CABERNET FRANC, JERUSALEM MOUNTAINS, 2002: Made entirely from Cabernet Franc grapes, this deep ruby towards garnet wine shows good balance between medium to full-body, generous soft tannins and currant and berry fruits together with the lead-pencil sensation one often finds in the wines of Bordeaux. Drink now–2007. Score 88. K

REGIONAL, LIMITED EDITION, 2003: A Bordeaux blend, this year of 50% Cabernet Sauvignon, 33% Petit Verdot, 16% Merlot and 1% Cabernet Franc. Somewhat more wood than in the 2002 release, but that balanced nicely by soft tannins and complex aromas and flavors of gooseberries, raspberries, currant, spice and cedar wood. Still a bit rough around the edges. Best 2007–2012. Score 90. K

REGIONAL, LIMITED EDITION, 2002: Deep royal-purple in color with orange reflections, a Bordeaux blend of 60% Cabernet Sauvignon, 30% Merlot and 10% Cabernet Franc, each variety vinified separately and developed for fourteen months in French oak before the final blend was made. Medium to full-bodied, with soft tannins integrating nicely and good balance between sweet and smoky wood, aromas and flavors of blackcurrants, berries, dark chocolate and a long finish. One of the best ever from Carmel. Drink now–2012. Score 92. K

REGIONAL, PETITE SIRAH, JUDEAN HILLS, 2004: Deep ruby towards garnet, this is an intense and vibrant wine, full-bodied, still rough around the edges but worth watching as it should open to reveal ample tannins well balanced by wood, and flavors and aromas of black cherries, currant and mocha. Best 2007–2010. Score 89. K

REGIONAL, CHARDONNAY, HAR TAVOR, 2004: Medium-bodied, buttery, and with appealing aromas and flavors of bitter oranges and tropical fruits. Good balance between acidity, wood and fruits. Drink now. Score 86. K

REGIONAL, CHARDONNAY, GALILEE, 2003: Oak fermented and then developed *sur lie* for nine months, this light gold, medium-bodied white offers up a generous mouthful of summer and tropical fruits, those matched nicely by crisp minerals and just the right feel of oak. Drink now. Score 88. K

REGIONAL, SAUVIGNON BLANC-CHARDONNAY, UPPER GALILEE AND RAMAT ARAD, 2003: A blend of 80% Sauvignon Blanc from Ramat Arad and 20% Chardonnay from the Upper Galilee, this wine was fermented in stainless steel and then transferred to new French oak *barriques* to develop *sur lie* for six months. Clean, light to medium-bodied, with generous acidity and appealing grapefruit and melon flavors. Drink now. Score 86. K

Private Collection

PRIVATE COLLECTION, CABERNET SAUVIGNON, 2003: Dark royal-purple in color, medium to full-bodied, with tannins integrating nicely and appealing aromas and flavors of currants, wild berries, spicy oak. Drink now–2007. Score 85. K

PRIVATE COLLECTION, CABERNET SAUVIGNON, 2002: Dark royal purple, this medium to full-bodied oak-aged red shows appealing aromas and flavors of currants, black cherries and spices. Good balance between moderate tannins, acidity and wood. Drink now–2007. Score 87. K

PRIVATE COLLECTION, CABERNET SAUVIGNON, 2001: Medium to full-bodied, this dark cherry red toward garnet wine shows firm tannins and a rather generous hand with the oak beyond. Given time to open in the glass the wine shows wild berry, currant and lightly spicy aromas and flavors. Drink up. Score 85. K

PRIVATE COLLECTION, CABERNET SAUVIGNON, 2000: Medium to full-bodied, the wine shows firm but well-integrated tannins along with appealing currant, cedar wood and earthy aromas and flavors. Not overly complex. Drink up. Score 86. K

PRIVATE COLLECTION, CABERNET SAUVIGNON, RAMAT ARAD, 1999: Medium to full-bodied, well-balanced and deep royal purple in color, the wine has plenty of smooth tannins and good black fruit including currants and plums as well as a nice herbal-vegetable overlay. Drink up. Score 88. K

PRIVATE COLLECTION, CABERNET SAUVIGNON, 1999: Ripe, with good firm tannins and a solid core of black cherry and cedary oak flavors but now showing age and no longer scoreable. K

PRIVATE COLLECTION, CABERNET SAUVIGNON, NO. 1, RAMAT ARAD, 1998: Made entirely from Cabernet Sauvignon grapes harvested at Ramat Arad and the Yatir Forest, this medium to full-bodied wine spent 12 months in French oak casks and shows nice flavors of vanilla and fresh herbs, but lacks a core of ripe fruits that might have added to its charm. Drink up. Score 85. K

PRIVATE COLLECTION, CABERNET SAUVIGNON, 1988: Now rapidly browning in color, the first sip of this wine still reveals some fruits but after a few minutes in the glass it yields somewhat acidic aromas and caramelized flavors. Showing age and no longer scoreable. K

PRIVATE COLLECTION, CABERNET SAUVIGNON, RAMAT ARAD, 1997: Spicy and peppery in character, the wine has a supple texture and smooth ripe tannins along with a nice core of currant, black cherry and wild berry flavors. After ten months of barrel aging, this well focused wine has appealing overlays of oak. Past its peak. Drink up. Score 86. K

PRIVATE COLLECTION, MERLOT, 2003: Deep garnet in color, medium-bodied, reflecting its ten months in oak with hints of vanilla and spices along with firm tannins that may yield in time but now hold back the plum and berry fruits. Drink now–2007. Score 85. K

PRIVATE COLLECTION, MERLOT, 2002: This medium-bodied soft and round wine has stingy aromas but offers up generous and appealing flavors of black cherries and plums. Drink up. Score 85. K

PRIVATE COLLECTION, MERLOT, 2001: Medium-bodied, soft and round, with generous berry, cherry and currant fruits along with light hints of oak and fresh herbs. Not overly complex but pleasant. Drink up. Score 85. K

PRIVATE COLLECTION, MERLOT, 2000: Not a classic Merlot but a solid and well made wine that boasts plenty of currant, wild berry, black cherry and spicy flavors as well as good balance and abundant firm tannins. Drink up. Score 86. K

PRIVATE COLLECTION, MERLOT, NO 1, 1999: This generous wine that was aged in French oak barrels for 10 months is firm and tannic but has plenty of herbal, oak and fruit flavors, primarily cherries and wild berries. Lingers nicely on the palate. Drink up. Score 87. K

PRIVATE COLLECTION, MERLOT, 1999: Firm and tannic, but with plenty of cherry, herb and oak flavors that come through on the palate. Drink up. Score 84. K

PRIVATE COLLECTION, MERLOT, NO. 1, RAMAT ARAD, 1998: More tannic and sharper than one usually expects from a pure Merlot, this is nevertheless a pleasant medium-bodied wine with herb and wild berry flavors and appealing mineral accents. Somewhat past its peak. Drink up. Score 85. K

PRIVATE COLLECTION, CABERNET SAUVIGNON-MERLOT, 2003: Medium to full-bodied, with soft tannins and appealing currant and plum fruits backed up by hints of spices and sweet herbs. Drink now. Score 85. K

PRIVATE COLLECTION, CABERNET SAUVIGNON-MERLOT, 2002: This medium-bodied red shows just enough cherry, plum and spicy notes on a smooth, moderately tannic background. Drink now. Score 86. K

PRIVATE COLLECTION, CABERNET SAUVIGNON-MERLOT, 2000: Medium-bodied, with an attractive ruby-garnet color, this lightly herbal wine shows a modest range of plum, cherry, earth and anise aromas and flavors as well as a cedary, moderately tannic finish. Drink up. Score 85. K

PRIVATE COLLECTION, CABERNET-MERLOT, 1999: Earthy, lean and tight, the wine shows currant and cherry notes that struggle, not fully successfully, to break through. The finish is packed with oak. Drink up. Score 85. K

PRIVATE COLLECTION, CABERNET SAUVIGNON-SHIRAZ, 2002: The abundant wood and tannins are backed up by enough berry, black

95

cherry and earthy-herbal aromas and flavors to pull the wine together. Needs time to open in the glass. Drink now. Score 86. **K**

PRIVATE COLLECTION, CABERNET SAUVIGNON-SHIRAZ, 2001: Crisp and tannic but slightly too acidic, this ruggedly country-style wine has aromas and flavors of unripe cherries and currants. Drink up. Score 82. **K**

PRIVATE COLLECTION, CHARDONNAY, 2002: Fermented in the barrels and allowed to develop *sur lie* for eight months, the wine has attractive aromas and flavors of citrus fruits and peel, a hint of pineapple, and a light underlying spiciness. Somewhat past its peak. Drink now. Score 86. **K**

PRIVATE COLLECTION, CHARDONNAY, 2001: Soft, generous and fresh, with an abundance of spicy citrus, pineapple and floral aromas and flavors Well past its peak and no longer scoreable. **K**

PRIVATE COLLECTION, SAUVIGNON BLANC, 2003: After undergoing long, low temperature fermentation to keep its fresh fruity character, this crisply refreshing unoaked white shows a core of nectarine, citrus, floral and light grassy aromas and flavors. Full of flavor and charming. Drink now. Score 88. **K**

PRIVATE COLLECTION, SAUVIGNON BLANC, 2001: Light spices and floral aromas and flavors that come together with hints of pears and citrus make this medium-bodied wine lively. Past its peak. Drink up. Score 80. **K**

PRIVATE COLLECTION, CHARDONNAY-SAUVIGNON BLANC, 2003: Medium-bodied, clean and crisp, the wine shows summer fruit, pineapple and citrus aromas and flavors. Drink now. Score 84. **K**

PRIVATE COLLECTION, CHARDONNAY-SAUVIGNON BLANC, 2001: An appealing fresh white with peach, apple and citrus flavors. Drink up. Score 82. **K**

PRIVATE COLLECTION, CHARDONNAY-SAUVIGNON BLANC, 2000: Already darkening in color, the wine still shows a few citrus flavors but now taking on a light caramelized personality. Well past its peak and no longer scoreable. **K**

PRIVATE COLLECTION, EMERALD RIESLING, 2004: Light golden straw in color, light to medium-bodied, floral on the nose, with thankfully restrained sweetness, good liveliness and flavors citrus and tropical fruits. Drink now. Score 80. **K**

PRIVATE COLLECTION, EMERALD RIESLING, 2003: Flowery on the nose, medium-bodied and with refreshing grapefruit and lemon fruits, this straightforward semi-dry wine is not overly sweet. Drink up. Score 82. K

Selected (Vineyard)

SELECTED, CABERNET SAUVIGNON, 2004: Dark garnet, medium-bodied, with somewhat coarse tannins and rather stingy currant and plum notes. Drink up. Score 82. K

SELECTED, CABERNET SAUVIGNON, 2003: Dark in color, medium-bodied and with soft tannins and appealing plum, currant and black cherry fruits, those with appealing hints of spices and Mediterranean herbs. Drink now. Score 83. K

SELECTED, CABERNET SAUVIGNON, 2002: Deep garnet in color, this pleasant medium-bodied wine reflects its nine months in oak with only moderate wood and tannins, and shows aromas and flavors of currants, herbs and anise. Drink up. Score 82. K

SELECTED, MERLOT, 2004: Medium-bodied, with soft tannins and forward black fruits. A simple entry-level wine. Drink now. Score 82. K

SELECTED, MERLOT, 2003: Medium-bodied, with silky tannins and generous black fruits and a hint of spiciness. Somewhat one dimensional but good with food. Drink now. Score 83. K

SELECTED, MERLOT, 2002: Appealing royal purple in color, this medium-bodied red opens slowly in the glass to reveal plum, currant and black cherry fruits along with a hint of spiciness but lacks enough tannins or wood to give it a backbone. Drink up. Score 81. **K**

SELECTED, PETITE SIRAH, 2004: Medium-bodied, with country-style tannins and a hint of overall coarseness but generous berry and earthy aromas and flavors. Drink now. Score 83. **K**

SELECTED, PETITE SIRAH, 2003: Dark cherry-red, this medium-bodied wine offers up somewhat chunky tannins and appealing plum and berry flavors. Not complex but an appealing country-style wine. Drink now. Score 84. **K**

SELECTED, PETITE SIRAH, 2002: Light to medium-bodied, with moderate tannins but somewhat stingy with its black fruit flavors. Drink up. Score 82. **K**

SELECTED, ARGAMAN, 2002: Deep royal purple in color, medium-bodied and with generous plum and berry fruits. Low in tannins and lacking depth or breadth but a pleasant little quaffer. Drink up. Score 80. **K**

SELECTED, ZINFANDEL, 2003: A semi-dry blush Zinfandel of medium body with some appealing fresh berry-cherry aromas and flavors but with sweetness that is not matched by acidity or depth. Drink up. Score 80. **K**

SELECTED, HAR ADIR RED, 2001: Based on Cabernet Sauvignon and Merlot grapes, this medium-bodied red offers up firm layers of tannins that tend to hide the red and black fruit flavors. Somewhat one-dimensional. Drink up. Score 81. **K**

SELECTED, CHARDONNAY, 2004: A simpe little wine, light in color, with citrus and pineapple flavors. Drink now. Score 82. **K**

SELECTED, CHARDONNAY, 2003: Simple and fruity, the wine shows hints of apples, pears and spices along with a short grassy-herbal finish. Lacking depth or length. Drink up. Score 81. **K**

SELECTED, SAUVIGNON BLANC, 2003: Light straw colored, with a few citrus and tropical fruits but lacking liveliness or charm. Drink up. Score 79. **K**

SELECTED, EMERALD RIESLING, 2003: This clean semi-dry wine has grape and floral aromas and flavors but lacks crispness or depth. Drink up. Score 78. **K**

Zichron Ya'akov

ZICHRON YA'AKOV, MERLOT, 2003: Dark garnet in color, medium-bodied, with soft, well-integrated tannins and appealing black cherry and currant fruits. Lacking complexity, but a good everyday wine. Drink now. Score 84. K

ZICHRON YA'AKOV, MERLOT, 2002: Bright purple toward garnet in color, the wine has up-front plum, black cherry and light spicy aromas and flavors, but lacks a balance between those fruits, tannins and wood. Drink up. Score 79. K

ZICHRON YA'AKOV, MERLOT, 2001: Not complex but smooth and lively with berry and black cherry flavors and moderate tannins, this wine was destined for early drinking and is now starting to show age. Drink up. Score 80. K

ZICHRON YA'AKOV, CABERNET SAUVIGNON-SYRAH, 2001: This medium bodied wine with not fully ripe currant and plum flavors is somewhat tart and stingy. Drink up. Score 79. K

ZICHRON YA'AKOV, CABERNET SAUVIGNON-MERLOT, 2000: Light to medium-bodied, the wine is low in tannins even though it spent 8 months in oak and has hardly any aromas and only moderate hints of berries and currants flavors. Well past its peak and no longer scoreable. K

ZICHRON YA'AKOV, RED, 2004: An unoaked blend of Merlot, Carignan, Cabernet Sauvignon and Petit Sirah. Garnet to purple in color, medium-bodied with soft tannins and berry-cherry fruits. An appealing quaffer. Drink up. Score 85. K

ZICHRON YA'AKOV, SAUVIGNON BLANC, 2004 (ADVANCE TASTING): Light straw towards gold in color, medium-bodied, this unoaked blend of 87% Sauvignon Blanc and 13% Chardonnay proves acidic but refreshing, with crisp, clean citrus, pear and pineapple aromas and flavors matched by an appealing hint of bitterness. Drink now. Score 86. κ

ZICHRON YA'AKOV, CHADONNAY-SEMILLON, 2002: Medium-bodied, clean, fresh with citrus and summer fruits. Drink up. Score 82. κ

ZICHRON YA'AKOV, CHARDONNAY-SEMILLON, 2001: This medium-bodied wine shows plenty of floral, lime and litchi aromas and flavors, but leaves a rather sharp and sour sensation on the palate. Well past its peak and no longer scoreable. κ

ZICHRON YA'AKOV, EMERALD RIESLING-FRENCH COLOMBARD, 2002: A semi-dry white that is low in aroma, low in flavor and low in acidity. Drink up. Score 75. κ

ZICHRON YA'AKOV, WHITE, 2004: A somewhat disconnected potpourri of Sauvignon Blanc, French Colombard, Chardonnay, Emerald Riesling and Semillon. Very fruity and flowery, with tropical fruits, citrus and a hint of sweetness. An acceptable entry-level wine. Drink up. Score 80. κ

Not Part of a Specific Series

CARMEL, SYRAH, 2001: With an alcohol content of only 11%, only a few black cherry and herbal flavors and lacking in tannins and oak, this light, one-dimensional and too sour blend of 85% Sirah and 15% Cabernet Sauvignon fails to excite. Drink up. Score 78. κ

CARMEL, EMERALD RIESLING, GVAT ZAMARIN, 2004: A blend of just about every white grape (Sauvignon Blanc, French Colombard, Chardonnay, Semillon and Emerald Riesling), this dry white offers up clean aromas and flavors of tropical fruits, pears and melons, all with just enough natural acidity to keep it lively. Drink up. Score 84. κ

CARMEL, HILULEEM, ADOM, 2004: A super-light, super-fruity young blend of Merlot, Syrah and Petite Sirah, with clean aromas of raspberry, cherries and strawberries. Serve chilled. Drink up. Score 82.

CARMEL, HILULEEM, WHITE, 2004: A blend of Sauvignon Blanc, Semillon and a bit of Chardonnay, this straw colored wine is light in body, flowery on the nose and yields flavors of tropical fruits. A bit more acidity might have helped. Drink up. Score 79.

CARMEL, MUSCAT DESSERT WINE, 2002: Made from late harvested Muscat of Alexandria grapes that were fermented slowly and then reinforced with alcohol to stop the fermentation, this sweet, fruity and fresh wine offers up ripe pear, litchi and honeyed aromas and flavors.

Balanced, elegant and a good match to fruit based desserts. Drink now. Score 88. **K**

CARMEL, THE PRESIDENT'S WINE, N.V.: Carmel's attempt at producing a sparkling wine has far too much acidity, its flavors and aromas are too similar to a nectar made from tropical fruits, lemon and grapefruit, and its bubbles are far too "fat" and not long-lasting enough. Score 75. **K**

Castel ★★★★★

Starting as a boutique winery, Castel grew gradually and now produces approximately 100,000 bottles annually. That change in output, however, has not affected the quality of the wines, and since releasing a mere 600 bottles of his first wine in 1992, owner-winemaker Eli Ben Zaken has consistently made some of the best wines in the country. The physically beautiful winery, with an exquisite cellar holding more than 500 *barriques*, is located in Moshav Ramat Raziel in the Jerusalem Mountains. Currently Ben Zaken and his son Ariel rely entirely on grapes grown in the area of the winery, mostly in their own vineyards, some in vineyards under their full supervision. Grape varieties include Cabernet Sauvignon, Merlot, Petit Verdot, Cabernet Franc and Chardonnay.

The winery produces wines in three series—the first label, Grand Vin Castel, is an often exquisite Bordeaux-style blend with distinct Italian overtones; a very good second label, Petit Castel, is meant for earlier drinking; and then there is "C", which is consistently one of the most exciting Chardonnay wines produced in the region. The winery produced a first kosher version of its Grand Vin in 2002 and from the 2003 vintage all of Castel's wines have been kosher.

Grand Vin Castel

GRAND VIN CASTEL, 2004: Not yet a final blend at this tasting but already showing deep garnet in color with orange and purple reflections, full-body and the kind of balance and structure that bode well for the future. Raspberries, blackcurrants, vanilla and chocolate all here on first attack, those followed by plums and a gentle influence of the wood. On the finish, berries, licorice and tobacco. Destined for complexity and elegance. Best 2007–2012. Tentative Score 93–95. K

GRAND VIN CASTEL, 2003: Still tight because of its youth, but with the clear potential for focused elegance. Deep garnet towards royal purple in color, full-bodied, with firm tannins integrating well. On first attack currant, plum, spices and an appealing earthy-herbal overtone and a finish on which you will find white chocolate and a hint of mint. Perhaps Castel's best red ever. Best 2007–2012. Tentative Score 93–95. K

GRAND VIN CASTEL, 2002 (KOSHER EDITION): Full-bodied, bold, concentrated, and with layer after layer of aromas and flavors that linger on. Look for currants, cherries, plums and spices on first attack, those yielding nicely to cedar, minerals and tobacco leaf. Still showing some rough edges because of its youth, but with balance and structure that bode very well for its future. Drink now–2009. Score 91. K

GRAND VIN CASTEL, 2002: Rich and round, with ripe currant, black cherry and anise, with still firm tannins on a green olive, cedar and mineral background. Full-bodied, intense and long. Drink now–2008 Score 91.

GRAND VIN CASTEL, 2001: Developing beautifully, this still young wine is now showing earthy currant, black cherry, sage and cedar wood aromas and flavors. Full-bodied and concentrated, the wine possesses great elegance and features long lingering flavors rich in hints of coffee and chocolate. Drink now–2007. Score 91.

GRAND VIN CASTEL, 2000: With once firm tannins now well-integrated, this medium to full-bodied wine is showing excellent balance between spicy blackcurrant, plum and blackberry fruits, those matched nicely by hints of Mediterranean herbs and clean earthy aromas and flavors. Muscular, with firm tannins with as well as a long, spicy finish. Drink now. Score 92.

GRAND VIN CASTEL, 1999: This full-bodied, deep ruby toward dark purple wine reveals good balance between generous, well-integrated tannins and elegant black fruits including currants, plums and blackberries. Look also for aromas and flavors of mint and red licorice, all coming together in a just spicy enough finish with tobacco aromas and flavors. Drink now. Score 90.

GRAND VIN CASTEL, 1998: A near-elegant wine, slow to open during its youth but now aging somewhat more quickly than anticipated. With now softened tannins, some spicy-smoky wood and plum and currant fruits, all leading to a moderately-long vanilla flavored finish. Drink now. Score 90.

GRAND VIN CASTEL, 1997: Perhaps Castel's most luxurious wine in its youth, with remarkably intense blackcurrant and black cherry fruits, Mediterranean herbs, an abundant but very well balanced oak and a long finish with pepper and anise. Supple and harmonious but now starting to fade. Drink up. Score 89.

GRAND VIN CASTEL, 1996: Fully mature now, this complex full-bodied wine shows excellent balance between wood, ample tannins, and an array of aromas and flavors of currants, herbs, tobacco and hints of mint and sweet cedar that unfold nicely on the palate. Drink up. Score 91.

GRAND VIN CASTEL, 1995: Concentrated, intense and elegant, this medium to full-bodied wine shows deep currant, purple plum and black cherry fruits on a background of chocolate, and what has developed into earthy, tobacco and cedar wood flavors. Still harmonious but now fully mature and not meant for further cellaring. Drink up. Score 90

GRAND VIN CASTEL, 1994: Since its release this wine showed a lace-like delicate texture and a somewhat atypical (for Castel) sweet finish. During its heyday it was packed with currants, cherries, plums and vanilla, showing good balance with moderate tannins and wood. Now well beyond its peak and no longer scoreable.

GRAND VIN CASTEL, 1993: Now taking on a deep adobe brick red color, this still rich and round wine with ample blackcurrants, a light bitter nuttiness and deeper herbaceousness than it had earlier is clearly past its peak and not meant for further cellaring. Drink up. Score 90.

GRAND VIN CASTEL, 1992: This very first wine released by Castel, more Italian than Bordeaux in style, was delicious and complex, but now is well past its prime. Still showing dark fruits but reflecting only a shadow of its once fine balance, the wine drinks well when first poured but then quickly fades in the glass. No longer scoreable.

Petit Castel

PETIT CASTEL, 2003: Softer, smoother and more approachable than the Grand Vin of this vintage. Medium to full-bodied, with forward black fruits, soft tannins already integrating nicely and a pleasing array of currant, wild berry and earthy-herbaceous aromas and flavors. Mouthfilling and moderately long. Drink now–2008. Score 90. K

PETIT CASTEL, 2002: Dark ruby toward garnet in color, this medium-bodied red shows soft, well-integrated tannins and generous currant and wild berry fruits together with generous touches of sweet cedar, spices and herbs on the moderately long finish. Drink now–2008. Score 89.

PETIT CASTEL, 2001: Medium to full-bodied, with soft and well-integrated tannins and excellent balance between wood and fruit, this wine is living up to its earlier promise. Blackcurrant and blackberry fruits come together very nicely with lightly smoky cedar and an appealing underlying hint of earthiness. Drink now–2008. Score 91.

PETIT CASTEL, 2000: Medium to full-bodied, this deep garnet toward royal purple wine reveals smooth, well-integrated tannins and an attractive array of fruits including currants, black cherries and plum to which generous hints of oak and a dash of spiciness add charm. Drink now. Score 89.

PETIT CASTEL, 1999: Medium to full-bodied, this appealing wine offers currant and cherry-berry notes integrated well with lightly smoky-toasty and spicy aromas and flavors. With moderate levels of smooth tannins, tantalizing bittersweet and herbal notes that emerge at the finish, and just the right touch of oak. Drink now. Score 89.

PETIT CASTEL, 1998: Well balanced and with a spicy finish, this wine is living up to its full potential. Ripe, rich and harmonious, the wine shows fine balance between smooth tannins, smoky wood and blackcurrant-black cherry fruits. Drink now. Score 90.

"C" Chardonnay

"c", CHARDONNAY, 2004: Light golden in color, full-bodied, with fresh citrus, melon and tropical fruits. Creamy and long on the finish, another triumph for this wine. Best 2007–2010. Tentative Score 92–94. K

"c", CHARDONNAY, 2003: A Burgundy style Chardonnay, full-bodied, showing complex ripe pear, green apple and hazelnut aromas and flavors on a lightly smoky background. Drink now–2008. Tentative Score 90–92. Score 91. K

"c", CHARDONNAY, 2002: A full-bodied, elegant Burgundy style white, showing citrus, pineapple, green apple, toasted bread and fig aromas and flavors along with a comfortably nutty finish. Drink now–2008. Score 91.

"c", CHARDONNAY, 2001: Medium to full-bodied, mouth-filling and showing depth, length and elegance, this somewhat lighter but no less delicious Chardonnay than Castel's earlier releases offers up tempting white peach, nectarine, pineapple and citrus aromas and flavors, all on a just firm enough toasty oak background and with an appealing nut and vanilla flavored long finish. Not showing as rich now as it did during its youth. Drink now. Score 90.

"c", CHARDONNAY, 2000: Medium to full-bodied, now taking on a somewhat darker golden straw color, the wine boasts generous pear, fig and citrus aromas and flavors, all on a background that at one moment feels like butterscotch and at another like toasty bread. An elegant wine. Drink now. Score 91.

"c", CHARDONNAY, 1999: This complex, elegant and full-bodied white calls to mind the Burgundy whites of Montrachet and Meursault with its nutty, mineral and summer fruit aromas and flavors, all unfolding beautifully on the palate. The wine continues to develop very nicely in the bottle. Drink now. Score 94.

"C", CHARDONNAY, 1998: Deep golden in color, this full-bodied, velvety and lush wine continues to show rich summer fruit and pear along tempting spicy oak flavors. Long on the palate, with a welcome hint of bitter almonds creeping in. Drink up. Score 93.

The Cave ★★★

Founded in 1997 as a daughter company of Binyamina Wineries, this small winery has its barrel storage facilities in a cave at the foothills of Mount Carmel, not far from the town of Zichron Ya'akov. The artificial cave, which was built in the sixteenth century at the foothills of Mount Carmel, is 9 meters high and maintains a constant natural temperature. The winery is releasing 6,000 bottles annually of a Cabernet Sauvignon-Merlot blend, the grapes coming from a single vineyard in Kerem Ben Zimra in the Upper Galilee.

THE CAVE, CABERNET SAUVIGNON, 2002: Dense and compact but smooth and generous, with chewy tannins and a rich array of berry, currant, vanilla and spices that come together in a long finish. Drink now–2007. Score 88. K

THE CAVE, MERLOT, 2002: Firm, concentrated and well balanced with a tight band of toasty oak, currant, and herbal aromas and flavors. Drink now–2007. Score 87. K.

THE CAVE, CABERNET SAUVIGNON-MERLOT, 2001: This deep garnet, well balanced, full-bodied, oak-aged Bordeaux blend of Cabernet Sauvignon and Merlot shows tempting aromas and flavors of currants, plums and berries, those with overlays of coffee, Mediterranean herbs and spicy oak. Drink now–2007. Score 88. K

THE CAVE, CABERNET SAUVIGNON-MERLOT, 2000: This blend of 60% Cabernet Sauvignon and 40% Merlot was aged in small oak barrels for 24 months. The barnyard-aromas and somewhat firm tannins felt when the wine is first poured are somewhat distracting, but given time in the glass those will yield to ripe plum and blackberry aromas and flavors. Full-bodied and sturdy, the wine offers generous oak and a perhaps overly herbal finish. Drink up. Score 85. K

Chateau Golan ✶✶✶✶

A fully modern winery located on Moshav Eliad in the Golan Heights, Chateau Golan released their first wines from the 2000 vintage under the hand of Oregon and California trained winemaker Uri Hetz. Vineyards owned by the winery currently yield Cabernet Sauvignon, Merlot, Cabernet Franc, Petite Sirah, Petit Verdot, Pinot Noir, Grenache, Sauvignon Blanc, Mouvredre and Viognier. Other grapes are being planted, these including Rousanne and Grenache Blanc. Production is currently about 48,000 bottles and future production is estimated at somewhat over 100,000 bottles annually. To date the winery has released wines in one series, Royal Reserve, and only one wine, the proprietary blend known as Eliad, has been released outside of that series.

Royal Reserve

ROYAL RESERVE, CABERNET SAUVIGNON, 2003: Deep and tannic, young and tight, but showing excellent focus and concentration. Full-bodied, packed with tannins waiting to integrate but with the inherent balance to develop beautifully into a smooth and supple wine. With aromas and flavors of currant, black cherries and anise along with attractive earthy-herbal overtones and hints of green olives. Drink from release–2012. Tentative Score 89–91.

ROYAL RESERVE, CABERNET SAUVIGNON, 2002: Still young but already showing medium to full-body and good balance, concentration and length, this blend of Cabernet Sauvignon and about 9% Cabernet Franc offers an appealing array of ripe cherry, currant, red plum, jammy strawberry and spicy flavors overlaid by light toasty oak, and a moderately long, near-sweet finish. Look as well for a hint of tobacco on the finish. Drink now–2007. Score 89.

ROYAL RESERVE, CABERNET SAUVIGNON, 2001: Oak-aged for ten months, this deep garnet toward purple wine is surprisingly light to medium-bodied. Smooth tannins, just the right hints of earth and spices and appealing blackberry and blackcurrant fruits lead to a clean and medium-long finish. Drink now. Score 88.

ROYAL RESERVE, CABERNET SAUVIGNON, 2000: Intense and deep with cherry, currant and mocha aromas and flavors, and with good balance between tannins and fruits, this medium to full-bodied 100% Cabernet fills the mouth nicely and with near-elegance. Drink now. Score 88.

ROYAL RESERVE, CABERNET SAUVIGNON, 1999: Medium to full-bodied, with an appealing royal purple color, this Cabernet Sauvignon was blended with 4% Merlot to give it some softness. Reflecting ten months in new French oak barrels, the wine is rich and well balanced, with smooth tannins and with currant, mineral, pepper and smoky oak aromas and flavors. Drink now. Score 89.

ROYAL RESERVE, MERLOT, 2003: Dark garnet in color, medium to full-bodied, with generous but yielding tannins and tempting layers of plum, currant and black cherry fruits matched nicely by a light hint of herbaceousness. Rich and long. Drink now–2009. Score 90.

ROYAL RESERVE, MERLOT, 2002: This deep royal-purple oak-aged blend of 85% Merlot and 15% Cabernet Sauvignon shows firm, well-integrated tannins and appealing currant, wild berry and plum aromas and flavors, together with gentle overlays of spicy chocolate and vanilla. Drink now. Score 88.

ROYAL RESERVE, MERLOT, 2001: Medium to full-bodied, this elegant and intense Merlot, blended with 15% of Cabernet Sauvignon, was aged in French oak casks for one year. Dark in color, the wine has deep, still firm tannins, well balanced by raspberry, plum and currant fruits, those on a complex background of dark chocolate and vanilla, and a long, sweet finish. Drink now–2008. Score 91.

ROYAL RESERVE, MERLOT, 2000: Remarkably similar in style to the Merlot-based wines of Bordeaux, this medium to full-bodied, ripe and juicy oak-aged blend of 89% Merlot and 11% Cabernet Sauvignon has plenty of ripe cherry and currant fruits along overlays of vanilla, green olives and toasted oak. Drink now. Score 88.

ROYAL RESERVE, SYRAH, 2003: Blended with 15% of Grenache to flush out the elegance of the wine, this is a classic Syrah with distinct Mediterranean overtones. Combining assertiveness with complexity, this spicy, gamy wine offers up appealing smoke and black pepper along with deep raspberry and floral aromas and flavors. Drink now–2008. Score 90.

ROYAL RESERVE, SYRAH, 2002: Big, rich, dense and tannic, and already showing roundness and richness, this wine is a deep garnet to purple color and has generous plum, herbal and earthy aromas and flavors. Somewhat astringent in its youth but integrating very nicely now. Drink now–2008. Score 90.

ROYAL RESERVE, SYRAH, 2001: Dark royal purple in color, this medium to full-bodied blend of 85% Syrah and 15% Cabernet has inherent good balance and structure. Still young but already showing soft tannins and tempting plum and berry fruits with generous hints of earthiness and herbaceousness. In time it will show olive and mushroom aromas as well. Drink now–2008. Score 91.

ROYAL RESERVE, SYRAH, CUVEE NATUREL, 2001: Intense, tannic and concentrated, medium to full-bodied. Deep purple in color, reflecting its 14 months in French oak with spices and a generous dash of vanilla, those complemented nicely by jammy black fruits. Drink now–2007. Score 90.

ROYAL RESERVE, GRENACHE, 2003: Loyal to its varietal traits, an attractive pale ruby wine, medium-bodied, with soft tannins and tempting blackberry, black cherry and red currant fruits as well as spicy oak. Drink from release–2009. Tentative Score 87–89.

ROYAL RESERVE, CABERNET FRANC, 2003: Full-bodied, earthy and aromatic, with an appealing array of currant, vanilla and herbal flavors that fold together well. A long, deep and concentrated finish showing richness and concentration. Drink from release–2011. Tentative Score 88–90.

ROYAL RESERVE, CABERNET FRANC, 2002: Earthier and less tannic than Cabernet Sauvignon, this medium-bodied and well balanced wine shows good body, weight and structure, with tempting plums and blackberries and a generous touch of herbaceousness. Drink now–2007. Score 88.

ROYAL RESERVE, MERLOT-CABERNET, 2000: Dark purple toward black in color, this medium to full-bodied blend of 65% Cabernet and 35% Merlot was aged in French and American oak barrels for 12 months. Well balanced and with tempting black cherry, currant, plum and hazelnut aromas and flavors, this smooth wine has just a hint of coffee on the finish. Drink now. Score 89.

ROYAL RESERVE, CABERNET FRANC, ROSÉ, 2004: Somewhere in color between bright cherry red and that of red rose petals and far deeper than a standard rosé, this medium-bodied, soft and round rosé shows appealing aromas and flavors of raspberries, cassis and cranberries, turning almost sweet on the surprisingly long finish. Drink up. Score 87.

ROYAL RESERVE, SAUVIGNON BLANC, 2003: Made entirely from Sauvignon Blanc grapes from the northern Golan, fermented in stainless steel and then partly oak aged, a multi-layered wine, showing at first citrus and pineapple, those yielding nicely to pear, floral and herbal aromas and flavors. Generous alcohol (14%) but that balanced by natural acidity. Long, mouthfilling and elegant. Drink now–2007. Score 91.

ROYAL RESERVE, SAUVIGNON BLANC, 2002: Fermented partly in stainless steel vats and partly in oak and then allowed to rest *sur lie* for six months, this medium-bodied, deep golden straw white offers up aromas and flavors of melons and pears on the first attack, those then yielding to tropical fruits, all with generous herbal-tobacco overlays. Crisp, long and elegant. Drink now–2007. Score 91.

Eliad

ELIAD, 2003: A barrel-aged,deep garnet blend of 66% Cabernet Sauvignon, 20% Merlot and 14% Cabernet Franc. Rich, intense and complex, with concentrated fruits and spices on the noise and palate. Look for layers of plums, blackberries, currants and spicy oak. Needs time to show its elegance. Best 2007–2012. Tentative Score 90–92.

ELIAD, 2002: Still young and tight, this blend of 91% Cabernet Sauvignon and 9% Merlot has crisp tannins and generous currant, black cherry and cedar as well as leathery-earthy aromas and flavors, with a long finish in which the tannins and wood meld beautifully. Drink now–2010. Score 90.

ELIAD, 2001: A blend of Cabernet Sauvignon, Merlot and Syrah (85%, 10% and 5% respectively), each aged separately, some in French and some in American oak. This dark, almost inky royal purple medium-bodied wine shows soft tannins that are nicely balanced by jammy plum and blackberry fruits, and appealing layers of chocolate and smoky-toasty aromas and flavors. Drink now–2008. Score 90.

Chillag ★★★★

After studying oenology in Piacenza, Italy and working at the Antinori wineries in Tuscany, Chillag released her first wines in Israel in 1998. Temporarily located at the winery of Barry Saslove on Kibbutz Eyal, and relying on Merlot and Cabernet Sauvignon grapes from the Upper Galilee, production jumped from 4,000 bottles in 2002 to 12,000 each in 2003 and 2004. Anticipated future production is 20,000 bottles. In addition to her regular releases, which are in three series—Riserva, Primo Riserva and Primo—Chillag also now produces a line of kosher wines under the label "Orna" at Carmel in Rishon Letzion. Made from hand-selected grapes grown in the Zar'it vineyards in the Upper Galilee, 15,000 bottles of Chillag's first kosher Cabernet Sauvignon were released in mid-2005.

Riserva

RISERVA, CABERNET SAUVIGNON, 2004: Still in embryonic form but already rich, ripe and intense, with a tight core of currant, plum and black cherry aromas and flavors, those complemented nicely by hints of anise. Plush tannins promise to settle in nicely. Best 2007–2010. Tentative Score 89–91.

RISERVA, CABERNET SAUVIGNON, 2003: Harmonious and supple, with a generous array of currants, cherries and plums, those with tempting overlays of toasty oak, spices and soft but mouth-coating tannins. Drink now–2009. Score 90.

RISERVA, CABERNET SAUVIGNON, CASTELLANA, 2002: Dark royal purple in color, this full-bodied wine was made by blending 70% Cabernet Sauvignon and 30% Merlot together in the same oak barrels. Aromas and flavors of spicy currants, anise and cedary oak come together in a complex, mouth-filling, supple wine. Lacks the depth for long-term aging. Drink now–2007. Score 89.

RISERVA, CABERNET SAUVIGNON, 2001: Full-bodied, with real weight and grip and with plenty of tannins, this concentrated blend of 90% Cabernet Sauvignon and 10% Merlot shows a deep purple color and a still muscular structure. Give it time and it will open to reveal its fine balance between tannins, wood and fruit, yielding currants, plums and blackberries with meaty and toasty accents. Drink now–2007. Score 89.

RISERVA, CABERNET SAUVIGNON, 2000: Medium to full-bodied, with soft tannins and generous plum, currant and berry fruits backed up by ample sweet vanilla from the wood. Drink up. Score 88.

Primo Riserva

PRIMO RISERVA, MERLOT, GIOVANNI, 2004: Deep purple, with sweet, soft tannins, well balanced by currant, plum and spicy aromas and flavors. Soft, round and long. Drink from release–2009. Tentative Score 88–90.

PRIMO RISERVA, MERLOT, GIOVANNI, 2003: Dark royal purple with orange and violet reflections, needing some time for the still firm tannins to integrate but already showing an elegant array of currant, cherries and spices along with a gentle modicum of oak. On the finish hints of coffee and herbs. Drink now–2009. Score 90.

PRIMO RISERVA, MERLOT, 2001: Smooth, supple, and with a fascinating core of toasted oak, currant, tea, sage and mineral flavors, this medium to full-bodied wine offers up ample but gentle and well-integrated tannins, and a lingering finish yielding lightly sweet berry flavors. Drink now. Score 89.

PRIMO RISERVA, MERLOT, 2000: Smooth, ripe, complex and combining strength with softness, the wine has abundant currant, berry and plum fruits along with light spicy notes. Well-balanced, with plenty of soft tannins, its flavors develop in the glass and then linger nicely on the palate. Drink now. Score 91.

Primo

PRIMO, CABERNET SAUVIGNON, 2002: This medium to full-bodied blend of 90% Cabernet Sauvignon and 10% Merlot is smooth, round and well-balanced. The wine has soft tannins and moderate oak along with spicy currants, cherry and cedar nuances and a moderately long finish. Drink now. Score 89.

PRIMO, 2002: Smooth and polished, with an attractive but somewhat delicate style, this blend of Merlot and Cabernet Sauvignon shows cherry, currant, coffee and herbal aromas and flavors as well as hints of green olive and cedar wood on the finish. Drink now. Score 88.

PRIMO, 2000: A blend of 92% Merlot and 8% Cabernet Sauvignon that aged for 13 months in French oak barrels, this lithe and supple wine has plenty of blackberry, raspberry and anise flavors that linger gently on the palate. A delicious wine with good balance between tannins and fruit. Drink now. Score 90.

PRIMO, 1998: This medium-bodied blend of 90% Merlot and 10% Cabernet Sauvignon is packed with aromas and flavors of wild berries, dark cherries and a light hint of eucalyptus. Soft and seductive but also bold, the wine is well balanced and has a long, fruity finish. Drink up. Score 89.

Orna

ORNA, CABERNET SAUVIGNON, RESERVE, 2003: Made from grapes specially selected at the Zar'it Vineyard in the Kadesh Valley of the Upper Galilee and aged in French oak casks for 14 months. Ripe and chewy, with soft tannins and plum and blackcurrant aromas and flavors that linger nicely on the palate. Drink now–2007. Score 89. **K**

Clos de Gat ✶✶✶✶

Located on Kibbutz Har'el in the Jerusalem Mountains, this new winery, a joint project of the *kibbutz* and Australian-trained winemaker Eyal Rotem, released its first wines from the 2001 vintage. The name, "Clos de Gat" is a play on words—the French *clos* being an enclosed vineyard surrounded by stone walls or wind-breaks, while the Hebrew *gat* is an antique wine press. With the exception of the Chardonnay grapes in the 2002 wine, all the grapes have come from the winery's own vineyards, which now include Cabernet, Merlot, Petit Verdot, Syrah and most recently the winery's own Chardonnay. Production in 2002 was 22,000 bottles and in 2004 approximately 60,000 bottles. Second label wines are labeled Har'el and, starting with the 2003 vintage, will rely entirely on wild yeasts.

2003
CLOS de GAT
CLOS de GAT
HAR'EL
Cabernet Sauvignon
Grown, Produced & Estate Bottled by Clos de Gat Winery
14% vol.   PRODUCE OF ISRAEL   750 ml.

CLOS DE GAT, 2003: A complex, rich, ripe blend of 66% Cabernet Sauvignon, 30% Merlot and 4% Petit Verdot. Spicy cherry, currant, anise and oak flavors fold togther seamlessly even at this early stage. Full-bodied, still quite tannic but with the potential to show elegance and harmony. Drink now–2012. Score 91.

CLOS DE GAT, 2002: A very good effort considering the problematic 2002 vintage. Good touches of the wood and somewhat firm tannins, but those well balanced by ripe currant and plum fruits as well as sage, cedar and vanilla flavors. Drink now–2008. Score 89.

CLOS DE GAT, 2001: A deep ruby-garnet full-bodied unfiltered blend of 70% Cabernet Sauvignon and 30% Merlot, with generous soft tannins that integrate beautifully, this is a wine that can honestly be said to reflect its *terroir*. Overlaying traditional Cabernet blackcurrants are generous hints of green olives, basil, tarragon and other Mediterranean herbs. The wine shows good balance and structure, with chocolate and leather coming in on the long finish. Drink now–2009. Score 90.

CLOS DE GAT, CHARDONNAY, 2003: Delicious medium to full-bodied Chardonnay with ripe pineapple, citrus, apple and spicy notes. Enough mineral crispness here to make one think of fine Chablis, with a good touch of toasty oak but with balancing acidity that carries the wine very well indeed. Drink now–2007, perhaps longer. Score 91.

CLOS DE GAT, CHARDONNAY, 2002: Full-bodied with ripe pear and pineapple aromas and flavors on the first attack, these yielding beautifully to citrus flowers, apple, and ripe apricots, all on a spicy background. Fermented and aged *sur lie* in French oak barrels, the wine has very good balance between lively acidity, intentionally underplayed oak and minerals, and a creamy, mouth-filling sensation. Drink now–2007. Score 91.

Har'el

HAR'EL, CABERNET SAUVIGNON, 2003: An oak-aged blend of 93% Cabernet Sauvignon, 4% Merlot and 3% Petit Verdot, this medium-bodied, softly tannic wine shows abundant raspberry, ripe cherry and currant fruits, those matched nicely by moderate oak and a hint of anise. Surprisingly complex and inviting for a second wine. Drink now–2007. Score 89.

HAR'EL, SYRAH, 2003: A blend of 85% Syrah and 15% Cabernet Sauvignon, this dark garnet, medium-bodied wine has soft, already well-integrating tannins. Well-balanced and structured, spicy, with an earthy overtone to its plum and wild berry flavors, and with a light leathery hint on the finish. Drink now–2009. Score 91.

Dahlia *

Founded in 2000 by Rosanna and Uzi Braun on Kibbutz Dahlia on Mount Carmel, the winery draws on a wide variety of grapes from the *kibbutz* as well as from nearby Moshav Amikam, those including Cabernet Sauvignon, Merlot, Carignan, Argaman, white and red Muscat, and French Colombard. Production is currently about 1,000 bottles annually.

DAHLIA, CABERNET SAUVIGNON, 2003: Medium to full-bodied, with a basic imbalance between coarse tannins, high acidity and overripe black fruits. Drink up. Score 77.

DAHLIA, CABERNET SAUVIGNON, 2002: Medium-bodied, with flat tannins and herbal and weedy overtones overlaying the berry-cherry flavors that never quite manage to make themselves fully felt. Drink up. Score 72.

DAHLIA, MERLOT, 2002: Medium-bodied, with spicy and peppery accents to the cherry and strawberry flavors. A simple wine. Drink up. Score 74.

DAHLIA, CABERNET SAUVIGNON-MERLOT, NOBLE, 2003: Unripe fruit aromas mark this medium-bodied wine, those followed by herbal and beefy flavors. Even though the wine was aged in oak barrels for only 4 months, the finish is woody and resinous. Drink up. Score 70.

DAHLIA, MERLOT-ARGAMAN, 2003: Light and simple, with earthy, leathery accents to rhubarb and plum flavors. Drink up. Score 74.

DAHLIA, MUSCAT DESSERT WINE, 2003: Flowery, fruity and sweet, but without the balancing acidity that might have made the wine lively or refreshing. Score 69.

Dalton ✴✴✴✴

Founded by Mat Haruni in 1993, this fully modern winery located in the industrial park of Dalton in the Upper Galilee has vineyards in Kerem Ben Zimra and several high altitude sites along the Lebanese border. Australian and Californian trained winemaker Na'ama Mualem is currently producing wines in three series, Reserve, Dalton and Canaan, the first of age-worthy Cabernet Sauvignon, Merlot, Chardonnay and Sauvignon Blanc, the second, of similar varieties, is intended for earlier drinking, and the third, a popularly priced series. First production was of 50,000 bottles, current production has risen to about 800,000 and the target for 2007 is one million bottles. Dalton has earned an especially good name for quality wines providing excellent value for money. The winery is also currently engaged in development of vineyards containing Barbera and Shiraz grapes.

Reserve

RESERVE, CABERNET SAUVIGNON, 2003: Deep ruby towards garnet in color, medium-bodied, with generous oak well balanced by soft tannins and appealing blackcurrant, black cherry and herbal-spicy aromas and flavors. Drink now–2008. Score 88. K

RESERVE, CABERNET SAUVIGNON, 2002: Medium-bodied, ripe and harmonious, with black plums overlaying currants, cherries, and reflecting its 18 months in French oak with sweet cedar, and an herbal-spicy but somewhat short finish. Drink now. Score 87. K

RESERVE, CABERNET SAUVIGNON, 2001: Medium-bodied, with barely any tannins and marked too strongly by the oak in which it aged, the black fruits here fail to make themselves felt adequately. Drink up. Score 84. K

RESERVE, CABERNET SAUVIGNON, 1999: After two years in oak, this deep royal purple, medium to full-bodied wine opens in the glass to reveal aromas and flavors of ripe wild berry, black cherry and currant fruits along with generous hints of mint and vanilla. Focused, concentrated and well balanced. Drink now. Score 89. K

RESERVE, CABERNET SAUVIGNON, 1998: This medium to full-bodied wine opens nicely in the glass to reveal ripe black cherry, currant, vanilla and light spicy overtones. Well focused and with smooth tannins and good balance. Drink up. Score 86. K

RESERVE, CABERNET SAUVIGNON, 1997: Aged for over 12 months partly in American and partly in French oak barrels, this well-made medium to full-bodied wine has plenty of plum, currant and cherry flavors, along with vanilla and oak notes and just the right hint of herbs and spices that linger on the palate. Somewhat past its peak. Drink up. Score 89. K

RESERVE, MERLOT, 2003: Ripe, polished and smooth, with an attractive array of flavors including currants, raspberries and cherries as well as herbs and vanilla-tinged oak. Medium to full-bodied, finishing off with complexity and finesse. Drink now–2007. Score 89. K

RESERVE, MERLOT, 2002: Smooth and elegant, with a core of ripe plum and black cherry fruits, those on a background of toasty oak, spices and very appealing hints of sage and tea. As the wine continues to develop, look for a leather note on the long finish. Drink now. Score 89. K.

RESERVE, MERLOT, 2001: Not fully living up to its earlier promise, the toasty oak seems to overshadow the plum, berry and currant fruits and a rather strong white chocolate overlay now hiding the anise and cedar wood that were once there. Drink up. Score 85. K

RESERVE, MERLOT, 2000: Intense and lively, with generous plum, wild berry and light hints of oak and vanilla, this rich and complex wine borders comfortably on elegance. The wine aged in small oak casks for a year and has a nice lingering finish. Drink up. Score 90. K

RESERVE, SHIRAZ, 2003: Medium to full-bodied and solidly tannic, reflecting its 10 months in new American oak with generous hints of smoke and vanilla, those on tempting black fruits, mint and earthiness. Needs time to open and show its elegance. Drink from release–2009. Tentative Score 88–90. K

RESERVE, CHARDONNAY, 2003: After 8 months *sur lie* in new French oak *barriques*, this medium-bodied white shows appealing earthy, buttery and vanilla aromas backed up nicely by flavors of melons and pears. Drink now. Score 88. Ⰽ

RESERVE, CHARDONNAY, 2002: Deep, complex and harmonious, this tempting wine shows ripe, rich pear, spice, apple and hazelnut aromas and flavors, with an elegant finish yielding notes of figs, butterscotch and spices. Drink now. Score 88. Ⰽ

RESERVE, CHARDONNAY, 2001: Fresh, lively and elegant, the wine shows an abundance of citrus, ripe pear, melon and spicy flavors. Light toasty oak and hints of minerals add charm to the long finish. Drink now. Score 90. Ⰽ

RESERVE, CHARDONNAY, 2000: Medium-bodied with appealing aromas and flavors of ripe pear, citrus and nutmeg. Drink up. Score 85. Ⰽ

RESERVE, CHARDONNAY, 1999: This smooth and polished medium-bodied wine is packed with aromas and flavors of pears, hazelnuts and melon, and with just enough vanilla, reflecting 9 months in oak barrels. Good natural acidity makes it still lively and as the flavors linger on the palate look for a hint of honey. Past its peak. Drink up. Score 86. Ⰽ

RESERVE, SAUVIGNON BLANC, 2004: Unoaked, fresh, crisp and aromatic, with light herbal hints. On first sip dominated by grapefruit flavors but those yielding to aromas and flavors of apples, melons, spices and minerals. Drink now. Score 87. Ⰽ

RESERVE, SAUVIGNON BLANC, 2003: The color of golden straw, with appealing tropical fruits, citrus and melon flavors, those on a lightly floral-herbaceous background; a very nice wine indeed. Drink now. Score 88. Ⰽ

RESERVE, SAUVIGNON BLANC, 2002: Light gold in color, this un-oaked white has hints of tropical fruits and a low-keyed grassiness felt on the long finish. Drink up. Score 89. K

RESERVE, SAUVIGNON BLANC, 2001: One of the best Sauvignon Blanc varietals made in Israel. Pale gold in color, this unoaked white is smooth and elegant, with fresh herbal aromas and flavors overlaying citrus and peach notes. Look for light hints of grass as the wine lingers on the palate. Somewhat past its peak. Drink up. Score 91. K

RESERVE, SAUVIGNON BLANC, 2000: Smooth and refreshing, this well made wine has just enough citrus, pear and earthy mineral flavors to make it appealing. Somewhat past its peak. Drink up. Score 87. K

Dalton

DALTON, CABERNET SAUVIGNON, 2003: Medium-bodied, with soft, well-integrated tannins and a solid core of currant, wild berry and minty flavors. An appealing wine. Drink now. Score 88. K

DALTON, CABERNET SAUVIGNON, 2002: Well focused and with good balance between moderate tannins and plum, cherry and currant flavors, this appealing wine has a medium-long finish with hints of mocha and cedar wood. Drink now. Score 87. K

DALTON, CABERNET SAUVIGNON, 2001: Medium-bodied and with smooth tannins, this deep ruby toward garnet red offers good currant and plum fruits. Drink up. Score 86. K

DALTON, CABERNET SAUVIGNON, 2000: Young, fresh and supple, this medium-bodied, not overly complex white shows well-focused earthy, currant, black cherry and cedar flavors. Drink up. Score 85. K

DALTON, MERLOT, 2003: Showing better than at barrel tastings, with moderate levels of complexity, soft tannins, medium-body and a band of berry and black cherry fruits and a tempting hint of spices. Good backbone here. Drink now. Score 87. K

DALTON, MERLOT, 2002: Distinctly New World in style, this medium to full-bodied fruit-driven wine shows generous plum, currant and blackberry flavors on a firm tannic background. A nice hint of bitterness on the finish. Drink now. Score 88. K

DALTON, MERLOT, 2001: Showing soft tannins, hints of sage and tea and a medium-long finish, the wine needs time to open in the glass to reveal its currant and berry flavors. Drink up. Score 87. **K**

DALTON, MERLOT, 2000: Aged in French oak barrels for 14 months and blended with 5% Cabernet Sauvignon, this tempting medium-bodied wine offers smooth tannins and generous aromas and flavors of wild berries and plums with appealing toasty, vanilla overtones. Somewhat past its peak. Drink up. Score 87. **K**

DALTON, SHIRAZ, 2003: Deep, almost impenetrable purple in color, medium to full-bodied, with generous but yielding tannins, this lightly oak-aged wine shows a generous array of earthiness, tobacco and milk chocolate on a background of wild berries and plums. Drink now–2007. Score 88. **K**

DALTON, CHARDONNAY, 2004: Unoaked, medium-bodied, with tempting tropical fruits, citrus and minerals, a crisply dry, lightly floral and delicious wine meant for early consumption. Drink now. Score 86. **K**

DALTON, CHARDONNAY, 2003: As we have come to anticipate, this unoaked, medium-bodied white is crisp and fresh, with citrus, pineapple and green apple fruits, minerals, and a light floral overlay. Delicious. Drink now. Score 87. **K**

DALTON, CHARDONNAY, 2002: This unoaked medium-bodied white shows lovely pineapple, green apple and citrus aromas and flavors along with a light flinty-mineral overlay that calls to mind a simple but delicious Chablis. Drink up. Score 86. **K**

DALTON, CHARDONNAY, 2001: This medium-bodied, unoaked white has generous citrus and pineapple aromas and flavors along with appealing mineral overlays and plenty of natural acids to keep it lively. Somewhat past its peak. Drink up. Score 85. **K**

DALTON, SAUVIGNON BLANC FUME, 2004: Fresh and lively, light in color, medium-bodied, with grapefruit, melon and tropical fruits and an appealing hint of freshly baked bread. Drink now. Score 86. **K**

DALTON, SAUVIGNON BLANC FUME, 2003: Light in color but packed with fresh tropical fruit and citrus flavors, those with a lightly smoky overlay and hints of roasted nuts. Meant for youthful drinking. Drink up. Score 86. **K**

DALTON, SAUVIGNON BLANC FUME, 2002: Toasty-smoky aromas and flavors along with appealing peach and apricot fruits on a clean, just lively enough background. Drink up. Score 86. **K**

DALTON, SAUVIGNON BLANC FUME, 2001: Well balanced, medium-bodied, with plenty of summer fruits and pineapple as well as hints of toasted white bread and vanilla reflecting the wood in which it was aged for 3 months. Drink up. Score 85. **K**

DALTON, SAUVIGNON BLANC FUME, 2000: This medium-bodied, light golden straw white shows aromas and flavors of white peaches, citrus and spring flowers, as well as a hint of the famous "cat's pee" aroma that gives Sauvignon Blanc its good name. Showing age. Score 83. **K**

DALTON, ROSE, 2004: Made from a pot-pourri of all of the red grapes available to the winery that spent 12 hours on the skins to gain its rich strawberry to rose-red color. Semi-dry, medium-bodied with strawberry and plum fruits but lacking the natural acidity to keep it truly lively. Drink now. Score 84. **K**

DALTON, MUSCAT DESSERT, 2002: Aromatic, with gently honeyed sweetness and aromas and flavors of citrus and tropical fruits, the wine is also appropriate as an aperitif. Drink now. Score 84. **K**

Canaan

CANAAN, RED, 2004: A not complex but plesant little blend of Cabernet Sauvignon and Merlot. Soft, round and with appealing black fruits. Drink now. Score 85. **K**

CANAAN, RED, 2003: A basic Cabernet-Merlot blend, light to medium-bodied, with soft tannins and generous fruits. A good quaffing wine. Drink up. Score 85. **K**

CANAAN, RED, 2002: This country-style blend of Cabernet Sauvignon, Merlot and a small amount of Shiraz shows deep garnet-purple color, medium-body and chunky tannins, those joining together nicely with black plum and berry flavors. Drink up. Score 86. **K**

CANAAN, RED, 2001: Ruby-red in color, this low tannic, light to medium-bodied blend of Cabernet Sauvignon and Merlot has a pleasant berry-cherry personality and just a few hints of oak. Somewhat past its peak. Drink up. Score 84. **K**

CANAAN, RED, 2000: Smooth, fruity and with plenty of red fruits and vanilla in its youth, this medium-bodied wine is somewhat past its peak. Drink up. Score 83. **K**

CANAAN, SAUVIGNON BLANC, 2001: Light to medium-bodied, with grassy, floral overtones to fresh apple and citrus aromas and flavors in its youth but now past its peak. Drink up. Score 83. **K**

CANAAN, CHARDONNAY-WHITE RIESLING, 2001: Not complex but pleasantly fruity, with ripe pear, apple and citrus aromas and flavors. Somewhat past its peak. Drink up. Score 84. **K**

CANAAN, SAUVIGNON BLANC-CHARDONNAY-WHITE RIESLING, 2002: Light straw in color, this semi-dry, light to medium-bodied white offers simple and low-level citrus, pineapple and apple aromas and flavors. Drink up. Score 83. K

CANAAN, SAUVIGNON BLANC-CHARDONNAY-WHITE RIESLING, 2001: Light and refreshing, with clean aromas and flavors of citrus, pears, green apples and an appealing hint of spiciness on the finish. Past its peak. Drink up. Score 82. K

CANAAN, WHITE, 2004: Pale straw in color, light to medium-bodied, with citrus and melon fruits on a lightly spicy background. Drink now. Score 84. K

Deux Paysans ✸✸✸

Founded by Hugh and Isabelle Levenbach and located in Moshav Kochav Ya'ir in the Sharon region, the winery released its first wine in 2001. Producing only red wines and drawing on Cabernet Sauvignon, Merlot and Syrah grapes from vineyards in the Upper Galilee, the Jerusalem Mountains and the Golan Heights, the winery's regular series, Deux Paysans, is meant for short-term aging, and their new Al Tiruni wine is meant for early drinking. Production for 2001 was 2,500 bottles and for 2003 was about 2,000 bottles. In 2004 the winery ceased production.

DEUX PAYSANS, CABERNET SAUVIGNON, 2001: Medium to full-bodied, with plenty of oak, and smooth tannins along with appealing blackcurrant, anise and black cherry aromas and flavors, the wine is somewhat rough on the palate when first poured but smooths out nicely after a short time in the glass. Drink now. Score 88.

DEUX PAYSANS, MERLOT, 2003: Aged in oak *barriques*, this blend of 95% Merlot and 5% Syrah has well-integrated soft tannins, a generous hint of spiciness, and appealing aromas and flavors of currants, raspberries and blackberries. Soft, generous and moderately long. Drink now–2007. Score 87.

DEUX PAYSANS, MERLOT, 2001: This medium-bodied wine offers plenty of vanilla-flavored oak, balanced nicely by appealing overlays of rich cherry and red currant fruits and smooth tannins. Drink now. Score 87.

DEUX PAYSANS, SYRAH, 2003: With 2% of Viognier grapes added to the final blend, this round, soft and tempting wine offers up a generous mouthful of black cherry and blackberry fruits, those matched nicely by appealing nutty, peppery and light earthy overtones. Drink now–2008. Score 88.

DEUX PAYSANS, MERLOT-SHIRAZ, N.V.: Made from 1999 vintage Merlot grapes and 2000 vintage Shiraz, this is a medium-bodied country-style wine with an appealing deep ruby red color, smooth tannins, and plenty of black fruits along with a warm, long finish. Drink up. Score 86.

DEUX PAYSANS, AL TIRUNI, 2002: A blend of Cabernet Sauvignon, Merlot and Syrah, this garnet toward purple medium-bodied wine offers up soft tannins, generous currant and berry fruits, a nice layer of spiciness and a hint of dark chocolate on the medium-long finish. Meant for early drinking, the wine is round and generous. Drink up. Score 88.

DEUX PAYSANS, AVEC BARBERA, 2002: A blend of 61% Cabernet Sauvignon, 25% Merlot, 10% Barbera and small amounts each of Syrah and Malbec, this medium-bodied red spent 12 months in oak barrels. Young and vibrant, the wine shows ripe cherry, currant, herb and tea flavors along with soft tannins. Somewhat on the tart side. Drink up. Score 85.

Dico's *

Founded by David Ben-Arieh in 2001 on Moshav Ginaton on the central plains, this winery relies on Cabernet Sauvignon grapes from Kerem Ben Zimra and Merlot from the Gedera area. Current production is about 1,000 bottles annually.

DICO'S, CABERNET-MERLOT, 2003: A country-style wine, deep cherry red towards purple, medium-bodied, with chunky tannins, smoky wood and aromas and flavors of ripe berries and plums. Drink up. Score 79.

DICO'S, CABERNET-MERLOT, 2002: A medium-bodied blend of 85% Cabernet Sauvignon and 15% Merlot, this soft, simple country-style wine has a ripe black cherry flavor, somewhat coarse tannins and a vague hint of sweet cedar wood. Drink up. Score 78.

DICO'S, CABERNET-MERLOT, 2001: Medium-bodied, with a modest array of cedar and cherry flavors that fade on the too-short finish. Drink up. Score 79.

Efrat ***

Founded in 1870 by the Teperberg family, in the Jewish quarter of the old city of Jerusalem, and then relocating outside of the walls, the winery moved in 1964 to Motza, on the outskirts of the city. For many years the winery produced primarily sacramental wines for the ultra-Orthodox community, but in the 1990s they also started producing table wines. More recently, under the supervision of California-trained winemaker Shiki Rauchberger, the winery has been trying to appeal to a more sophisticated audience and with the recent release of their Teperberg Reserve series may be succeeding.

The winery currently releases wines in several series—Teperberg Reserve, Teperberg Selection, Israeli and Jerusalem Mountains. Annual production is currently about 3.7 million bottles. Grapes are drawn from the Judean Mountains, the Central Plain and other regions, including several new and well tended vineyards. Construction of a new modern winery to replace the largely outmoded existing facilities is now underway, and anticipated production within five years is scheduled to attain 7,000,000 bottles. With the exception of the wines in the Teperberg series, all of the wines are *mevushal*.

Teperberg Reserve

TEPERBERG RESERVE, CABERNET SAUVIGNON, 2004: Deep royal purple in color, still in embryonic form but already showing full-body with soft tannins in good balance with wood and fruits. On the nose and palate, blackcurrants, plums and tantalizing hints of lead-pencils, tobacco and asphalt leading to a long, mouthfilling finish. Perhaps the very best to date from Efrat. Drink from release–2008. Tentative Score 88–90.K

TEPPERBERG RESERVE, CABERNET SAUVIGNON, 2003: Deep garnet towards purple, still reflecting its youth with firm tannins and somewhat closed aromas and flavors but with balance and structure that bode very well for the future. Needs time in the glass but when it does open look for aromas and flavors of blackcurrants, blackberries and black cherries, those yielding gently to reveal Oriental spices and hints of leather and earthiness on what promises to be a very long finish. Best 2007–2012. Tentative Score 88–90. **K**

TEPERBERG RESERVE, CABERNET SAUVIGNON, 2002: A youthful royal purple in color, full-bodied, with soft, well-integrated tannins and appealing aromas and flavors of currants, black cherries and wild berries. Well balanced. Drink now–2007. Score 86. **K**

TEPERBERG RESERVE, MERITAGE, 2003: This full-bodied Bordeaux blend of 50% Cabernet Sauvignon, 40% Merlot and 10% Cabernet Franc shows deep ruby towards garnet in color, with spicy oak, soft tannins and appealing plum, currant and berry fruits. Full-bodied, round and well-balanced. Drink now–2007. Score 87. **K**

TEPERBERG RESERVE, CHARDONNAY, 2004: Deep golden yellow in color, medium-bodied, with citrus and summer fruits on a crisply-dry, mineral-rich background. Calls to mind Chablis. Drink from release–2007. Tentative Score 87–89. **K**

TEPERBERG RESERVE, CHARDONNAY, 2003: Fermented and developed on its lees *sur lie* in French oak *barriques* for six months, this medium to full-bodied white shows appealing citrus, pear and melon fruits, those on a round and creamy background. Drink now. Score 87. **K**

TEPERBERG RESERVE, CHENIN BLANC, 2004: Light gold in color, medium-bodied, with rich aromas and flavors of peaches, pears, melon and heather. Round, crisp and refreshing with hints of citrus peel on the finish. Drink from release–2007. Tentative Score 86–88. **K**

TEPERBERG RESERVE, CHENIN BLANC, 2003: Golden-straw colored, medium to full-bodied, with good balance between tropical fruits and citrus, crisp acidity and light creamy and nutty overtones from the oak in which the wine was aged. Bordering on elegance. Drink now. Score 87. K

Teperberg Selection

TEPERBERG SELECTION, CABERNET SAUVIGNON, 2004: Dark garnet towards royal purple in color, medium to full-bodied, with still firm tannins but those showing signs of integrating nicely with smoky wood, purple plums, currants and an appealing herbaciousness. Drink from release–2007. Tentative Score 87–89. K

TEPERBERG SELECTION, MERLOT, 2004: Dark ruby towards garnet in color, medium-bodied with soft, almost sweet tannins well balanced by wood and fruits. Look for aromas and flavors of plums and cassis as well as hints of chocolate and fresh herbs on the finish. Drink from release–2007. Tentative Score 86–88. K

TEPERBERG SELECTION, CHARDONNAY-SAUVIGNON, 2003: Light straw in color, with lively acidity, a hint of oak and appealing citrus and tropical fruits as well as a hint of grassiness. A good quaffer. Drink now. Score 84. K

TEPERBERG SELECTION, EMERALD RIESLING, 2003: Light in color and body, semi-dry, with floral and citrus aromas and flavors. An appealing entry-level wine. Drink up. Score 84. K

1870

1870 SERIES, MERLOT, 2003: Even though this wine spent one year in new French oak casks, it remains simple, not quite ripe and not balanced enough. Moderately tart berry and leathery flavors fail to come together. Drink up. Score 78. K

1870 SERIES, CHARDONNAY, 2003: Fermented in stainless steel vats and then aged for two months in new oak barrels, this pleasant little wine has attractively understated flavors of pears and citrus fruits supported by light hints of oak. Drink up. Score 82. K

1870 SERIES, SAUVIGNON BLANC, 2003: Light and refreshing but without the grassy, earthy traits one hopes for in wines made from this variety. Citrus, pear and delicate herbal flavors add some interest. Drink up. Score 80. K

1870 SERIES, EMERALD RIESLING, 2003: Light and fruity but with a somewhat bitter aftertaste. Drink up. Score 78. K

1870 SERIES, MUSCAT DESSERT WINE, N.V.: Somewhere between dark molasses and ruby Port in color, this wine is so cloyingly sweet that the fruits are all but hidden. Drink up. Score 70. K

Israeli Series

ISRAELI SERIES, CABERNET SAUVIGNON, 2004: Dark royal purple in color, medium-bodied, with soft tannins and berries and black cherry fruits. A simple entry-level wine. Drink now. Score 85. K

ISRAELI SERIES, CABERNET SAUVIGNON, 2003: Medium-bodied, with soft tannins and basic berry-cherry fruits. Drink up. Score 82. K

ISRAELI SERIES, CABERNET SAUVIGNON, 2002: Light to medium-bodied, this simple and unpretentious blend of 85% Cabernet Sauvignon and 15% Merlot is fresh and fruity. Drink up. Score 82. K

ISRAELI SERIES, MERLOT, 2004: Dark cherry red, medium-bodied with dusty tannins, perhaps too generous acidity and hints of spices. A bit skimpy on its currant and berry fruits. Drink up. Score 83. K

ISRAELI SERIES, MERLOT, 2003: Light to medium-bodied, with very soft tannins and uncomplicated berry-plum fruits. Drink up. Score 80. K

ISRAELI SERIES, MERLOT, 2002: Medium-bodied and low in tannins, this wine has a high level of acidity and only stingy fruits. Drink up. Score 65. K

ISRAELI SERIES, SHIRAZ, 2004: Bright garnet in color, medium-bodied, with country-style chunky tannins but those opening nicely in the glass to reveal pleasant enough plum and wild berry fruits. Drink now. Score 84. K

ISRAELI SERIES, CABERNET SAUVIGNON-MERLOT, 2004: Young, fresh and lively, with soft tannins and an appealing berry-cherry personality. Hints of spices and Mediterranean herbs add complexity. Drink now. Score 85. K

ISRAELI SERIES, ZINFANDEL, BLUSH, 2004: Light, fresh and fruity, off-dry and packed with berry, cherry and strawberry flavors. A pleasant picnic wine. Drink up. Score 83. K

ISRAELI SERIES, CHARDONNAY, 2004: Light golden straw in color, medium-bodied, with appealing citrus and tropical fruits backed up nicely by good natural acidity and hints of spiciness. Drink now. Score 85. K

ISRAELI SERIES, SAUVIGNON BLANC, 2003: Lively straw colored, light to medium-bodied, somewhat floral on the nose and with peach and citrus flavors. Drink up. Score 80. K

ISRAELI SERIES, EMERALD RIESLING, 2004: A pleasant little wine, light to medium-bodied, with floral and citrus overtones on a semi-dry background. Drink now. Score 83. K

Efrat

EFRAT, CABERNET SAUVIGNON-MERLOT, 2004: Light to medium-bodied, with almost unfelt tannins. Appealing berry and currant fruits and a hint of spices. Drink now. Score 83. K

EFRAT, CABERNET SAUVIGNON-MERLOT, 2003: Light, fresh and fruity, this unoaked blend of 60% Cabernet and 40% Merlot is a step up for Efrat. Not complex, but quite pleasant, with low tannins and appealing black fruit and cherry flavors. Drink up. Score 84. K

EFRAT, MERLOT, 2003: Light, with simple and modest flavors of black cherries and herbs, this red wine will probably be at its best when served lightly chilled. Drink up. Score 78. **K**

EFRAT, WHITE MUSCAT, DESSERT WINE, N.V.: After 18 months in oak casks, this sweet dessert wine has subtle aromas of peaches, melon and honey. Light in body and with a light acidity but with flavors that fade too quickly after the wine has been swallowed. Drink up. Score 82. **K**

Harei Yehuda (Judean Mountains)

HAREI YEHUDA, MERLOT, 2003: Light to medium-bodied, with soft tannins and generous fruits. A simple entry-level wine. Drink up. Score 78. **K**

HAREI YEHUDA, PETITE SIRAH, N.V.: Dark purple, medium-bodied with chunky tannins and appealing aromas and flavors of plums, berries and earthiness. A pleasing country-style wine. Drink up. Score 84. **K**

HAREI YEHUDA, ARGAMAN. N.V.: Despite its deep purple color, this wine lacks body, depth or fruit. Score 68. **K**

HAREI YEHUDA, EMERALD RIESLING, 2004: Light straw in color, light in body, with floral, pineapple and citrus aromas and flavors. Moderately sweet. Drink up. Score 80. **K**

HAREI YEHUDA, ZINFANDEL, N.V.: Flat on the palate and nose, not so much a true Zinfandel as the label implies but a pale cherry colored, semi-sweet "white Zin" that lacks fruit or other charms. Drink up. Score 72. **K**

Ella Valley ★★★★

Located on Kibbutz Netiv Halamed Hey in the Jerusalem Mountains, the winery has vineyards that might well serve as a model of efficiency and beauty anywhere in the world. Cultivation started in 1997 in the Ella and Adulam Valleys in the Judean Hills, and now includes Cabernet Sauvignon, Cabernet Franc, Merlot, Shiraz, Pinot Noir, Petite Sirah, Chardonnay, Sauvignon Blanc, Semillon and Muscat grapes. Under the supervision of French-trained winemaker Doron Rav Hon, the winery released its first wines, 90,000 bottles, from the 2002 harvest, and then nearly doubled that number in 2003 and 2004. Projected production for 2010 is 300,000 bottles. At this stage wines are being released in three series: Vineyard's Choice, Ella Valley and Ever Red.

Vineyard's Choice

VINEYARD'S CHOICE, CABERNET SAUVIGNON, 2003: Deep royal purple in color, full-bodied, with ripe, rich and complex fruits showing true harmony and finesse. Abundant layers of currants, juicy cherries and tempting oak shadings. Soft, supple and well-balanced tannins promise for a wine that although ready for early drinking should cellar very nicely. Drink from release–2011. Tentative Score 91–93. **K**

VINEYARD'S CHOICE, CABERNET SAUVIGNON, 2002: Medium to full-bodied, with good balance between toasty oak, near-sweet tannins and blackcurrant, berry, cherry fruits, those on a background of Mediterranean herbs. Drink now–2009. Score 90. **K**

VINEYARD'S CHOICE, MERLOT, 2003: Full-bodied, firmly structured with dark black cherry, berry, anise and spice flavors that stand up nicely to the firm tannins and moderate oak influences. Needs time but promises to soften and develop beautifully. Drink from release–2008. Tentative Score 89–91. K

VINEYARD'S CHOICE, MERLOT, 2002: Full-bodied, with deep but soft and sweet tannins and a complex array of plum, currant and berry fruits, together with rewarding black olive and earthy overlays. Excellent balance between oak, tannins and fruits that bodes well for the future. Drink now–2008. Score 92. K

Ella Valley Vineyards

ELLA VALLEY VINEYARDS, CABERNET SAUVIGNON, 2004: Big, ripe, complex and shows good balance between ripe cherry, currant and plums, those with a dash of anise and oak. Developing nicely, with supple tannins and overall excellent balance. Best 2007–2010. Tentative Score 90–92. K

ELLA VALLEY VINEYARDS, CABERNET SAUVIGNON, 2003: Firm and tight, big and somewhat rustic, with notes of minerals and sweet cedar all on a background of chewy tannins. Deeply concentrated, but with the balance that gives it the promise to soften with time and reveal its rich plum and currant fruits. Drink now–2008. Score 89. K

ELLA VALLEY VINEYARDS, CABERNET SAUVIGNON, 2002: Dark garnet toward purple, this medium to full-bodied wine shows medicinal aromas and flavors when first poured, but those fade somewhat as the wine opens in the glass, yielding rich, ripe currant, plum, cherry, anise and mint aromas and flavors. Rich and long, but with a light bitterness that runs through and then lingers on the finish. Drink now–2007. Score 88. K

ELLA VALLEY VINEYARDS, MERLOT, 2004: Supple and with good balance between generous and still firm tannins and spicy wood and fruit, with the promise to yield a graceful full-bodied red in which black cherry, currant and cedary oak flavors will come together very nicely indeed. Drink from release–2008. Tentative Score 90–92. K

ELLA VALLEY VINEYARDS, MERLOT, 2003: Medium to full-bodied, supple and well balanced, striving for elegance with just the right balance between plum, berry, currant and wood aromas and flavors. Graceful and not overwhelming, with cedar and spices on the finish. Drink now–2009. Score 90. K

ELLA VALLEY VINEYARDS, MERLOT, 2002: Dark in color, full in body and with firm tannins for a Merlot, the wine is rich, ripe and harmonious, showing an elegant array of cherry, currant and spice aromas and flavors, a generous but well balanced hand with the oak, and a long fruity finish highlighted by hints of coffee and herbs. Drink now–2009. Score 91. K

ELLA VALLEY VINEYARDS, PINOT NOIR, 2004: Rich, dark and concentrated, with a complex range of cherry, blackberry, plum, spice and toasty oak flavors that fold together nicely. Delicious and with the tannic concentration to bode well for comfortable aging. Best starting from 2007. Tentative Score 89–91. K

ELLA VALLEY VINEYARDS, CABERNET FRANC, 2004: Medium to full-bodied with austere tannins but already showing finesse. Sharply focused cherry, currant and wild berry flavors open slowly on the palate along with a generous but well-tempered dose of smoky oak. Needs time to show its depth and complexity. Drink from release–2008. Tentative Score 88–90. K

ELLA VALLEY VINEYARDS, SHIRAZ, 2004: Full-bodied, dark, rich and complex with an array of spicy, smoky and meaty plum, berry, currant and anise notes set off nicely by near sweet tannins. Well-balanced and flavorful. Drink from release 2008. Tentative Score 88 90. K

ELLA VALLEY VINEYARDS, CHARDONNAY, 2004: Soft in texture but generous with pear, citrus and mineral flavors that develop a very appealing creamy note on the finish. Light wood and just the right amount of zingy acidity makes this a solid, complex wine with long, lingering flavors. Drink now–2007. Score 90. K

ELLA VALLEY VINEYARDS, CHARDONNAY, 2003: Ripe and complex, with spicy pear, spice, apple and hazelnut notes. Reflecting its 10 months *sur lie*, this deep golden wine fills the palate with complex and long lingering flavors and just the right hints of toasted white bread and yeast. A good dose of oak here but that well integrated. Drink now- 2008. Score 91. K

ELLA VALLEY VINEYARDS, SAUVIGNON BLANC, 2004: Smooth, rich and buttery, with good spices, a light grassiness matched by good spices and appealing layers of pear, honey and minerals. A very appealing hint of light bitterness comes in on the long finish. Drink now–2008. Score 91. K

ELLA VALLEY VINEYARDS, MUSCAT OF ALEXANDRIA, DESSERT WINE, 2002: Medium-bodied, with honeyed sweetness set off nicely by lively acidity, the wine offers generous and ripe apricot, peach and dried apple fruits matched nicely by spices and floral aromas and flavors. Equally good as an aperitif. Drink now. Score 89. K

Ever Red

ELLA VALLEY VINEYARDS, EVER RED, 2003: Deep purple in color, medium-bodied, this blend of Cabernet Sauvignon and Merlot opens in the glass to reveal gentle wood, soft tannins and appealing currant and wild berry fruits. A lightly spicy finish. Drink now. Score 87. **K**

ELLA VALLEY VINEYARDS, EVER RED, 2002: A medium to full-bodied oak-aged blend of 80% Cabernet Sauvignon and 20% Merlot, this supple and harmonious wine has an attractive core of plum, berry and cherry fruits. Finishes with a nice touch of spices, mild tannins and toasty oak. Drink now. Score 87. **K**

Essence *

Located in the community of Ma'aleh Tsvi'a in the Western Galilee, the winery was founded by Yaniv Kimchi, Eitan Rosenberg and Itzhak Avramov, and released its first wines in 2001. Grapes, including Cabernet Sauvignon, are raised in the winery's organic vineyards at the foothills of Mount Kamon. The winery produced 3,000 bottles in 2001 and 5,000 in 2002 and 2003.

ESSENCE, CABERNET SAUVIGNON, 2003: Deep ruby towards garnet, medium-bodied, with chunky tannins, spicy cedar wood and aromas and flavors primarily of ripe berries. Pleasant but somewhat one dimensional. Drink now. Score 84.

ESSENCE, CABERNET SAUVIGNON, 2002: Medium to dark garnet in color, this medium-bodied oak-aged wine shows soft tannins and appealing black cherry and blackberry fruits, but is a bit too acidic and shows none of the varietal traits of Cabernet. Drink up. Score 83.

ESSENCE, MERLOT, 2003: Cloudy purple in color, with chunky tannins that seem not to want to integrate and stingy black fruits dominated by an overly alcoholic finish. Drink up. Score 79.

ESSENCE, MERLOT, 2002: Dark garnet toward purple in color, this medium-bodied wine has firm tannins that fail to integrate along with some appealing black fruit aromas and flavors and a hint of smoky oak. Somewhat past its peak. Drink up. Score 82.

ESSENCE, MERLOT, 2001: The wine has only stingy aromas, body and tannins, a few black fruit flavors and is so acidic that some will consider it sour. Score 72.

ESSENCE, ELECTRUM, 2002: This medium-bodied oak-aged blend of Cabernet Sauvignon and Merlot offers up soft tannins and generous blackcurrant and plum flavors. Drink now. Score 84.

Flam ✶✶✶✶✶

MERLOT
VINTAGE 2001
RESERVE

PRODUCED AND
BOTTLED BY FLAM
BROS. HAGEFEN LTD

I S R A E L

750 ML   13,5% ALC. BY VOL.

PRODUCT OF ISRAEL

Located in a sparkling new state-of-the-art facility not far from the town of Beit Shemesh at the foothills of the Jerusalem Mountains, the Flam winery has produced consistently excellent and exciting wines since its first releases from the 1998 vintage. Established by brothers Golan and Gilad Flam, Golan being the winemaker, after having trained and worked in Australia and Tuscany, and Gilad in charge of the business aspects, the winery now relies on grapes from vineyards in the Jerusalem Mountains and the Upper Galilee. The winery is currently producing age-worthy varietal Cabernet Sauvignon and Merlot wines in their Reserve series, and also has a second wine, Classico, a blend of Cabernet Sauvignon and Merlot that is meant for relatively early drinking. Production from the 1998 vintage was less than 1,000 bottles, 25,000 bottles were released in 2002, 45,000 in 2003 and 55,000 in 2004.

Reserve

RESERVE, CABERNET SAUVIGNON, 2004: Rich, ripe and complex, full-bodied, with firm but already well integrating tannins and an abundance of cherry, currant, anise and spicy oak. Smooth and harmonious. Drink from release–2010. Tentative Score 91–93.

RESERVE, CABERNET SAUVIGNON, KEREM DISHON, UPPER GALILEE, 2003: Dark garnet towards royal purple, with spicy Cabernet fruits on a generous background of minerals, earthiness, herbs and spices, with the wine showing as well a generous splash of toasty oak. A firm wine that already shows great complexity and depth. Best starting from 2007. Tentative Score 90–92.

RESERVE, CABERNET SAUVIGNON, KARMEI YOSEF VINEYARD, 2003: This full-bodied, deep purple towards black wine, made from grapes raised in the Karmei Yosef vineyards, shows rich, ripe and complex fruit and appealing influences of wood. Lots of currants and cherries together with hints of spicy oak. Smooth tannins and a long finish. Drink now–2012. Score 92.

RESERVE, CABERNET SAUVIGNON, 2002: Made primarily from Cabernet Sauvignon grapes from Kerem Dishon and Kerem Ben Zimra, blended with a small amount of Merlot from Karmei Yosef, this elegant deep garnet towards black wine already shows good integration between wood, soft tannins and fruit, and generous currant and ripe red fruits. On the finish complex overlays of sweet cedar. Drink now–2010. Score 92.

RESERVE, CABERNET SAUVIGNON, 2001: Deep royal purple toward garnet, with excellent extraction but still showing a remarkable softness, this full-bodied, distinctly Mediterranean red has excellent balance between wood, tannins and fruit. Traditional Cabernet blackcurrants are the dominant fruits but these well set off by black cherries, spices and generous hints of black olives and leather. Drink now–2009. Score 94.

RESERVE, CABERNET SAUVIGNON, 2000: Well focused and balanced, this remarkably deep purple, medium to full-bodied blend of 90% Cabernet Sauvignon and 10% Merlot spent 15 months in oak casks. A wine so deep you feel you can get lost in it, with traditional Cabernet flavors and aromas of red currants, ripe red fruit and delicious spices. Drink now–2008. Score 94.

RESERVE, CABERNET SAUVIGNON, 1999: This deep and profound blend of 85% Cabernet Sauvignon and 15% Merlot has intense berry, mint and cassis aromas and flavors, along with ample hints of the oak in which it aged for 14 months. Full-bodied, elegant and refined, with silky tannins and a succulent finish. Drink now–2008. Score 94.

RESERVE, CABERNET SAUVIGNON, 1998: Aged in new oak casks for 14 months, this delicious blend of 85% Cabernet Sauvignon and 15% Merlot is as assertive, rich and lush today as it was during its youth. Spicy and peppery tones overlay deep aromas and flavors of currants, black cherries and plums, along with floral accents and a clean, long finish. Drink now–2007. Score 92.

RESERVE, MERLOT, 2004: Deep garnet towards purple, full-bodied, with a complex array of currant, plum and berry aromas and flavors, this graceful, well-balanced and mouth-filling wine shows adequate cedar and spice flavors and an appealing earthy hint on the finish. Drink from release–2010. Tentative Score 89–91.

RESERVE, MERLOT, 2003: Dark, deep and intense, with soft, almost sweet tannins and layer after layer of berry, black cherry, anise and spice aromas and flavors that linger nicely on the palate. Still marked wood influence here but with the balance and structure that bode well for the future. Needs time to soften in the bottle. Best from 2007–2012. Score 92.

RESERVE, MERLOT, 2002: Deep royal purple, full-bodied, and with excellent extraction, this dark, rich and luxurious wine has an array of flavors that open in the glass to reveal spicy currants, wild berries, mocha and herbs. Still somewhat tannic, reflecting its 15 months in oak, the wine needs time to integrate and in the near future will begin to show anise and light tar overtones on a long smooth finish. Drink now–2010. Score 91.

RESERVE, MERLOT, 2001: Subdued but with marked elegance, this full-bodied wine shows smooth, well-integrated tannins together with delicious plum, black cherry and light olive fruits, all coming together with just the right impact of the oak casks in which it was aged. An appealing, almost sweet herbal finish adds to the charm of the wine. Drink now–2008. Score 92.

RESERVE, MERLOT, 2000: Made entirely from Merlot grapes and aged for 15 months in small oak casks, the wine shows deep, concentrated and luscious black fruits overlaid with generous mocha, chocolate and vanilla aromas and flavors, as well as a pleasing sensation of herbaceousness that comes in on the long finish. With smooth tannins and excellent balance, this is a mouth-filling, ripe and elegant wine. Drink now–2007. Score 93.

RESERVE, MERLOT, 1999: This medium to full-bodied wine has silky tannins and remarkably harmonious aromas and flavors of cassis, violets, berries and toasty oak. Rich, with flavors that linger on and on, Merlot lovers will find this wine irresistible. Drink now–2007. Score 91.

RESERVE, SYRAH, 2004: Youthful royal purple, packed with purple plums and red berries as well as generous soft tannins. Medium to full-bodied, with spicy chocolate, vanilla and an herbal-tobacco finish. Drink from release–2010. Tentative Score 90–92.

RESERVE, SYRAH, 2003: Perhaps the Israeli wine that to date most typifies true Syrah. Aged in oak for about 10 months, this deep purple wine shows tempting earthy, mineral aromas and flavors, those backed up nicely by berries, currants and spices. Drink now–2009. Score 91.

RESERVE, CHARDONNAY-SAUVIGNON BLANC, 2004: The first white wine from Flam. Unoaked and retaining the fresh and unalloyed aromatic flavors of both varieties (70% Chardonnay, 30% Sauvignon Blanc), this crisply dry, medium-bodied wine shows delicious citrus, pear and summer fruit aromas and flavors, those with tempting overlays of melon, herbs and flowers. Harmonious and expressive. Drink now–2007. Score 90.

Superieur

SUPERIEUR, 2003: A blend of 77% Syrah and 23% Cabernet Sauvignon, each fermented separately in French oak before blending. Medium to full-bodied, with soft tannins and a generous earthy-herbal Syrah background coming together nicely with plum, tobacco and blackberry fruits. Round, long, and elegant. Calls to mind a Rhone Cornas. Drink now–2009. Score 90.

Classico

CLASSICO, 2003: A medium-bodied blend of equal parts of Cabernet Sauvignon and Merlot, with soft already well integrated tannins, a well balanced dose of wood and aromatic red berries and currants all coming together nicely with light smoky vanilla and a hint of spices. Drink now–2007. Score 90.

CLASSICO, 2002: This medium to full-bodied Cabernet Sauvignon-Merlot blend shows plenty of smooth tannins, just the right influence of the wood to pass on generous smoky and vanilla flavors, and fruits that include red currants and wild berries along with a nice hint of herbaceousness. Drink now. Score 90.

CLASSICO, 2001: This medium-bodied Cabernet Sauvignon-Merlot blend spent 7 months in small oak casks and shows generous smooth tannins and tempting flavors of currants, plums, wild berries and spices. A well-balanced and seductive wine. Drink now. Score 91.

CLASSICO, 2000: Surprisingly full-bodied and tannic but simultaneously smooth, elegant and well balanced, this blend of Cabernet and Merlot has vanilla, berry and coffee aromas and flavors, and a long delicious finish. Drink up. Score 90.

CLASSICO, 1999: A blend of 50% each of Cabernet Sauvignon and Merlot that was aged for 6 months in new French oak barrels, this medium to full-bodied wine is remarkably smooth for its age, well balanced and packed with ripe black cherry, currant and berry flavors that linger nicely on the palate. Drink up. Score 88.

Gadot *

Set on Kibbutz Gadot in the Upper Galilee, this small winery was founded in 2001. Drawing on Merlot, Cabernet Sauvignon, Shiraz and Carignan grapes from vineyards in Binyamina, on the Lebanese border, and on the Golan Heights, as well as the Santa Catarina grapes that are said to have originated in the Sinai Desert, the winery is currently releasing about 500 bottles annually.

GADOT, SANTA CATARINA, 2003: Garnet red, medium-bodied, with chunky, country-style tannins. Generous ripe berry and black cherry fruits but not much in the way of balance, depth or length. Drink up. Score 78.

GADOT, SANTA CATARINA, 2002: A dark cherry-red medium-bodied wine with far too coarse tannins and with aromas and flavors of overripe plums and crushed berries. Drink up. Score 76.

GADOT, SANTA CATARINA, 2001: This medium-bodied blend of Cabernet Sauvignon, Merlot and Santa Catarina grapes has somewhat coarse tannins and far too forward, hyper-sweet fruits. Give it time to settle down in the glass and it becomes somewhat more subdued. Drink now. Score 79.

Galai **

GALAI
ESTATE WINE

2002

Cabernet Sauvignon

12.5% vol.   Unfiltered   e 750 ml.

Sigalit and Asaf Galai established this small winery at Moshav Nir Akiva in the northern part of the Negev Desert in 2002. The winery has vineyards containing Cabernet Sauvignon and Merlot as well as experimental sections of Cabernet Franc, Shiraz and Zinfandel. Production was 3,000 bottles in 2002, 5,000 in 2003 and 7,500 in 2004.

GALAI, CABERNET SAUVIGNON, 2004: Dark ruby towards royal purple, medium to full-bodied, with chunky country-style tannins. Appealing currant, plum and smoky oak flavors but somewhat one-dimensional. Drink from release–2007. Tentative Score 84–86.

GALAI, CABERNET SAUVIGNON, 2003: Deep garnet in color, with firm tannins integrating nicely, this soft and round medium-bodied wine is a blend of Cabernet Sauvingon, Merlot and Cabernet Franc (85%, 11% and 4% respectively). Well balanced, with appealing black fruits and a moderately long finish. Drink now–2007. Score 86.

GALAI, CABERNET SAUVIGNON, 2002: Medium-bodied, with the once firm tannins now nicely integrated. Supple and fruity, with just enough plum and cherry flavors to hold your interest. Drink now. Score 84.

GALAI, MERLOT, 2004: Medium to full-bodied, with firm tannins integrating nicely and an appealing array of berry, cherry and plum, those matched nicely by hints of spices and smoke. A bit of bitterness creeps in on the finish. Not meant for cellaring. Drink from release. Tentative Score 84–86.

GALAI, MERLOT, 2003: Dark ruby towards garnet, this medium-bodied wine blended with 15% Cabernet Sauvignon spent 13 months in oak. There are some nice berry and cherry flavors here but with flabby tannins and high acidity the wine fails to come together. Drink now. Score 83.

GALAI, MERLOT, 2002: Medium-bodied, with soft almost unfelt tannins. Berry-cherry flavors and a hint of spices but short and one-dimensional. Drink up. Score 79.

GALAI, CABERNET SAUVIGNON-SHIRAZ, 2003: Aged for 20 months in oak, this medium to full-bodied blend of 67% Cabernet Sauvignon and 33% Shiraz offers appealing currant, plum and earthy-mineral aromas and flavors, all leading to a moderately long finish. Drink now. Score 85.

GALAI, CABERNET SAUVIGNON-SHIRAZ, 2002: Deep cherry-red in color, medium to full-bodied, with soft tannins, a hint of smoky oak, and generous plum and berry fruits. Drink now. Score 83.

GALAI, BACCHUS, 2003: Light to medium-bodied, this blend of 60% Cabernet Sauvignon and 40% Merlot has light tannins and somewhat diluted flavors and aromas of berries and black cherries. Short and one-dimensional. Drink up. Score 83.

Galil Mountain ✦✦✦✦

With its state-of-the-art winery located on Kibbutz Yiron in the Upper Galilee, this joint venture between the Golan Heights Winery and the *kibbutz* has vineyards located in some of the best wine-growing areas of the Upper Galilee, including Yiron, Meron, Misgav Am, Yiftach and Malkiya. Californian and French trained winemaker Gaby Sadan is currently producing distinctly *terroir*-based wines in two series. The first label, Yiron, is a blend of Cabernet Sauvignon and Merlot, and the second, the Galil Mountain series, contains varietal releases of Cabernet Sauvignon, Merlot, Pinot Noir, Syrah, Sangiovese, Chardonnay and Sauvignon Blanc. Production from the 2000 vintage was about 300,000 bottles. Since then the winery has grown to an output of 800,000 and expects to meet its target production of 1–1.2 million bottles annually with the 2005 harvest.

Yiron

YIRON, 2003: A blend this year of 60% Cabernet Sauvignon, 35% Merlot and 5% Syrah. Young and vibrant but already showing potential complexity. Dark royal purple, with firm but nicely integrating tannins, generous but judicious wood and layers of spicy currant, anise, tar and cedary oak aromas and flavors blending nicely on the long finish. Drink from release–2009. Tentative Score 90–92. K

YIRON, 2002: A medium to full-bodied oak-aged blend of 54% Cabernet Sauvignon and 46% Merlot. Deeply aromatic, dark purple toward black in color, with still muscular tannins but those now integrating well, the wine shows an abundance of blackcurrant, cassis and berry fruits as well as sweet-cedar wood. Generous, with a long mouth-filling finish. Currently developing appealing light herbal-earthy overtones. Drink now–2008. Score 90. K

YIRON, 2001: Dark garnet in color, this medium to full-bodied red, a blend of 78% Cabernet Sauvignon and 22% Merlot, offers up generous tannins, those well balanced by oak and a tempting array of fruits including black cherries, blackberries and currants, all lingering nicely on the palate. Delicious and sophisticated. Drink now–2007. Score 90. K

YIRON, 2000: Deep red toward purple, this medium to full-bodied blend of 60% Cabernet Sauvignon and 40% Merlot shows smooth, well-integrating tannins, and generous but not overpowering oak, reflecting 16 months in small oak barrels. Plum, cherry-berry and eucalyptus aromas and flavors are felt on the first attack, yielding to an appealing and gentle herbal-earthy overlay and a moderately long finish. Drink now–2007. Score 90. K

Galil Mountain

GALIL MOUNTAIN, CABERNET SAUVIGNON, 2004: Dark garnet red, with tannins already integrating nicely, and traditional Cabernet currant, berry and light herbal aromas and flavors. Drink from release–2008. Tentative Score 87–89. K

GALIL MOUNTAIN, CABERNET SAUVIGNON, 2003: Inky-black in color, full-bodied, with muscular tannins that have started to soften and with good balance and excellent structure. Tempting currant, cranberry and rhubarb aromas and flavors make this a long, round and quietly elegant wine. Drink now–2008. Score 89. K

GALIL MOUNTAIN, CABERNET SAUVIGNON, 2002: Medium to full-bodied, with generous well-integrated tannins, those well balanced by cassis and blackberry fruits. Drink now. Score 87. K

GALIL MOUNTAIN, CABERNET SAUVIGNON, 2001: Deep royal purple, medium-bodied and aromatic, this unoaked 100% Cabernet Sauvignon shows plenty of soft tannins as well as aromas and flavors of wild berries, black plums and herbs, along with a hint of cigar tobacco. Drink now. Score 87. K

GALIL MOUNTAIN, CABERNET SAUVIGNON, 2000: Medium to full-bodied, this smooth, ripe and fruity wine has generous wild berry, plum and currant flavors along with soft tannins. Well balanced and graceful. Drink up. Score 87. K

GALIL MOUNTAIN, MERLOT, 2004: Dark ruby towards garnet, medium-bodied, with soft tannins, and with berry and plum fruits, all on a light peppery background. Round and smooth. Drink from release–2008. Tentative Score 86–88. K

GALIL MOUNTAIN, MERLOT, 2003: Medium to full-bodied and rich in currant, berry and grapefruit peel aromas and flavors, smoky overlays and generous soft tannins, this unoaked wine promises to develop nicely. Drink now–2008. Score 88. K

GALIL MOUNTAIN, MERLOT, 2002: Deep, almost inky purple in color, medium to full-bodied, with generous aromas and flavors of herbs, berries and spring flowers on a softly tannic background and a medium-to-long, almost sweet finish highlighted by cedar and chocolate. Drink now. Score 86. K

GALIL MOUNTAIN, MERLOT, 2001: Deep purple, medium-bodied, and with appealing fruit, vanilla, light oak and peppery aromas and flavors, this distinctly Mediterranean wine has hints of orange and lemon peel on the finish. Drink up. Score 87. K

GALIL MOUNTAIN, MERLOT, 2000: A stylish, medium-bodied Merlot, generous in flavors of berries, with light overtones of Mediterranean herbs and vanilla, all with bare hints of tobacco and coffee. Drink up. Score 86. K

GALIL MOUNTAIN, PINOT NOIR, 2004: With the potential for European elegance, an intentionally understated style that appeals with its subdued oak allowing free reign to spice, black cherry, and strawberry flavors as well as subtle herbal notes. Drink from release–2008. Tentative Score 87–89. ᴋ

GALIL MOUNTAIN, PINOT NOIR 2003: With six months in oak, this medium- bodied wine shows well-integrated soft tannins and appealing plum, cherry and wild berry fruits together with a bare meaty-herbal overtone. Drink now–2007. Score 86. ᴋ

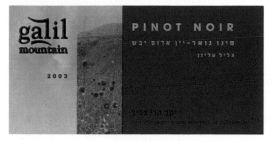

GALIL MOUNTAIN, PINOT NOIR, 2002: The darkest, most deeply extracted and most fruity of the Pinot Noir wines from Galil Mountain, with hints of cedar wood, soft and well-integrated tannins, and black cherry and Oriental spices now showing nicely. Drink now. Score 86. ᴋ

GALIL MOUNTAIN, PINOT NOIR, 2001: The first and the lightest of the Pinot Noirs made by the winery, aged in oak for six months, its once youthful ruby color now darkening, the plummy, floral aromas and flavors still in place but now starting to show a few earthy-meaty hints. Drink up. Score 87. ᴋ

GALIL MOUNTAIN, SYRAH, 2003: Deep and tannic, soft but powerful, medium to full-bodied, integrating well and showing generous peppery black fruits and hints of grilled meat, tobacco and chocolate. Developing beautifully. Drink from release–2008. Tentative Score 88–90. ᴋ

GALIL MOUNTAIN, SHIRAZ-CABERNET, 2003: Dark garnet, medium-bodied, with good balance between soft tannins, sweet-and-spicy oak, and showing smooth and supple aromas and flavors of creamy currants, black cherries and coffee. Distinctly New World in style, the wine is surprisingly approachable. Drink now–2007, Score 88. ᴋ

GALIL MOUNTAIN, ROSÉ, 2004: A blend of Sangiovese, Cabernet Sauvignon and Syrah (92%, 5% and 3% respectively), this crisply dry light to medium-bodied rosé is refreshing, lively and fruity while maintaining a surprising level of sophistication. Not recognizable as Sangiovese but you cannot miss the berry and light spices here. Lightly *frizzante* when well chilled. Drink up. Score 86. ᴋ

GALIL MOUNTAIN, CHARDONNAY, 2004: Bright golden straw in color, medium-bodied, with tempting aromas and flavors of loquats, tropical fruits and minerals. Good balance between light wood, crisp balancing acidity and mouthfilling fruits. Drink now–2007. Score 88. K

GALIL MOUNTAIN, CHARDONNAY, 2003: The color of golden straw, with grapefruit, green apple and floral aromas and flavors and good balancing acidity to keep it lively, this is a refreshing wine, with appealing hints of vanilla and minerals. Give the wine ten minutes to open in the glass to show its best. Drink now. Score 86. K

GALIL MOUNTAIN, CHARDONNAY, 2001: Light to medium-bodied, well balanced, and with appealing aromas and flavors of citrus, pineapple and green apples. Drink up. Score 85. K

GALIL MOUNTAIN, CHARDONNAY, 2000: Crisp, with lemon, grapefruit and passion fruit aromas and flavors, and with just a hint of the oak in which it was aged for a short while, this near-elegant wine lingers nicely on the palate. Drink up. Score 86. K

GALIL MOUNTAIN, SAUVIGNON BLANC, 2004: A light straw color with orange and green reflections, this medium-bodied unoaked white offers up crisp balancing acidity to highlight its primarily melon and peach fruits. Floats in a tantalizing manner on the palate. Drink now. Score 88. K

GALIL MOUNTAIN, SAUVIGNON BLANC, 2003: Light, shiny straw colored, this medium-bodied, unoaked white has appealing floral, grapefruit and mineral aromas and flavors. Lively, refreshing and long. Drink now. Score 88. K

Gat Shomron ✴

Founded by Avigdor Sharon and Limor Nachum on the settlement of Karnei Shomron, not far from Kfar Saba, in 2003, and releasing their first wines from that harvest in 2005, this small winery is currently producing about 2,000 bottles annually of oak-aged Cabernet Sauvignon, Merlot and Chardonnay.

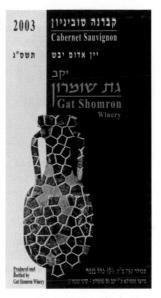

GAT SHOMRON, CABERNET SAU-VIGNON, 2003: Dark ruby towards garnet, with somewhat overgenerous tannins and oak, and ripe plum and berry fruits. Drink now. Score 82. K

GAT SHOMRON, MERLOT, 2003: Garnet red, medim-bodied, with chunky country-style tannins and generous oak set off nicely by aromas and flavors of plums, cassis and sweet herbs. Drink now. Score 84. K

GAT SHOMRON, CHARDONNAY, 2004: Medium-bodied, light golden in color, with aromas and flavors of pineapple, citrus and spring flowers. Somewhat alcoholic and coarse on the palate. Drink up. Score 82. K

Gefen Adderet *

Founded by Meir Kfir in the village Gan Yavne in the southern Coastal Plain, this small winery draws Cabernet Sauvignon, Merlot and Chardonnay grapes from the vineyards of Karmei Yosef, the Jerusalem Mountains and the Galilee. The winery released about 900 bottles in 2003.

GEFEN ADDERET, AVICHAI, 2003: A medium-bodied blend of 79% Merlot, 13% Cabernet Sauvignon and 8% Petite Sirah. Dark garnet, with soft tannins and appealing aroma and flavors of plums, black cherries and currants all on a lightly spicy background. Drink now–2007. Score 85.

GEFEN ADDERET, ZOHARA, 2003: Deep ruby towards garnet, this medium-bodied blend of Cabernet Sauvignon, Merlot and Argaman (68%, 22% and 10% respectively) shows light tannins and a fresh, lightly spicy berry-cherry personality. Drink now. Score 84.

GEFEN ADDERET, BICURIM, 2003: Made from Petite Sirah grapes by the process of carbonic maceration and meant to be consumed very young, the wine has already lost whatever cherry-berry fruits it once possessed. Score 65.

GEFEN ADDERET, CHARDONNAY, 2003: Light golden in color and medium-bodied, with hints of oak and vanilla and aromas and flavors of citrus and melon. A pleasant quaffer. Drink now. Score 85.

GEFEN ADDERET, ROSEMARINE, 2003: Made from Gewurztraminer grapes but without any of the spiciness, litchi or tropical fruits that often typify that variety, the wine is defined as half-dry but feels cloying on the palate, yielding more honey than fruits. Score 62.

Gesher Damia *

Founded in 1999 by Moshe Kaplan in the town of Pardess Hannah on the northern Coastal Plain, this small winery receives Cabernet Sauvignon, Merlot, Argaman, Petite Sirah, Gewurztraminer and Chardonnay grapes from Gush Etzion, the Jerusalem Hills and the center of the country. Production in 2002 was 4,000 bottles and the winery released 5,000 bottles in 2003.

GESHER DAMIA, CABERNET SAUVIGNON, 2003: Deep ruby in color, medium-bodied, with gripping tannins and generous sweet and smoky oak and a few berry-cherry fruits. Drink up. Score 78.

GESHER DAMIA, CABERNET SAUVIGNON, 2002: This medium-bodied wine has firm tannins and abundant sweet cedar wood but lacks the fruits, depth or length to carry it. Drink up. Score 77.

GESHER DAMIA, CABERNET SAUVIGNON, 2001: Medium-bodied, with soft tannins and an appealing fruity character of currants and red plums, this country-style wine shows exaggerated wood that adds an unnecessary coarseness. Drink now. Score 84.

GESHER DAMIA, CABERNET SAUVIGNON, 2000: This dark purple medium-bodied amateurish effort is now oxidizing rapidly. No longer scoreable.

GESHER DAMIA, MERLOT, 2002: Smooth and soft, this dark ruby toward garnet wine shows appealing currant, berry and cherry fruits but proves somewhat one-dimensional and short. Drink up. Score 78.

GESHER DAMIA, MERLOT, 2001: This deep garnet, medium-bodied, moderately tannic red with berry-black cherry fruits is faulted by a somewhat musky barnyard-like finish and now showing age. Score 78.

GESHER DAMIA, MERLOT, 2000: Medium-bodied and with barely discernible tannins, the wine lacks fruit in its aromas and flavors and now oxidizing rapidly. Score 65.

Ginaton **

Founded in 1999 by Doron Cohen and Benju Duke on Moshav Ginaton on the central plains not far from the city of Lod, and drawing Cabernet Sauvignon, Muscat and Chardonnay grapes from Karmei Yosef and Kerem Ben Zimra, the first commercial releases of the winery were 3,000 bottles from the 2000 vintage. Production from the 2003 vintage was about 5,500 bottles and the winery is holding temporarily at that number.

GINATON, CABERNET SAUVIGNON, KEREM BEN ZIMRA, 2003: Clear ruby towards purple, medium-bodied, with soft, almost unfelt tannins. Aromas and flavors of berries, cassis and black cherries on a ligtly herbaceous background. Drink now–2007. Score 84.

GINATON, CABERNET SAUVIGNON, KEREM BEN ZIMRA, 2002: Medium-bodied, with currant, berry and cherry fruits all on a lightly spicy background and with hints of Mediterranean herbs that come in on the finish. Drink now. Score 85.

GINATON, CABERNET SAUVIGNON, KEREM BEN ZIMRA, 2001: Medium-bodied, with berry, cherry and some currant fruits and a hint of toasty oak. Simple but appealing. Drink up. Score 83.

GINATON, CABERNET SAUVIGNON, KEREM YOSEF, 2001: Ripe plum and cherry flavors make this medium-bodied and moderately tannic wine just engaging enough to hold your interest. Drink now. Score 83.

GINATON, CABERNET SAUVIGNON, KEREM YOSEF, 2000: Medium-bodied, firm and with berry and chocolate notes but with too many earthy, cedary flavors. Somewhat past its peak. Drink up. Score 82.

GINATON, MERLOT, KEREM YOSEF, 2003: Medium-bodied, with soft, well integrating tannins and appealing aromas and flavors of blackberries and purple plums on a lightly spicy background. Drink now. Score 84.

GINATON, MERLOT, KEREM YOSEF, 2002: Medium-bodied, with good focus and nice wild berry and herbal flavors, but turning thin on the finish where it picks up a smoky, mineral accent. Drink up. Score 80.

GINATON, MERLOT, KEREM YOSEF, 2001: Medium-bodied and with very soft tannins, with some ripe plum and cherry flavors, but turning simple on the finish. Drink up. Score 83.

GINATON, MERLOT, KEREM YOSEF, 2000: Not complex but with juicy ripe cherry and berry flavors and hints of cedar. Soft tannins make this an acceptable quaffer. Past its peak. Drink up. Score 82.

Givon *

Established by Nir Ernesti and Shuki Segal in the village of Givon, north of Jerusalem in the Judean Mountains, and relying on Cabernet Sauvignon and Merlot grapes from nearby vineyards, this winery released its first wines from the 2002 vintage. Current production is about 2,000 bottles annually.

GIVON, CABERNET SAUVIGNON, 2003: Medium-bodied, with soft tannins and simple but appealing flavors of berries and black cherries, but faulted somewhat by a too generous acidity. Drink now. Score 80.

GIVON, CABERNET SAUVIGNON, SOLO, 2003: Made entirely from Cabernet Sauvignon grapes, this medium-bodied, softly tannic red is somewht one-dimensional but with appealing plum and berry fruits. Drink up. Score 84.

GIVON, MERLOT, 2003: This simple country-style wine, a blend of 90% Merlot and 10% Cabernet Sauvignon, has forward black fruits and medium-body but with its somewhat chunky tannins and rasping acidity it is not at all reminiscent of Merlot. Drink now. Score 78.

GIVON, MERLOT, 2002: Dark cherry red, this medium-bodied, simple wine offers up soft tannins and light but pleasant plum and berry flavors. Drink up. Score 78.

Golan Heights Winery *****

From the moment they released their first wines in 1984, there has been no doubt that the Golan Heights Winery was and is still today largely responsible for placing Israel on the world wine map. The winery, with its state-of-the-art facilities located in Katzrin on the Golan Heights, and fine vineyards in the Upper Galilee and on the Golan, is owned by eight of the *kibbutzim* and *moshavim* that supply them with grapes. By maintaining rigorous control over the vineyards and relying on a combination of New and Old World knowledge and technology, senior winemaker Victor Shoenfeld and his staff of winemakers, all of whom trained in California or France, produce wines that often attain excellence.

The winery produces three regular series, Yarden, Gamla and Golan, the wines in the first two series often being age-worthy while those in the Golan series are meant for early drinking. There is also the top-of-the-line Katzrin series that includes a red Bordeaux-style blend that is released only in years considered exceptional and a Chardonnay that has been released annually since 1995.

The winery is currently producing more than five million bottles annually and is increasing its output by ten to twenty percent annually. Of this production nearly thirty percent is destined for export. Among the regularly released varietal wines are Cabernet Sauvignon, Merlot, Sauvignon Blanc, Chardonnay, Johannisberg Riesling, Muscat Canelli and Gewurztraminer. Recent additions to the winery's output have been successful releases of Pinot Noir, Sangiovese and Gamay. Look in the future for results of now experimental plantings of Nebbiolo and Malbec. The winery also produces sparkling Blanc de Blanc and Brut, which are made in the traditional Champenoise method, Heightswine (a play on the words "Ice Wine") and several dessert wines.

Katzrin

KATZRIN, 2000: Elegant, ripe, bold and concentrated, with still tight tannins reflecting its youth but with the kind of balance and structure that bodes very well for the future, the wine shows currants, black cherries and purple plums along with spices and smoky wood. Drink now–2015. Score 94. K

KATZRIN, 1996: Vibrant and complex, with an array of aromas and flavors that include currants, cherries and plums overlaid by smoky oak, chocolate, spices and tobacco, this full-bodied, young tannic red is only now beginning now to reveal its charms. Excellent integration between fruit, tannins and oak indicates that the wine will continue to develop beautifully. Drink now–2015. Score 94. K

KATZRIN, 1993: Deep, broad, long and complex, this full-bodied Cabernet-Merlot blend continues to live up to its promise. Abundant tannins are well balanced by wood and fruits that include cassis, black cherries and orange peel, along with generous overlays of milk chocolate and toasty oak. Elegant and graceful, the wine is drinking nicely now and will cellar comfortably until 2012. Score 95. K

KATZRIN, 1990: A blend of 90% Cabernet Sauvignon and 10% Merlot, this deep, elegant full-bodied wine has a dark garnet color and excellent balance between fruits, wood, acidity and tannins. Look for a complex array of aromas and flavors, including blackcurrants, cherries, vanilla, cloves and chocolate. Lingering long on the palate, the wine is drinking beautifully now and should continue to cellar well until 2010. Score 95. K

KATZRIN, CHARDONNAY, 2003: Rich, ripe, concentrated and complex with generous layers of figs, tangerines, summer fruits and hazelnuts. Generous but not imposing oak on the finish makes it especially elegant as does a hint of butterscotch that comes in on the long finish. Drink now-2011. Score 92. K

KATZRIN, CHARDONNAY, 2002: Full-bodied, concentrated and complex, the wine was fermented in French oak *barriques* and then allowed to age *sur lie* for seven months. It shows layer after layer of fruits, those including orange, grapefruit, ripe pears and passion fruit, along with tiers of hazelnuts, minerals, vanilla and smoky, toasty oak. Rich, mouth-filling and long. Drink now–2009. Score 93. K

KATZRIN, CHARDONNAY, 2000: Aged for 10 months *sur lie*, this full-bodied, elegant and complex white still maintains a young and enthusiastic deep golden color and has layers of aromas and flavors that include poached pears, apples and passion fruit. Intense and concentrated, it shows tantalizing hints of spices, vanilla and oak, all culminating in a long finish. Drink now–2010. Score 94. K

KATZRIN, CHARDONNAY, 1999: Featuring complex pear, vanilla, apple and buttery notes, this full-bodied wine was aged *sur lie* and now shows enviable depth, balance and richness. Just enough hints of spices and vanilla come together to make the wine stylish and appealing. Drink now. Score 91. K

KATZRIN, CHARDONNAY, 1998: Generous, round and beautifully proportioned, this buttery, full-bodied wine has an abundance of spicy pear and apple flavors on a frame of rich oak, as well as hints of minerals and earthiness. Drink now. Score 91. K

KATZRIN, CHARDONNAY, 1997: This full-bodied deep golden wine was aged *sur lie* in new French barrels for nine months. Remarkably deep, concentrated and complex, it reveals an intense bouquet of cooked apples and pears, plenty of buttery overtones, and just the right amount of oak. Drink now. Score 94. K

KATZRIN, CHARDONNAY, 1996: Rich, full-bodied and buttery, this lovely wine continues to show toast, vanilla and smoky aromas and flavors that are complemented by pears, pineapples and apples. Once concentrated, and with flavors that linger on and on but now fading rapidly and no longer scoreable. K

KATZRIN CHARDONNAY, 1995: Intensely fruity, the wine shows aromas and flavors of ripe pears and apples as well as of dried apricots, along with a few spicy notes and plenty of moderate oak. Tight and concentrated, it lingers on and on long after it has been swallowed. Somewhat past its peak. Drink up. Score 88. **K**

Yarden

YARDEN, CABERNET SAUVIGNON, 2004: Young and vibrant, showing complex layers of cherries, earthy currants, tar and smoky oak. Plenty of tannins here but those yielding nicely and leaving room for a hint of green olives on the finish. Best starting in 2008. Tentative Score 89–91. **K**

YARDEN, CABERNET SAUVIGNON, 2003: Dark garnet red, showing an appealing balance between ripe soft tannins, spicy currant, anise and cedar wood, all leading to a long and complex finish. Drink from release–2010. Tentative Score 91–93. **K**

YARDEN, CABERNET SAUVIGNON, 2002: Dark garnet towards royal purple in color, full-bodied, with firm tannins and spicy oak both yielding nicely to reveal flavors and aromas of red currants and berries on first attack, those giving way to layers of sweet cedar, vanilla, leather and, on the long finish a hint of anise. Needs a bit of time but promises to be round, elegant and long. Drink now–2012. Score 92. **K**

YARDEN, CABERNET SAUVIGNON, ELROM VINEYARD, 2001: Dark, almost impenetrable garnet-purple in color, full-bodied and with finely-tuned balance between generous well-integrated tannins and judicious oak, this exquisite wine shows complex tiers of aromas and flavors of red currants, berries, and spices on the first attack those later opening to include light earthy and herbal overlays. Plush and opulent, with a long, complex finish. Among the best ever made in Israel. Drink now–2013. Score 95. **K**

YARDEN, CABERNET SAUVIGNON, 2001: This delicious full-bodied red has good balance between wood, tannins and fruits. Still young but already showing plum, wild berry and currant fruits, reflecting its 18 months in oak, with appealing overlays of vanilla, cedar and violets. Drink now–2010. Score 91. **K**

YARDEN, CABERNET SAUVIGNON, 2000: This full-bodied young red has firm tannins and abundant oak well balanced by currants, black cherries and what at one moment feels like plums, at another like black cherries, all matched nicely with vanilla and an appealing herbal overlay, and followed by a long finish. Drink now–2012. Score 92. K

YARDEN, CABERNET SAUVIGNON, 1999: Still young, this full-bodied red is quite marked by its tannins, but those are well balanced by wood and fruit. The wine promises to open very nicely, but at this stage one might be tempted to describe it as "still brooding." Deep royal purple toward garnet in color with delicious aromas and flavors of black berries and cherries on a background of vanilla and sweet cedar wood as well as a hint of freshly roasted coffee on its long finish. Drink now–2009. Score 92. K

YARDEN, CABERNET SAUVIGNON, 1998: Full-bodied, deep in color and remarkably intense, the wine shows aromas and flavors of currant, plum, black cherry, vanilla and lightly toasted oak as well as excellent balance between fruits, wood and tannins. The long finish yields mineral-earthy overtones and a very appealing hint of anise. Drink now–2008. Score 91. K

YARDEN, CABERNET SAUVIGNON, 1997: This traditional Yarden blend of 94% Cabernet Sauvignon, 5% Merlot and 1% Cabernet Franc has now opened and continues to show an overall firm structure and good balance between soft tannins, fruits, wood and acidity. Plenty of Cabernet currants along with blackberries and plums on the first attack, those yielding to gentle overlays of spices and Mediterranean herbs. Drink now–2008. Score 91. K

YARDEN, CABERNET SAUVIGNON, 1996: A blend of 98% Cabernet Sauvignon and 2% Cabernet Franc, this concentrated and intense medium to full-bodied wine is now showing plum, currant and cherry fruits, those complemented nicely by vanilla and anise on the mid-palate, and appealing herbal sensations on the finish. If any wine can be said to have "sweet tannins" this is that wine. Drink now 2007. Score 91. K

YARDEN, CABERNET SAUVIGNON, 1995: The wine needs time to open in the glass but as it does it reveals luscious layers of aromas and flavors of blackcurrants, plums, tobacco and vanilla. Full-bodied, with concentrated but well-integrated tannins, and a hint of raspberries on the long finish, the wine promises to continue developing nicely in the bottle. Drink now–2008. Score 92. K

YARDEN, CABERNET SAUVIGNON, 1994: Because 1994 was not a great vintage year in Israel, this wine never attained the heights of the best wines of this series. Medium-bodied, it shows flavors of stewed prunes, black fruits and floral-earthy overtones. Drink up. Score 87. K

YARDEN, CABERNET SAUVIGNON, 1993: Royal purple in color, this full-bodied wine is one of the very best Cabernet wines ever produced in Israel. It is concentrated, full-bodied and powerful, and has now attained enviable levels of roundness, depth and complexity along with impeccable balance and an elegant bouquet. Silky tannins that give the wine just the right bite, flavors that unfold comfortably on the palate and a long finish assure that the wine will continue to cellar well. Drink now. Score 94. K

YARDEN, CABERNET SAUVIGNON, 1992: Full-bodied, with fully integrated tannins and abundant black fruits, vanilla and appealing herbal, earthy, and tobacco overlays, this well balanced and generous wine shows a moderately long near-sweet finish. Drink up. Score 90. K

YARDEN, CABERNET SAUVIGNON, 1991: Perhaps somewhat past its peak, this deep purple medium to full-bodied wine continues to reveal traditional Cabernet aromas and flavors of blackcurrants, cedar wood and black cherries along with herbal-mineral overtones on the finish. Drink up. Score 87. K

YARDEN, CABERNET SAUVIGNON, 1990: When young, this superb wine showed almost massive tannins and such intensity that some wondered if it would ever be more than searingly deep. Yet due to its excellent structure and good balance it has maintained its rich concentration along with its traditional blackcurrant, oak and vanilla aromas and flavors, those overlaid by aromatic cedar, leather and tobacco, and a remarkably long finish. Drink now–2007. Score 94. K

YARDEN, CABERNET SAUVIGNON, 1989: Now at its peak, this delicious and elegant wine shows a remarkable array of aromas and flavors that open seemingly without end on the palate. Look for blackberries, cherries, coffee, leather, toasted bread, smoky oak, vanilla and a hint of tobacco that is now creeping in. Drink up. Score 92. K

YARDEN, CABERNET SAUVIGNON, 1988: Not one of the best of the series. Darkening and starting to brown at the rim, and with dark fruits, currants, vanilla and spices now clearly overlaid with aromas and flavors of damp earth, herbs and smoked meats, the wine continues to drink nicely even though it is perhaps somewhat past its peak. Drink up. Score 87. K

YARDEN, CABERNET SAUVIGNON, 1987: Never attaining excellence, the wine blossomed for a short while several years ago in what may have been its swan song. Still showing some currants and a few black fruits, the leather now starting to have a rather sweaty aroma, the cinnamon and vanilla becoming just a bit caramelized. Past its peak. Drink up. Score 85. K

YARDEN, CABERNET SAUVIGNON, 1986: Far lighter than most of the other Cabernet wines in this series, this wine has now passed whatever peak it may have attained and is now browning. Well past its peak. Drink up. Score 84. K

YARDEN, CABERNET SAUVIGNON, 1985: Deep and warm, concentrated, heady and exotic, with spicy plums, blackcurrants and blackberries all overlaid with stewed fruits, chocolate and leather, along with flavors of coffee and chocolate that linger nicely, this is a wine that belies its age. Drink up. Score 92. K

YARDEN, CABERNET SAUVIGNON, 1984: A slight "off" aroma on first pouring that fades after a short while indicates that the wine is still struggling to stay alive. Despite its deep red color and the fact that it does manage to open somewhat in the glass, it is well past its peak and no longer scoreable. K

YARDEN, CABERNET SAUVIGNON, 1983: This landmark wine that forever changed the face of Israeli winemaking is still alive but has lost most of its appeal. Showing age. No longer scoreable. K

YARDEN, MERLOT, 2004: Still in embryonic form but showing the potential to be smooth and polished. In addition to cherry, strawberry, and cassis aromas and flavors look as well for spices, cedar, tar and light herbal notes. Best 2007–2010. Tentative Score 88–90. K

YARDEN, MERLOT, 2003: Smooth, polished and ripe, with an array of aromas and flavors including currants, cherries, herbs, vanilla and lightly smoky oak, this is a complex wine with a long finish. Drink from release–2009. Tentative Score 89–91. K

YARDEN, MERLOT, 2002: Deep ruby towards garnet, medium to full-bodied, with soft, already well-integrating tannins and generously spicy oak. Shows tempting sweet black plum and wild berry fruits on an appealing herbal and chocolate background as well as black cherries on the medium long finish. Drink now–2008. Score 88. K

YARDEN, MERLOT, ORTAL VINEYARD, 2001: Loads of character in this rich, plush, full-bodied wine. On the first attack, a tempting array of currant, mocha, hazelnut and spices, those later joined by almost jammy plum and berry fruits. Reflecting its 14 months in new and used *barriques* with seamless tannins, generous but not at all overpowering oak and a long and complex milk chocolate and herbal finish. Drink now–2014. Score 94. K

YARDEN, MERLOT, 2001: Garnet toward royal purple in color, this medium to full-bodied wine has soft, integrated tannins and a tempting array of black fruits, vanilla and spices on the first attack, these yielding nicely to almost sweet cassis and light Mediterranean herbs on the finish. Drink now–2007. Score 89. K

YARDEN, MERLOT, 2000: Somewhat less full-bodied than in its youth but still a rich and tempting wine, generous in plum, berry and black cherry fruits as well as in overlays of chocolate and even a hint of citrus on its finish. Good spices and an almost ideal interplay between vanilla, wood and soft tannins. Drink now. Score 89. K

YARDEN, MERLOT, 1999: Silky smooth tannins, and upfront fruit aromas and flavors of wild berries and currants, along with generous hints of vanilla and spices make this medium to full-bodied wine smooth and tempting. Drink now. Score 88. K

YARDEN, MERLOT, 1998: Ripe, complex, and simultaneously bold and elegant, the wine has tiers of rich plum, currant and blackberry aromas and flavors, overlaid by vanilla, chocolate and tobacco, together with smooth tannins and a deep long finish. Drink now. Score 92. K

YARDEN, MERLOT, 1997: Smooth, bright and striving for elegance, this blend of 85% Merlot and 15% Cabernet Sauvignon was aged for 14 months in oak. Full-bodied and with still chewy tannins, it offers tempting black cherry, raspberry, currant, floral and chocolate notes that open nicely on the palate. Drink now. Score 90. K

YARDEN, MERLOT, 1996: A blend of 85% Merlot, 14% Cabernet Sauvignon and 1% Cabernet Franc, this now fully mature wine continues to reflect rich prunes, berries and Oriental spices in its aromas and flavors. With sweet tannins integrated nicely, the wine continues to drink well but is not appropriate for further cellaring. Drink up. Score 90. K

YARDEN, MERLOT, 1995: Now mature, the fully integrated tannins and oak make the wine round and comfortable on the palate. Still showing appealing wild berry, currant and spicy flavors and a moderately long finish. Drink now. Score 87. **K**

YARDEN, MERLOT, 1994: From a mediocre vintage year, this is not the most exciting Merlot released by the winery. The wine is now showing age, its black fruits quite subdued and somewhat shadowed by what seems to be a light caramelization process. No longer scoreable. **K**

YARDEN, MERLOT, 1993: This well-balanced, well-structured wine is now showing a hint of browning and has hints of leather and coffee sneaking in at the end, but still maintains its ample plums and blackcurrants as well as a long, lightly herbal finish. Drink up. Score 89. **K**

YARDEN, MERLOT, 1992: Full-bodied and tannic in its youth, the wine has evolved beautifully from deep royal purple to an adobe brick red with a hint of browning at the rim. Still showing generous plum, vanilla, orange peel and spices, it now has hints of herbs and earthiness coming in. At the far edge of its peak. Drink up. Score 90. **K**

YARDEN, MERLOT, 1991: Leaving the grapes in the autumn sun for a prolonged time in order to attain a good level of ripeness contributed to the special success of this wine. Full-bodied and concentrated, with aromas and flavors of black cherries, currants, orange peel, chocolate and exotic spiciness, the wine is still drinking well. Drink up. Score 91. **K**

YARDEN, SYRAH, 2004: Showing medium to full-body and good balance. along with aromas and flavors of blackberry, currant, anise and cedar. Still tightly closed and needs time. Best starting in 2007. Tentative Score 88–90. **K**

YARDEN, SYRAH, 2003: Supple, with fresh and appealing sweet berry and vanilla flavors as well as peach pits, spring flowers and light earthiness. Look for a hint of tar on the moderately long finish. Drink now–2009. Score 90. **K**

YARDEN, SYRAH, 2002: Medium to full bodied, concentrated and packed with tannins but those soft and already integrating nicely. Multiple layers of green berry, plums and hints of spices, chocolate and vanilla. Plenty of oak here but that will settle down in time and the wine will soften and show increased complexity with tobacco and floral overtones. Drink now–2010. Score 91. **K**

YARDEN, SYRAH, 2001: Medium to full-bodied, with youthful firm tannins, this dark garnet wine already shows excellent balance and opens in the glass to reveal black cherry and plum fruits, together with appealing earthy, floral and licorice flavors that arise and then linger nicely on the finish. Drink now–2009. Score 90. **K**

YARDEN, SYRAH, 2000: Dark, still youthful royal-purple in color, this soft tannic medium to full-bodied wine features aromas and flavors of red currants, plums and spices. Now showing tobacco, herbal and an appealing light meaty-earthy sensation, reflecting its 18 months in oak. Long and mouth-filling. Drink now–2008. Score 91. K

YARDEN, PINOT NOIR, 2004: Still in embryonic form but already showing itself as a tasty fruit-driven wine with complex flavors including toasted pine nuts and herbs, plums and black cherries. As this one develops look as well for anise and wild berry on a long mouthfilling finish. Best starting in 2007. Tentative Score 89–91. K

YARDEN, PINOT NOIR, 2003: Dark black-cherry in color, this smooth, rich, concentrated and complex wine shows layer after layer of plum, black cherry, blackberry and spicy flavors, all wrapped nicely in spicy oak. Medium to full-bodied, seamless, long and elegant. Drink from release–2010. Tentative Score 90–92. K

YARDEN, PINOT NOIR, 2002: This medium to full-bodied wine, with soft, almost sweet tannins and good balance between gentle wood and fruit is still young but already shows the potential for elegance. On the palate are wild red berry, cherry, sweet cedar and a light spicy overlay, as well as a hint of espresso coffee on the finish. Not as Burgundian in style as was when first tasted. Best 2007–2010. Score 90. K

YARDEN, PINOT NOIR, 2001: Medium-bodied, with well-integrating soft tannins, a nice hint of sweet cedar wood and cassis, cherry and raspberry fruits. Floral on the nose, with hints of spices running through, but needs time to show its true elegance and to open to reveal the earthy and dark chocolate aromas and flavors that are still lying dormant. Drink now–2009. Score 91. K

YARDEN, PINOT NOIR, 2000: Dark garnet in color, with silky tannins, and a generous set of aromas and flavors, those including black cherries, sweet cedar wood, blackberries and spices. Given time in the glass the wine begins to reveal its spicy-earthy background. Drink now–2008. Score 90. K

YARDEN, PINOT NOIR, 1999: Just starting to attain its peak, this medium-bodied red is darkening in color now and in addition to the berry-cherry fruits, chocolate and minerals that it showed during its youth now taking on an earthy, nutty, almost fresh-mushroom personality. Complex, moderately-long and delicious. Drink now–2008. Score 91. K

YARDEN, MOUNT HERMON RED, 2004: Cherry towards garnet red, medium-bodied with soft tannins, this blend of Merlot, Cabernet Sauvignon and Cabernet Franc shows appealing plum and berry fruits along on a light herbal background. Not complex but a good quaffer. Drink now. Score 85. K

YARDEN, MOUNT HERMON RED, 2003: This smooth, medium-bodied softly tannic blend of 48% Merlot, 42% Cabernet Sauvignon and 10% Cabernet Franc has a lightly spicy and appealing berry-cherry personality. Drink up. Score 85. K

YARDEN, MOUNT HERMON RED, 2002: As always, this medium-bodied blend (this year of 48% Cabernet Sauvignon, 42% Merlot and 10% Cabernet Franc) has a generous cherry-berry and light currant personality along with a hint of Mediterranean herbs. Drink up. Score 85. K

YARDEN, MOUNT HERMON RED, 2001: This medium-bodied Cabernet-based blend has soft tannins along with delicate flavors of currants, blueberries, black cherry and vanilla. Past its peak. Drink up. Score 85. K

YARDEN, MOUNT HERMON RED, 2000: This wine's traditional blend of Cabernet Sauvignon, Merlot and Cabernet Franc supplemented by 5% of Sangiovese is somewhat fuller in body than in the past and with a more chewy texture, but now the once appealing aromas and flavors of currants, black cherries and herbs are less pronounced. Well past its peak and no longer scoreable. K

YARDEN, CHARDONNAY, ODEM ORGANIC VINEYARD, 2003: A rich and elegant wine with ripe pear, honeysuckle and melon flavors all coming together beautifully with minerals, nutmeg and hazelnut hints on the long finish. Drink now–2010. Score 91. K

YARDEN, CHARDONNAY, 2003: Medium to full bodied, fresh, vibrant and complex with an array of pear, fig, citrus, honey and melon aromas and flavors that come together nicely with toasty oak and hints of spices. Drink now–2009. Score 90. K

YARDEN, CHARDONNAY, ODEM ORGANIC VINEYARD, 2002: Deep golden straw in color, this single-vineyard, full-bodied and elegant white made from organically raised grapes is showing ripe and complex flavors of pears, tropical fruits, hazelnuts and spices, those opening on the palate to reveal flinty and floral overtones along with generous but well-integrated oak and a long and creamy finish. Drink now–2009. Score 93. **K**

YARDEN, CHARDONNAY, 2002: Light gold in color, this complex, medium to full-bodied oak-aged white offers up abundant pear, spice, hazelnut and citrus flavors, as well as hints of minerals, spicy oak and earth on the finish. Drink now–2007. Score 90. **K**

YARDEN, CHARDONNAY, 2001: Medium to full-bodied and aged *sur lie* for seven months in partly new, partly old French oak barrels, this tempting light golden wine shows excellent balance between wood, natural acidity and fruits. Notable pear aromas and flavors yield comfortably to apples, lightly toasted bread and vanilla. Drink now–2008. Score 91. **K**

YARDEN, CHARDONNAY, 2000: Smooth and rich, this medium to full-bodied white shows subtle pear, fig and citrus aromas and flavors along with the barest hints of butter and spices, and an appealing overlay of smoke imparted by the oak barrels in which it aged for seven months. Drink now. Score 89. **K**

YARDEN, CHARDONNAY, 1999: Subtle and delicious, this deep golden colored wine has lovely spice and butterscotch aromas, all on a solid core of apple, quince and pear flavors. Well balanced and bordering on elegance. Drink now. Score 89. **K**

YARDEN, CHARDONNAY, 1998: After having spent seven months in small oak barrels, this delicious medium to full-bodied wine has aromas and flavors of pears, grapefruits, lemons and kiwis, as well as charming hints of vanilla. Drink up. Score 88. **K**

YARDEN, CHARDONNAY, 1997: Deep and long, with stewed pear, yeasty and nutty flavors all overlaid by generous hints of oak, minerals and earthiness, this full-bodied deep golden wine continues to drink nicely. Drink up. Score 91. **K**

YARDEN, SAUVIGNON BLANC, 2004: Light straw in color, medium-bodied, with straightforward aromas and flavors of lemon and lime and ripe peaches. Marred somewhat by unwanted hints of bitterness and earthiness that develop on the palate. Score 85. **K**

YARDEN, SAUVIGNON BLANC, 2003: Not showing as well now as during earlier tastings. Straw-colored, medium-bodied, with muted tropical fruit aromas and flavors and what many will perceive as personality that is crisply dry but somewhat flat. Drink up. Score 85. K

YARDEN, SAUVIGNON BLANC, 2002: Fresh and lively, with light grassy-stony overtones on pear, apple and grapefruit flavors. Plenty of acidity to add zest to a wine that will remind many of the Sauvignon Blanc wines of Sancerre. Drink now. Score 88. K

YARDEN, SAUVIGNON BLANC, 2000: This medium-bodied wine has rich aromas and flavors of citrus and tropical fruits, and just the right hints of grassiness and spring flowers. Drink up. Score 87. K

YARDEN, SAUVIGNON BLANC, 1999: Ripe and aromatic, the wine has good pear, apple and melon flavors complemented by hints of spices. Somewhat past its peak. Drink up. Score 86. K

YARDEN, SAUVIGNON BLANC, 1998: A medium-bodied blend of 85% Sauvignon Blanc and 15% Semillion grapes, this crisp and refreshing wine has a core of green apple, melon and floral flavors along with minor mineral and spice overtones. Past its peak. Drink up. Score 85. K

YARDEN, VIOGNIER, 2004: Round and ripe, aged partly in oak, partly in stainless steel, with the classic spicy, litchi and lime aromas and flavors of the variety, those set off nicely by hints of coconut, a gentle spiciness and just the right amount of acidity to add liveliness and balance. Harmonious, long, and complex. All in all an enchanting wine. Drink now–2007. Tentative Score 89–91. K

YARDEN, VIOGNIER, 2003: The winery's first Viognier, released only in very limited amounts. Fermented partly in new oak and partly in stainless steel, this medium-bodied rich and ripe wine shows spring flowers, vanilla and orange blossoms on a background of pineapple, nectarine and apricots, all complemented by lively acidity. There is an appealing bitterness that comes in from mid-palate and a hint of pepper that comes in at the end. Some may consider the hint of bitterness that comes in from mid-palate a fault. I do not. Drink now. Score 88. K

YARDEN, MOUNT HERMON WHITE, 2004: An unoaked blend of Chardonnay, Sauvignon Blanc and a small amount of Semillon that shows pleasant aromas and flavors of citrus and tropical fruits that come together with a light spiciness. Drink up. Score 83. K

YARDEN, MOUNT HERMON WHITE, 2003: A simple entry-level wine. Medium-bodied, with generous pineapple, orange and melon fruits and good balancing acidity to set off the hint of sweetness that runs throughout. Drink up. Score 83. K

YARDEN, JOHANNISBERG RIESLING, 2003: Medium-bodied, semi-dry, with a light golden-straw color and appealing summer fruits well balanced by good acidity. On the moderately-long finish look for green apples and a hint of spiciness. Drink now-2006. Score 87. K

YARDEN, JOHANNISBERG RIESLING, 2002: Pale yellow toward gold in color, this medium-bodied semi-dry wine shows appealing aromas and flavors of peaches and apricots along with a long mineral laden finish. Plenty of natural acidity setting off the light sweetness makes it a good choice as an aperitif. Drink now. Score 89. K

YARDEN, JOHANNISBERG RIESLING, 2001: Even though this wine is categorized as semi-dry, it has just the barest hint of sweetness on the palate. Lively, well balanced and delicious, the wine has tempting aromas and flavors of peaches, apples and citrus. Drink now. Score 87. K

YARDEN, JOHANNISBERG RIESLING, 2000: Flowery and semi-dry but with enough natural acidity to keep it lively, the wine has aromas and flavors of white peaches, green apples and grapefruit. Drink up. Score 85. K

YARDEN, GEWURZTRAMINER, 2004: Perhaps the most representative Gewurztraminer released by the winery, semi-dry but crisp, medium-bodied but mouthfilling, with traditional litchi and tropical fruits set off nicely by an appealing spiciness. Well balanced and generous. Drink now–2007. Score 88. K

YARDEN, GEWURZTRAMINER, 2003: An appealing semi-dry, medium-bodied white with litchi, summer fruits and spices but lacking the acidity that might have made it more refreshing. Best as an aperitif. Drink now. Score 86. K

YARDEN, GEWURZTRAMINER, 2002: Young and frisky, this semi-dry medium-bodied white shows moderate Gewurztraminer traits of spiciness and litchis along with the more dominant aromas and flavors of pears, citrus and even gentle hints of pineapple and earthiness. Also good as an aperitif. Drink now. Score 86. K

YARDEN, GEWURZTRAMINER, 2001: Medium-bodied, light golden in color, with peach, nectarine and melon fruits along with, just a hint of spiciness. Medium-sweet and mouth-filling. Drink up. Score 87. K

YARDEN, GEWURZTRAMINER, 2000: Hints of litchis, apricots, cinnamon and honey come together in a wine that has a nice level of spiciness, good acids to keep it lively and a moderate level of dryness that makes it appropriate equally as an aperitif. Drink up. Score 86. K

YARDEN, GEWURZTRAMINER, 1999: The wine shows traditional Gewurztraminer litchis and spices and plenty of acidity to keep it lively but lacks depth and is now showing age and no longer scoreable. K

YARDEN, NOBLE SEMILLON, BOTRYTIS, 2002: Made by exposing late-harvested Semillon grapes to botrytis in the winery, this golden towards orange, medium to full-bodied white shows generous honeyed sweetness complemented nicely by aromas and flavors of orange peel and apricots. Soft, round and creamy on the palate, with good balancing acidity and hints of heather and white pepper on the moderately-long finish. Drink now–2009. Score 89. K

YARDEN, NOBLE SEMILLON, BOTRYTIS, 2001: This lively golden medium-bodied dessert white offers up unabashed honeyed sweetness along with aromas and flavors of orange marmalade, pineapple and ripe apricots that meld comfortably into a soft, almost creamy texture. It has plenty of balancing natural acidity as well as a medium-long finish boasting hints of spring flowers and spices, and promises to darken and attain greater complexity and depth in the future. Drink now–2008. Score 90. K

YARDEN, HEIGHTSWINE, 2003: As always, a tantalizing dessert wine, light to medium-bodied with delicate honeyed apricot and peach aromas and flavors, good balancing acidity and an elegantly lingering finish. Drink now–2008. Score 90. K

YARDEN, HEIGHTSWINE, 2002: Light gold in color, medium-bodied, and with excellent balance. Plenty of natural acidity to back up the sweetness and keep it lively while allowing the peach, apricot, and quince fruits to make themselves nicely felt. Honeyed and floral, generous and round. Drink now–2008. Score 90. K

YARDEN, HEIGHTSWINE, 2001: Well balanced, generous and elegant, this honeyed dessert wine is made entirely from Gewurztraminer grapes treated to sub-freezing temperatures at the winery. It has a lively golden color and offers up a generous array of yellow peaches, apricots, melon, orange marmalade and quince, all on a floral and just spicy enough background. Drink now–2008. Score 91. K

YARDEN, HEIGHTSWINE, 2000: Well chilled, this delicious sweet wine reveals honeyed flavors of pears and quince. Let it warm in the glass and you will feel ripe apricots and white peaches. Let it linger on the palate and you will sense kiwi, pineapple and other tropical fruits. Made entirely from Gewurztraminer grapes, the wine is well balanced by plenty of natural acidity. Drink now–2008. Score 92. K

YARDEN, HEIGHTSWINE, 1999: Unlike German or Canadian ice wines, in which grapes are allowed to freeze on the vine, the Gewurztraminer grapes used in this wine were frozen at the winery. The result is a sweet, almost thick mineral-rich dessert wine packed with aromas of peaches, apples, mangoes and pineapple that sit very comfortably on the palate. Drink now. Score 88. K

YARDEN, HEIGHTSWINE, 1998: Showing 40% sugar content to the pressed grape juice, this pleasingly sweet dessert wine offers up aromas and flavors of ripe peaches, apricots and tropical fruits. Drink up. Score 88. K

YARDEN, MUSCAT DESSERT WINE, 2003: Reinforced lightly with brandy, this floral wine shows tempting aromas and flavors of citrus and summer fruits. Good balance between generous sweetness, acidity and fruits. Drink now–2007. Score 87. K

YARDEN, MUSCAT DESSERT WINE, 2002: Lightly reinforced with brandy, this remains as it has in past years, a floral wine, rich with citrus peel, pineapple and white peach aromas and flavors. Smooth and round, with generous sweetness and good balancing acidity to keep it fresh and lively. Drink now. Score 87. K

YARDEN, MUSCAT DESSERT WINE, 2000: Since its first release in 1997, this brandy-reinforced wine has shown a remarkable consistency in its flower-rich bouquet and flavors of orange peel, pineapple jam and ripe summer fruits. It is smooth, round and unabashedly sweet, but with plenty of balancing acidity, and calls to mind the French *Muscat de Beaumes de Venise*. Drink now. Score 86. K

YARDEN, MUSCAT DESSERT WINE, 1999: Aromas and flavors of orange marmalade, ripe peaches and wild flowers make this a pleasing after-dinner drink, its abundant sweetness balanced nicely by natural acidity. Drink up. Score 85. K

YARDEN, BLANC DE BLANCS, 1998: Showing better now than at earlier tastings, this ripe and vibrant wine has crisp apple and citrus aromas and flavors along with hints of vanilla, toasted white bread and nuts. The mousse is somewhat short but the bubbles are long-lasting and the lingering nutty-grapefruit finish lingers nicely. Drink now–2007. Score 90. K

YARDEN, BLANC DE BLANCS, 1997: Made entirely from Chardonnay grapes in the traditional *Champenoise* method, this lovely and sophisticated sparkling wine has just the right hint of yeast on a background of delicious citrus, white peach, spring flowers and mint. Look for sharp, concentrated bubbles, a long lasting mousse and a lingering nutty finish. Drink now–2007. Score 90. K

YARDEN, BLANC DE BLANCS, 1996: Made entirely from Chardonnay grapes, this medium-bodied sparkling wine is simultaneously rich and subdued. With concentrated long-lasting bubbles, a bouquet of dried and exotic fruits, spring flowers and the barest hints of coffee beans and herbs, this remains a refined, fresh and vibrant wine. Drink now–2009. Score 93. K

YARDEN, BLANC DE BLANCS, 1994: Made entirely from Chardonnay grapes in the traditional Champenoise method this luxurious sparkling wine was fermented in the bottle for 32 months together with its yeasts. Now fully mature, it remains fresh and vibrant with lemon, apple and vanilla flavors under attractive overlays of toasted brad, nuts and a bare hint of honey. Its creamy smooth texture seems to almost melt in the mouth. Drink up. Score 92. K

YARDEN, BLANC DE BLANCS, N.V.: Made from 95% Chardonnay grapes and 5% Pinot Noir, this medium-bodied sparkling wine feels marvelously alive in the mouth, and the bouquet, although light, has a comfortable hint of yeast. Nicely fruity, the wine has a fresh unalloyed taste and long-lasting bubbles. Score 89. K

YARDEN, BRUT, N.V.: Made in the traditional *Champenoise* method from a blend of Chardonnay and Pinot Noir grapes, this wine shows good balance, an abundance of citrus and white peach fruits, nutty flavors, just the right hints of yeast and sharp, long-lasting bubbles. Score 89. K

YARDEN, LATE HARVEST SAUVIGNON BLANC, 1988: Not many bottles are left, a few still drinking beautifully but most well past their peak. Best examples are almost caramel in color now but still maintain their elegant and luscious mouth-filling character. The wine is somewhat less sweet than during earlier years but still shows delicious honeyed apricot, *crème brule* and flowery aromas and flavors. Surely the best dessert wine ever produced in Israel. Drink up. At its best it scores 94. K

Gamla

GAMLA, CABERNET SAUVIGNON 2003: Always reliable, this oak aged medium to full-bodied blend of Cabernet Sauvignon, Merlot and Cabernet Franc shows good balance between tannins, wood and black fruits, all with hints of vanilla and an appealing spicy finish. Drink now–2008. Score 87. K

GAMLA, CABERNET SAUVIGNON, 2002: The usual Bordeaux blend of Cabernet Sauvignon, Merlot and Cabernet Franc. Medium to full-bodied, a gentle touch of oak, soft tannins and with appealing blackcurrant, blackberry and vanilla aromas and flavors. Drink now. Score 87. K

GAMLA, CABERNET SAUVIGNON, 2001: This Bordeaux blend of Cabernet Sauvignon, Merlot and Cabernet Franc was oaked for about 12 months. Medium to full-bodied with soft tannins, generous currant and berry fruits and hints of spices and vanilla running throughout. On the moderately-long finish light earthy overtones. Drink now–2008. Score 88. K

GAMLA, CABERNET SAUVIGNON, 2000: A Bordeaux blend of 85% Cabernet Sauvignon, 11% Merlot and 4% Cabernet Franc, this medium to full-bodied red was aged for 12 months in oak and is now showing tempting currant, berries and black cherry fruits along with light vanilla and spicy overtones imparted by wood and a long, lightly spicy finish. Drink now. Score 89. K

GAMLA, CABERNET SAUVIGNON, 1999: A blend of 85% Cabernet Sauvignon, 12% Merlot and 3% Cabernet Franc, this deep red, medium to full-bodied wine spent one year in small oak barrels and is now showing appealing red fruit, currant and herbal notes, those overlaid by vanilla and white pepper. Drink now. Score 87. K

GAMLA, CABERNET SAUVIGNON, 1998: A blend of Cabernet Sauvignon, Merlot and Cabernet Franc (88%, 8%, and 4% respectively), very much in the Bordeaux style, this well balanced and complex medium to full-bodied wine has a core of currant, cherry, and light oak aromas and flavors. The generous tannins are well integrated now and the wine is starting to show herbal and tobacco flavors. Drink up. Score 89. K

GAMLA, CABERNET SAUVIGNON, SPECIAL RESERVE, 1997: This ripe and harmonious blend of Cabernet Sauvignon and Merlot (85% and 15% respectively) that spent 14 month in small oak casks shows fresh plum, red cherry and spice aromas and flavors along with plenty of tannins and nice hints of tobacco and vanilla. Drink up. Score 89. K

GAMLA, CABERNET SAUVIGNON, 1997: This medium-bodied, well-balanced wine shows generous plum and cherry fruits on a background of vanilla, cinnamon and tobacco, as well as a long finish. Somewhat past its peak. Drink up. Score 89. K

GAMLA, CABERNET SAUVIGNON, 1996: This medium to full-bodied wine is at its peak now, showing good balance between well-integrated tannins, wood and a broad array of aromas and flavors, those including blackcurrant and black cherry fruits, vanilla and herbs. Somewhat past its peak. Drink up. Score 87. K

GAMLA, CABERNET SAUVIGNON, 1995: Starting to show its age but still deep, fragrant and well focused, with layers of red and blackcurrants, stewed cherries and toasted oak, along with appealing hints of cigar tobacco and eucalyptus. Past its peak. Drink up. Score 87. K

GAMLA, CABERNET SAUVIGNON, 1990: In its youth the wine was more tannic and full-bodied than most Cabernet wines in this series and therefore took time to reach its peak. Now showing fine balance between acids and tannins, a concentrated flavor and barely browning deep purple color, it has an aromatic freshness that belies its age and flavors that linger on and on. Drink up. Score 90. K

GAMLA, MERLOT, 2003: Deep garnet, medium to full-bodied, with still firm tannins but with balance and structure that bode well for the future. Generous berry, currant and plum fruits here, with overlays of sweet cedar, hints of milk chocolate and an appealing herbaceous overlay. Drink now–2010. Score 89. K

GAMLA, MERLOT, 2002: Dark ruby towards garnet, medium to full-bodied, with tannins well-balanced by spicy wood, black plum and wild berry fruits. Not overly complex and not for long-term cellaring. Drink now–2007. Score 86, K

GAMLA, MERLOT, 2001: Elegant, well balanced and supple, this deep garnet medium-bodied wine offers up tempting berry and plum fruits, those complemented nicely by aromas and flavors of milk chocolate, vanilla and sweet cedar wood. Drink now–2008. Score 89. K

GAMLA, MERLOT, 2000: Lean and with still-taut tannins, this deep royal purple toward garnet wine is more in the country-style than one usually anticipates from the Golan Heights Winery. Somewhat coarse and earthy, the wine shows plenty of plum and blackberries, and hints of orange peel and mint to carry it. Drink now. Score 87. K

GAMLA, MERLOT, 1999: This medium-bodied garnet to purple blend of 93% Merlot and 7% Cabernet Sauvignon was aged for 9 months in small oak barrels and shows plenty of black fruit and currants. Drink up. Score 86. K

GAMLA, MERLOT, 1998: This medium-bodied deep garnet wine is just starting to brown but still reflects inherent good balance and complexity, its firm tannins and moderate wood set off nicely by currant and plum fruits, those matched by herbal, tobacco and light earthy flavors. Drink up. Score 89. K

GAMLA, MERLOT, 1996: Somewhat beyond its peak, the wine is still concentrated and nicely balanced, with plenty of tannins and appealing blackcurrant, plum and vanilla flavors and aromas as well as underlying hints of herbs and earthiness. Drink up. Score 87. K

GAMLA, MERLOT, 1995: This medium to full-bodied red continues to show appealing layers of currants, plums and herbs but is now taking on a lightly off-beat earthy-leathery background. Drink up. Score 87. K

GAMLA, PINOT NOIR, 2003: Dark cherry red towards garnet, medium-bodied, reflecting its 7 months in oak with a hint of spicy wood.

Well-balanced, smooth and ripe, with cherry, raspberry and cola aromas and flavors on a lightly spicy background. Long and rich, with soft, well-integrated tannins. Drink now–2007. Score 88. K

GAMLA, PINOT NOIR, 2002: Light colored and medium-bodied, this smooth wine shows aromas and flavors of currants, berries and spring flowers as well as gentle overlays of oak and a hint of chocolate on the finish. Drink now. Score 86. K

GAMLA, SANGIOVESE, 2004: Still in its infancy but already showing excellent extraction, and tempting blackberry, raspberry and black cherry aromas and flavors. Medium-bodied with soft tannins and a long, smooth and fruity finish. Drink from release–2008. Tentative Score 88–90. K.

GAMLA, SANGIOVESE, 2003: Medium-bodied, with round tannins and tempting aromas and flavors of plums, blueberries and violets. Gentle flavors lead to a long ripe fruit finish. Drink now–2008. Score 89. K

GAMLA, SANGIOVESE, 2002: Surprisingly concentrated considering the vintage. Dark, deep and rich with intense berry and black cherry fruits, smoky aromas and flavors. Medium to full-bodied with fine tannins and a long finish. Drink now. Score 88. K

GAMLA, SANGIOVESE, 2001: Dark garnet toward purple, this medium-bodied red offers up generous but smooth and well-integrated tannins on a background of ripe plums, black cherries, currants and tobacco. Reflecting its 12 months in small oak barrels, the wine also shows nice hints of sweet oak and a charming tinge of coffee on the long finish. Drink now. Score 86. K

GAMLA, SANGIOVESE, 2000: A blend of 85% Sangiovese and 15% Cabernet Sauvignon, both harvested in the northern part of the Golan Heights, this medium-bodied oak-aged wine shows many of the traditional Sangiovese traits such as blackberries, chocolate and cinnamon along with distinctive and generous Mediterranean hints of black cherries and sage. Look for smooth tannins, good overall balance, and a long finish highlighted by hints of mocha. Drink now. Score 88. K

GAMLA, CHARDONNAY, 2004: Light gold, medium-bodied, with generous summer fruit, citrus and citrus flower aromas and flavors, those on a lightly spicy background. Good balancing acidity to keep it lively. Drink now–2007. Score 87. K

GAMLA, CHARDONNAY, 2003: Medium-bodied, with appealing citrus, summer fruit and mineral aromas and flavors. Drink now–2007. Score 87. K

GAMLA, CHARDONNAY, 2002: Light golden straw in color, medium-bodied, with refreshing natural acidity and appealing peach, pineapple and tropical fruits. Not a complex wine but a very pleasing one. Drink now. Score 87. K

GAMLA, CHARDONNAY, 2001: Clean, medium-bodied and fruity, the wine was aged for four months in small oak barrels and shows tempting pear, melon, fig and citrus aromas and flavors. Drink now. Score 88. K

GAMLA, CHARDONNAY, 2000: The best Chardonnay ever in the Gamla series. Medium to full-bodied and golden in color, the wine offers up aromas and flavors of citrus, pears and green apple fruits as well as spicy oak, all on a well-balanced frame, with an intense finish yielding spicy fig notes. Drink up. Score 89. K

GAMLA, SAUVIGNON BLANC, 2004: Light straw in color, medium-bodied, with appealing pear, tropical fruit and melon flavors, those with a nice hint of spiciness and a light herbaceousness. Drink now. Score 87. K

GAMLA, SAUVIGNON BLANC, 2003: Light golden straw colored, medium-bodied, with generous aromas and flavors of tropical fruit, melon and a light overlay of grassiness. Good balancing acidity makes for a refreshing drink. Drink now. Score 86. K

GAMLA, SAUVIGNON BLANC, 2002: Unoaked and fresh, this round and rich wine shows pear, melon and pineapple aromas and flavors on a background of a clean after-rain grassiness. Drink up. Score 87. K

GAMLA, SAUVIGNON BLANC, 2001: When young, this medium-bodied white had lively acidity along with aromas and flavors of citrus, pear and tropical fruits, but is now past its peak. Drink up. Score 85. K

GAMLA, WHITE RIESLING, 2004: Frankly sweet even though categorized as semi-dry, the wine has enough natural acidity to keep it lively and to highlight tempting citrus, pineapple and apricot flavors. Look for a hint of mint on the moderately-long finish. Drink now–2007. Score 87. K

GAMLA, MUSCAT CANELLI, 2001: Light to medium-bodied, pale straw in color, with hints of flowers, nuts and spices, this appealing white semi-dry wine has plenty of natural acids to keep it lively and refreshing. Best as an aperitif or a dessert wine. Drink up. Score 86. K

Golan

GOLAN, CABERNET SAUVIGNON, 2003:
Ruby red towards purple in color, medium-bodied, with bare hints of oak and soft, well-integrated tannins and appealing spicy cherry-berry aromas and flavors. A nice quaffer. Drink now. Score 86. K

GOLAN, CABERNET SAUVIGNON, 2002:
Made entirely from Cabernet Sauvignon grapes and aged in American oak for six months, this medium-bodied red boasts soft tannins and tempting berry, currant and plum fruits, along with hints of spices and vanilla. Drink now. Score 87. K

GOLAN, CABERNET SAUVIGNON, 2001:
Six months in American oak give this medium-bodied, simple but pleasant wine, appealing smoky cedar-oak flavors all sitting nicely on generous plum, wild berries and currants, along with a hint of green olives in the medium finish. Drink up. Score 86. K

GOLAN, CABERNET SAUVIGNON, 2000: Made entirely from Cabernet Sauvignon grapes and aged in oak for six months, this young and fruity wine has soft tannins and an abundance of currant, black cherry and vanilla aromas and flavors. Somewhat past its peak. Drink up. Score 86. K

GOLAN HEIGHTS WINERY, GAMAY NOUVEAU, 2004:
Made from Gamay Noir grapes and by the process of carbonic maceration, as is the case with the Beaujolais Nouveau wines of France, this cherry-red wine shows simple but generous and appealing raspberry and cassis fruits. A

bit more tannic and more medium-bodied than most of the hyper-young wines from France, but no less pleasant. Drink lightly chilled. Drink up. Score 85. K

GOLAN, SION CREEK, RED, 2004: A simple entry-level wine, light to medium-bodied, with soft tannins, a floral aroma and a berry-cherry personality. Drink up. Score 80. K

GOLAN, SION CREEK, RED, 2003: Meant to replace the Har Avital wines in this series, this unlikely blend of Sangiovese, Shiraz, Gamay Noir and Pinot Noir grapes lacks sophistication but is refreshing, with low tannins and a cherry-berry personality. Drink up. Score 80. K

GOLAN, CHARDONNAY, 2003: Clean, crisp and refreshing, medium-bodied, with aromas and flavors of green apples, citrus and spring flowers. Drink now. Score 85. K

GOLAN, CHARDONNAY, 2002: This unoaked, medium-bodied white has appealing aromas and flavors of citrus and green apples, along with a flowery overlay and plenty of balancing acidity to keep it crisp and refreshing. Drink up. Score 86. K

GOLAN, CHARDONNAY, 2001: This unoaked medium-bodied crisp wine shows appealing citrus, nectarine and tangerine fruits along with floral and green apple overtones. Drink up. Score 85. K

GOLAN, SION CREEK, WHITE, 2004: A light to medium-bodied potpourri of white grapes with citrus, pineapple aromas and flavors. Drink up. Score 80. K

GOLAN, SION CREEK, WHITE, 2003: A rather unlikely blend of Sauvignon Blanc, Gewurztraminer, Johannisberg Riesling and Muscat of Alexandria, this semi-dry white shows tropical fruits and pineapple aromas and flavors. Drink up. Score 79. K

GOLAN, MOSCATO, 2004: Fresh, lightly alcoholic, just barely *frizzante* in the style of Moscato d'Asti. Generously sweet but with good natural acidity to keep it lively and appealing, with pineapple, melon, and citrus flavors. Drink up. Score 87. K

GOLAN, MOSCATO, 2003: Lightly *frizzante*, light on the palate and rich in pineapple, lime, melon and green apple fruits along with a hint of white pepper and just the right level of refreshing acidity. Drink up. Score 87. K

GOLAN, EMERALD RIESLING, 2004: As to be anticipated with this grape, half-dry, floral and fruity. Drink up. Score 80. K

Goshen *

Located in the southern Negev Desert, this winery released its first wines in 1998. Current production is about 1,500 bottles annually.

GOSHEN, CABERNET SAUVIGNON, RESERVE, 2001: Medium-bodied, with soft tannins and aromas and flavors of far too ripe berries and plums. Drink up. Score 75. **K**

GOSHEN, CABERNET SAUVIGNON, RESERVE, 2000: Medium-bodied, with chunky tannins and aromas and flavors of hyper-ripe berry and cherry. Lacks depth and length. Score 68. **K**

GOSHEN, CABERNET SAUVIGNON, RESERVE, 1999: Light to medium-bodied and far too acidic, the wine shows flavors that call to mind concentrated fruit juice. Showing age. Score 65. **K**

GOSHEN, CABERNET SAUVIGNON, RESERVE, 1998: Somewhat thin and tannic, with blackberry and cassis flavors that struggle to make themselves felt. Showing age. Score 70. **K**

GOSHEN, MERLOT, RESERVE, 2001: Dull garnet red, alcoholic, almost searing tannins and minimal fruit. Score 68. **K**

GOSHEN, MERLOT, RESERVE, 2000: Tannic, acidic and thin, with flavors reminiscent of cranberry juice which then turn bitter and earthy on the finish. Score 66.

GOSHEN, MERLOT, RESERVE, 1999: Now past its peak, this medium-bodied wine still maintains its cherry red toward garnet color and its soft tannins, appealing berry and black cherry fruits along with a hint of spices at the finish. Drink up. Score 82.

GOSHEN, MERLOT, RESERVE, 1998: Light, but with tough tannins, this is a simple red with a few berry and herbal flavors, hardly deserving its self-proclaimed title Grand vin Rouge d'Israel. Showing age. Score 69.

GOSHEN, PETITE SIRAH, SIBONY SELECTION, 2000: A simple, medium-bodied country-style red, with chunky tannins and a few berry, currant and plum aromas. Drink up. Score 81. **K**

Greenberg **

Located in the town of Herzliya Pituach, not far from Tel Aviv, this micro-winery, owned by Motti Greenberg, is now producing about 750 bottles annually. First wines were released from the 2003 vintage, using Shiraz and Merlot grapes from Karmei Yosef and Cabernet Sauvignon from Kerem Ben Zimra in the Galilee.

GREENBERG, CABERNET SAUVIGNON, 2003: Deep garnet toward purple, this medium to full-bodied red is a fine first effort, the wine showing generous but well integrating tannins, and blackcurrant and wild berry fruits with moderate overlays of spicy oak, vanilla and a light herbaceousness. Drink now–2007. Score 86.

GREENBERG, MERLOT, 2003: Medium-bodied, with soft, sweet tannins. Blackberry and cherry fruits are complemented nicely by spiciness and hints of vanilla and eucalyptus. Drink now–2008. Score 87.

GREENBERG, SHIRAZ, 2003: This tempting medium-bodied wine shows floral and earthy aromas and flavors matched well by moderate tannins, wood and appealing black fruits. Mouthfilling and long. Drink now–2007. Score 87.

Gush Etzion ✳✳✳

Located at the Gush Etzion Junction near Jerusalem and owned largely by vintner Shraga Rozenberg and partly by the Tishbi family, the winery has its own vineyards in the Jerusalem Mountains, those with Cabernet Sauvignon, Merlot, Pinot Noir, Shiraz, Cabernet Franc and Petit Verdot as well as Chardonnay and Johannisberg Riesling grapes. The winery released its first wines in 1998 when production was about 3,000 bottles. Current production is about 10,000 bottles annually, but the new winery has the potential for future production of up to 100,000 bottles.

GUSH ETZION WINERY
Cabernet Sauvignon 70% Merlot 30%
2000 | Judean Hills

Bottle No. **2890** of 7900   13% Alcohol by Volume 750 ml ⓊP

GUSH ETZION WINERY, CABERNET SAUVIGNON, 2001: Dark, almost inky garnet toward royal purple, this full-bodied wine shows excellent balance between generous but soft tannins, just the right touch of smoky-spicy oak and elegant blackcurrant and wild berry fruits and spices, as well as Mediterranean herbs and green olives coming in toward the finish and then lingering nicely. Drink now–2008. Score 89. K

GUSH ETZION WINERY, CABERNET SAUVIGNON, 2000: Deep ruby medium to full-bodied wine with generous tannins and wood blending well with currant, plum and herbal aromas and flavors. Look for light hints of spices and smoky wood as well. Drink now. Score 86. K

GUSH ETZION WINERY, CABERNET SAUVIGNON, 1999: Aged in new oak barrels for 12 months, this medium-bodied, hearty and somewhat herbal wine yields appealing plum, black cherry and olive flavors, and has a lightly smoky character. Drink now. Score 86. **K**

GUSH ETZION WINERY, CABERNET SAUVIGNON-MERLOT, 2000: Medium to full-bodied, this country-style wine shows chunky tannins, plenty of wood, plum and black cherry fruits, all with hints of dill and other Mediterranean herbs. Drink now. Score 85. **K**

GUSH ETZION WINERY, CHARDONNAY, 2002: A lively golden color, this ripe and full flavored wine shows a pleasant earthy accent to its pineapple, hazelnut and citrus aromas and flavors as well as a surprisingly long and complex finish. Drink now. Score 88. **K**

GUSH ETZION WINERY, CHARDONNAY, 2001: Clean, ripe and fruity, the wine has a solid core of pear, apple and melon flavors as well as hints of spices that linger nicely on the palate. Drink now. Score 87. **K**

GUSH ETZION WINERY, CHARDONNAY, 2000: Made from organically grown grapes, this lightly *frizzante* wine has a nice core of pear, apple and citrus aromas and flavors that linger nicely on the palate, and a light, toasty finish. Somewhat past its peak. Drink up. Score 86. **K**

GUSH ETZION WINERY, SEMI DRY WHITE, 2000: Made entirely from Sauvignon Blanc grapes and with light flowery and grassy aromas to complement its rich apple and pear flavors, the wine is faulted somewhat by not having sufficient natural acids to balance out its sweetness. Past its peak. Drink up. Score 82. **K**

GUSH ETZION WINERY, DESSERT WINE, 2000: This blend of organically raised Chardonnay and Sauvignon Blanc grapes spent 8 months in small oak barrels. Deep gold toward orange in color, this markedly sweet wine has plenty of natural acids to keep it lively. Drink now. Score 85. **K**

Gustavo & Jo ✶✶✶✶

Located in the village of Kfar Vradim in the Western Galilee and drawing on grapes from the Golan Heights, this small winery was founded in 1995 by Gideon Boinjeau and produces wines made entirely from Cabernet Sauvignon grapes. In addition to a regular release, the winery also produces a Premium

series and total production is 3,500–4,000 bottles annually, with a future target of 20,000 bottles. Starting with the 2006 vintage the wines will be kosher.

Premium

PREMIUM, CABERNET SAUVIGNON, 2001: Made entirely from Cabernet grapes, this full-bodied, deep ruby toward garnet red has firm tannins but also balance and structure that will allow it to develop nicely over time and reveal deep cassis, black cherry and plum fruits, spiciness, and a long herbal-oaky finish. Drink now–2007. Score 91.

PREMIUM, CABERNET SAUVIGNON, 2000: Full-bodied and with its once firm tannins now well integrated, the wine reveals a complex set of aromas and flavors that include currants, wild berries, leather and spices. Deep, rich, and bordering on elegance. Drink now. Score 90.

Gustavo & Jo

GUSTAVO & JO, CABERNET SAUVIGNON, 2003: Dark garnet towards black, full-bodied, with still firm tannins well balanced by spicy wood and blackcurrant, blackberry and cassis fruits all on a background of minty-chocolate. Long and complex. Best 2007–2010. Tentative Score 89–91.

GUSTAVO & JO, CABERNET SAUVIGNON, 2002: This deep inky purple full-bodied still young red has firm, somewhat tight tannins but shows fine balance and structure that bode well for its future. Given time to open in the glass the wine reveals a tempting array of currant and black cherry fruits, those coming together nicely with spicy oak, eucalyptus and generous hints of chocolate and tobacco on the long finish. Long, complex and mouth-filling. Drink now–2008. Score 89.

GUSTAVO & JO, CABERNET SAUVIGNON, 2001: Dark purple toward garnet, full-bodied, with distinct Cabernet aromas and flavors including blackcurrants, black cherries, and a generous hint of mint on firm but well-integrated tannins, the wine shows good balance between wood and tannins and has a long appealing herbal finish. Drink now–2007. Score 89.

GUSTAVO & JO, CABERNET SAUVIGNON, 2000: Full-bodied, well rounded, with already soft tannins and good blackcurrant, plum and cherry aromas and flavors that linger very nicely on the palate, the wine also shows an appealing overlay of oak. Drink now. Score 89.

GUSTAVO & JO, CABERNET SAUVIGNON, 1999: Full-bodied and with fine balance between fruits, acids and smooth tannins, the wine shows a ripe, complex core of berries, currants, leather and spices, all blended together nicely and lingering comfortably on the palate. Drink now. Score 89.

GUSTAVO & JO, CABERNET SAUVIGNON, 1998: Perhaps not quite as heavy as the 1997 but with better balance. Intense and concentrated, with smooth tannins and a very attractive earthy streak that runs through currant and berry aromas and flavors. Drink now. Score 90.

GUSTAVO & JO, CABERNET SAUVIGNON, 1997: Full-bodied, ripe and complex, with blackcurrant, cherry, and raspberry flavors coming together with a supple texture and an intriguing finish. Well balanced, with a nice core of tannins and oak, and mild hints of anise and cedar wood. Drink now. Score 90.

Hakerem **

Founded in 2001 by Isaac Herskovitz in Beit-El near Hebron, this small winery produces unoaked Cabernet Sauvignon and Merlot wines, drawing on grapes from various vineyards. Annual production is currently 3,000 bottles.

HAKEREM, CABERNET SAUVIGNON, 2004: Deep ruby towards garnet, medium-bodied, with soft tannins and hints of spicy oak coming together nicely with aromas and flavors of currants, black cherries and earthiness. Drink from release–2007. Tentative Score 85–87. K

HAKEREM, CABERNET SAUVIGNON, 2003: Medium-bodied, with soft, nicely integrated tannins and plum, cherry, berry and spice notes, this smooth wine ends with an appealing fruity finish. Drink now. Score 86. K

HAKEREM, CABERNET SAUVIGNON, 2002: Dark garnet in color with hints of adobe brick browning, this medium to full-bodied oak-aged wine shows firm tannins and generous vanilla and smoky aromas and flavors, those well balanced by black fruits and hints of herbs and tobacco. Drink now. Score 86. K

HAKEREM, MERLOT, 2004: Medium-bodied, round and soft with plum, berry and currant fruits, the wine is somewhat one dimensional. Drink now. Score 84. K

HAKEREM, MERLOT, 2003: Deep cherry red toward purple, this medium-bodied wine shows good balance between soft tannins and ripe berry and currant fruits, along with a nice hint of spice on the finish. Drink now. Score 85. K

Hamasrek **

HAMASREK

2 0 0 2

CHARDONNAY
שרדונה

Alc 12.5% Vol 750 ml. Prod & Bot.
By HAMASREK Winery, ISRAEL.

Established by the Greengrass brothers in 1999 on Moshav Beit Meir in the Jerusalem Mountains, this kosher boutique winery draws on grapes from their own area as well as from Zichron Ya'akov and the Upper Galilee. First releases in 2000 included 5,000 bottles of Merlot and Chardonnay. Since then the winery has added Cabernet Sauvignon and Gewurztraminer to their line, and current production is about 9,000 bottles.

HAMASREK, CABERNET SAUVIGNON, 2003: Deep ruby towards garnet, medium to full-bodied, with firm tannins and generous wood but those yielding nicely to show blackcurrant and plum fruits on a lightly spicy background. Drink from release–2007. Tentative Score 85–87. **K**

HAMASREK, CABERNET SAUVIGNON, 2002: Dark garnet toward purple, medium to full-bodied with generous oak and firm tannins that tend to hide the currant and plum fruits. Somewhat one-dimensional. Drink now. Score 83. **K**

HAMASREK, CABERNET SAUVIGNON, 2001: Deep garnet red in color, this medium to full-bodied wine that was developed in French oak barrels for 19 months is somewhat dominated by dusty, smoky oak at this stage, but those well balanced by soft tannins and appealing currant and berry fruits. Drink now. Score 85. **K**

HAMASREK, MERLOT, 2002: Dark royal purple, medium-bodied and with soft, well-integrating tannins opening to reveal generous blackberry, black cherry and cassis aromas and flavors. Drink now–2007. Score 86. **K**

HAMASREK, MERLOT, 2001: Aged in French oak for 18 months, this deep purple, medium-bodied red has generous but well-integrated tannins and appealing berry, currant and herbal flavors and aromas. Drink now. Score 85. **K**

HAMASREK, MERLOT, 2000: Made entirely from Merlot grapes, this deep purple, medium-bodied, country-style wine has soft tannins, light earthy overtones and aromas and flavors of currants and mint. Pleasant but lacking depth or breadth. Drink now. Score 84. **K**

HAMASREK, CHARDONNAY, 2003: Golden-straw in color, medium-bodied, with buttery overtones from the generous oak treatment, that matched nicely by natural acidity and aromas and flavors of melon, pears and tropical fruits. Drink now. Score 86. **K**

HAMASREK, CHARDONNAY, 2002: Developed *sur lie* in oak barrels for eight months, this medium-bodied, light golden wine shows appealing pineapple, citrus and pear aromas and flavors. The generous oak is nicely balanced by fruits and acidity. Drink now. Score 85. **K**

HAMASREK, CHARDONNAY, 2000: After having spent 10 months in new oak barrels, this rather heavy-handed wine has far too much feel of smoky oak and not nearly enough of fruit. Lacking character and balance, the wine's flavors fade while still in the glass. Past its peak. Drink up. Score 82. **K**

Hans Sternbach ✶✶

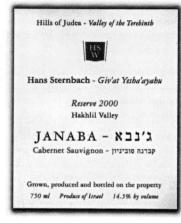

Hills of Judea - *Valley of the Terebinth*

HS W

Hans Sternbach - *Giv'at Yesha'ayahu*

Reserve 2000
Hakhlil Valley

JANABA - ג׳נבא
Cabernet Sauvignon - קברנה סוביניון

Grown, produced and bottled on the property
750 ml   *Produce of Israel*   *14.5% by volume*

Founded by Gadi and Shula Sternbach in Moshav Givat Yeshayahu in the Judean Hills, the winery's first release was of 1,800 bottles from the 2000 harvest. With a new winery located on the Moshav and relying primarily on Cabernet Sauvignon grapes from their own nearby vineyards, production from the 2003 vintage was about 3,000 bottles and from the 2004 vintage about 10,000 bottles. The winery produces wines in three series: Janaba Reserve, Nachal Hakhlil and Emek Haella.

Janaba Reserve

JANABA RESERVE, CABERNET SAUVIGNON, HAKHLIL VALLEY, 2003: Made entirely from Cabernet Sauvignon grapes, this deep garnet towards royal purple, medium to full-bodied red shows firm tannins that yield slowly to reveal blackcurrant and wild berry fruits. Marred somewhat by a bit of unwanted residual sugar. Drink now. Score 84.

JANABA RESERVE, CABERNET SAUVIGNON, HAKHLIL VALLEY, 2001: Aged in Bulgarian oak casks for 18 months, this dark cherry-red wine shows generous smoky and spicy oak, that well balanced by soft tannins, vanilla, and appealing currant, berry and black cherry fruits. Drink now. Score 85.

JANABA RESERVE, CABERNET SAUVIGNON, HAKHLIL VALLEY, 2000: Dark royal purple in color, medium to full-bodied, with firm tannins and a perhaps overly generous dose of wood, but with an array of currant, plum and berry fruits that open nicely in the glass. Drink now. Score 85.

Nachal Hakhlil

NACHAL HAKHLIL, CABERNET SAUVIGNON 2003: Deep purple, medium to full-bodied, with firm, chunky tannins and aromas and flavors of currants and berries, this blend of 90% Cabernet Sauvignon and 10% Petite Sirah reflects its 12 months in oak with spicy and vanilla overtones. Drink now. Score 85.

Emek Haella

EMEK HAELLA, CABERNET SAUVIGNON, VALLELLA CLASSICO SUPERIORE, 2002: The name of the wine, a take-off on Valpolicella Classico Superiore has a certain logic, as both wines are made by the *ripasso* method. Unfortunately, the grapes of this wine are not adequate for the method. Light cherry colored, light to medium-bodied, the wine shows far too bitter overtones to the plum flavors that are here and therefore lacks balance. Drink up. Score 79.

Har-Noy **

Founded in 1998 by Michal and Benny Har-Noy on Moshav Karmei Yosef at the foothills of the Jerusalem Mountains, this winery receives its grapes from the surrounding vineyards. Current production is 1,400 bottles annually and the winery is hoping to double its production in the coming years.

HAR-NOY, MERLOT, 2003: Cherry-red towards garnet, medium-bodied, with sweet tannins and appealing smoky oak, opening in the glass to reveal generous blackberry and currant fruits. A good quaffer. Drink now. Score 84.

HAR-NOY, MERLOT, 2002: Dark royal purple in color, this medium-bodied wine shows good balance between black fruits, moderately soft tannins and oak. Lacking complexity. Drink now. Score 84.

HAR-NOY, MERLOT, 2001: A pleasant medium-bodied country wine, chunky and alcoholic, with appealing smoky oak overlays on a background of plum, black cherry and currant fruits. Somewhat past its peak. Drink up. Score 82.

HAR-NOY, MERLOT, 2000: A biting, country-style blend of 85% Merlot and 15% Cabernet Sauvignon, this medium-bodied wine is stingy in its black fruit flavors and far too one-dimensional. Well past its peak and no longer scoreable.

HAR-NOY, TENE, 2001: This medium-bodied oak-aged blend of Cabernet Sauvignon and Merlot shows firm but well-integrated tannins, smoky oak, and aromas and flavors of blackcurrants, cherries and vanilla, along with a nice hint of spiciness on the finish. Drink up. Score 86.

HAR-NOY, TENE, 2000: An oak-aged blend of 60% Cabernet Sauvignon and 40% Merlot, this garnet colored medium-bodied wine offers up soft tannins and aromas and flavors of currants, plums and vanilla. Somewhat short and one-dimensional. Drink up. Score 84.

Hatabor **

Located in the village of Kfar Tabor in the lower Galilee, this small winery was founded by Shimi Efrat in 1999 and released its first wines from the 2002 harvest. Grapes come primarily from nearby vineyards, and production is currently about 3,500 bottles annually.

HATABOR, CABERNET SAUVIGNON, 2002: Dark cherry-red toward garnet in color, medium-bodied, with moderately firm tannins and up-front berry, currant and cherry fruits. Lacking complexity but appealing. Drink now. Score 84.

HATABOR, MERLOT, 2002: Medium-bodied, with soft, well-integrated tannins and appealing berry and plum fruits set off by the hint of fresh herbs. Pleasant, without pretensions, and a good quaffer. Drink now. Score 84.

HATABOR, CHARDONNAY, 2003: Light straw colored, medium-bodied, and with citrus, pineapple and melon flavors. Not traditional of Chardonnay but a pleasant little quaffing wine. Drink now. Score 85.

HATABOR, SAUVIGNON BLANC, 2003: Light to medium-bodied, with refreshing litchi, melon and citrus aromas and flavors. Not complex but pleasant. Drink now. Score 84.

Hevron Heights *

Located in Kiryat Arba, not far from the heart of the city of Hebron, this winery was founded in 2001 by a group of French investors and intially produced about 150,000 bottles per year, the target audience being observant Jews abroad. The winery reports current production of about 400,000 bottles annually, and produces a line of varietal and blended wines of Cabernet Sauvignon, Merlot, French Colombard, Sauvignon Blanc, and Malbec grapes, drawing largely on grapes from the Judean Hills as well as vineyards near Hebron. The winery has a broad and somewhat confusing labeling system, various labels and brands including Hevron Heights, Noach, Hevron, Tevel, Efron's Cave, Shemesh, Pardess, Judea and Jerusalem Heights, some of which are produced as private labels.

HEVRON HEIGHTS, CABERNET SAUVIGNON, SDEH CALEV, 2003: Deep garnet in color, medium to full-bodied, with soft tannins and currant and berry fruits matched nicely by hints of spices and mint. Drink now. Score 85. K

HEVRON HEIGHTS, MEGIDDO, 2002: The flagship wine of the winery, this unfiltered blend of Cabneret Sauvignon, Merlot and Syrah, aged in new French oak for 24 months and reflects that by a heavy dose of sweet and smoky wood. Gripping tannins that at least so far do not seem to integrate are hiding the currant, berry and very ripe plum flavors that are trying to make it to the surface. Drink now. Score 84. K

HEVRON HEIGHTS, SPECIAL RESERVE, 2001: A firmly tannic and far too oaked blend of Cabernet Sauvignon, Merlot and Shiraz. The vegetal and oak flavors dominate while the fruits never quite make it to the surface, and the wine lacks balance. Drink up. Score 72. K

HEVRON HEIGHTS, CABERNET SAUVIGNON, ISAAC'S RAM, 2001: Deep but not clear garnet in color, this medium to full-bodied wine is packed with tannins and has such a high level of acidity that it makes the mouth pucker. Precious few fruits here; those present on a somewhat muddy background. Score 68. K

HEVRON HEIGHTS, CABERNET SAUVIGNON, GIDEON, NOACH 2002: Dark, inky purple in color and medium-bodied, the wine has chunky tannins, too much acidity and an overbearing influence of what appears to be oak. Over ripe and cloying. Showing better than at earlier tastings but still failing to excite. Drink up. Score 78. K

HEVRON HEIGHTS, CABERNET SAUVIGNON, TEVEL, NOACH, 2002: Deep ruby towards garnet in color, with soft tannins and clean aromas and flavors of currants and raspberries. Not complex but an acceptable entry-level wine. Drink now. Score 82. K

HEVRON HEIGHTS, MERLOT, NOACH, 2002: Dark ruby towards garnet, medium-bodied, with chunky country-style tannins and generous wood. Appealing black fruits and a hint of tobacco here. Drink now. Score 84. K

HEVRON HEIGHTS, MERLOT, ESTATE, 2002: Not a typical Merlot, this is a simple country style red with medium-body, nearly unfelt tannins and a few berry and plum fruits. Drink up. Score 74. K

HEVRON HEIGHTS, MERLOT, PARDESS, 2001: Deep garnet toward purple and with a pleasant aroma when first poured, but that fading rather quickly and revealing a coarse texture yielding searing tannins and acidity as well as flavors of stewed black fruits. Drink up. Score 74. K

HEVRON HEIGHTS, CABERNET-SAUVIGNON-MERLOT, JERUSALEM HEIGHTS, 2002: This unfiltered medium to full-bodied blend of 50% each Cabernet Sauvignon and Merlot, aged for 18 months in new American and French oak barrels, shows aromas and flavors of blackcurrants, wild berries and chocolate on a lightly spicy background. Drink now–2007. Score 85. K

HEVRON HEIGHTS, CABERNET SAUVIGNON-MERLOT, MAKHPELAH, 2001: With a very strong oak influence that reflects its 20 months in French and American casks, this coarse wine is stingy in fruits. Drink up. Score 72. K

JUDEAN VINEYARDS

5761

Cabernet - Merlot

2001

MAKHPELAH

HEVRON HEIGHTS WINERY

13% vol.   *750 ml*

PRODUCED IN ISRAEL

HEVRON HEIGHTS, CABERNET SAUVIGNON-MERLOT, TEVEL, NOACH, 2002: Medium-bodied, with soft tannins and perhaps too generous acidity but with appealing aromas and flavors of currants and wild berries. Drink now. Score 83. K

HEVRON HEIGHTS, CABERNET SAUVIGNON-MERLOT, JUDEA, JERUSALEM HEIGHTS, 2001: After 18 months in barrels, this country-style wine is far too oaky, has coarse tannins and a lingering sensation of sawdust. Drink up. Score 76. K

HEVRON HEIGHTS, TRIPLE RED, EFRON'S CAVE, 2003: Dark garnet in color, this medium-bodied, unoaked blend of one-third each Cabernet Sauvignon, Merlot and Syrah offers up soft tannins and forwards berry-cherry fruits. Drink up. Score 79. K

HEVRON HEIGHTS, TRIPLE PLUM, EFRON'S CAVE, 2003: A light to medium-bodied one dimensional blend of Cabernet Sauvignon, Merlot and Syrah (35%, 35% and 30% respectively) with forward plum and black cherry fruits. Drink up. Score 78. K

HEVRON HEIGHTS, VINYAMINA 160, N.V.: A half-dry red far too much like cough syrup in flavor and aromas. Score 60. K

HEVRON HEIGHTS, VILLAGE SUPERIOR, NOACH VILLAGES, N.V.: Dark cherry colored, light to medium-bodied, with far too ripe red fruits and unpleasant hints of bitterness and earthiness. Score 68. K

HEVRON HEIGHTS, CABERNET-MERLOT BLUSH WINE, MESSOPY, NOACH, 2001: Pale pink turning to brown in color, the wine is far too acidic and calls to mind pink grapefruit juice. Score 60. K

HEVRON HEIGHTS, CHARDONNAY, 2002: Too generously oaked and somewhat flat on the palate, this wine reveals only stingy pineapple and grapefruit flavors and none of the traits of Chardonnay. Drink up. Score 72. K

HEVRON HEIGHTS, SAUVIGNON BLANC FUME, SHEMESH, 2004: Straw-colored, medium-bodied, with smoky oak and appealing citrus peel, tropical fruits, light herbal and grassy aromas and flavors. Not complex but pleasant. Drink now. Score 84. K

HEVRON HEIGHTS, MOSCATO, SHEMESH, 2004: Light lively golden straw in color, light in body, with moderate sweetness and distinctly floral on the nose and with an abundance of citrus and tropical fruits. Drink now. Score 83. K

HEVRON HEIGHTS, WHITE, EFRON'S CAVE, 2003: Unoaked Sauvignon Blanc, light in color and body with refreshing citrus and herbal-mineral aromas and flavors. A simple entry-level wine. Drink up. Score 80. K

Israel Wine Institute *

The Israel Wine Institute released more than 10,000 bottles of twenty different experimental wines under the label Duran from the 1999 and 2002 vintages. With offices, laboratories and experimental wine-making facilities located in the town of Rehovot on the southern Coastal Plain, the wines include among others, Cabernet Sauvignon, Argaman, Nebbiolo,

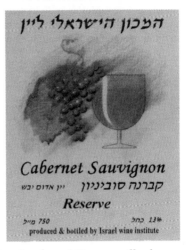

Sangiovese, Barbera, Merlot, Syrah and Tempranillo drawn from nearly every region throughout the country.

DURAN, CABERNET SAUVIGNON, 2000: Deep garnet toward purple, this medium-bodied, moderately tannic wine shows cassis and wild berry fruits, but lacks depth or true Cabernet traits. Drink up. Score 82.

DURAN, MERLOT, 2000: Not a typical Merlot, with only modest cherry and plum flavors and tannins, and a light pickle barrel sensation that comes in from mid-palate. Somewhat past its peak. Drink up. Score 78.

DURAN, TEMPRANILLO, 2000: A rustic wine, with an earthy and mineral sensation hiding whatever berry-cherry flavors exist here. This austere wine fails to reflect the quality of the vintage. Somewhat past its peak. Drink up. Score 80.

DURAN, BARBERA, 2000: A few cherry and plum fruits are felt along with low tannins and a green tobacco edge. Drink up. Score 78.

DURAN, SANGIOVESE, 2000: As light in color as it is in body, the wine is dominated by dill pickle flavors. Somewhat past its peak. Drink up. Score 73.

DURAN, NEBBIOLO, 1999: Dilute, with "dirty" aromas and flavors and a low level of berry and anise. Well past its peak and no longer scoreable.

DURAN, 2000: This medium-bodied Bordeaux blend of 45% Cabernet Sauvignon, 40% Merlot and 15% Cabernet Franc shows modest cedar, currant and herbal aromas and flavors on a lightly spicy background, but lacks somewhat in focus. Drink up. Score 84.

Kadesh Barnea *

This Negev Desert winery was established in 1999 by Alon Tzadok on Moshav Kadesh Barnea and has its own vineyards near the ruins of the Byzantine city of Nitzana, near the Egyptian border. Although releases to date have included only Cabernet Sauvignon and Merlot mouth-fillings, the winery is developing further vineyards containing Petit Verdot and Shiraz grapes. Production for 2000 and 2001 was 2,000 bottles; 3,700 bottles were produced in 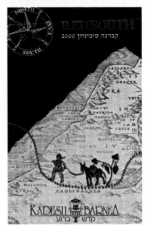 the 2002 and 2003 vintages, and 4,500 in 2004. The wines have been kosher since the 2002 harvest.

CABERNET SAUVIGNON, RED SOUTH, 2004. Medium-bodied, with chunky tannins that seem not to want to integrate and only skimpy black fruits on a too herbal background. Drink from release. Tentative Score 80–82. K

CABERNET SAUVIGNON, RED SOUTH, 2003: Medium to full-bodied, firmly tannic, with hints of black cherry and plum fruits, those coming together with hints of green olives, herbs and chocolate. Drink now. Score 84. K

CABERNET SAUVIGNON, RED SOUTH, 2002: Medium bodied, young and tight with soft tannins and green olive notes on the cherry and currant flavors along with hints of herbs. Drink now. Score 83. K

CABERNET SAUVIGNON, RED SOUTH, 2001: After eight months in oak, this medium-bodied red is fairly stingy but has appealing currant, mineral and cedary oak aromas and flavors. Somewhat acidic and not a typical Cabernet. Drink up. Score 84.

CABERNET SAUVIGNON, RED SOUTH, 2000: Light to medium-bodied, with only modest hints of currant, cherry and berry fruits, along with hints of tea and rhubarb. Somewhat past its peak. Drink up. Score 79.

KADESH BARNEA, MERLOT, 2004: A simple country-style wine with chunky tannins, generous wood influence and skimpy black fruits. Drink up. Score 79. **K**

KADESH BARNEA, MERLOT, 2003: Soft and generous, with tart black cherry, cedar and spice flavors. Somewhat tannic on the finish, but promises to settle down with time. Drink up. Score 84. **K**

Kadita ***

Jonathan Goldman made wines at his home in Bikta Bekadita in the Upper Galilee for several years before he released his first commercial output of 600 bottles in 2001, a blend of Cabernet Sauvignon and Merlot. Grapes are currently drawn from the winery's own nearby vineyards and from Kerem Ben Zimra. Production doubled in 2002 and again in 2003 with the release of 2,400 bottles. Production in 2004 was 3,000 bottles and anticipated future production is 22,000 bottles annually.

KADITA, CABERNET SAUVIGNON, 2004: Youthful deep royal-purple in color, full-bodied, with generous soft tannins integrating nicely and concentrated black fruits, Mediterranean herbs, eucalyptus and hints of spicy cedar wood from the oak barrels. Long, concentrated and mouthfilling. Drink from release–2009. Tentative Score 88–90.

KADITA, CABERNET SAUVIGNON, 2003: A blend of grapes from two vineyards, one with volcanic soil, one with red soil, this still youthful deep royal-purple wine shows full body, firm tannins promising to integrate nicely and a tempting array of blackcurrant and wild berry fruits, those on a long, spicy tobacco and chocolate finish. Best starting in 2007. Tentative Score 87–89.

KADITA, MERLOT, 2004: Full-bodied and aromatic, with firm but already well-integrating tannins and even at this early stage showing a tempting array of blueberry, raspberry and purple plum fruits, those on a background of chocolate and Mediterranean herbs. Drink from release–2008. Tentative Score 88–90.

KADITA, MERLOT, 2003: Full-bodied, concentrated, and intense, with generous soft tannins well balanced by near-sweet and smoky oak. Look for aromas and flavors of black cherries, blackberries and cassis as well as for hints of mocha and cigar tobacco on the long finish. Drink from release–2008. Tentative Score 86–88.

KADITA, SHIRAZ, 2002: Made from grapes from a largely untended vineyard, this intense and concentrated wine is blended with 10% of Cabernet Sauvignon and aged in French oak for 20 months. Medium to full-bodied, with firm but well-integrating tannins and an appealing array of plum, berry and cassis fruits all on a background of generous black pepper, light earthiness and herbaceousness. Drink now–2008. Score 89.

KADITA, CABERNET SAUVIGNON-MERLOT, 2003: Dark ruby toward garnet in color, medium to full-bodied, showing generous ripe berry and plum fruits and soft tannins, all balanced by vanilla, spices and herbal overtones. Drink now. Score 87.

KADITA, CABERNET SAUVIGNON-MERLOT, 2002: Medium to full-bodied, with generous tannins, those integrating nicely and set off well by blackcurrant, plum and wild berry fruits. Look as well for overlays of spices and toasty oak. Drink now. Score 86.

KADITA, CABERNET SAUVIGNON-MERLOT, 2001: Dark garnet toward purple in color, medium to full-bodied, with good balance between tannins, wood and acidity, this successful first release offers up appealing currant and berry fruits together with hints of vanilla and spices. Drink now. Score 86.

Karmei Yosef ★★★★

Founded in 2001 by Ben-Ami Bravdo and Oded Shosheyov, both professors of oenology at the Hebrew University of Jerusalem, the winery sits in the heart of a vineyard at Karmei Yosef on the western slopes of the Judean Mountains. This small winery released 2,800 bottles of its first wine in 2001, 7,500 bottles in 2002 and about 10,000 each for 2003 and 2004. Anticipated production by 2006 is for 17,000–20,000 bottles annually.

Among the varieties under cultivation in the winery-owned vineyards are Cabernet Sauvignon, Merlot, Chardonnay, Carignan, French Colombard, Emerald Riesling and Muscat of Alexandria grapes. From 2001 to 2003 releases included red wines only, and the winery's first Chardonnay is from the 2004 vintage. The winery will also be releasing a Muscat-based ice wine.

KARMEI YOSEF, CABERNET SAUVIGNON, BRAVDO, 2004: In its infancy now but showing good balance between sweet tannins, spicy wood, and berry, black cherry and cassis aromas and flavors. Needs time to develop. Best 2007–2012. Tentative Score 90–92.

KARMEI YOSEF, CABERNET SAUVIGNON, BRAVDO, 2003: A well-balanced, well structured blend of 80% Cabernet Sauvignon and 20% Merlot. Still young but already showing ripe, generous and mouthfilling aromas and flavors of plums, currants, black cherries and berries, with hints of minty spice and wood. On its way to becoming an elegant and graceful wine. Drink now–2010. Score 91.

KARMEI YOSEF, CABERNET SAUVIGNON, BRAVDO, 2002: This blend of 90% Cabernet Sauvignon and 10% Merlot, full-bodied, young and tight, but already well focused and lively, has a leathery base with a complex array of ripe aromas and flavors of currants, black cherries and a tantalizing hint of anise, as well as an appealing hint of bitterness that makes itself felt on the long, fruity finish. Generous soft tannins and good balance. Drink now–2007. Score 92.

KARMEI YOSEF, CABERNET SAUVIGNON, BRAVDO, 2001: Deep garnet toward purple, this oak-aged, unfiltered blend of 85% Cabernet Sauvignon and 15% Merlot is now showing excellent balance between soft, well-integrated tannins, natural acidity, wood and a tempting array of currant, blackberry and black cherry fruits, those on a background of toasted nuts, black licorice and Mediterranean herbs. Mouth-filling, long and delicious, the wine opens beautifully in the glass and on the palate, and then lingers long and gently. Drink now–2008. Score 91.

KARMEI YOSEF, MERLOT, BRAVDO, 2003: A rich, generous Merlot, with minty and licorice accents to ripe blackberry, currant, spice and anise flavors. Soft tannins well in balance with fruits and the first influence of the wood bode very nicely for the future development of this wine. Drink now–2010. Score 91.

KARMEI YOSEF, MERLOT, BRAVDO, 2002: Ripe, bold, well focused and delicious, with layer after layer of blueberry, plum and currant fruits, this medium-bodied wine boasts soft tannins along with hints of mocha and Mediterranean herbs that seem to dart in and out on the palate, all culminating in a long, near-sweet finish. Drink now–2007. Score 91.

KARMEI YOSEF, CHARDONNAY, BRAVDO, 2004: Medium to full-bodied, rich, concentrated, complex and somewhat bold, with crisply dry aromas and flavors of citrus and citrus peel, melon, and apple fruits together with light oak shadings. Drink now–2007. Score 91.

Katlav ✳

Owner-winemaker Yossi Yittach founded this small winery on Moshav Nes Harim in the Jerusalem Mountains in 1996, and first commercial releases were from the 2000 vintage. The winery draws on Cabernet Sauvignon, Merlot and Syrah grapes from local vineyards and is currently releasing about 6,000 bottles annually.

KATLAV, CABERNET SAUVIGNON, 2003: Deep garnet towards purple, medium to full-bodied, with still firm tannins, this blend of 60% Cabernet Sauvignon and 40% Merlot reveals simple but appealing aromas and flavors of cassis and blackberries as well as hints of smoky, spicy oak. Drink now. Score 83. **K**

KATLAV, CABERNET SAUVIGNON, 2002: Dark purple in color, this medium-bodied oak-aged wine, a blend of Cabernet Sauvignon with a small amount of Shiraz, offers up generous aromas and flavors of currants and wild berries, those complemented by a hint of spiciness. Somewhat one-dimensional. Drink up. Score 81. **K**

KATLAV, CABERNET SAUVIGNON, 2001: An oak-aged medium-bodied red made primarily from Cabernet Sauvignon with some Shiraz added, this dark garnet wine shows good balance between wood, soft tannins and generous plum, blackberry and herbal aromas and flavors. Drink up. Score 82. **K**

KATLAV, CABERNET SAUVIGNON, 2000: A deep royal purple medium-bodied blend of 95% Cabernet Sauvignon and 5% Shiraz aged in oak for about 12 months, the wine has moderate levels of black fruits, moderate tannins and an herbal overlay. Now well past its peak and no longer scoreable. **K**

KATLAV, CABERNET SAUVIGNON-MERLOT, 2003: Full-bodied, with somewhat firm tannins and a bit hot on the palate but given time to open in the glass the wine reveals tempting currant, plum and berry fruits along with hints of spices and Mediterranean herbs. Not showing as well as at an earlier tasting. Drink up. Score 84. **K**

KATLAV

Cabernet Sauvignon
2003

750 ml. 14.5 Alc.
Katlav Winery, Nes Harim 99885, Israel

Kella David *

Founded in 1995 by Amos Barzilai and Smadar Kaplinsky on Moshav Givat Yeshayahu in the Jerusalem Mountains, this small winery produces about 10,000 bottles annually.

Kella David, Dry White, Semi-Dry White, Semi-Sweet White, 2004: As in previous vintages, each of these wines is a blend of French Colombard and Emerald Riesling. Remarkably similar in aroma and flavor, the wines vary primarily in their level of sweetness. Floral on the nose, with tutti-frutti flavors and lacking acidity, there is little here to charm. Drink up. Score for each of the wines 71.

Kfira ✳✳✳✳

Founded in 1995 by microbiologist Ronnie Shapira on Moshav Nataf in the Jerusalem Mountains. Until he closed the winery in 2003, Shapira produced mouth-filling oak-aged Cabernet Sauvignon and Merlot wines from grapes grown in his own vineyards on the *moshav* as well as from Kerem Ben Zimra in the Upper Galilee. Production was several thousand bottles annually.

KFIRA, CABERNET SAUVIGNON, 2000: Deep garnet toward purple in color, full-bodied and with generous but well integrating tannins, this muscular but elegant wine shows very appealing aromas and flavors of cassis, ripe berries and sweet cedar wood on the first attack, those opening to reveal undertones of spices and Mediterranean herbs. Well crafted. Drink now–2007. Score 90.

KFIRA, CABERNET SAUVIGNON, 1999: Dark royal purple, medium to full-bodied and with now soft tannins and traditional Cabernet currant, lead pencil and spicy vanilla aromas and flavors complemented nicely by hints of freshly turned earth on the long finish. Drink now. Score 89.

KFIRA, CABERNET SAUVIGNON, 1998: Firm and lively, with deep and concentrated aromas and flavors of black and red currants, black cherries, plums and vanilla, this medium to full-bodied wine has plenty of smooth tannins and good overall balance. Drink now. Score 88.

KFIRA, CABERNET SAUVIGNON, 1997: With its tannins now fully integrated, the wine shows mature aromas and flavors in which an earthy-herbal sense has risen to match the still rich currant, stewed plum and cherry flavors, but with the vanilla now yielding to caramel and licorice. A bit past its peak. Drink up. Score 88.

KFIRA, CABERNET SAUVIGNON, 1996: Medium to full-bodied, with an almost chewy texture and good balance and structure, this now fully mature wine reveals aromas and flavors of dark fruits and herbs, and continues to show good concentration and elegance although now somewhat past its peak. Past its peak. Drink up. Score 86.

KFIRA, CABERNET SAUVIGNON, 1995: The winery's first release. Medium-bodied, with good balance between blackcurrant and plum fruits, vanilla and spices. Was a delight in its youth but now well past its peak and no longer scoreable.

KFIRA, MERLOT, 2000: Garnet toward purple in color and medium to full-bodied, this well balanced and elegant wine shows firmer than usual tannins for a Merlot, but those integrating nicely with aromas and flavors of plums, currants and wild berries, supported by layers of spicy oak, vanilla and a light herbaceousness. Drink now. Score 90.

KFIRA, MERLOT, 1999: Dark, firm, rich and tannic, this chewy and hearty Merlot has appealing mineral and herbal accents to its plum, currant and spicy oak flavors and aromas. Harmonious and well balanced, with flavors that linger nicely on the palate. Drink now. Score 91.

KFIRA, MERLOT, 1997: Deep garnet, but now fully mature and starting to brown. Still warm, soft and with a velvety texture. Look for aromas and flavors of berries, plums, chocolate and tobacco. Somewhat past its peak. Drink up. Score 89.

KFIRA, MERLOT, 1996: As it has been since its youth, a firmly tannic and somewhat astringent wine, but now fully mature, its once appealing fruit aromas and flavors giving way to dominant earthy and herbal aromas. Well past its peak and no longer scoreable.

KFIRA, WHITE MERLOT, 1999: Although it lacks any of the traits of more normal Merlot, this was a pleasant little white wine in its youth, medium-bodied and with aromas and flavors that called to mind peaches, nectarines and grapes. Showing age. Score 84.

La Terra Promessa ***

Parma born Sandro Pelligrini, who comes from a family of winemakers, founded this small winery in 1998 at his home in Moshav Shachar in the northern Negev Desert. Pelligrini relies on Cabernet Sauvignon and Merlot grapes from the Upper Galilee and Ramat Arad, as well as from a vineyard he is developing near the winery with Shiraz, Zinfandel and Sangiovese. Currently he produces about 3,000 bottles annually under the premium Rubino Reserva and three La Terra Promessa labels.

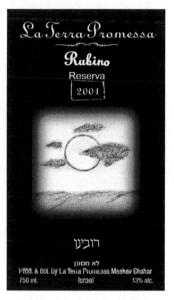

Rubino Reserva

RUBINO RESERVA, 2002: Full-bodied, with generous but soft tannins well balanced by spicy wood and aromas and flavors of black cherries, berries and currants. Long and mouthfilling. Drink now–2008. Score 88.

RUBINO RESERVA, 2001: A lightly oak-aged, dark garnet towards purple, medium to full-bodied blend of Cabernet Sauvignon and Merlot, with soft tannins now integrating nicely, hints of smoky oak from the wood and generous aromas and flavors of currant, wild berries and plums. A moderately-long, just spicy enough finish adds charm. Drink now. Score 88.

RUBINO RESERVA, 2000: Deep garnet-red, medium to full-bodied, with tannins now well integrated, showing an appealing herbal overlay over currant and plum fruits. Moderately long and mouth-filling. Drink now. Score 87.

RUBINO RESERVA, 1999: Medium to full-bodied, with still chunky country-style tannins and hints of berry, currant and plum fruits. A bit past its peak. Drink up. Score 85.

RUBINO RESERVA, 1998: Full-bodied, with tannins that have never quite softened and currant fruits now staring to caramelize. Well past its peak and no longer scoreable.

La Terra Promessa

LA TERRA PROMESSA, CABERNET SAUVIGNON, 2003: Medium to full-bodied, dense royal-purple towards black in color, with firm tannins now starting to integrate, this wine shows a gentle hand with the wood, and currant and black cherry fruits on a lightly spicy and herbal background. Drink from release–2008. Tentative Score 86–88.

LA TERRA PROMESSA, CABERNET SAUVIGNON, 2002: Dark garnet toward purple, this medium-bodied red has firm and chunky country-style tannins, those matched nicely by plum, berry and black cherry fruits and light spiciness. Drink now. Score 85.

LA TERRA PROMESSA, CABERNET SAUVIGNON, 2001: An appealing deep purple in color, this medium-bodied wine has soft tannins and soft, smoky oak to match currant, wild berry and light herbal aromas and flavors that linger nicely on the palate. Drink now. Score 86.

LA TERRA PROMESSA, MERLOT, 2003: Made entirely from Merlot grapes and with 8 months in oak, this calls to mind a Tuscan Merlot. Medium-bodied, unfiltered, with soft, sweet and already well-integrating tannins. Good plum, berry and black cherry fruits and a light hint of spices that linger nicely on the palate. Drink now–2007. Score 87.

LA TERRA PROMESSA, SYRAH, 2003: Dark and spicy, with earthy overlays to wild berry, currant and cherry fruits, all of those with hints of anise and a light anise-leathery edge on the finish. Firm tannins here but those yielding beautifully to highlight the wine's intrinsically good balance and structure. Drink from release–2008. Tentative Score 89–91.

LA TERRA PROMESSA, ZINFANDEL, 2003: Deep garnet in color, medium-bodied, with fresh blackberry and plum fruits. Pleasant, with very soft tannins, but a bit too acidic and thus lacking balance for bottle aging. Drink now. Score 82.

LA TERRA PROMESSA, ZINFANDEL, 2002: Light cherry red in color, with only the barest hints of tannins and oak, this light to medium-bodied wine yields modest raspberry and cherry flavors, much like wines made from Gamay grapes rather than from Zinfandel. Drink up. Score 84.

LA TERRA PROMESSA, LA CRIME, 2004: Still in its infancy, this blend of 40% each of Sangiovese and Shiraz with 20% of Cabernet Franc is already showing enviable balance and structure. Firm tannins but those promising to yield and come together nicely with spicy wood and wild berry-plum and light earthy-herbal aromas and flavors. Drink from release–2008. Tentative Score 88–90.

LA TERRA PROMESSA, LA CRIME, 2003: Dark, deep and rich, full-bodied and with still muscular tannins but those well balanced by smoky wood and generous berry-cherry and earthy aromas and flavors. Drink now–2007. Score 87.

LA TERRA PROMESSA, LA CRIME, 2002: An unfiltered, medium-bodied blend of half each of Sangiovese and Shiraz, reflecting its 14 months in oak with generous spicy oak and firm tannins, those nicely balanced by fresh berry, black cherry and earthy-mineral aromas and flavors. Drink now. Score 87.

LA TERRA PROMESSA, RUBINO, 2002: This dark ruby toward garnet, medium-bodied, generous blend of Cabernet Sauvignon and Merlot has soft, well-integrated tannins along with appealing currant and wild berry fruits. Smooth and mouth-filling, with just the right hint of spiciness. Drink now. Score 86.

LA TERRA PROMESSA, RUBINO, 2001: An oak-aged, deep purple, medium-bodied blend of Cabernet Sauvignon and Merlot, with soft tannins, gentle smoky oak from the wood barrels, and generous currant, blackberry and plum fruits. Look as well for hints of spices and Mediterranean herbs here. Drink up. Score 86.

LA TERRA PROMESSA, RUBINO, 2000: A blend of 60% Cabernet Sauvignon and 40% Merlot, this medium-bodied, lively and fresh wine developed in one and two-year-old oak *barriques* for about 14 months has deep ruby color and ample currant, plum and spicy aromas and flavors. Somewhat past its peak. Drink up. Score 85.

LA TERRA PROMESSA, DRY EMERALD RIESLING, 2003: Light golden straw in color, light to medium-bodied, with crisply refreshing acidity and aromas and flavors of pineapple, grapefruit and limes. Drink up. Score 85.

Lachish **

Established on Moshav Lachish on the Central Plain by Oded Yakobson, Oscar Meisels and Gai Rosenfeld, this small winery relies entirely on Cabernet Sauvignon and Shiraz grapes from their own vineyards. The winery's first releases, in 2002 were of 500 bottles and current production is about 3,000 bottles annually.

LACHISH, CABERNET SAUVIGNON, 2003: Dark ruby towards garnet in color, medium-bodied, with light oak influences and chunky country-style tannins. Appealing currant and berry fruits overlaid with light spices and a hint of herbaceousness. Drink now. Score 84.

LACHISH, SHIRAZ, 2003: Deep royal purple in color, showing soft tannins and a hint of spicy wood, along with aromas and flavors of ripe plums, wild berry and freshly picked mushrooms. Drink now. Score 84.

Latroun *

Located in an idyllic setting at the foothills of the Judean Mountains midway between Jerusalem and the coast, the Trappist monks at this monastery have been producing wine since their arrival from France in the 1890s. With over 400 dunams of land adjoining the monastery planted in grapes, the winery was the first to introduce Gewurztraminer, Riesling, Pinot Noir and Pinot Blanc grapes to the country and is currently producing about 300,000 bottles annually from twenty varieties of grapes.

LATROUN, CABERNET SAUVIGNON, 2004: Deep garnet red, medium-bodied, a distinctly country-style wine with simple currant and berry aromas and flavors. Drink now. Score 83.

LATROUN, CABERNET SAUVIGNON, 2003: Dark royal purple in color, medium to full-bodied and with plenty of alcohol and chunky tannins, this country-style wine offers up appealing berry, currant and herbal aromas and flavors. Drink now. Score 84.

LATROUN, MERLOT, 2004: Royal purple, medium-bodied, with chunky tannins and simple berry-cherry aromas and flavors. Drink up. Score 79.

LATROUN, MERLOT, 2003: Light to medium-bodied, cherry red, with somewhat coarse tannins and stingy fruits. Drink up. Score 77.

LATROUN, PINOT NOIR, 2004: Dark ruby in color, medium-bodied, with soft tannins. An odd sour aroma and flavor tends to hide the plum and berry fruits here. Drink up. Score 79.

LATROUN, PINOT NOIR, 2003: Deep ruby toward garnet in color, medium-bodied, with soft tannins but marred by somewhat stingy fruits and slightly exaggerated acidity. Drink now. Score 84.

LATROUN, GRENACHE, 2003: A light rosé wine, with perhaps too much residual sweetness and alcohol, and not nearly enough fruits. Drink up. Score 74.

LATROUN, CHARDONNAY, 2004: Medium-bodied, light golden in color, with pineapple and citrus fruits. A pleasant quaffer. Drink up. Score 84.

LATROUN, CHARDONNAY, 2003: Golden straw in color, medium-bodied, with generous citrus and tropical fruits and good acidity to keep it lively. Drink now. Score 84.

LATROUN, SAUVIGNON BLANC, 2004: As light in color as in body, and dominated by grapefruit and bitter orange aromas and flavors. Drink up. Score 76.

LATROUN, SAUVIGNON BLANC, 2003: Pale golden straw in color, medium-bodied and crisply dry, but overly dominated by grapefruit aromas and flavors. Drink up. Score 78.

LATROUN, DRY RIESLING, 2003: Straw colored, light to medium-bodied and with appealing citrus, mineral and floral aromas. Drink now. Score 81.

LATROUN, RIESLING, SEMI-DRY, 2003: Honey colored and with far too much sweetness that tends to hide whatever fruit and mineral flavors that might be found here. Drink up. Score 74.

LATROUN, GEWURZTRAMINER, 2004: Light gold in color, medium-bodied and with generous aromas and flavors of citrus and summer fruit. Not traditional for Gewurztraminer . Drink now. Score 84.

LATROUN, GEWURZTRAMINER, 2003: A pleasant enough light to medium-bodied white but lacking litchis or any other aromas and flavors typical of this variety. Drink now. Score 83.

LATROUN, PINOT BLANC, 2003: Pale straw in color, light to medium-bodied, with citrus and floral notes. Drink up. Score 77.

Lavie **

Located in the community of Ephrata not far from Jerusalem, owner-wine-maker Asher Lavie's first wine was from the 2002 vintage. Drawing largely on grapes from the Jerusalem Mountains, the winery is currently producing about 1,000 bottles annually.

LAVIE, CABERNET SAUVIGNON, 2002: Deep purple in color, this medium-bodied oak-aged wine shows clean and appealing aromas and flavors of blackberries, currants and spices on the first attack, those then complemented by light overtones of spices and green olives. A solid first effort. Drink now. Score 85. K

Maccabim**

Founded in 2002 by Eytan Rosenthal, Gari Hochwald, Yo'av Heller and Ami Dotan in the community of Maccabim, at the foothills of the Jerusalem Mountains, and drawing grapes from that area as well as from the Galilee and the Ella Valley, this start-up winery's first release was of 1,200 lightly oak-aged bottles of Cabernet Sauvignon. The winery released 3,000 bottles from the 2003 vintage, those including their first Merlot.

MACCABIM, CABERNET SAUVIGNON, 2003: Dark ruby towards garnet, medium-bodied, with gentle oak influences and appealing currant and wild berry fruits. On the moderately-long finish look for hints of spices and vanilla. Drink now. Score 84. **K**

MACCABIM, CABERNET SAUVIGNON, BIN 9, 2002: Dark cherry red toward garnet in color, this medium-bodied, lightly oaked red shows soft tannins and appealing cherry-berry and currant fruits along with hints of spicy oak. Refreshing and pleasant. Drink up. Score 84. **K**

MACCABIM, MERLOT, 2003: Garnet red, medium-bodied, with soft tannins integrating nicely to reveal cassis, plum and berry fruits on a lightly herbal background. Drink now. Score 84. **K**

Maor *

Established by Danny Maor on Moshav Ramot on the Golan Heights, the winery's first release was of 3,200 bottles from the 2003 vintage. Current production is about 10,000 bottles annually and drawing on grapes from the Golan Heights and the Upper Galilee, those including Cabernet Sauvignon, Merlot, Syrah, and Cabernet Franc, the winery plans to release 30,000 bottles by the 2008 vintage.

MAOR, CABERNET SAUVIGNON, 2003: Deep, almost impenetrable royal purple in color, full-bodied and concentrated, with rather firm tannins and a somewhat heavy hand with the oak, the wine shows aromas and flavors of very ripe plums and berries as well as hints of mocha and chocolate in the background. Somewhat tight. Drink now. Score 85.

Margalit ✶✶✶✶✶

Among the first boutique wineries in the country, and the first to capture the imagination of sophisticated wine lovers. Founded in 1989, it was first located in Moshav Kfar Bilu near the town of Rehovot, and since 1994 has been set in a larger winery near the town of Hadera, at the foothills of Mount Carmel. Father and son team Ya'ir and Assaf Margalit are most renowned for their Bordeaux-style reds that are released in both a regular and a reserve series. In his role as a physical chemist, Ya'ir Margalit has published several well-known textbooks. Assaf, who studied in the agriculture faculty of Hebrew University at Rehovot, also trained in California.

Margalit's earliest release, in 1989, was of 900 bottles of Cabernet Sauvignon. More recent releases, including Cabernet, Merlot, Petite Sirah and Syrah are made primarily from grapes in their own vineyards in Kadita in the Upper Galilee, while the Cabernet Franc is grown in their Binyamina vineyard. Starting with the 2003 harvest, the winery released Enigma, its first Bordeaux-style blend. Most definitely not a second wine but one that stands on its own within the Margalit repertoire. Production, including the occasional Chardonnay, currently varies at between 17,000–21,000 bottles annually.

2003
Cabernet Sauvignon
Special Reserve
Kadita · Single Vineyard
C. Sauvignon 87% / Petite Sirah 13%
Galilee Mountains / Product of Israel

Special Reserve

SPECIAL RESERVE, CABERNET SAUVIGNON, 2004: Still in embryonic form and not yet even a final blend but already showing balance and structure necessary for aging. Full-bodied, with still firm tannins that promise to integrate nicely, sweet oak, and tempting aromas and flavors of blackcurrants, chocolate, espresso, purple plums and Mediterranean herbs. Best 2008–2012. Tentative Score 90–92.

SPECIAL RESERVE, CABERNET SAUVIGNON, 2003: Rich, ripe and concentrated, with layer after layer of dark plum, currant, anise, mocha, black cherrries and sage. An oak-aged blend of Cabernet Sauvignon and Petite Sirah (87% and 13% respectively), this distinctly Old World wine has excellent balance between wood, lively acidity and well-integrated tannins. Complex and long. Best 2008- 2013. Score 93.

SPECIAL RESERVE, CABERNET SAUVIGNON, 2002: This blend of 80% Cabernet Sauvignon, 12% Petite Sirah and 8% Cabernet Franc is remarkably concentrated, intense, and heavy enough to chew, but through its muscles shows great elegance. Ripe currants, spices and cedar flavors on a complex leathery core and a long intense finish make this a wine difficult to match with food but excellent on its own or with fine aged cheeses. Drink now–2012. Score 93.

SPECIAL RESERVE, CABERNET SAUVIGNON, 2001: Dense and concentrated, this firmly tannic, full-bodied and rich blend of 85% Cabernet Sauvignon and 15% of Margalit's very special Petite Sirah needs time to develop, but as it does look for multiple layers of currants, wild berries, plums and black cherries along with toasty oak, minerals and just the right hints of earthiness and sage on the very long finish. Drink now–2012. Score 94.

SPECIAL RESERVE, CABERNET SAUVIGNON, 2000: Delicious, complex and so deep in color that it is almost black, this remarkably full-bodied, deep and concentrated blend of 80% Cabernet Sauvignon, 15% Petite Sirah and 5% Merlot boasts earthy currant, sage, black cherry and cedary oak flavors. As it develops look for coffee and tobacco notes. Drink now–2010. Score 93.

SPECIAL RESERVE, CABERNET SAUVIGNON, 1999: Harmonious, dense and tannic, this full-bodied and elegant blend of 87% Cabernet Sauvignon and 13% Carignan offers tempting spices and ripe fruit aromas and flavors of currants, plums, chocolate and coffee. Drink now–2012. Score 93.

SPECIAL RESERVE, CABERNET SAUVIGNON, 1998: This blend of 90% Cabernet Sauvignon and 10% remarkably concentrated Petite Sirah offers up a luxurious mouthful of ripe black cherry, currant, anise and plum flavors. Dark, hearty, rich and tannic, the wine is now beginning to turn silky and polished and has a long, mouth-filling finish. Drink now–2009. Score 92.

SPECIAL RESERVE, CABERNET SAUVIGNON, 1997: A blend of 85% Cabernet Sauvignon and 15% of the very special Petite Sirah that Margalit has managed to isolate and cultivate, this ripe, complex and full-bodied red has a lovely balance between currant, black cherry, spice, chocolate and cedary oak flavors, all of which seem to burst forth and blend together on the palate. Its once rough tannins are now integrating nicely and the wine shows a long, mouth-filling finish. Drink now–2008. Score 93.

SPECIAL RESERVE, CABERNET SAUVIGNON, 1995: Having lost its youthful rough edges, this full-bodied and harmonious wine now shows well-integrated tannins blending nicely with deep oak, tobacco, cherry and spicy flavors. Drink now. Score 91.

SPECIAL RESERVE, CABERNET SAUVIGNON, 1994: From a problematic vintage, and thus lacking the concentration and intensity felt in the 1993 wine, but still showing tempting currant, plum and berry aromas and flavors, those on a background of smoky oak and fresh forest. Somewhat past its peak. Drink up. Score 89.

SPECIAL RESERVE, CABERNET SAUVIGNON, 1993: Deep violet toward garnet, this remains one of Margalit's finest efforts. A blend of Cabernet Sauvignon with 15% of an extraordinarily deep and smooth Petite Sirah that Margalit found almost accidentally in a partially abandoned vineyard, this full-bodied wine boasts multiple layers of blackcurrants, dried fruits and vanilla as well as violets and plums. This seductive, tempting and well-structured wine with an appealing earthy-herbal finish is somewhat past its peak now. Drink up. Score 92.

Margalit

MARGALIT, CABERNET SAUVIGNON, 2003: Full-bodied and intense, but rich and well balanced, this blend of 88% Cabernet Sauvignon and 12% Cabernet Franc, both from the Kadita vineyard, is loaded with complex earthy currant, black cherry, anise and mocha aromas and flavors, those well set off by generous but smooth tannins. Look for an appealing leathery sensation on the long finish. Drink now–2012. Score 91.

MARGALIT, CABERNET SAUVIGNON, 2002: This full-bodied, well-balanced blend of 85% Cabernet Sauvignon, 8% Merlot and 7% Cabernet Franc is concentrated, its once firm tannins softening now and showing tempting aromas and flavors of blackcurrants, berries and game meat, together with a long finish. A complex and sophisticated wine. Drink now–2008. Score 92.

MARGALIT, CABERNET SAUVIGNON, 2001: A distinctly Old World wine, this dark, dense and richly flavored oak-aged blend of 90% Cabernet Sauvignon and 10% Merlot has generous currant, blackberry, sage and mineral aromas and flavors. Still firm tannins but those integrating nicely now, showing structure and balance that bodes well for future development. The long finish yields tempting coffee, dark chocolate and hints of licorice and mint. Drink now–2012. Score 93.

MARGALIT, CABERNET SAUVIGNON, LOT 37, 2001: Vastly different in style from every other Margalit wine released to date. The wine was aged in *barriques* for 2 years (all of Margalit's other wines have been aged for only 1 year), the blackcurrants that typify so many of the wines of this winery have been replaced here by plums, and the often-searing tannins that sometimes take years to integrate in the usual releases are already soft and well integrated and are now showing a sweet and dusty nature. All in all, a fascinating wine. Drink now–2012. Score 92.

MARGALIT, CABERNET SAUVIGNON, 2000: This full-bodied, still tannic blend of 88% Cabernet Sauvignon and 12% Merlot still has some rough edges but is finally beginning to come into its own. Look for an abundance of raspberry, black cherry, sage, and spicy aromas and flavors, all with delicious leathery, cedar wood overtones. Drink now–2008. Score 91.

MARGALIT, CABERNET SAUVIGNON, 1999: A blend of 84% Cabernet Sauvignon, 12% Merlot and 4% Petite Sirah, this oaked, full-bodied, ripe and complex wine shows good balance between wood and ripe cherry and berry flavors that all come together in a long finish. Drink now–2008. Score 92.

MARGALIT, CABERNET SAUVIGNON, 1998: A blend of 90% Cabernet and 10% Merlot, this chewy, full-bodied red is packed with spicy currant and blueberry flavors alongside notes of pepper and cola for additional dimension. Still showing youthful and firm tannins, but those now softening and rounding off nicely. Drink now–2010. Score 91.

MARGALIT, CABERNET SAUVIGNON, 1997: Deep garnet-purple, this full-bodied blend of 85% Cabernet Sauvignon, 13% Merlot and 2% Petite Sirah has a complex core of currant, spices and cedar flavors along with hints of anise, tobacco and ripe cherries. Good balance, now well-integrated tannins and a long finish. Drink now–2008. Score 92.

MARGALIT, CABERNET SAUVIGNON, 1996: Full-bodied but neither as tannic nor as heavy as some of Margalit's earlier efforts. Deep garnet red now, this distinctly Bordeaux-style red shows good balance between fruits, tannins and acidity, and is fleshy, elegant and long. Drink now. Score 91.

MARGALIT, CABERNET SAUVIGNON, 1995: Medium to full-bodied, with soft and well-integrated tannins and generous aromas and flavors of black fruits, coffee and tobacco along with earthy-herbal notes, this well-balanced and well-structured wine offers up a generous mouthful. At its peak now and not meant for further cellaring. Drink up. Score 91.

MARGALIT, CABERNET SAUVIGNON, 1994: Reflecting an overall poor vintage year, this wine is much lighter in style than Margalit's earlier efforts. Despite that, during its heyday the wine showed a deep purple color and intense blackcurrant aromas and flavors on a background of black pepper. Somewhat past its peak so drink up. Score 89.

MARGALIT, CABERNET SAUVIGNON, 1993: One of the best Cabernet wines ever made in Israel, this deep, concentrated and remarkably full-bodied wine was backward in its youth but when it did come into its own revealed delicious black and red fruits including cherries, plums and currants, as well as generous overtones of chocolate and cedar. Somewhat past its peak. Drink up. Score 92.

MARGALIT, CABERNET SAUVIGNON, 1992: Margalit's only disappointing effort. The wine is far too one-dimensional. Lacking balance, its aromas are too musky and it is now clearly well past its peak and no longer scoreable.

MARGALIT, CABERNET SAUVIGNON, 1991: Whether this or Margalit's 1993 Cabernet is the best wine they ever produced is still debated. With a clean, intense bouquet, deep color and complex mouth-filling flavors, this concentrated and tannic wine is holding its peak nicely but not for much longer. Drink up. Score 94

MARGALIT, CABERNET SAUVIGNON, 1990: Full-bodied, fragrant and rich, the wine still shows deep fruits and hints of cloves, cinnamon and oak, as well as good balance between soft tannins and low acidity, but is somewhat past its peak. Drink up. Score 90.

MARGALIT, CABERNET SAUVIGNON, 1989: At its best this was a seductive, complex and elegant wine with remarkable color and intense aromas and flavors of black fruits, chocolate and cigar box all on a velvety, almost chewy texture. Now past its peak and no longer scoreable.

MARGALIT, MERLOT, 2002: Full-bodied, deep purple toward inky black in color and blended with 10% Cabernet Sauvignon to add backbone, this ripe, bold and delicious wine shows well-integrated tannins that give it a welcome softness, those matched nicely by aromas and flavors of plums, currants and black cherries, and a long spicy and cedar-flavored finish. Drink now–2012. Score 92.

MARGALIT, MERLOT, 2001: This complex, intense and well-balanced 85% Merlot and 15% Cabernet Sauvignon blend has abundant soft tannins and plenty of earthy and mineral notes overlaying spicy currant, wild berry and coffee aromas and flavors. Look for a long lingering finish with an array of hazelnuts, coffee and anise. Drink now–2010. Score 91.

MARGALIT, MERLOT, 2000: Remarkably tannic for a Merlot, this full-bodied wine which also contains 10% of Cabernet Sauvignon grapes is rich, ripe and concentrated, with layer after layer of currants, plums and black cherries, all with generous hints of tobacco, smoky oak and vanilla. Drink now–2008. Score 92.

MARGALIT, MERLOT, 1999: With smooth tannins and rich flavors that fill the mouth and then linger nicely, this well-balanced, full-bodied, bold, ripe and delicious wine shows layer after layer of plum, currant, and black cherry flavors as well as a long finish on which you will find nice herbal overtones. Drink now. Score 90.

MARGALIT, MERLOT, 1998: A full-bodied blend of 87% Merlot, 10% Cabernet Sauvignon and 3% Petite Sirah, with layers of ripe, spicy black cherry, currant, plum and mineral aromas and flavors. This rich, smooth, elegant and complex wine has remarkable depth and concentration. Drink now. Score 90.

MARGALIT, MERLOT, 1997: Bold, ripe and delicious, with multiple layers of plum, currant and black cherry aromas and flavors, smooth, nicely polished tannins, and a rich, deep finish. Drink now. Score 91.

MARGALIT, MERLOT, 1995: With a core of black cherry, currant, tea, herb and cedary oak flavors, this well-balanced, full-bodied and elegant red has ripe, well-rounded tannins and a long finish. Drink up. Score 90.

MARGALIT, CABERNET FRANC, 2003: Almost impenetrable deep purple in color, full-bodied, with excellent balance between soft, almost luxurious tannins and a tempting array of dark plum, wild berry and herbal aromas and flavors. Oak-aged, with the addition of 10% of Cabernet Sauvignon, the wine is mouthfilling and long, showing a tantalizing hint of mint on the finish. Drink now–2010. Score 90.

MARGALIT, CABERNET FRANC, 2002: This deep royal purple, full-bodied, concentrated Cabernet Franc with 12% Cabernet Sauvignon blended in, shows aromas and flavors of spicy plums and earthiness on first attack that yield to an array of currant, anise, chocolate and sweet cedar, all coming together in a long mouth-filling finish. The wine has soft tannins, generous oak, plenty of acidity and overall good balance. Drink now–2010. Score 92.

MARGALIT, CABERNET FRANC, 2001: This full-bodied, heavily oaked blend of 90% Cabernet Franc and 10% Cabernet Sauvignon is at the same time seductive, well balanced and supple. The wine has generous cherry, anise and currant fruits along with spicy and toasty aromas and flavors and a generous hint of mocha. The long finish boasts earthy and cedar wood flavors typical of the best wines made from this variety. Drink now–2009. Score 91.

MARGALIT, CARIGNAN, 1999: A delightful surprise because Carignan rarely produces a fine wine on its own. This full-bodied wine which also contains 5% of Cabernet Sauvignon grapes to round it out is still young, but given time to open in the glass it will burst with raspberry and chocolate flavors and an almost floral bouquet. Drink now. Score 90.

2003
ENIGMA
Red Table Wine
C. Sauvignon 70% / Merlot 18% / C. Franc 12%
Galilee Mountains / Product of Israel

MARGALIT, ENIGMA, 2003: Containing 70% Cabernet Sauvignon, 18% Merlot and 12% of Cabernet Franc, this is the first true Bordeaux-style blend from the winery. Rich, ripe and polished, remarkably round and approachable even in this stage, the wine is already showing complex currant, plum and wild berry aromas and flavors, those well focused and long. Drink now–2010. Score 91.

MARGALIT, CHARDONNAY, 2001: This complex, full-bodied white, fermented in new oak barrels and developed *sur lie* shows ripe tropical fruits, citrus, toasty oak flavors and aromas, all coming together in a long fruit-rich finish. Drink now. Score 90.

MARGALIT, CHARDONNAY, 2000: Complex and full-bodied, the wine at first shows generous ripe pear, citrus, spice, hazelnut and honey flavors, those making way for appealing hints of minerals and earth on the palate. Rich and elegant, with just the right touch of oak. Drink now. Score 90.

MARGALIT, CHARDONNAY, 1998: At its best this full-bodied, earthy and mineral-rich wine was smooth, supple and ripe, with citrus, melon and ripe pear fruits and a spicy-honeyed finish. Now beyond its peak and no longer scoreable.

Meishar ★★★

Founded in 1991 by Ze'ev and Chaya Smilansky on Moshav Meishar in the southern coastal plains, this small winery relies entirely on its own vineyards of Cabernet Sauvignon, Merlot, Shiraz and Muscat grapes and currently produces about 6,000 bottles annually of red wines in a reserve and in a Meishar series.

Reserve

RESERVE 730, CABERNET SAUVIGNON, 2002: Medium to full-bodied, dark garnet red, with still firm tannins but those starting to integrate nicely to reveal aromas and flavors of smoky oak, all well balanced with black fruits, Oriental spices and hints of chocolate and cigar tobacco on the moderately-long finish. Drink now–2007. Score 88.

RESERVE 730, CABERNET SAUVIGNON, 2001: Dark cherry red toward garnet in color, this medium to full-bodied Cabernet was blended with 4% of Merlot to round it out. Its generous tannins balanced nicely with wood and fruits, the wine shows aromas and flavors of red currants and berries together with smoky oak and anise, as well as chocolate and mocha on the long finish. Drink now–2007. Score 90.

RESERVE, CABERNET SAUVIGNON, 2000: Medium to full-bodied, with a rich array of berry, currant and plum fruits on a spicy oak background, the wine has good balance and tannins that are integrating nicely, as well as a long near-sweet finish. Drink now–2008. Score 89.

RESERVE 730, CABERNET SAUVIGNON, 1999: A blend of Cabernet Sauvignon and Merlot, with the Cabernet dominating and now showing ripe blackcurrants and cherries along with tempting spicy and cedar aromas and flavors. Good balance between oak, fruits and smooth tannins, as well as a comfortably long finish. Drink now. Score 90.

RESERVE, CABERNET SAUVIGNON, 1998: Medium to full-bodied, ripe and intense, with good balance between soft tannins and generous black cherry, currant, plum and anise flavors, those complemented nicely by light toasty oak. Supple and harmonious, the wine borders on elegance. Drink now. Score 88.

Meishar

MEISHAR, CABERNET SAUVIGNON, 2004: Dark garnet in color, medium to full-bodied, with generous but soft tannins and smoky oak opening nicely to reveal aromas and flavors of blackcurrants, purple plums, white chocolate and spices. Long and mouthfilling. Drink from release–2009. Tentative Score 88–90.

MEISHAR, CABERNET SAUVIGNON, 2003: Medium to full-bodied, with soft tannins and appealing currant and black cherry fruits set off nicely by hints of vanilla and spices. Drink now–2009. Score 89.

MEISHAR, CABERNET SAUVIGNON, 2002: Deep ruby toward garnet in color, full-bodied and with surprisingly soft tannins. Black cherry, currant and plum fruits here, along with generous vanilla. An appealing wine, but lacking the depth or balance for more than short-term cellaring. Drink now–2007. Score 87.

MEISHAR, CABERNET SAUVIGNON, 2001: Deep garnet, with generous but well-integrated tannins balanced nicely by smoky oak, this medium-bodied red offers up appealing plum, black cherry and blackcurrant aromas and flavors. Look as well for a hint of Oriental spices on the finish. Drink now–2007. Score 88.

MEISHAR, CABERNET SAUVIGNON, 2000: This firm, intense and well-balanced red reveals currant and toasty oak flavors on a not overly imposing background of herbs and earthiness. Drink now. Score 88.

MEISHAR, CABERNET SAUVIGNON, 1999: Medium to full-bodied and with spicy, toasty oak flavors overlaying currant, berry and cherry flavors, the wine has a strong tannic finish. Drink up. Score 88.

MEISHAR, CABERNET SAUVIGNON, 1998: A medium to full-bodied blend of 75% Cabernet Sauvignon and 25% Merlot with blackcurrant and black cherry fruits on a background of Mediterranean herbs, spices and more recently hints of earthiness and tobacco. Drink up. Score 87.

MEISHAR, CABERNET SAUVIGNON, 1997: Deep purple and showing signs of browning, but still has good mineral and black fruit aromas and flavors together with now fully integrated tannins. Somewhat past its peak. Drink up. Score 86.

MEISHAR, CABERNET SAUVIGNON, 1996: Medium to full-bodied, now fully mature but with still attractive and lively plum, cherry and currant fruits, those now overlaid by hints of dill, Mediterranean herbs and spicy oak. Somewhat past its peak. Drink up. Score 87.

MEISHAR, MERLOT, 2003: Brick-red, the color reflecting the wine's extreme youth, it has the potential to develop beautifully. Medium to full-bodied, with still-firm tannins that need time to settle down, but under those tempting plum and black cherry fruits and an appealing hint of licorice and chocolate. Drink now–2009. Score 89.

MEISHAR, MERLOT, 2002: Blended with 15% of Cabernet Sauvignon, this deep ruby toward garnet and full-bodied red shows good balance between firm but already well-integrating tannins, wood and fruits. Look for appealing plum, berry and blackcurrant fruits together with generous overlays of smoke and spices. Drink now–2008. Score 89.

MEISHAR, MERLOT, 1996: Soft and supple and with an attractive array of cherry, currant and cedar aromas in its youth, becoming somewhat tannic and austere as it has matured. Somewhat past its peak. Drink up. Score 85.

MEISHAR, CHARDONNAY, 2002: Medium to full-bodied, generously oaked, with a buttery texture and aromas and flavors that include grassy-floral overtones together with citrus and pineapple. Good balancing acidity keeps the wine lively. Drink up. Score 87.

MEISHAR, TACSUM, 2003: Perhaps the winemakers were in a playful mood when they named this wine by spelling "Muscat" backward. Made from Muscat-Canelli grapes that were sun-dried and then frozen before pressing, this is a wine as much in the Italian *appasimento* style as it is an ice wine. Not so much full-bodied as it is "thick", the wine shows unabashed sweetness and a dark, burnished bronze color. Good balancing acidity and flavors of apricots, ripe peaches and honeydew melon keep it lively. Drink now–2009. Score 89.

Meister ∗

קברנה סוביניון
יין אדום יבש

m
e
i
s
t
e
r

מ
י
י
ס
ט
ר

2004
יקב מייסטר

13% אלכוהול-ראש פינה- תכולה 750 מ"ל

Founded by Ya'akov Meister in Rosh Pina and drawing on grapes from his own vineyards as well as from other Galilee vineyards, this small winery released its first wines to the market in 2003. The winery is currently producing about 2,000 bottles of Cabernet Sauvignon annually and will be releasing about 6,000 from the 2005 vintage.

MEISTER, CABERNET SAUVIGNON, 2004: Developed partly in used wood barrels and partly in stainless steel with the addition of oak chips, this medium-bodied, somewhat cloudy dark garnet wine shows chunky tannins and only skimpy berry and black-cherry fruits. Drink from release. Tentative Score 73–75.

MEISTER, CABERNET SAUVIGNON, 2003: Despite its youth the wine is already oxidizing, caramel and chocolate flavors dominating whatever black fruits struggle to make themselves felt. Coarse and biting. Score 65.

Meron ***

Founded in 1987 in Mitzpe Charashim in the Upper Galilee, this was the first true boutique winery in the country. Relying primarily on Cabernet Sauvignon, Merlot, and occasionally on Chardonnay grapes drawn largely from Kerem Ben Zimra and a small amount from his own vineyard, part owner and winemaker Alex Bertan was producing about 6,000 bottles annually until the winery ceased production in 2004.

MERON, CABERNET SAUVIGNON, 2000: Perhaps the best wine ever from this winery. Dark, ripe, intense and spicy, with good balance between already well-integrating tannins and sweet cedar flavors from the oak, those blended nicely with cassis, berry and plum fruits. Look as well for hints of Mediterranean herbs on the mouth-filling finish. Drink now–2008. Score 90.

MERON, CABERNET SAUVIGNON, 1999: A well-rounded, oak-aged wine made entirely from Cabernet Sauvignon grapes. Deep royal purple in color, this medium to full-bodied red is smooth, supple and harmonious, with layers of currant, berry, and spices (look for anise and black pepper), and with good balance between tannins and hints of smoke from the oak casks. Drink now–2007. Score 89.

MERON, CABERNET SAUVIGNON, 1998: Medium-bodied, with smooth tannins and currant flavors as well as a hint of tobacco, this appealing wine has a long and comfortable herbal and tea finish that lingers nicely. Drink up. Score 87.

MERON, CABERNET SAUVIGNON, 1997: After two and a half years in small French oak casks, this deep royal purple wine is concentrated and full-bodied, showing polished tannins that complement currant, cherry, chocolate and herbal aromas and flavors. Complex on the palate and with an appealing peppery and cedar wood finish. Drink now. Score 89.

MERON, CABERNET SAUVIGNON, 1996: With generous blackcurrants, black cherries and overlays of spices (look especially for allspice and pepper), this appealing wine is now at its peak, its tannins softened and well integrated, with a long mouth-filling finish. Somewhat past its peak. Drink up. Score 87.

MERON, CABERNET SAUVIGNON, 1995: As it has been since its youth, a well-balanced, soft, round and fruity wine with just enough firm tannins and herbal notes to give it character. Past its peak. Drink up. Score 86.

MERON, CABERNET SAUVIGNON, 1994: Medium to heavy-bodied and with intrinsic good balance between tannins, acids, fruits, oak and tobacco flavors. Well past its peak and no longer scoreable.

MERON, CABERNET SAUVIGNON, 1993: During its youth and at its peak this was a rich, well-balanced wine but now it is well past its peak and no longer scoreable.

MERON, MERLOT, 2000: Very generously oaked and tannic for a Merlot, the wine opens slowly to reveal currant, oak and spicy flavors. Drink now. Score 88.

MERON, CHARDONNAY 1999: Fresh, fruity and lightly *frizzante* when well chilled, still showing fig, pear and melon flavors but past its peak and now somewhat dominated by earthy-mineral notes. Drink up. Score 86.

Miles **

Founded by vintner Eyal Miles in 2001 on Moshav Kerem Ben Zimra in the Upper Galilee, with its own vineyards containing Cabernet Sauvignon, Merlot, Sauvignon Blanc and Gewurztraminer, this winery is currently producing 3,000 bottles annually.

MILES, CABERNET SAUVIGNON, 2003: A medium-bodied, quaffing wine, garnet towards purple in color, with soft tannins, red fruits and a near-sweet finish. Drink now. Score 83. K

MILES, CABERNET SAUVIGNON, 2002: Aged in oak for 14 months, this medium to full-bodied deep garnet wine shows chunky tannins, generous wood, and currant, berry and pepper aromas and flavors, those somewhat hidden under earthy and herbal notes. A pleasant country-style wine. Drink now. Score 84. K

MILES, CABERNET SAUVIGNON, 2001: A country-style oak-aged wine, perhaps too rustic, with deep earthy and herbal notes almost hiding the plum, blackberry and vanilla flavors. Not meant for further cellaring. Drink up. Score 75. K

MILES, MERLOT, 2003: Garnet towards royal-purple, medium-bodied with soft well integrated tannins and not at all complex but rewarding aromas and flavors of blackberries, black cherries and plums. A good quaffer. Drink now. Score 85. K

MILES, MERLOT, 2002: Dark cherry red toward purple, this medium-bodied moderately tannic country-style wine offers up straightforward but appealing aromas and flavors of berries and plums on a light herbal background. Drink up. Score 85. K

MILES, MERLOT, 2001: After having spent 14 months in French oak casks, this young and intense medium-bodied wine is now showing cherry, anise, currant and cedar aromas and flavors. Plenty of tannins here but those nicely integrated in a well-balanced wine. Drink up. Score 86. **K**

MILES, SAUVIGNON BLANC, 2003: A light straw-colored medium-bodied white with appealing apple, grapefruit, and pineapple fruits, a light hint of spring flowers and good balancing acidity to add liveliness. Not complex but pleasant. Drink up. Score 85. **K**

MILES, SAUVIGNON BLANC, 2002: This light golden medium-bodied wine offers up generous summer fruit, citrus and floral notes all balanced nicely by fresh acidity. Somewhat past its peak. Drink up. Score 84. **K**

MILES, GEWURZTRAMINER, 2004: Light golden straw with a hint of bronze, medium-bodied and with good balancing acidity to show off the appealing spicy tropical fruits. Drink now–2007. Score 86. **K**

Mony **

Located in the scenic foothills of the Jerusalem Mountains, on the grounds of the Dir Rafat Monastery, the winery was operated for many years by the resident monks. About three years ago the winery was transferred to the Artoul family, long-time vintners for the monastery. Grapes in the vineyards include Cabernet Sauvignon, Merlot, Zinfandel, Argaman, Petite Sirah, Chardonnay, Emerald Riesling and

other varieties. Annual production is about 22,000 bottles. The winery is currently producing wines in two series, Reserve and Mony.

Reserve

RESERVE, CABERNET SAUVIGNON, 2002: Medium to full-bodied with soft tannins, a marked but pleasant influence of smoky oak, well balanced by generous currant, berry and herbal aromas and flavors, all with a light spiciness to the moderately long finish. Not elegant but a tempting country style wine. Drink now–2007. Score 86.

RESERVE, MERLOT, 2002: Dark garnet red, medium to full-bodied, with still firm tannins but those set off nicely by spicy-smoky oak and generous currant and berry aromas and flavors. Drink now–2007. Score 85.

RESERVE, CHARDONNAY, 2003: Made entirely from Chardonnay grapes, and with 60% of the wine aged in oak, this light golden-colored wine offers clean and fresh aromas and flavors of citrus, pineapple and melons, those just spicy enough and with just enough acidity to keep the wine lively. A hint of bitter almonds on the finish adds charm. Drink now. Score 86.

Mony

MONY, CABERNET SAUVIGNON, 2003: Deep garnet red, medium to full-bodied, with firm but well-integrating tannins and with traditional Cabernet aromas and flavors of currants, berries and a hint of spicy cedar wood. Well balanced and moderately long. Drink now. Score 85.

MONY, CABERNET SAUVIGNON 2002: Somewhat cloudy dark red in color, medium-bodied and with firm tannins that tend to hide the berry and currant fruits. A simple but pleasant country-style wine. Drink up. Score 83.

MONY, MERLOT, 2003: Dark ruby towards garnet, medium to full-bodied, with firm tannins that need time to open to reveal the berry, black cherry and currant flavors that lie underneath as well as spicy oak and light herbal overlays. Drink now–2007. Score 86.

MONY, MERLOT, 2002: Deep royal purple, with soft tannins and generous smoky oak, the wine shows berry and black cherry flavors. Drink now. Score 84.

MONY, SHIRAZ, 2003: Dark cherry towards garnet red, with chunky, country-style tannins and reflecting its 12 months in oak with spices and hints of vanilla. Aromas and flavors of currants, black cherries and plums backed up by a hint of freshly tanned leather. An appealing entry-level wine. Drink now–2007. Score 84.

Nachal Amud *

Established by Avi Abu in 1998 and located on Moshav Kfar Shamai near Sefad in the Upper Galilee, the winery draws on grapes from its own vineyards, those including Cabernet Sauvignon, Cabernet Franc, Merlot and Petite Sirah. The winery produced 2,500 bottles in 2002 and double that in 2003 and 2004.

NACHAL AMUD, CABERNET SAUVIGNON, 2003: Developed partly in oak barrels and partly in glass demijohns, this unfiltered country style wine is more heavy than full-bodied and is lacking balance between its chunky tannins, high acidity and overripe fruits. Drink up. Score 72. K

NACHAL AMUD, CABERNET SAUVIGNON, 2002: With an unwanted hint of sweetness that runs throughout and with intense herbal and earthy aromas and flavors and only stingy fruits, this wine lacks balance. Score 68. K

Nachshon ✱✱✱

Founded by Ariel Padawer in 1996 on Kibbutz Nachshon in the Ayalon Valley at the foot of the Jerusalem Hills, the winery, now under the supervision of winemaker Shlomi Zadok, raises its own Cabernet Sauvignon, Merlot, Shiraz, Cabernet Franc and Argaman grapes. Current production is about 16,000 bottles annually and anticipated growth within five years is 50–60,000 bottles. Until 2003 the winery produced wines in four series, Ayalon, Sela, Alma, Pushkin and Nachshon. With the 2004 vintage, the Nachshon series was dropped.

Ayalon

AYALON, CABERNET SAUVIGNON, 2004: Tastings from two different barrels, one used French barrels and the other of new American oak, both perfectly dry but the first showing firm and almost sensually sweet tannins, a bare hint of vanilla and traditional blackcurrant fruits, the second softer and more round with comfortably yielding tannins and in addition to currant and berry fruits gentle overlays of sweet herbs and dark chocolate. Best 2007–2009. Tentative Score 87–89.

AYALON, CABERNET SAUVIGNON, 2003: Dark garnet red, medium to full-bodied, with a good touch of sweet cedar wood nicely set off by soft tannins and currant and berry fruits. Drink now–2007. Score 86.

AYALON, CABERNET SAUVIGNON, 2002: Youthful dark cherry red in color, this medium to full-bodied red shows good balance between tannins, sweet and smoky wood and berry-cherry fruits. Drink now. Score 86.

AYALON, CABERNET SAUVIGNON, 2001: Deep royal purple and medium-bodied, the wine shows moderately firm tannins and generous, perhaps overly ripe flavors of currants and berries, but is a bit heavy on the oak. Drink now. Score 84.

AYALON, CABERNET SAUVIGNON, 2000: This firmly tannic, dark-colored medium to full-bodied wine has still firm tannins but those are well balanced with the fruits. The wine needs some time to open in the glass to reveal its ripe and peppery flavors of currants, herbs and oak. Drink up. Score 86.

AYALON, MERLOT, 2004: Deep cherry-ruby red in color, medium-bodied, with soft tannins, aromas and flavors of raspberries and cherries, the wine promises to be gently oaked, well rounded and nicely balanced. Drink from release–2007. Tentative Score 86–88.

AYALON, MERLOT, 2002: Dark royal purple in color, this blend of 66% Cabernet Sauvignon and 34% Merlot shows generous sweet cedar wood, currants, and plums, all with an appealing overlay of Mediterranean herbs. Drink now. Score 85.

AYALON, MERLOT, 2001: With the addition of 4% Cabernet Sauvignon to add a bit of backbone, this deep ruby toward purple, medium to full-bodied wine shows soft tannins, Mediterranean herbs and a light earthiness overlaying blackcurrant and black cherry fruits. Shows a bit of bottle stink when first poured but this fades quickly in the glass. Drink up. Score 86.

AYALON, MERLOT, 2000: Medium to full-bodied, with herb and wild berry aromas and flavors backed up nicely by spices and mint. On the medium finish you will find mineral and smoky accents. Somewhat past its peak. Drink up. Score 85.

AYALON, SYRAH, 2004: Youthful royal-purple in color, already showing a nice touch of sweet cedar wood, with firm but nicely yielding tannins. Aromas and flavors of currants, red berries, plums and hints of vanilla-scented oak. Good balance between tannins and wood ensures medium-term aging. Drink from release–2008. Tentative Score 86–88.

AYALON, SYRAH, 2003: Medium-bodied, deep ruby in color, with soft tannins integrating well and ripe purple plum, blackberry and cherry fruits. Good balance between wood, tannins and acidity and an appealing spicy-earthy finish. Drink now–2007. Score 87.

AYALON, SYRAH, 2002: Dark purple in color, medium-bodied, with good balance between soft tannins, smoky wood, raspberries and black fruits. Moderately long. Drink now. Score 86.

AYALON, CABERNET SAUVIGNON-MERLOT, 2002: Medium-bodied, a blend of 66% Cabernet Sauvignon and 34% Merlot that spent two years in oak. Rich and round, with tannins nicely integrating and overall good balance. Drink now. Score 86.

AYALON, CABERNET SAUVIGNON-MERLOT, 2001: Showing somewhat better than earlier this medium-bodied blend of 60% Cabernet Sauvigon and 40% Merlot offers soft tannins nicely set off by ripe cherry and plum flavors as well as crisp acidity and a generous and medium-long mouth filling finish. Drink up. Score 85.

Sela

SELA, FRENCH BLEND, 2003: A blend this year of Cabernet Sauvignon, Merlot, Cabernet Franc and Syrah (37%, 33%, 25% and 5% respectively), this full-bodied red shows smooth tannins well balanced by smoky oak and aromas and flavors of raspberries and blackberries. Drink now. Score 85.

SELA, FRENCH BLEND, 2002: Dark garnet toward purple, this blend of 50% Merlot, 33% Cabernet Sauvignon, 10% Syrah and 7% Cabernet Franc is medium-bodied and moderately tannic, showing an appealing touch of oak together with currant and berry fruits. Soft and generous but lacking depth. Drink now. Score 86.

SELA, AUSTRALIAN BLEND, 2002: A blend of 60% Shiraz and 40% Cabernet Sauvignon, this bright and supple wine offers up nice smoke-tinged berry and currant flavors. It has smooth tannins, moderate use of oak, and flavors that are tight and spicy through a medium-long finish. Drink now. Score 86.

SELA RESERVE, CABERNET SAUVIGNON, 2000: With its once chunky tannins now far smoother and better integrated, this appealing, somewhat country-style red has ample currant, plum and berry fruits, plenty of spices on a gentle background of Mediterranean herbs, and hints of tobacco on the finish. Drink up. Score 85.

SELA, MERLOT-CABERNET SAUVIGNON, 2001: An oak-aged blend of 50% each of Merlot and Cabernet Sauvignon. Low in both tannins and acidity, with the oak somehow dominating the too stingy berry and cherry aromas and flavors. Drink up. Score 80.

Alma

ALMA, CABERNET SAUVIGNON-MERLOT, 2001: Dark royal purple, medium-bodied, with smooth tannins and generous currant, plum, mint and tobacco flavors. Drink up. Score 85.

Nachshon

NACHSHON, CABERNET SAUVIGNON-MERLOT, 2002: A simple country-style wine with chunky tannins and a somewhat coarse influence of the wood and skimpy black fruits. Drink up. Score 84.

NACHSHON, CABERNET SAUVIGNON-MERLOT, 2000: Medium bodied, smooth, with well-integrated tannins, those nicely balanced by currant, plum and tobacco aromas and flavors. Drink up. Score 84.

NACHSHON, MERLOT, 2002: Medium-dark garnet in color, medium-bodied with soft, well-integrated tannins and appealing blackberry, currant and cherry fruits. Look for hints of Oriental spices on the moderately-long finish. Drink now. Score 86.

NACHSHON, MERLOT, 2000: Garnet toward purple in color, this medium-bodied oak-aged wine shows good balance between soft tannins, natural acidity and fruits. Look for plums, currants and berries on a lightly spicy background. Drink up. Score 85.

NACHSHON, MERLOT, 1999: Dominated by earthy and herbal aromas and flavors and a touch of unwanted bitterness, the wine does not have nearly enough fruits. Showing age. Score 72.

NACHSHON, YOUNG MERLOT, 1999: With unusual and unwelcome flavors of milk and cooked herbs that hide its fruitiness, this wine is now showing age and no longer scoreable.

NACHSHON, ARGAMAN DESSERT WINE, 2003: As most wines produced from Argaman grapes, deep ruby towards garnet in color. The wine has far too much cloying sugar and not nearly enough fruit or balancing acidity. Drink now. Score 72.

Pushkin

NACHSHON, PUSHKIN, 2004: A deep garnet red, medium-bodied blend of 60% Cabernet Sauvignon, 30% Merlot, 6% Argaman and 4% Syrah, with light oak influence, soft tannins and appealing berry-cherry and currant fruits. Not a long but a pleasant finish with wild berries and hints of sage and tar. Drink now. Score 86.

NACHSHON, PUSHKIN, 2002: Medium-bodied, this oak-aged blend of Cabernet Sauvignon and Merlot offers up clean, round flavors of currants and berries on a lightly tannic and spicy background. Drink now. Score 84.

NACHSHON, PUSHKIN, 2001: A medium-bodied blend of Cabernet Sauvignon and Merlot with soft tannins and fresh black fruits. Drink up. Score 84.

NACHSHON, PUSHKIN, 2000: This simple light to medium-bodied Merlot-Cabernet blend has a deep ruby color and aromas and flavors of raspberries, cranberries and currants. Well beyond its peak and no longer scoreable.

Nashashibi **

Owned by brothers Munir and Nashashibi Nashashibi. Located in the village of Eehbelin in the heart of the Carmel Mountains and on a site where wine has been made since Roman times, this winery is now producing 5,000 bottles annually, those from Chardonnay and Cabernet Sauvignon grapes. The winery is currently drawing on grapes from the Upper Galilee and planting their own vineyards at the foothills of the Carmel Mountains.

NASHASHIBI, CABERNET SAUVIGNON, 2003, SPECIAL RESERVE: Dark ruby towards garnet, medium to full-bodied, with soft tannins and forward berry and black cherry fruits and a hint of spices that runs throughout. Drink now. Score 85.

NASHASHIBI, CABERNET SAUVIGNON, 2002, SPECIAL RESERVE: Perhaps not truly up to the title of "Special Reserve" but a nice effort. Medium to full-bodied with rich aromas and flavors of blackcurrants, chocolate and tobacco, the wine is mouth-filling and moderately long. Drink now. Score 85.

NASHASHIBI, CABERNET SAUVIGNON, 2001, SPECIAL RESERVE: Dark garnet with some browning, medium to full-bodied with plum, currant and herbal aromas but somewhat flat on the palate. Drink now. Score 84.

NASHASHIBI, CHARDONNAY, RESERVE, 2002: Fresh, crisp and aromatic, this oak-aged white shows pineapple, green apple and melon flavors. Drink up. Score 84.

Natuf **

**CABERNET
SAUVIGNON**
2001

CONT. 750 ml   12.5 ALC by VOL

Founded by Meir Akel and Ze'ev Cinamon on Moshav Kfar Truman in the Central Plains not far from Ben Gurion Airport, this winery draws on grapes from the Ayalon Valley, and its first releases have been of Cabernet Sauvignon and a sweet, Port-style Merlot from the 2000 vintage. Currently the winery produces about 3,000 bottles annually.

NATUF, CABERNET SAUVIGNON, 2003: Ruby towards garnet red, medium-bodied, with chunky tannins and aromas and flavors of ripe berries, plums and cassis as well as a bare hint of sweet chocolate on the finish. An appealing country-style wine. Drink now. Score 85.

NATUF, CABERNET SAUVIGNON, 2002: A pleasant country-style wine, medium to full-bodied with chunky tannins, firm texture, and appealing cassis, berry and plum fruits. Drink now. Score 85.

NATUF, CABERNET SAUVIGNON, 2001: With somewhat chunky tannins, this medium to full-bodied wine offers up a pleasing berry-cherry and plum personality and good length. Drink now. Score 87.

NATUF, CABERNET SAUVIGNON, 2000: A blend of 85% Cabernet Sauvignon and 15% Merlot, this deep purple wine spent 14 months in small oak barrels and shows medium to full-body and good balance between moderate, well-integrated tannins, currants and plum fruits, as well as an appealing hint of spiciness at the end. Drink up. Score 85.

Neot Smadar **

This small winery, located in an oasis on Kibbutz Neot Smadar in the Jordan Valley, sixty kilometers north of Eilat, released their first wines from the 2001 vintage. The winery relies entirely on organically raised grapes of Cabernet Sauvignon, Merlot, Chardonnay, Sauvignon Blanc and Muscat Canelli, all grown in vineyards on the *kibbutz*. Due to the unique climate conditions, theirs is invariably the earliest harvest in the country. Winemakers Orit Idan and Anat Gan'or released about 7,000 bottles in 2002 and 6,000 in 2003 and 2004.

קברנה סוביניון
Cabernet Sauvignon
2002

יין אורגני אדום יבש
Organic Dry Red Wine

13% Alc. By Vol. 750 ml.
Prod. & bot. By Neot Semadar Wine Cellars

נאות סמדר
אורגני מן המדבר

NEOT SMADAR, CABERNET SAUVIGNON, 2003: Moderately tannic, medium-bodied and with fresh berry-cherry flavors, but somewhat flabby and lacking in liveliness, this wine raises the question of whether Cabernet Sauvignon is a good choice for lowland-desert cultivation. Drink now. Score 83.

NEOT SMADAR, CABERNET SAUVIGNON, 2002: Medium-bodied, with soft tannins and currant, cassis and light herbal-spicy aromas and flavors. Drink now. Score 84.

NEOT SMADAR, MERLOT, 2003: Medium to full-bodied, deep royal purple in color and with generous mineral, herbal and green olive overlays. Somewhat atypical for Merlot, this wine has good balance and depth, and a surprisingly long and tannic finish. Drink now. Score 87.

NEOT SMADAR, MERLOT, 2002: Medium-bodied and rather light in color, with soft tannins and appealing black fruits, those perhaps somewhat too dominated by the wood in which the wine developed. Drink now. Score 84.

NEOT SMADAR, CABERNET SAUVIGNON-MERLOT, 2003: A blend of 85% Cabernet and 15% Merlot, still somewhat tannic and rough because of its youth, but showing good balance and a promise to reveal nice currant, berry and herbal aromas and flavors. Drink now. Score 87.

NEOT SMADAR, CHARDONNAY, 2003: Light golden straw in color, this medium-bodied, gently oaked Chardonnay shows refined citrus, green apple and pineapple fruits, those complemented nicely by crisp acidity and appealing mineral undertones. Drink up. Score 86.

NEOT SMADAR, CHARDONNAY, 2002: This pleasant light-gold colored medium-bodied white has clean and refreshing citrus and green apple fruits along with a nice hint of spiciness. Past its peak. Drink up. Score 85.

NEOT SMADAR, CHARDONNAY, 2001: Lacking the typical traits of Chardonnay grapes, but light and fruity in its youth, the wine is now showing age. Score 70.

NEOT SMADAR, SAUVIGNON BLANC FUME, 2003: Golden straw in color, medium-bodied and reflecting just the right hint of smoky-toasted oak on a background of grassy and citrus aromas and flavors. Drink up. Score 85.

NEOT SMADAR, SAUVIGNON BLANC, 2003: Light golden straw in color, this light to medium-bodied wine offers up appealing peach and melon fruits along with mineral-crisp acidity. Drink up. Score 83.

NEOT SMADAR, SAUVIGNON BLANC, 2001: Light to medium-bodied, with appealing summer fruit and apple aromas and flavors on a lightly spicy background. Somewhat past its peak. Drink up. Score 84.

NE'OT SMADAR, MUSCAT, 2002: Light to medium-bodied, with generous underlying sweetness to dried apricot and honeyed fruits, and with good balancing acidity, this is an appealing aperitif or dessert wine. Drink up. Score 85.

NE'OT SMADAR, MUSCAT, 2001: Sweet, flowery and with plenty of tropical fruits, the wine has a honeyed-caramelized nose, but lacks balance, depth or breadth. Score 65.

Odem Mountain ✦✦✦

Founded by Michael Elfasi and his sons Adam and Yishay in 2003 and situated in a newly constructed and thoroughly modern facility on Moshav Odem in the northern Golan Heights, the winery relies on grapes grown in its own vineyards, including one organic vineyard, as well as from other vineyards on the Golan and in the Upper Galilee. Currently producing wines based on Cabernet Sauvignon and Merlot, the winery is considering future releases of Sauvignon Blanc and Pinot Noir. Production for 2003 was 6,500 bottles and for 2004 about 24,000. Current target production is 30,000 bottles. Wines are currently being produced in a Reserve series, the mid-range Nimrod and Odem Mountain series' and the Volcanic label for wines made from organic grapes.

Reserve

RESERVE, CABERNET SAUVIGNON, 2004: Dark garnet towards black in color, full-bodied and already reflecting soft tannins and moderate wood influence. Traditional Cabernet Sauvignon aromas and flavors of blackcurrants and blackberries come together with hints of lead-pencil and sweet cedar. Best from 2007–2009. Tentative Score 88–90.

RESERVE, CABERNET SAUVIGNON, 2003: Dark ruby towards garnet in color, medium to full-bodied, with generous tannins and wood influence now starting to integrate. Needs time in the glass to open but when it does look for appealing black fruits, spices and chocolate leading to a long and mouthfilling finish. Drink now–2007. Score 87.

RESERVE, MERLOT, 2004: Deep purple, with gentle spices and hints of vanilla from the oak and an appealing array of aromas and flavors that includes wild berries, black cherries, and chocolate. Long and mouthfilling. Drink from release–2008. Tentative Score 87–89.

RESERVE, MERLOT, 2003: Dark almost impenetrable garnet towards purple, medium to full-bodied, reflecting firm tannins and smoky oak from its 15 months in new and used oak *barriques*. Look for aromas and flavors of currants, plums and blueberries, those with hints of tobacco and vanilla on the finish. Drink now–2007. Score 87.

Volcanic

VOLCANIC, 2004: Fermented partly in stainless steel and then allowed to undergo malolactic fermentation in French oak *barriques*, this medium to full-bodied, deep garnet colored wine shows primarily herbal aromas and flavors when first poured but then opens nicely in the glass to reveal currant and purple plum fruits. Drink now–2007. Score 86.

Odem Mountain

ODEM MOUNTAIN, CABERNET SAUVIGNON, 2004: Medium to full-bodied, deep garnet in color, with firm tannins just starting to reside, those balanced nicely by smoky oak and aromas and flavors of blackcurrants, plums and chocolate. Drink from release–2008. Tentative Score 86–88.

ODEM MOUNTAIN, CABERNET SAUVIGNON, 2003: Deep royal purple in color, medium-bodied and reflecting its 6 months in oak with an overlay of spices and vanilla. Look for aromas and flavors of blackcurrants and blackberries on a background of citrus peel and chocolate. Drink now. Score 86.

ODEM MOUNTAIN, MERLOT, 2004: Dark garnet towards purple, medium to full-bodied, with firm tannins already integrating nicely and generous ripe plum, black cherry and berry fruits backed up nicely by hints of spices and vanilla. Drink from release–2008. Tentative Score 86–88.

ODEM MOUNTAIN, MERLOT, 2003: Medium-dark purple in color, medium to full-bodied, with well-integrating tannins and aromas and flavors of black cherries, berries and vanilla. Lacking backbone and somehow one dimensional. Drink now. Score 84.

Nimrod

NIMROD, 2004: Medium to full-bodied, with soft tannins integrating nicely, with flavors and aromas of black fruits along with hints of anise and chocolate. Round and generous. Drink from release. Tentative Score 86–88.

NIMROD, 2003: Dark ruby towards garnet in color, medium-bodied with light tannins and a bit of excess acidity, this blend of 60% Cabernet Sauvignon and 40% Merlot spent 15 months in oak. Opens nicely on the palate to reveal berry, plum and red currant fruits. A good quaffer. Drink now. Score 85.

Pelter ✴✴✴

Established in 2000 by Tel Pelter, who studied oenology and worked at several wineries in Australia, and located on Moshav Tsofit in the Sharon region, the winery receives grapes from the Jerusalem Mountains and Kerem Ben Zimra in the Upper Galilee. His releases to date have been Sauvignon Blanc and blends of Shiraz and Cabernet Sauvignon. Production in 2002 was 2,000 bottles and for 2003 and 2004 about 4,000 bottles.

PELTER, CABERNET SAUVIGNON-SHIRAZ, 2003: Deep ruby towards garnet, medium-bodied, with good balance between soft, well-integrating tannins, vanilla and herbal overtones and appealing currant, blackberry and red plum fruits. Long, but with a hint of bitterness that creeps in on the finish. Drink now. Score 86.

PELTER, CABERNET-MERLOT-CABERNET FRANC, 2002: Dark garnet in color, medium to full-bodied, and with an appealing berry-black cherry personality. Soft tannins, overall good balance, and a mouth-filling finish. Drink now. Score 86.

PELTER, SHIRAZ-CABERNET, 2002: Medium-bodied, deep garnet toward purple, this blend of 35% Shiraz and 65% Cabernet Sauvignon offers up good balance between oak, moderate tannins and black fruits, those coming together nicely with spicy and just earthy enough sensations on an appealingly sweet finish. Drink now. Score 87.

PELTER, SAUVIGNON BLANC, 2004: Light golden straw, medium-bodied, with good balancing acidity on melon, pear and citrus fruits and an appealing hint of grassiness. Drink now. Score 86.

PELTER, SAUVIGNON BLANC, 2003: Golden straw in color, this medium-bodied, crisply acidic and almost flinty-dry white offers up generous aromas and flavors of citrus and melon fruits, those on a background of a light hint of freshly mown grass. Drink up. Score 86.

PELTER, SAUVIGNON BLANC, 2002: An Australian-style blend of 90% Sauvignon Blanc and 10% Semillon, this white wine is far too light in body and color, showing stingy grassy, grapefruit and pineapple aromas and flavors, followed by a hint of grassy bitterness on the finish. Somewhat past its peak. Drink up. Score 82.

Ra'anan **

Established by Ra'anan Margalit in 1994 on Moshav Ganei Yochanan in the Southern Plains and utilizing Cabernet Sauvignon, Merlot and Chardonnay grapes from his own vineyards, those located near the winery as well as at Karmei Yosef, current production of the winery is about 8,000 bottles annually. In order to avoid confusion with the Margalit winery, the owner changed the name from Ra'anan Margalit to Ra'anan with the releases of the 2003 vintage and re-labeled several of the earlier releases.

RA'ANAN, CABERNET SAUVIGNON, RESERVE, 2003: A country style wine, the best to date from this winery. Medium-bodied, with chunky and firm tannins but those yielding in the glass to reveal smoky wood, black plums and cassis flavors. Drink now. Score 85.

RA'ANAN MARGALIT, CABERNET SAUVIGNON, 2002: Dark garnet and medium-bodied, this red has generous tannins, wood and cherry, plum and spices. A pleasant country-style wine. Drink now. Score 83.

RA'ANAN MARGALIT, CABERNET SAUVIGNON, 2001: Medium-bodied, with firm tannins that promise to integrate nicely and appealing black cherry and currant fruits as well as hints of spicy oak. Drink now. Score 84.

RA'ANAN MARGALIT, CABERNET SAUVIGNON, 2000: A country-style, medium-bodied wine with chunky tannins that go nicely with black fruits, spices and a light earthy-herbal overlay. Drink up. Score 81.

RA'ANAN, MERLOT, 2002: Garnet towards purple, medium-bodied, with soft tannins and a pleasant berry-cherry personality. Drink now. Score 84.

RA'ANAN MARGALIT, MERLOT, 2001: Dark cherry red toward purple, medium-bodied, with moderate tannins and appealing flavors of black cherries and wild berries. Lacking depth or complexity but a pleasant quaffer. Drink up. Score 84.

RA'ANAN MARGALIT, MERLOT, 2000: Garnet colored and medium-bodied, with soft tannins and forward berry, cherry and currant fruits, but those hindered by a not entirely clean and somewhat overly alcoholic finish. Drink up. Score 78.

RA'ANAN, MERLOT-CABERNET SAUVIGNON, 2002: A medium-bodied blend of 80% Merlot and 20% Cabernet Sauvignon. Sweet tannins, light wood influence and ripe berry-cherry fruits. Drink now. Score 84.

RA'ANAN, CHARDONNAY, 2003: Dark golden straw in color, medium-bodied, with aromas and flavors of citrus, pineapple and green apples. Drink now. Score 84.

Ramim ✻✻

Founded in 1999 by Nechemia Ya'akobi and Nitzan Eliyahu—who is also the winemaker—and producing their first wines from the 2000 harvest, this winery is located on Moshav Shachar in the Southern Plains. Grapes are planted in three of the winery's vineyards, some in Kfar Yuval and Safsofet, both on the Lebanese border of the country, and others on Moshav Shachar. Red varieties include Cabernet Sauvignon, Merlot, Sangiovese, Cabernet Franc, Syrah from France and Shiraz from Australia, as well as early plantings of Barbera, and Nebbiolo. White varieties include Zinfandel, Chardonnay, Gewurztraminer, Riesling, Semillon and Muscat.

The winery, which relies on Hungarian, French and American oak barrels, releases wines in three series: Reserve, Ramim and Yuval. Production in 2000 was 2,500 bottles, in 2001, 7,000 bottles, in 2002, 22,000 bottles, in 2003, 55,000 bottles and in 2004 about 75,000 bottles. Projected production for 2005 is for 100,000 bottles. From the 2003 vintage the wines have been kosher.

Reserve

RAMIM, SPECIAL RESERVE, CABERNET SAUVIGNON, 2002: This blend of 85% Cabernet Sauvignon, 10% Merlot and 5% Cabernet Franc is best described as wood-driven, the smoky oak and tannins so dominant that they all but surpress whatever black fruits struggle to make themselves felt. Drink from release. Tentative Score 81–83.

RAMIM RESERVE, CABERNET SAUVIGNON, 2002: Aged for 15 months in 400 liter Hungarian oak barrels, this deep cherry-red toward garnet wine shows solid tannins, those well balanced by vanilla and spiciness from the wood and a generous array of blackcurrant and blackberry fruits. Just enough spiciness here to gain your attention. Drink now–2007. Score 86.

YUVAL, MERLOT 2003: Deep cherry towards garnet red, medium-bodied, with soft tannins, this smooth, well-balanced wine shows lightly spicy berry, cherry and plum aromas and flavors. Somewhat internationalized in style. Drink from release–2007. Tentative Score 85–87. **K**

RAMIM SPECIAL RESERVE, MERLOT, 2002: Dark, almost impenetrable garnet towards black, aged in barrels for a lengthy 29 months, now so dominated by wood that it is difficult to find either the tannins or the fruits here. Drink up. Score 82.

RAMIM RESERVE, MERLOT, 2002: Aged for 14 months in new Hungarian oak barrels, the wine shows a few off aromas when first poured, but those fade quickly in the glass making place for aromas and flavors of plums and black cherries, vanilla and sweet cedar. Somewhat acidic. Drink now. Score 84.

Ramim

RAMIM, CABERNET SAUVIGNON, 2003: Oak-aged in 165-liter Hungarian oak barrels, this medium to full-bodied red shows firm tannins, which promise to integrate nicely with time, and an array of currant and plum fruits on a spicy background with appealing herbal hints coming in on the finish. Drink now–2007. Score 86. **K**

RAMIM, CABERNET SAUVIGNON, 2002: Deep garnet in color, medium-bodied, and when first poured showing somewhat coarse tannins that tend to dominate, reflecting its 15 months in oak. However, given considerable time in the glass these recede and allow the currant, berry and black cherry flavors to show through. Drink now–2007. Score 85.

RAMIM, CABERNET SAUVIGNON, 2001: Blended with 14% of Merlot and aged in oak for 18 months, this medium to full-bodied country-style wine shows generous chunky tannins, those melding nicely with plum, blackberry and cassis flavors. Some spices coming in from mid-palate and leading to a medium-long finish. Drink now. Score 85.

RAMIM, MERLOT, 2003: Aged in small oak casks, with just firm enough tannins balanced nicely by vanilla and spices from the wood, the wine shows good spicy plum and black cherry fruits as well as hints of tobacco and cocoa on the long finish. Drink from release–2008. Tentative Score 85–87. **K**

RAMIM, MERLOT, 2002: Oak-aged for 18 months, with 5% of Cabernet Sauvignon blended in to add backbone, this soft, medium-bodied deep garnet wine has silky tannins now integrated nicely. Appealing raspberry and black cherry fruits. Somewhat too acidic. Drink now. Score 85.

RAMIM, MERLOT, 2001: With the addition of 14% Cabernet Sauvignon to add backbone, this medium-bodied, moderately tannic wine shows a modest band of currant and plum fruits, those on a background of spices and Mediterranean herbs. An unwelcome note of earthiness comes in on the finish. Drink up. Score 82.

RAMIM, MERLOT, 2000: A pleasant blend of 95% Merlot and 5% Cabernet Sauvignon that was oak aged for 18 months, deep purple in color, country-style, with somewhat coarse tannins but those set off nicely by generous berry, cherry and currant flavors and an appealing herbaceousness that comes in from mid-palate. Drink up. Score 82.

RAMIM, SANGIOVESE, 2003: Aged in 165-liter Hungarian oak barrels, this deep garnet toward royal purple, medium-bodied red has generous but soft and well-integrated tannins, but hardly any aromas, and flavors of plum, berry and cassis that fade too quickly. Drink now. Score 84. **K**

RAMIM, CABERNET FRANC, 2004: Deep ruby towards garnet, with gripping tannins that need time to settle down, but intrinsic good balance that promises that the plum, wild berry and wood-inspired spices and vanilla will show through nicely. Drink from release–2007. Tentative Score 86–88.**K**

RAMIM, CABERNET FRANC, 2003: Reflecting its development in 165-liter Hungarian oak barrels, this dark ruby toward garnet, medium to full-bodied red shows appealing black fruit, cassis and spicy flavors but hardly any aromas. Drink up. Score 84. **K**

RAMIM, CABERNET SAUVIGNON-MERLOT, 2004: A deep garnet, medium-bodied blend of 55% Cabernet Sauvignon and 45% Merlot, aged in oak for about six months. Soft tannins and good balance with tempting aromas and flavors of ripe berries and plums as well as hints of sweet cedar and vanilla that make themselves nicely felt. Drink from release–2008. Tentative Score 86–88. **K**

RAMIM, CABERNET SAUVIGNON-MERLOT, 2003: Aged in small oak barrels for six months, this blend of Cabernet Sauvignon, Merlot, Pinot

Noir and Syrah (54%, 31%, 8% and 7% respectively) has dark purple color, medium body, soft tannins and berry, currant and plum fruits on a lightly earthy-vanilla background. Somewhat short on the finish. Drink now. Score 85. K

RAMIM, CABERNET SAUVIGNON-MERLOT 2002: Garnet toward purple in color, this medium to full-bodied oak-aged blend of 52% Cabernet Sauvignon and 48% Merlot shows generous and well integrating tannins and an appealing array of blackberry, currant and plum fruits, those coming together nicely with lightly spicy and herbal overtones. Drink now–2007. Score 86.

RAMIM, MERLOT-CABERNET, 2001: Deep cherry toward purple in color and medium-bodied, with somewhat chunky tannins and a bitter overlay to the black fruit aromas and flavors. Hints of vanilla and smoky oak let us know the wine aged in small barrels for 16 months. Pleasant enough, but lacking complexity. Drink up. Score 84.

RAMIM, SANGIOVESE-MERLOT, 2004: Dark royal purple in color, medium-bodied,with chunky country style tannins integrating nicely to reveal blackberry, cassis and plum fruits. Drink from release–2007. Tentative Score 85–87. K

RAMIM, ROSÉ DE CABERNET FRANC, 2003: Orange-pink in color, with unabashed sweetness and some grapefruit and strawberry aromas and flavors, but without the balancing acidity to keep it lively. Drink up. Score 82. K

RAMIM, CHARDONNAY, 2002: This light golden straw, medium to full-bodied white was aged partly in French and Hungarian oak barrels, partly in stainless steel. When first poured, it is completely flat on the nose and palate, but given time in the glass it does open somewhat, but only to reveal stingy lemon-lime aromas and flavors and none of the true Chardonnay crispness. Somewhat past its peak. Drink up. Score 81.

RAMIM, CHARDONNAY DESSERT WINE, 2003: An appealing bright gold in color, this generously sweet and moderately full-bodied wine was made in the style of ice wine but with the grapes frozen in the winery and not in the fields. It has appealing aromas and flavors of honeyed apricot, those matched by gentle acidity. Generous on the palate but somewhat short. Drink now. Score 85. K

RAMIM, RIESLING, 2004: Crisp and fruity, light on the palate, with generous acidity to keep it lively. Flavors of citrus and tropical fruits. Drink now. Score 85. K

RAMIM, DESERT ICE, 2003: Not one but five separate wines, one each of Gewurztraminer, Riesling, Chardonnay and Muscat Grapes and the fifth an unlikely blend of all those grapes, all frozen at the winery and developed in oak casks for eight months, and all similar enough to deserve a single review. Extremely flowery, with honeyed flavors dominating and holding back the apricot fruits that never quite make themselves felt. Lacking adequate acidity to balance the forward sweetness and not destined for aging. Drink now. Score 81. K

Yuval

YUVAL, CABERNET SAUVIGNON, 2003: Medium-bodied, with gripping tannins and generous wood but those yielding nicely to reveal currant, berry and herbal aromas and flavors. A rather standard but pleasant wine. Drink now. Score 85. K

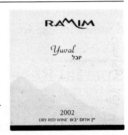

YUVAL, MERLOT, 2003: Deep cherry towards garnet red, medium-bodied, with soft tannins, this is a smooth, well-balanced wine showing lightly spicy berry, cherry and plum flavors and aromas. Somewhat internationalized in style. Drink now. Score 85. K

YUVAL, CABERNET SAUVIGON-MERLOT, 2002: This medium-dark garnet-red, medium-bodied blend of 58% Cabernet Sauvignon and 42% Merlot was aged in small oak barrels for 15 months. With tannins integrating nicely and good balance between tannins, wood and black fruits, this is a soft and smooth if not overly complex wine. Drink up. Score 86.

YUVAL, CABERNET SAUVIGNON-MERLOT, 2001: Dark cherry towards garnet, medium-bodied, with soft tannins, this blend of 80% Cabernet Sauvignon and 20% Merlot shows light but appealing aromas and flavors of black cherries and currants. Drink up. Score 85.

Recanati ✶✶✶✶

Established in 2000, this fully modern winery located in the Hefer Valley in the north part of the Sharon region relies on grapes from their own as well as contract vineyards, primarily in the Upper Galilee. Under the supervision of California trained winemaker Lewis Pasco, the winery currently produces wines in several series: the top-of-the-line Special Reserve wines, which are often blends of Cabernet Sauvignon and Merlot; and two varietal series, Reserve and Recanati, which now include Cabernet Sauvignon, Merlot, Syrah, Petite Sirah, Chardonnay and most recently Sauvignon Blanc. The winery has also introduced a popularly priced series named Yasmine. Production in 2002 was 230,000 bottles and in 2003, 500,000. Output for 2004 is 700,000 bottles and future target production is 1–1.2 million bottles, 30% of which is destined for export.

Special Reserve

SPECIAL RESERVE, 2003: A blend of grapes from vineyards at Manara, Alma and Kerem Ben Zimra, this deep, broad wine shows traditional Cabernet currants, cassis and spicy-herbal overtones. Good balance between wood, tannins and fruit and a long finish. Needs time to show its elegance. Drink from release–2012. Tentative Score 92–94. **K**

SPECIAL RESERVE, 2002: A blend of 50% each of Cabernet Sauvignon and Merlot, this dark, solid, medium to full-bodied wine overall has a good balance, appealing black fruit and herbal overtones, spicy oak and a generously tannic and fruity finish, but due to its problematic vintage lacks the depth or structure for long-term aging. Drink now–2007. Score 88. **K**

SPECIAL RESERVE, 2001: A blend of 96% Cabernet Sauvignon and 4% Merlot, this full-bodied, deep garnet toward purple wine offers tempting currant, blackberry and raspberry fruits, those backed up nicely by generous but soft and well-integrated tannins and a nice touch of oak. Drink now– 2008. Score 90. K

SPECIAL RESERVE, 2000: Aged 18 months in new French oak, this full-bodied young blend of 50% each of Cabernet Sauvignon and Merlot with its once tight tannins now softening nicely shows good balance between tannins, fruit and smoky oak, along with tempting currant, black cherry and vanilla aromas and flavors and herbal, earthy and leathery notes on the long finish. Drink now–2007. Score 92. K

Reserve

RESERVE, CABERNET SAUVIGNON, 2004: Deep garnet in color, this medium to full-bodied wine with still firm tannins softening nicely now shows aromas and flavors of currants and black cherries as well as hints of spicy wood and Mediterranean herbs. Drink from release–2010. Tentative Score 88–90. K

RESERVE, CABERNET SAUVIGNON, 2003: Ripe and rich, well balanced, with medium to full-body and soft tannins, traditional Cabernet currant and berry fruits as well as hints of anise and light toasty oak flavors. Drink now–2010. Score 90. K

RESERVE, CABERNET SAUVIGNON, 2002: Still firm tannins make this young wine very tight, but given time to open it will show cedar, oak, currant, plum and anise flavors. Somewhat short and perhaps lacking the structure for long-term cellaring. Drink now. Score 86. K

RESERVE, CABERNET SAUVIGNON, 2001: Dark in color, and firmly tannic but with concentrated currant, berry and spicy aromas and flavors, the wine has a welcoming hint of raspberries on the long finish. Elegant and complex. Drink now–2007. Score 90. K

RESERVE, CABERNET SAUVIGNON, 2000: Having lost the first flush of youth, now with hints of browning but still fresh and with plenty of oak and tannins balanced nicely by rich black fruits and overlays of freshly picked truffles, espresso and leather. Drink now. Score 89. K

RESERVE, MERLOT, 2004: Medium to full-bodied with firm tannins already yielding nicely and well balanced by sweet oak, black cherry, currant and herbal aromas and flavors. Moderately long. Best 2007–2011. Tentative Score 87–89. **K**

RESERVE, MERLOT, 2003: Already showing concentrated and complex ripe currant, cherry and sweet oak aromas and flavors, this graceful wine is true to its variety and promises a long and generous finish. Drink now–2008. Score 89. **K**

RESERVE, MERLOT, 2002: Tight and somewhat austere, with cherry and wild berry fruits backed up by hints of tea, herbs and cedar wood, the wine lacks complexity and has a tannic edge that may or may not settle down with time. Drink now. Score 86. **K**

RESERVE, MERLOT, 2001: Dark, deep and mysterious, this tempting medium to full-bodied wine has plenty of smooth tannins and abundant dark fruit, chocolate, vanilla and smoky-herbal aromas and flavors. Still somewhat tight when first poured, it needs time to open in the glass. Drink now–2008. Score 91. **K**

RESERVE, MERLOT, 2000: Deep royal purple, this medium to full-bodied red offers aromas and flavors of blackcurrants, purple plums, eucalyptus and sage. Still somewhat heavy on the oak, but well structured and balanced enough to carry that. Drink now–2007. Score 89. **K**

RESERVE, PETITE SIRAH-ZINFANDEL, 2003: Deep garnet toward purple, this concentrated, full-bodied and generously tannic wine has expressive spicy plums and black cherry fruits, those complemented nicely by spicy, earthy overlays as well as a light hint of asphalt that develops on the finish. Needs time for the tannins to settle down. Drink now–2008. Score 88. **K**

RESERVE, CHARDONNAY, 2003: Smooth and supple, with a pleasant earthy accent to pineapple and hazelnut notes, this stylish wine offers up nice oak seasoning on the finish, a light buttery note and a round and mouth-filling finish. Drink now–2007. Score 89. **K**

RESERVE, CHARDONNAY, 2002: With youthful zest and a bright golden color, the wine shows pear and hazelnut, as well as buttery-smoky oak aromas and flavors on the finish. Drink now. Score 88. **K**

RESERVE, CHARDONNAY, 2001: Medium to full-bodied with ample apple, summer fruits and pineapple aromas and flavors complemented nicely by buttery vanilla and spices, all on a well-balanced frame. Drink now. Score 90. **K**

Recanati

RECANATI, CABERNET SAUVIGNON, 2004: Deep ruby towards garnet, medium-bodied, with near-sweet tannins and generous currant and berry fruits, those backed up by smoky wood and earthiness. Drink now–2008. Score 87. **K**

RECANATI, CABERNET SAUVIGNON, 2003: Medium-bodied, with soft tannins and appealing berry, currant and plum fruits, all with a hint of spice on the background. Drink now. Score 85. **K**

RECANATI, CABERNET SAUVIGNON, 2002: Soft tannins, inviting currant and plum flavors, and hints of spices and herbs make this medium to full-bodied wine a good candidate for early drinking. Drink now. Score 87. **K**

RECANATI, CABERNET SAUVIGNON, 2001: Medium-deep garnet toward purple in color, the wine shows appealing plum, currant and blackberry fruits overlaid by pleasant spicy hints. Perhaps somewhat heavy on the oak but that settling in nicely with the tannins and fruits. Drink up. Score 85. **K**

RECANATI, CABERNET SAUVIGNON, 2000: Medium to full-bodied, with plum and currant flavors but now showing its wood rather heavily and with a caramel flavor that seems to be creeping in, the wine is drinking well but not meant for further cellaring. Drink up. Score 86. **K**

RECANATI, MERLOT, 2003: Smooth, ripe and fruity, with cherry, berry, earthy and herbal aromas and flavors. Young and vibrant, with good balance between tannins and fruits. Drink now. Score 86. **K**

RECANATI, MERLOT, 2002: Somewhat on the earthy side, with wild berry and juniper accents along with sweet cedar and spices. Firm and tight, this wine is not meant for long cellaring. Drink now. Score 85. **K**

RECANATI, MERLOT, 2001: After eight months in oak, this medium-bodied red may not have too many complexities but it is still an appealing wine, with cherry, currant and blueberry flavors along with a bit of toasty oak, and modest tannins that are felt mostly on the finish. Drink now. Score 86. **K**

RECANATI, MERLOT, 2000: Rather heavy on the oak, but fresh and packed with currant, berry and spices as well as a hint of caramel. Somewhat past its peak. Drink up. Score 85. **K**

RECANATI, SHIRAZ, 2003: Aged in new French and American oak, this dark ruby towards purple, medium-bodied wine shows moderate tannins and good balance along with enchanting aromas and flavors of jammy fruits, those with spicy, peppery and licorice overtones, all reflecting the judicious use of oak. Drink now–2008. Score 89. **K**

RECANATI, BARBERA, 2003: Aged for 9 months in used French *barriques*, this pleasant little cherry towards garnet colored, medium-bodied wine has light tannins allowing the cherry and berry flavors to come through nicely. Lacking complexity but pleasant. Drink now. Score 86. **K**

RECANATI, PETITE SIRAH, 2002: Medium-bodied, with lightly chunky, country-style tannins softening and integrating nicely, and with currant and berry fruits, those on an appealing background of earthiness and tobacco, the wine reflects its 8 months in oak with a smoky-vanilla finish. Drink now. Score 88. **K**

RECANATI, PETITE SIRAH-ZINFANDEL, 2003: Medium to full-bodied, with generous soft tannins, the wine offers up appealing blackberry and currant fruits together with an array of Mediterranean herbs, tobacco and, on the finish, mushroom and fruits. Drink now. Score 87. **K**

RECANATI, PETITE SIRAH, 2002: Medium-bodied, with firm tannins and generous currant, wild berry and spicy aromas and flavors, the wine also has touches of earth and tobacco on the finish. A lovely effort. Drink now. Score 88. **K**

RECANATI, CHARDONNAY, 2004: Golden straw in color, medium-bodied, with aromas and flavors of tropical fruits, melon and citrus. Lively, complex, round and long. Drink now–2007. Score 88. **K**

RECANATI, CHARDONNAY, 2003: Developed *sur lie* for 8 months, this medium to full-bodied Chardonnay reflects just a hint of wood over appealing citrus and tropical fruits. Good balancing acidity here and a nice hint of spiciness Drink now. Score 88. **K**

RECANATI, CHARDONNAY, 2002: Light golden straw in color, with generous litchis and pineapple fruits and good acidity. Drink up. Score 86. **K**

RECANATI, CHARDONNAY, 2001: An appealing golden straw in color, with apple, citrus, mineral and spicy flavors along with just the barest trace of oak. Somewhat past its peak. Drink up. Score 86. **K**

RECANATI, CHARDONNAY, 2000: Medium-bodied, with appealing lemon and lime flavors along with hints of orange peel and vanilla. Past its peak. Drink up. Score 86. **K**

RECANATI, SAUVIGNON BLANC, 2004: Light straw colored, medium-bodied, not specially aromatic but with very appealing summer fruits on a grassy, earthy background. Drink now. Score 87. **K**

RECANATI, SAUVIGNON BLANC, 2003: This unoaked, fresh and lively medium-bodied white starts off with earthy-mineral aromas, those yielding nicely to guava, grass and nectarine flavors. Good character. Drink now. Score 88. **K**

Yasmine

YASMIN, RED, 2004: Dark cherry red in color, medium-bodied, with soft tannins, gentle wood and blackberry and currant fruits. Drink now. Score 84. **K**

YASMINE, RED, 2003: This light to medium-bodied unoaked blend of Cabernet Sauvignon and Merlot has a deep cherry-red toward garnet color, fresh and abundant berry fruits, and low tannins. It is soft, clean and smooth. Drink up. Score 84. **K**

YASMIN, WHITE, 2004: A pleasant little white with aromas and flavors of citrus and summer fruit. Crisp, clean and refreshing. Drink up. Score 84. **K**

YASMINE, WHITE, 2003: Light and bright, this blend of Sauvignon Blanc and French Colombard has appealing summer fruits and the kind of crisp balancing acidity that makes it a pleasant summertime quaffer. Drink up. Score 85. **K**

Red Poetry *

Established in 2001 by Dubi Tal on Havat Tal in the Upper Galilee, the winery has its own vineyards with Cabernet Sauvignon, Merlot, Cabernet Franc, Petit Verdot, Shiraz, Petite Sirah, Sangiovese, Riesling and Gewurztraminer grapes. Their first releases have been of a varietal Cabernet Sauvignon and a blended white; currently production is 3,000 bottles annually.

RED POETRY, CABERNET SAUVIGNON, 2002: Dark garnet in color, medium-bodied, with near sweet ripe fruits and with an aroma of decaying mushrooms. Drink up. Score 75.

RED POETRY, CABERNET SAUVIGNON, 2001: Medium to full-bodied, deep garnet in color, and with simple plum and wood-imparted flavors that are hidden under biting tannins and a too herbal overlay that runs throughout. Drink up. Score 78.

RED POETRY, WHITE, 2002: Light to medium-bodied blend of 80% Johannisberg Riesling and 20% Chardonnay, this pale-straw colored wine offers up a rather odd mouthful of grapefruit, apple and earthy aromas and flavors, all followed by a too drying chalky finish. Drink up. Score 76.

Rosh Pina *

Set in the village of Rosh Pina in the Galilee, this small winery was founded by Ya'akov Blum in 2001 and released its first wines in 2002. The winery draws on grapes from the Galilee, those including Cabernet Sauvignon, Shiraz and Carignan. First releases were of 3,000 bottles and projected releases are 5,000 bottles annually.

ROSH PINA, CABERNET SAUVIGNON, 2003: Medium-bodied, with somewhat coarse tannins, but beyond that appealing currant and berry flavors and aromas. Drink now. Score 79.

ROSH PINA, CABERNET SAUVIGNON, 2002: An unfiltered, country-style wine with a modest band of dried cherry and berry fruits together with light toasty and spicy flavors. Simple but pleasant. Drink up. Score 80.

ROSH PINA, SHIRAZ, 2002: With modest tannins and an earthy, leathery character, but with enough cherry and wild berry flavors to give the wine some interest. Drink now. Score 78.

ROSH PINA, CABERNET-MERLOT-SHIRAZ, 2003: Ruby towards garnet in color, medium-bodied, far too acidic, with chunky tannins and skimpy berry and black fruit aromas and flavors. Drink up. Score 76.

ROSH PINA, SHIRAZ-CARIGNAN, 2002: A simple little wine without any varietal traits but with a few spicy cherry and berry flavors. Drink up. Score 78.

ROSH PINA, SHIRAZ-CARIGNAN, TEVA, 2002: Crisp and a bit tart, with spicy anise flavored black fruits. Drink now. Score 76.

Rota *

Established by Erez Rota on Moshav Tsafririm at the foothills of the Jerusalem Mountains in 2001 and re-located in 2005 to the Rota Ranch in the Negev Heights. Releasing its first wines in 2002, production for 2003 was about 2,500 bottles and for 2004 about 4,000.

ROTA, CABERNET-MERLOT, 2003: Unoaked, medium-bodied and somewhat on the simple side, but with just enough plum, black cherry and herbal aromas and flavors to hold interest. Drink up. Score 82.

ROTA, CABERNET-MERLOT, 2002: With clean aromas and flavors of berries and cherries, this soft, fresh and only moderately tannic wine is pleasant, although lacking complexity. Drink up. Score 83.

Rozenbaum *

Founded by Avi Rozenbaum in 1998, this small winery is located on Kibbutz Malkiya in the Upper Galilee near the Lebanese border. Grapes, including Cabernet Sauvignon, Merlot, Chardonnay and Muscat of Alexandria, come from the Kadesh Valley and production in 2002 was about 7,000 bottles. The winery also released its first Sangiovese from the 2002 harvest.

ROZENBAUM, CABERNET SAUVIGNON, 2002: Dark garnet in color, medium-bodied, with firm and almost searing tannins holding back whatever fruits struggle, not fully successfully, to make themselves felt. Drink up. Score 78.

ROZENBAUM, CABERNET SAUVIGNON, 2001: Herbal, earthy, astringent, thick on the palate and with almost sweet jam-like fruit flavors, the wine lacks depth or breadth. Score 62.

ROZENBAUM, CABERNET SAUVIGNON, 2000: Dark and brooding, its fruits are buried under an almost sweet overlay that confuses the palate. Drink up. Score 72.

ROZENBAUM, CABERNET SAUVIGNON, 1999: When young, this medium to full-bodied wine had firm tannins and a few black cherry, plum, currant and oak aromas and flavors. Now well past its peak and no longer scoreable.

ROZENBAUM, MERLOT, 2002: Chunky tannins, medium-body and aromas and flavors of black fruits, but reflecting a rather heavy hand with the oak. A country-style wine meant for early drinking. Drink up. Score 84.

ROZENBAUM, MERLOT, 2001: Light to medium-bodied, on the alcoholic side, and with plums and black cherries that bring to mind fruit-juice concentrates. Past its peak. Drink up. Score 70.

ROZENBAUM, MERLOT, 2000: Medium-bodied, with soft tannins, this wine is a bit flat on the nose but shows appealing flavors of berries and black cherries. Little here to call to mind Merlot but a pleasant little wine nevertheless. Somewhat past its peak. Drink up. Score 82.

ROZENBAUM, MERLOT, 1999: Tight and cedary, with cherry and currant flavors and moderate level of smooth tannins, this medium-bodied wine spent one year in oak. Look for hints of herbs, spices and plums on the medium finish. Showing age. Score 76.

ROZENBAUM, SANGIOVESE, 2002: Hard and acidic, with coarse tannins and not nearly enough balancing fruits, the wine calls to mind the cheap Chiantis of the 1950s. Two versions have been released simultaneously, one with a small percentage of Cabernet, but this does not help much either. Drink up. Score 72.

ROZENBAUM, CHARDONNAY, 2001: Light straw in color, with aromas and flavors of apples, lemons and vanilla, this unoaked wine shows few of the characteristics usually associated with Chardonnay. Drink up. Score 75.

Ruth **

Founded by Tal Ma'or and located in Kfar Ruth, adjoining the city of Modi'in, this family-owned winery produced several hundred bottles of wine from the 2002 vintage and 4,000 bottles from the 2003 and 2004 vintages. Grapes, including Cabernet Sauvignon, Merlot and Shiraz are harvested from vineyards on the central plain and in the hills of Jerusalem.

RUTH, MERLOT-SHIRAZ, 2003: Dark royal-purple in color, with generous acidity but only the barest traces of tannins, this medium-bodied blend of equal parts of Merlot and Shiraz was developed in oak for about 10 months. Appealing aromas and flavors of plums and black berries and, starting on mid-palate, an earthy-herbal overlay. Serve lightly chilled. Drink now. Score 85. K

RUTH, CABERNET SAUVIGNON, 2003: Dark ruby towards garnet, medium-bodied, with soft tannins, hints of smoky oak and berry, cherry and currant fruits that open nicely on the palate. Not complex but generous and satisfying. Drink now–2007. Score 86. K

Salomon *

Located on Moshav Amikam which is set in the Ramot Menashe forest not far from Zichron Ya'akov, this winery was founded in 1997 by Itamar Salomon. For several years the winery prepared only small quantities of wine for home consumption, and the first commercial release was from the 2002 vintage. Grapes are currently drawn from the Golan Heights but the winery is planting its own vineyards with Cabernet Sauvignon, Merlot and Shiraz grapes. Production for 2002 was 1,000 bottles and for 2003 and 2004 about 2,500 bottles.

SALOMON, CABERNET SAUVIGNON, 2003: Dark garnet but not fully clear, and medium-bodied with chunky, somewhat coarse tannins, but under those generous plum and black cherry fruits. Lacking complexity, but pleasant. Drink now. Score 84.

SALOMON, CABERNET SAUVIGNON, 2002: Deep cherry-red, this medium-bodied country-style wine shows slightly rough tannins but those well balanced by black fruits and an appealing hint of earthiness. Drink up. Score 83.

SALOMON, MERLOT, 2003: Somewhat over-extracted and showing hyper-ripe, almost sweet fruits, and fairly deep tannins for a Merlot. Simple but pleasant. Drink now. Score 84.

SALOMON, MERLOT, 2002: A simple little country-style wine, without complexities but with fresh plum and berry fruits and soft tannins. Drink up. Score 83.

Saslove ★★★★

Established by Barry Saslove in 1998 on Kibbutz Eyal in the Sharon region, this boutique winery has vineyards in the Upper Galilee currently planted with Cabernet Sauvignon, Merlot and Sauvignon Blanc grapes, and plans to grow Shiraz, Nebbiolo and Gewurztraminer grapes in the future. Current production of red wines is in three series: Reserved, Adom and Aviv, and the winery occasionally produces white wines as well. Production for 2002 was 35,000 bottles, for 2003, 40,000 and for 2004 55,000 bottles. Projected production by 2006 is about 80,000 bottles. Beginning with the 2003 harvest Saslove has also produced two kosher Cabernet Sauvignon wines under the label "K by Saslove", using the facilities of Carmel in Zichron Ya'akov. 2003 production for the kosher wines was 15,000 bottles.

Reserved

RESERVED, CABERNET SAUVIGNON, 2003: Elegant and sleek, with generous black cherry, raspberry, spice and toasty oak aromas and flavors. Medium to full-bodied, with firm tannins that show signs of integrating nicely, supple on the palate and with a long fruity-herbal finish. Drink from release–2010. Tentative Score 90–92.

RESERVED, CABERNET SAUVIGNON, 2002: Full-bodied, complex and inviting, with an appealing range of currant, vanilla, and herb flavors that come together nicely. Look for a deep, long and rich finish. Drink now–2008 . Score 89.

RESERVED, CABERNET SAUVIGNON, 2000: Full-bodied, deep garnet toward purple, showing good balance between wood, well-integrated tannins and fruits. The wine shows cassis and berry fruits together with appealing spices, and on the finish a generous overlay of Mediterranean herbs comes in. Drink now–2007. Score 91.

RESERVED, CABERNET SAUVIGNON, PRIVATE EDITION, SAGOL, 2000: Dark royal purple in color, this medium to full-bodied, well-balanced and moderately long wine spent 14 months in French oak barrels and now shows soft, well-integrated tannins, a gentle influence of smoky oak, and generous blackcurrant and plum fruits backed up nicely by Oriental spices, vanilla and chocolate. Drink now. Score 89.

RESERVED, CABERNET SAUVIGNON, 1999: Dark, deep and elegant, this delicious full-bodied wine has sweet plum, black cherry and red currant aromas and flavors, all opening slowly on the palate together with herbs, vanilla and a light hint of mint. Well balanced and with well-integrated tannins, the wine has a pleasingly long finish. Drink now–2007. Score 92.

RESERVED, CABERNET SAUVIGNON, 1998: With a generous core of ripe cherries, wild berries, red currants, plums, vanilla and spices, this well made and complex wine borders on elegance. After 21 months in new oak casks the wine has a fairly tannic finish. Drink now. Score 90.

RESERVED, MERLOT, 2003: Medium-dark garnet with orange reflections, medium to full-bodied, with generous but well integrating tannins set off nicely by spicy and vanilla hints from the wood and appealing black cherry, plum and berry fruits. Long and mouthfilling. Drink from release–2009. Tentative Score 87–89.

RESERVED, CHARDONNAY, 2002: This wine has generous oak on a tight firm frame, but given time to open in the glass it will reveal appealing flavors of citrus, pear and pineapple that fill the mouth nicely, and culminates in a lightly spicy finish. Somewhat past its peak. Drink up. Score 86.

Adom

ADOM, CABERNET SAUVIGNON, 2003: Still very young but already ripe and smooth, the wine shows an attractive array of flavors that include currants, cherries, herbs, and vanilla. The tannins of this well-balanced and complex red bode well for its aging potential. Drink now–2009. Score 90.

ADOM, CABERNET SAUVIGNON, 2002: Showing beautifully now with full body and with generous currant and berry fruits, those matched nicely by exotic spices and hints of sweet cedar. Tannins need a bit of time to recede. Drink now–2008. Score 90.

ADOM, CABERNET SAUVIGNON, 2001: Dark garnet red and full-bodied, this oak-aged wine shows good balance between generous but well integrating tannins, sweet wood and berry, currant and plum fruits. On the medium-long finish a hint of minty chocolate. Drink now. Score 90.

ADOM, CABERNET SAUVIGNON, 2000: Made entirely from Cabernet Sauvignon grapes and aged for 14 months in new and old French and American *barriques*, this attractive red shows currant, berry and smoky oak aromas and flavors. It has good balance, integrated tannins and a medium-long finish. Drink now. Score 88.

ADOM, CABERNET SAUVIGNON, 1999: A wine that opens beautifully and reveals a full body, firm but silky smooth tannins, deep flavors and aromas of blackcurrants, black cherries, and raspberries, along with hints of smoky oak, earthiness and mint chocolate. Drink now. Score 91.

ADOM, MERLOT, 2003: Shows exuberant blackberry and cassis fruits and a toasty oak accent as well as licorice and spice aromas and flavors. Look for hints of chocolate and coffee that will increase as the wine continues to develop. Drink now–2010. Score 90.

Aviv

AVIV, CABERNET SAUVIGNON, 2003: Deep garnet red, medium-bodied, with firm tannins that coat the mouth nicely, those balanced nicely by spicy oak and appealing currant and black cherry fruits. Drink now. Score 87.

AVIV, CABERNET SAUVIGNON, 2002: Dark and firmly tannic, with concentrated sweet cedar and smoke now blended comfortably with berry and currant fruits. Drink now. Score 88.

AVIV, CABERNET SAUVIGNON, 2001: A deep purple medium-bodied wine with red currants, black cherry, Oriental spices and a light welcome touch of earthiness. Drink now. Score 89.

AVIV, CABERNET SAUVIGNON, 2000: Made entirely from Cabernet Sauvignon grapes, this exuberant medium-bodied wine is packed with soft tannins, currant, cherry and plum flavors, and just the right hint of vanilla and spices. Drink now. Score 90.

AVIV, CABERNET SAUVIGNON, 1999: This deep purple medium-bodied Cabernet was aged in small oak casks with oak chips to add to its vanilla and spicy flavors, and now shows flavors of currants, raspberries, red and black cherries and cinnamon, along with moderate silky-smooth tannins. Drink up. Score 88.

AVIV, MERLOT, 2003: Medium-bodied, deep royal purple towards garnet in color, with soft tannins and light spicy oak set off well by currant, berry and cherry fruits. On the finish hints of white chocolate and mocha. Drink now–2007. Score 87.

AVIV, MERLOT, 2002: Fresh and exuberant, medium to full-bodied, and garnet toward purple in color, the wine was aged for 6 months in French and American oak and now shows tannins that start off firmly but open in the glass to reveal a pleasing berry and black cherry personality, the fruits complemented nicely by spicy chocolate and coffee flavors. Look as well for hints of smoky oak and toasted white bread on the medium-long finish. Drink now. Score 89.

AVIV, MERLOT, 2001: Comfortably reflecting the 5 months that it spent in small oak casks, this deep purple medium-bodied wine has plenty of black fruits, currant and spices. What gives the wine an appealing "twist" is its almost sweet finish, yielding vanilla beans and Mediterranean herbs. Drink now. Score 90.

AVIV, MERLOT, 2000: This medium-bodied blend of 85% Merlot and 15% Cabernet Sauvignon has plenty of vanilla and spices and an overlay of black cherry aromas and flavors. When it opens in the glass it also shows hints of cinnamon and tobacco. Drink up. Score 89.

AVIV, MARRIAGE, 2003: This deep royal purple, full-bodied blend of 60% Merlot, 39% Cabernet Sauvignon and 1% Syrah shows generous but almost sweet tannins coming together nicely with vanilla-rich American oak, spices and appealing berry, currant and black cherry fruits. On the pleasingly long finish look as well for hints of cigar tobacco. Drink now–2008. Score 88.

Saslove

SASLOVE, SAGOL, PRIVATE EDITION, 2000: Dark royal purple in color, this medium to full-bodied wine spent 14 months in French oak barrels. With soft, well-integrated tannins, a gentle influence of smoky oak and generous blackcurrant and plum fruits backed up nicely by Oriental spices, vanilla and chocolate, this is a well balanced and moderately long wine. Drink now. Score 89.

SASLOVE, SAUVIGNON BLANC, 2001: Light golden straw in color, this medium-bodied wine has appealing aromas and flavors of citrus and tropical fruits and just the right level of grassy herbaceousness. Past its peak. Drink up. Score 88.

SASLOVE, SAUVIGNON BLANC, 2000: During its youth this unoaked medium-bodied Sauvignon Blanc was crisp and refreshing, showing good balance between green apple and tropical fruits along with hints of freshly cut hay and citrus. Showing age. Score 85.

SASLOVE, BLANC DE NOIRS, 2004: Whether this is a vaguely blush or a white wine depends on how one holds it up to the light. Made entirely from Cabernet Sauvignon grapes that were allowed minimum skin contact, it has a medium body with a surprisingly high 14.7% alcohol and with aromas and flavors of red fruits and citrus. Young, fresh, frivolous and fun to drink, especially when well chilled. Drink now. Score 85.

SASLOVE, GEWURZTRAMINER DESSERT, RESERVED, JASMINE, 2002–2003: A blend of Gewurztraminer grapes from two harvest years that was aged in oak and reinforced to obtain a 14% alcohol content. This frankly sweet wine has good balancing acidity and generous aromas and flavors of litchis, pineapple, ripe peaches and lilacs, as well as a hint of bitterness on the finish that will appeal to some. Drink now. Score 87.

SASLOVE, JASMINE'S GEWURZTRAMINER, DESSERT WINE, 2001: Soft, sweet and gentle, this reinforced dessert wine has pleasing layers of pineapple, litchis, honey and apricot flavors and aromas that linger nicely on the palate. Drink up. Score 88.

K By Saslove

K BY SASLOVE, CABERNET SAUVIGNON, 2003: Light to medium-bodied, perhaps a bit thin on the palate, with some berry, currant, and herbal flavors but those somehow never coming together. Drink now. Score 84. K

K BY SASLOVE, CABERNET SAUVIGNON, MEDITERRANEAN, 2003: Made entirely from Cabernet Sauvignon grapes from the Kayumi Vineyard in the Galilee and aged in new French oak barrels for six months, this deep royal purple, medium-bodied wine seems fairly aggressive, with a green, herbal character that hids the cherry and plum flavors. Rough on the finish. Drink now. Score 83. K

Sassy *

Sasson Bar-Gig set up this small winery in 2000 after studying winemaking in Canada and Italy. Located in the town of Bat Yam on the outskirts of Tel Aviv, and drawing on grapes from Gush Etzion and the Golan Heights, the winery is currently producing about 4,000 bottles annually, the reds aged in oak for about 12 months.

SASSY, CABERNET SAUVIGNON, 2002: Showing better now than in its youth, this garnet red, medium-bodied wine continues to offer very earthy aromas and flavors but now also reveals some appealing plum and berry fruits. Drink up. Score 80.

SASSY, CABERNET SAUVIGNON, 2001: A medium-bodied country-style wine with chunky tannins, a high level of acidity, and a bitterness that overpowers the black fruits. Drink up. Score 74.

SASSY, CABERNET SAUVIGNON, 2000: A coarse wine with a few plum and currant fruits, that calls to mind homemade wines of Italian or French farmers. Score 68.

SASSY, MERLOT, 2002: Deep garnet in color, this medium to full-bodied wine is a step-up for Sassy. Generous tannins here, but those integrating nicely and coming together with aromas and flavors of sweet cedar, berries and black cherries, all backed up by hints of spices that lead to a moderately long finish. Drink now. Score 85.

SASSY, MERLOT, 2001: Medium-bodied, with soft tannins and an appealing deep purple color. Good fruits here but overall somewhat one-dimensional. Drink up. Score 78.

SASSY, MERLOT, 2000: Beyond its attractive, almost impenetrable purple color, there is little to appeal here, for this coarsely textured wine lacks freshness and its fruits are far too stingy. Score 65.

SASSY, PETITE SIRAH, 2000: Chunky and alcoholic, with only stingy black plum and berry flavors on a far too earthy background. Showing age. Score 75.

SASSY, SIRAH, 2000: A blend of Petite Sirah, Cabernet Sauvignon and Merlot. Despite an attractive dark purple color, the wine is watery and lacks either tannins or fruits. Score 60.

Sataf *

Founded in 1997 by Yosi Kursia, Benny and Arieh Bronstein and Peter Ludrikes on Moshav Aminadav in the Jerusalem Mountains, and drawing grapes from vineyards in the nearby Sataf forest and Har Meron, this winery is currently producing about 1,000 bottles annually.

SATAF, CABERNET SAUVIGNON, 2003: Dark ruby in color, medium-bodied, with chunky tannins and with somewhat stingy aromas and flavors of black fruits. Short and one-dimensional. Drink now. Score 80.

SATAF, CABERNET SAUVIGNON, 2002: Lean and on the herbal side, a rather austere wine with black fruits that make themselves felt mostly on the finish. Drink up. Score 84.

SATAF, MERLOT, 2003: Light to medium-bodied with soft, almost flabby tannins and watery on the palate. A few black fruits here. Drink up. Score 79.

SATAF, MERLOT, 2002: Very soft, with almost no tannins and with a sample array of herbal, tea and plum flavors. A simple wine meant for early drinking. Drink up. Score 82.

SATAF, CABERNET FRANC, 2003: Deep ruby towards purple in color, medium-bodied, with chunky tannins, spicy wood and generous blackberry and red currant fruits on a lightly herbal background. An appealing country-style wine. Drink now–2007. Score 84.

SATAF, SANGIOVESE, 2002: Medium-bodied, with a personality that is more of aromas and flavors of earth and leather than of fruits. The plum flavors that do emerge are rather stingy. Drink up. Score 80.

SATAF, CARIGNAN, 2002: A chewy young wine, somewhat tannic, with stingy plum and berry flavors. Drink up. Score 79.

SATAF, CABERNET SAUVIGNON-SANGIOVESE, 2003: Deep garnet in color, medium to full-bodied, somewhat too acidic, with still firm tannins that need time to integrate but already showing tempting currants and wild berries highlighted by a good level of spiciness. Drink now–2008. Score 84.

Savion ***

Founded in 2000 by Ashi Salmon and Eli Pardess on Moshav Nataf in the Jerusalem Mountains and with new vineyards in which they are raising their own Cabernet Sauvignon and Merlot, this winery is currently releasing about 2,000 bottles annually.

SAVION, CABERNET SAUVIGNON, 2003: Dark royal purple towards black, medium to full-bodied, with firm tannins well balanced by smoky wood and an array of red currants and wild berries. On the long finish hints of herbaceousness and chocolate. Drink from release–2009. Tentative Score 87–89.

SAVION, CABERNET SAUVIGNON, 2002: Deep youthful garnet towards royal purple in color, with still firm tannins that need time to integrate but with good balance between currant, berry and plum fruits and spicy wood, this tempting wine needs some time to show its elegance. Drink now–2008. Score 86.

SAVION, CABERNET SAUVIGNON, 2001: Full-bodied, with good balance between generous but soft tannins and fruits, this blend of 90% Cabernet Sauvignon and 10% Merlot spent 12 months in *barriques*, that reflected by hints of smoke, vanilla and cedar wood on a background of currant, plum and berry fruits. A long, just spicy enough finish. Drink now. Score 89.

SAVION, CABERNET SAUVIGNON, 2000: A blend of primarily Cabernet Sauvignon with small percentages of Merlot and Syrah, this deep purple toward black, rather Australian-style wine spent 12 months in small oak barrels and shows soft tannins and plenty of fruit on its medium to full-bodied frame. Drink now. Score 89.

Sde Boker ✶✶✶

Located on Kibbutz Sde Boker in the heart of the Negev Desert, this small winery was founded in 1998 by former Californian Tsvi Remick who studied winemaking at California's Napa Valley College. Relying on Cabernet Sauvignon, Merlot, Carignan, Zinfandel, Sauvignon Blanc and Chardonnay grapes grown entirely under desert conditions, production currently varies between 2,000–3,000 bottles annually.

SDE BOKER, CABERNET SAUVIGNON, 2003: Still tight because of its youth, this complex and well-balanced wine has a band of ripe currant, cherry, spice and anise flavors along with a refined long finish. Drink now–2009. Score 88.

SDE BOKER, CABERNET SAUVIGNON, 2002: A good effort considering the limitations of the 2002 vintage, with plenty of ripe plum, currant and berry flavors but not enough tannins or body. Drink now. Score 85.

SDE BOKER, CABERNET SAUVIGNON, 2001: Dark royal purple in color, this well-balanced, medium to full-bodied red reflects its 23 months in oak casks with abundant vanilla, toasty oak and cedar flavors, those with currant and berry fruits. Drink now–2008. Score 88.

SDE BOKER, CABERNET SAUVIGNON, 2000: Made entirely from Cabernet Sauvignon grapes, this medium-bodied red has ample soft tannins and an array of plum, currant and spicy flavors, as well as attractive overlays of vanilla and black olives that make themselves felt on the finish. Drink up. Score 86.

SDE BOKER, CABERNET SAUVIGNON, 1999: Somewhat on the rustic side, this medium-bodied, unfiltered wine has moderate tannins and green olive and herbal flavors, those matched with just enough cherry and plum flavors. Slightly past its peak. Drink up. Score 86.

SDE BOKER, MERLOT, 2003: Dark in color, with a tart accent to the currant and cherry fruits, those well focused and coming together nicely with what is now only a hint of spicy-toasty oak. Promises to develop appealing mineral and herbal flavors. Drink now–2009. Score 88.

SDE BOKER, MERLOT, 2002: An appealing medium-bodied wine with wild berry, herbal and mineral aromas and flavors and soft tannins, but turning somewhat thin on the finish. Drink now. Score 86.

SDE BOKER, MERLOT, 2000: Medium-bodied, gentle and well-balanced, with abundant black cherries and plums along with gentle hints of mint and spices. Drink now. Score 85.

SDE BOKER, MERLOT, 1999: Medium-bodied and with soft tannins, this wine had in its youth a good interplay between ripe currant, plum, spice and mint flavors, but is now showing age. Drink up. Score 84.

SDE BOKER, ZINFANDEL, 2003: Medium-bodied but with good solidity. Appealing wild berry, cherry and anise flavors that open nicely to a lightly tannic and mineral finish. Not a great Zinfandel but a very nice one indeed. Drink now–2007. Score 87.

SDE BOKER, CARIGNAN, 2003: Light to medium-bodied, with a nice chewy sensation and bright and lively on the palate, showing purple plum and spice flavors that linger nicely. An appealing little wine. Drink now. Score 86.

Sea Horse ✳✳✳✳

Ze'ev Dunie founded this small winery in 2000 on Moshav Bar Giora in the Jerusalem Mountains, after retiring from partnership in the Agur winery where he had made his first Elul wine. Now he has his own vineyards planted in Syrah and Zinfandel, and draws on Cabernet Sauvignon and Merlot from the Upper Galilee. The winery produced 1,800 bottles from the 2001 vintage, 5,000 from 2002, 9,000 from 2003 and 10,000 from 2004. Plans are to attain and hold at a temporary plateau of about 14,000 bottles. Releases to date have included a first wine, Elul, the Syrah-based Camus, the Zinfandel-based Lennon, the 100% Syrah Antoine and the Munch which is made from Petit Sirah. The winery also releases two blended wines, Fellini and TakeTwo.

Elul

SEA HORSE WINERY

ELUL
אֱלוּל
2000
JERUSALEM MOUNTAIN VINEYARDS

ELUL, 2003: A blend of 85% Cabernet Sauvignon, 10% Syrah and 5% Petite Sirah, this proves to be perhaps the best wine yet from Sea Horse. Rich, ripe and complex fruits include juicy berries, currants and black cherries, those with anise and light hints of oak that play nicely on the palate. Smooth and supple tannins and overall excellent structure. Drink from release–2012. Tentative Score 91–93.

ELUL, 2002: Deep garnet towards royal purple in color, this full-bodied blend of 85% Cabernet Sauvignon, 9% Merlot and 6% Syrah, shows generous but soft and well-integrating tannins and jammy currant and berry aromas and flavors, set off by spices and toast, all showing appealing overtones of Mediterranean herbs. Plush and elegant, with a long finish that yields bittersweet chocolate Drink now–2009. Score 92.

ELUL, 2001: Reflecting its 13 months in oak, this full-bodied, deep purple, non-filtered blend of 70% Cabernet Sauvignon, 28% Merlot and 2% Syrah starts off as somewhat chunky and tannic but, given time to open, smoothens out to reveal earthy and herbal currant, black cherry and mineral flavors and aromas, all with lightly toasty oak and tannins that promise to integrate well. Drink now 2007. Score 91.

ELUL, 2000: A blend of 70% Cabernet Sauvignon and 30% Syrah, this medium to full-bodied wine has opened beautifully and shows excellent balance between tannins, fruits and wood. Plenty of currant, cherry and plum flavors, all culminating in an enviably long and just spicy enough finish. Drink now. Score 91.

ELUL, 1999: A blend of 70% Cabernet Sauvignon and 30% Merlot, this full-bodied wine was aged for 14 months in small oak barrels. Tight, with firm but well-integrated tannins and with an appealing earthiness to its plum, currant and spicy flavors, the wine is now somewhat past its peak but is still showing good balance and finesse. Drink up. Score 87.

Sea Horse

SEA HORSE, ANTOINE, 2003: Made from 100% Syrah grapes, this is a rich and complex wine, with smoky, meaty overlays on a delicious array of berry, black cherry, spices and currants. Firm but supple tannins and tempting anise, leathery and earthy notes on the long finish. Only a single barrel was made. Drink now–2010. Score 91

SEA HORSE, ZINFANDEL, 2003: A complex and delicious medium to full-bodied, concentrated and well-balanced wine, with ripe and juicy aromas and flavors of wild berries, cherries, spices and a hint of Mediterranean herbs, all lingering nicely on the palate. Drink now–2007. Score 90.

SEA HORSE, PETITE SIRAH, 2003: Dark in color, full-bodied and concentrated, with generous but well-integrating tannins and oak that do not hold back the complex flavors of black cherry, chocolate and anise that come through and then linger nicely. Drink now–2009. Score 91.

SEA HORSE, MUNCH, 2003: Named as a tribute to artist Edward Munch, this 100% Petite Sirah spent 16 months in French and American oak. The best Petite Sirah ever from Israel, this exotic, spicy and complex wine shows layers of wild berry, plum, currant and black cherry fruits together with a generous peppery overlay and supple tannins. Drink now–2007. Score 91.

SEA HORSE, PETITE SIRAH, 2002: Dark, dense and rich, with aromas and flavors of wild berries, minerals and leather, those backed up nicely by crushed black pepper. Lots of tannins here, but those well in balance with the wood and fruits. Drink now–2007. Score 89.

SEA HORSE, FELLINI, 2003: This blend of 60% Syrah and 40% Cabernet spent 18 months in French and American oak. Complex, with tempting spiciness overlaying wild berry, blackcurrant and meaty plums, and with a tantalizingly sweet edge. Well balanced and moderately long. Drink now–2009. Score 90.

SEA HORSE, FELLINI, 2002: This medium to full-bodied blend of 90% Cabernet Sauvignon and 10% Petite Sirah is warm and elegant, and has distinctly Mediterranean aromas and flavors of fresh herbs and spicy vanilla notes that give an added dimension to the currant and black cherry fruits. Supple tannins, good balance and concentration come together nicely in this oak-aged blend. Drink now. Score 89.

SEA HORSE, CAMUS, 2003: Dark garnet red, full-bodied, with still firm tannins well balanced by spicy wild berry and cherry fruits, the wine boasts an appealing leathery edge on the finish. Rich and complex. Drink now–2009. Score 90.

SEA HORSE, CAMUS, 2002: Dark garnet toward royal purple, this medium to full-bodied red made primarily from oak-aged Shiraz shows deep raspberry flavors with floral accents, but with enough tannins to keep it firm. Clean and long, with hints of black pepper and licorice aromas and flavors, it has a moderately long, near-sweet finish. Drink now–2007. Score 90.

SEA HORSE, LENNON, 2003: A medium to full-bodied blend of 95% Zinfandel and 5% Petite Sirah. With 14 months in American oak this moderately tannic wine shows good concentration of ripe juicy cherry and wild berry flavors as well as an appealing pepper and anise edge. Drink now–2008. Score 90.

SEA HORSE, TAKE TWO, 2004: Dark ruby towards garnet, this blend of 90% Zinfandel and 10% Petite Sirah shows light meaty and leathery notes. Smooth and round, with wild berry fruits that make themselves felt nicely. Drink now–2008. Score 88.

SEA HORSE, TAKE TWO, 2003: A blend of 90% Zinfandel, 9% Petite Sirah and 1% Cabernet Sauvignon, this medium to full-bodied wine reflects its 8 months in American oak with good balance between tannins, wood and fruits. Look for a predominantly Zinfandel personality, round and juicy with spicy berry and cherry flavors on which you will find a firm tannic edge and a moderately-long tar and anise finish. Drink now–2008. Score 89.

SEA HORSE, TAKE TWO, 2002: A bow to the winemaker's background as a filmmaker, this second wine of the winery is a blend of 67% Merlot, 25% Cabernet Sauvignon and 8% Petite Sirah that spent 8 months in American and French oak. Dark cherry red in color and medium-bodied but somewhat light on the palate, the wine has low tannins, lively acidity, and raspberry and black cherry flavors. Drink now. Score 86.

Segal ★★★★

Established in the 1950s as Ashkelon Wines and later taking on the name of the family that owned it, Segal was until the mid-1980s one of the more up-market wineries of the country. In 2001 the company was bought out by Barkan Wineries, but kept its name. Under winemaker Avi Feldstein, with quality vineyards in several regions of the Upper Galilee, and operating now in Barkan's state-of-the-art facilities at Kibbutz Hulda, the winery is now producing several good wines, including unfiltered wines, Single Vineyard wines, and a periodically released Special Reserve, all from Cabernet Sauvignon grapes. Other series are Ben Ami, Marom Galil, Batzir and the low-priced Shel Segal series. The winery relies on Cabernet Sauvignon, Merlot, Argaman, Chardonnay, Sauvignon Blanc, Emerald Riesling, and French Colombard grapes, and current production is about 1.5 million bottles annually, of which nearly one million are in the Shel Segal series.

Single Vineyard

SINGLE VINEYARD, CABERNET SAUVIGNON, KEREM DISHON, 2002: Layers of jammy berry and strawberry fruits on spicy currants, anise, tar and sweet cedar, all along with a touch of green olive that works its way into the finish. Full-bodied and complex with firm but polished tannins. Drink now–2008. Score 89. **K**

SINGLE VINEYARD, KEREM DISHON, 2001: Deep royal purple in color, with blackberry, blackcurrant and plum fruits, this full-bodied wine was aged in oak for 18 months. Showing good balance between fruits, wood and moderately firm but well integrating tannins, this complex wine has a long, near-sweet finish. Drink now–2008. Score 91. **K**

SINGLE VINEYARD, CABERNET SAUVIGNON, KEREM DISHON, 2000: Made entirely from Cabernet Sauvignon grapes, this well-balanced, deep garnet toward royal purple wine reflects its 18 months in small oak casks by showing generous vanilla and smoke, those on a background of currant, berry, plum and spices. Drink now–2007. Score 91. **K**

SINGLE VINEYARD, MERLOT, DOVEV, 2002: Garnet towards black, medium to full-bodied, soft on the palate despite firm tannins and with tempting aromas and flavors of blackberries, plums and sweet herbs. Drink now–2008. Score 89. **K**

SINGLE VINEYARD, CHARDONNAY, DOVEV, 2004: Light gold in color, medium-bodied, with crisp minerals in the background yielding nicely to a rich array of spring flowers, summer fruits and melons. Tempting and long. Drink from release–2008. Tentative Score 88–90. **K**

Unfiltered

UNFILTERED, CABERNET SAUVIGNON, 2002: Rich and ripe, with a complex array of currant, plum and berry aromas and flavors, those set off nicely by smoky, dusty oak. Well focused and round, the wine reflects its 18 months in oak with generous but soft tannins and just the right hint of the oak. Long and mouthfilling. Drink now–2008. Score 90. **K**

UNFILTERED, CABERNET SAUVIGNON, 2001: Full-bodied, reflecting its 22 months in oak with generous vanilla and toasty oak, this still young, concentrated and complex wine is now quite tight and somewhat on the green side. What it needs is bottle aging, and when it does come into its own, look for tart plum, black cherry and berry fruits together with spice and anise aromas and flavors, leading to a long and complex fruited finish. Drink now–2008. Score 90. **K**

UNFILTERED, CABERNET SAUVIGNON, 2000: Made from grapes growing in the Upper Galilee, this deep royal purple toward garnet wine underwent a long skin contact for 35 days and then spent 20 months in new French and American oak barrels. Full-bodied, ripe, intense and with currant, earthy and herbal aromas and flavors, the wine has good balance between fruits, wood and firm tannins. Drink now–2007. Score 90. **K**

UNFILTERED, CABERNET SAUVIGNON, 1999: Full-bodied, well balanced, smooth and nicely focused, the wine shows tempting notes of anise and herbs overlaying basic berry, cherry and currant flavors. Drink now. Score 89. K

UNFILTERED, CABERNET SAUVIGNON, 1993: Now browning and barely showing its black fruits, with tannins and wood far too dominant, the wine is well past its peak. No longer scoreable. K

Special Reserve

SPECIAL RESERVE, CABERNET SAUVIGNON, 2000: Deep purple in color, this medium to full-bodied wine has smooth tannins that are matched well by generous hints of oak and abundant black fruits. Perhaps somewhat one-dimensional, and too plummy for a Cabernet. Drink up. Score 86. K

SPECIAL RESERVE, MERLOT, 2000: Dark garnet, but not completely clear in color, medium to full-bodied, with soft tannins and an array of berry, cherry and near-sweet cassis fruits. Lacking complexity and depth and starting to fade. Drink up. Score 85. K

Ben Ami

BEN AMI, CABERNET SAUVIGNON, 2003: Deep garnet towards royal purple, medium-bodied and with chunky, country style tannins. Appealing plum and berry fruits are matched nicely by a light herbaceousness. Drink now–2007. Score 85. K

BEN AMI, CABERNET SAUVIGNON, 2002: Dark garnet in color, medium-bodied, with generous soft tannins integrating nicely and aromas and flavors of currants, plums and berries as well as hints of wood and herbs. Drink now. Score 86. K

BEN AMI, CABERNET SAUVIGNON, 2001: Crisp, lean and moderately tannic, with an appealing herbal note running through the wild berry and plum flavors. Drink now. Score 85. K

BEN AMI, CABERNET SAUVIGNON, 2000: Medium to full-bodied, with somewhat coarse tannins but good backup of plum, berry and currant flavors. Drink up. Score 85. K.

BEN AMI, MERLOT, 2002: Dark garnet in color, medium-bodied, with chunky, country-style tannins and with aromas and flavors of plums and berries. Marred perhaps by a heavy herbal overtone. Drink up. Score 84. K

BEN AMI, MERLOT, 2001: Firm and tight when first poured, but after a few minutes in the glass it opens to show a compact personality with currant, herbal and cedar notes, all on a moderately tannic and cedar-wood background. Somewhat past its peak. Drink up. Score 85. K

BEN AMI, CABERNET-MERLOT, 2002: Dark royal purple in color, medium-bodied, with chunky, country-style tannins and straightforward currant, plum and berry flavors. Drink up. Score 84. K

Marom Galil

MAROM GALIL, CABERNET SAUVIGNON, 2002: Deep garnet towards inky purple, medium to full-bodied, with firm tannins comfortably balanced by sweet cedar wood, blackcurrants and ripe plum fruits. A long cola-berry finish. Drink now–2008. Score 87. K

MAROM GALIL, CABERNET SAUVIGNON, 2001: Inky purple to black in color, medium to full-bodied, and reflecting its 18 months in oak with generous sweet and smoky oak, those well balanced by firm but well integrating tannins and a rich array of blackcurrant, cassis and wild berry fruits. Long and complex. Drink now–2007. Score 89. K

MAROM GALIL, CABERNET SAUVIGNON, 2000: Dark purple, medium-bodied, with firm, almost hot tannins that tend to hold back the black fruits. Drink now. Score 85. K

MAROM GALIL, CABERNET SAUVIGNON, 1999: This medium-bodied, moderately tannic wine shows generous earthiness and moderate herbal aromas and flavors, together with wild berry, cherry and currant fruits and a pleasant cola-berry finish. Drink up. Score 85. K

MAROM GALIL, MERLOT, 2003: Deep ruby towards garnet, medium-bodied, with soft tannins integrating nicely and currant and wild berry fruits. A bit heavy on the oak. Drink now–2008. Score 87. K

MAROM GALIL, MERLOT, 2002: Medium to full-bodied, this blend of 85% Merlot and 15% Cabernet Sauvignon has firm tannins and generous wood, those balanced nicely by plum, berry and currant fruits. Round and mouthfilling. Drink now–2007. Score 87. K

MAROM GALIL, MERLOT, 2000: Soft, smooth, medium-bodied and fruity, you might never guess that this wine was made from Merlot grapes. Drink up. Score 84. K

MAROM GALIL, RED, 2003: Light to medium-bodied, with soft tannins this blend of Cabernet Sauvignon and Shiraz has a distinctly berry-cherry personality. Drink up. Score 83. K

MAROM GALIL, RED, 2002: A medium-bodied blend of Cabernet Sauvignon and Shiraz with somewhat chunky tannins and flavors of plums and black cherries. Drink up. Score 81. K

MAROM GALIL, CHARDONNAY, 2003: Not subjected to the usual process of malolactic fermentation, this rich, round and spicy white offers up toasty vanilla and caramel nuances to complement pineapple, melon and citrus fruits on a generous oaky background, culminating in a long finish. Drink now. Score 89. K

MAROM GALIL, CHARDONNAY, 2001: Aged in oak barrels for 6 months, this medium-bodied, quite pleasant wine is somewhat on the simple side, revealing only stingy tropical fruit, pear, green apple and vanilla aromas and flavors. Drink up. Score 85. K

MAROM GALIL, CHARDONNAY, 2000: Lacking depth and barely reflecting the 7 months it spent in oak casks, but smooth and refreshing, with citrus and apple flavors and aromas. Past its peak. Drink up. Score 82. K

MAROM GALIL, WHITE, 2003: Light golden straw in color, this simple blend of Sauvignon Blanc and Chardonnay shows some citrus and green apple aromas and flavors along with generous acidity to keep the wine lively. Drink up. Score 82. K

Shel Segal

SHEL SEGAL, CABERNET SAUVIGNON, 2003: Oak aged for about eight months, dark garnet in color, medium-bodied, with chunky, country-style tannins and a few berry and black cherry fruits. Drink now. Score 84. **K**

SHEL SEGAL, CABERNET SAU-VIGNON, 2002: Made entirely from Cabernet Sauvignon grapes and aged in oak barrels for eight months, this medium-bodied wine with black fruits and moderate tannins shows very few of the varietal traits of Cabernet Sauvignon. Drink up. Score 81. **K**

SHEL SEGAL, MERLOT, 2002: A medium-bodied blend of 90% Merlot and 10% Cabernet Sauvignon, this deep garnet-colored wine was aged for eight months in American oak casks and now shows plenty of vanilla and oak along with some black fruits but lacks backbone and depth. Drink up. Score 80. **K**

SHEL SEGAL, DRY RED, 2003: This blend of 65% Argaman filled out with Merlot and Petite Sirah has dark color but light body with no noticeable tannins and only a few black fruits. Drink up. Score 75. **K**

SHEL SEGAL, DRY RED, 2002: This year a blend of Argaman, Petite Sirah, Merlot and Cabernet, the wine has an attractive dark cherry toward garnet color but beyond that is low in aromas and flavors and lacks concentration or depth. Drink up. Score 75. **K**

SHEL SEGAL, DRY RED, 2001: With a dark cherry-red color and light to medium body this is a smooth, fruity and low tannic wine that makes for easy drinking. Drink up. Score 84. **K**

SHEL SEGAL, EMERALD RIESLING, 2003: This semi-dry, light and flowery white shows tropical and grapefruit flavors. Drink up. Score 82. **K**

SHEL SEGAL, EMERALD RIESLING, 2002: Light to medium-bodied, this semi-dry white has a flowery nose, some appealing summer and tropical fruits and a not exaggerated sense of sweetness. Drink up. Score 78. **K**

SHEL SEGAL, DRY WHITE, 2003: As it often is, this dry blend of Colombard, Sauvignon Blanc and Riesling has some appealing citrus and tropical fruits. Score 79. **K**

SHEL SEGAL, DRY WHITE, 2002: A blend of French Colombard, Sauvignon Blanc and Riesling, with good dryness and some citrus and pineapple flavors. Drink up. Score 79. **K**

SHEL SEGAL, SEMI-DRY WHITE, 2003: Far too sweet, without balancing acidity and with more floral than fruit aromas and largely grapefruit flavors. Drink up. Score 72. **K**

SHEL SEGAL, SEMI-DRY WHITE, 2002: Too sweet and floral, with only stingy fruits on the nose and palate. Drink up. Score 75. **K**

Smadar *

Established by Motti Sela in 1998 and located in Zichron-Ya'akov, this winery produces wines from nearby vineyards owned by the family, those containing Cabernet Sauvignon, Merlot and Carignan grapes. Production is currently about 6,000 bottles anually.

SMADAR, CABERNET SAUVIGNON, 2003: Dark ruby towards garnet, with firm tannins and perhaps too generous an impact from the wood, but with berry, currant and black cherry fruits and a light herbaceousness that make themselves felt. Somewhat short and one dimensional. Drink from release. Tentative Score 83–85.

SMADAR, CABERNET SAUVIGNON, 2002: Dark royal purple in color, medium to full-bodied, with chunky tannins and moderate wood influence, and aromas and flavors of blackberry and currant fruits as well as a hint of earthiness. Perhaps a bit coarse but a pleasant country-style wine. Drink now. Score 84.

SMADAR, MERLOT, 2002: Dark ruby with a hint of browning. Medium-bodied, with firm tannins and generous wood that tend to hide the black cherry and berry fruits. Drink now. Score 84.

SMADAR, CARIGNAN, 2003: Bright light garnet red, medium-bodied, with almost unfelt tannins and aromas and flavors of wild berries and cherries. Drink now. Score 82.

SMADAR, CARIGNAN, 2002: Deep ruby red, with soft tannins and aromas and flavors of blackberries, cherries and, on the finish an unwelcomed barnyard sensation. Drink up. Score 80.

Sode Hayain **

Founded by Reuven Cohen and located on Moshav Tirat Yehuda in the central plains, the winery produces about 3,500 bottles annually, drawing on Cabernet Sauvignon and Merlot grapes from vineyards in different parts of the country.

SODE HAYAIN, CABERNET SAUVIGNON, REUBEN'S WINE, 2002: Dark garnet towards purple in color, medium to full-bodied, with chunky, country-style tannins and perhaps too ample influence of the oak barrels, showing vanilla, spices and herbs overlaying the currant and berry fruits. Drink now. Score 85. **K**

SODE HAYAIN, MERLOT, REUBEN'S WINE, 2002: Medium-bodied, with soft tannins but with generous spicy and toasted bread from the oak in which it aged that tend to hide the plum and berry fruits. Drink now. Score 85. **K**

Soreq ✱✱✱

Originally a partnership of Yossi Shacham, his son Nir and
Barry Saslove, this small winery was founded in 1994 on
Moshav Tal Shachar, which is situated at the foot of the
Jerusalem Mountains between the Ayalon and Soreq Valleys.
After Saslove resigned to open his own winery in 1998, Nir
Shacham took over as winemaker and has recently taken
on full ownership. The winery relies entirely on Cabernet
Sauvignon and Merlot grapes grown in its own vineyards,
and releases wines in Special Reserve and regular editions.
The winery released 30,000 bottles from the 2002 vintage
but is now reexamining its policies and will release less than
1,000 bottles from the 2003 vintage. Production for 2004 was
about 5,000 bottles.

Special Reserve

SPECIAL RESERVE, CABERNET SAUVIGNON, 2001: Medium to full-
bodied, the wine shows generous tannins well balanced by spicy wood
and tempting currant, plum and berry fruits along with hints of smoke
and chocolate, on a medium-long finish. Drink now–2007. Score 89.

SPECIAL RESERVE, CABERNET SAUVIGNON, 2000: Full-bodied, the
wine shows generous tannins that are now integrating nicely, along
with rich aromas and flavors of blackcurrant and berry fruits, those
complemented nicely by toasted oak and spices. On the long finish look
for hints of chocolate and mint. Drink now. Score 88.

SPECIAL RESERVE, CABERNET SAUVIGNON, 1999: Rich, muscular
and full-bodied, but elegant and sophisticated, with currants, black
cherries, violets and dried herbs. Rich in tannins that promise to integrate nicely. Drink now. Score 92.

SPECIAL RESERVE, CABERNET SAUVIGNON, 1998: This deep purple
toward garnet, medium to full-bodied wine opens with an attack of
stewed, almost sweet black fruits. Given time in the glass, these yield
to appealing aromas and flavors of cassis, plums and herbs, all on a
moderately long finish. Drink up. Score 87.

SPECIAL RESERVE, CABERNET SAUVIGNON, 1997: Medium-bodied, dark, deep and long, with spicy currants running throughout, and a long finish yielding appealing hints of anise, peppermint and vanilla. Drink up. Score 87.

SPECIAL RESERVE, CABERNET SAUVIGNON, 1996: Dark ruby toward purple in its youth, this medium to full-bodied wine may be beginning to lighten slightly in color, but still shows deep fruit flavors, smooth tannins and appealing oak overtones. Long and gentle, with hints of spices on the finish. Somewhat past its peak. Drink up. Score 86.

SPECIAL RESERVE, CABERNET SAUVIGNON-MERLOT, 1999: This deep purple, medium to full-bodied blend of 60% Cabernet Sauvignon and 40% Merlot is somewhat stingy in its currant and berry fruits, and its tannins are almost unfelt, making the wine somewhat one-dimensional. Drink now. Score 86.

SPECIAL RESERVE, CABERNET SAUVIGNON-MERLOT, 1997: Medium to full-bodied and still showing generous dark fruit and vanilla aromas and flavors, these now overlaid nicely with generous hints of Mediterranean herbs and Oriental spices. Starting to show age. Drink up. Score 88.

SPECIAL RESERVE, MERLOT, 2001: Deep garnet red, medium to full-bodied, with generous soft tannins integrating nicely with generous oaky-vanilla aromas and flavors, those opening to reveal plum and blackberry fruits and a long, moderately sweet finish. Drink now. Score 89.

SPECIAL RESERVE, MERLOT, 1999: An almost inky dark medium to full-bodied Merlot, with excellent balance between soft tannins, ample but not exaggerated oak, well-delineated black fruits and enchanting herbal overtones. Drink up. Score 89.

Soreq

SOREQ, CABERNET SAUVIGNON, 2002: Reflecting its 18 months in *barriques* with generous sweet cedar, generous vanilla and firm tannins, those balanced well with currant, plum and wild berry fruits and an appealingly long finish rich in espresso and tobacco notes. Drink now–2008. Score 88.

SOREQ, CABERNET SAUVIGNON, TAL SHACHAR, 2001: 100% Cabernet Sauvignon aged for 18 months in French and American oak *barriques*, this medium-bodied red shows basic good balance between wood, soft tannins and somewhat dominating oak. The wine shows plum, blackcurrant and black cherry fruits on a generous smoky oak background. Drink now–2007. Score 86.

SOREQ, CABERNET SAUVIGNON, 1998: Deep purple toward garnet, this medium to full-bodied wine opens on the palate with stewed, almost sweet black fruits. Given time in the glass these will yield to appealing aromas and flavors of cassis, plums and herbs. With tannins now well integrated, and a comfortably long finish, the wine is beginning to show the first signs of age. Drink up. Score 89.

SOREQ, CABERNET SAUVIGNON, 1996: After having spent 21 months in oak barrels, the wine was blended with 5% of Merlot grapes. The wine starts off with a charming fruity character, but suffers from too high acidity and earthy flavors that tend to dominate. Showing age and no longer scoreable.

SOREQ, MERLOT, TAL SHACHAR, 2001: This medium-bodied, moderately tannic wine is dominated by wood that overshadows the plum and currant fruits. Drink up. Score 85.

SOREQ, MERLOT, 1998: Crisp and refreshing in its youth, with attractive raspberry, plum, currant and herbal aromas and flavors. Well past its peak and no longer scoreable.

Srigim *

Founded by Uriel Harari and Moti Mordechai on Moshav Srigim in the Ella Valley in 2000, this small winery released its first wines from the 2002 harvest. Drawing on grapes from the Judean Mountains, the Ella Valley and Gush Etzion, the winery has chosen to concentrate entirely on Cabernet Sauvignon. Production from 2002 was limited to 450 bottles, in 2003 to 1,100 bottles and in 2004 to 1,500 bottles. Target production is 2,500 bottles.

SRIGIM, CABERNET SAUVIGNON, 2003: Aged in oak for 12 months, this deep royal purple in color, full-bodied red offers firm tannins and generous oak, those complemented by super-ripe, almost jammy black plum and berry fruits. Drink now–2007. Score 85.

SRIGIM, CABERNET SAUVIGNON, BICURIM, 2002: Dark garnet but not as clear as one might hope for, with chunky tannins and raspberry, cherry and currant aromas and flavors. A simple country-style wine. Drink up. Score 82.

Tabor ✶✶✶✶

Founded in 1999 by several grape growing families in the village of Kfar Tabor in the Lower Galilee, and recently coming under the partial control of the UDV Beverage Corporation, this modern winery draws on white grapes largely from their own vineyards near Mount Tabor and on red grapes from the Upper Galilee. Initial production was of 20,000 bottles, but by 2003 had already jumped to 95,000, about half of which was committed to export. Production in 2004 was 150,000 bottles and the winery is striving to attain a maximum of 240,000–300,000 bottles annually.

European-trained winemaker Arieh Nesher is currently releasing wines in three series. The top-of-the-line label is Mes'cha, a series of varietal wines that now includes Cabernet Sauvignon, Merlot and Chardonnay, those to be joined shortly by Gewurztraminer. A second label, Tabor-Adama, reflects the type of soils in the vineyards. In reading the labels it may be useful to know that *adama* translates into soil; *gir* is chalky soil; *terra rosa* is red earth; and *bazelet* refers to volcanic soil. There is also a more basic series, the label Tabor.

Mes'cha

MES'CHA, CABERNET SAUVIGNON, 2003: Deep ruby towards garnet, medium to full-bodied, with still firm tannins but those yielding nicely to smoky wood and currant, berry and plum fruits. Generous and well-balanced. Drink from release–2008. Tentative Score 88–90. **K**

MES'CHA, CABERNET SAUVIGNON, 2002: Deep royal-purple in color, medium to full-bodied, with good balance between firm tannins, spicy oak and forward berry, currant and plum aromas and flavors. Moderately long, with a hint of spices on the finish. Drink now–2008. Score 88. **K**

MES'CHA, CABERNET SAUVIGNON, 2001: Dark garnet red, medium to full-bodied, with good balance betweeen firm but nicely integrating tannins, spicy oak and an appealing array of blackcurrant, plums, smoke and fresh earthy aromas and flavors. Long and mouthfilling. Drink now–2008. Score 90. K

MES'CHA, CABERNET SAUVIGNON, 2000: Full-bodied, concentrated and intense, this deeply tannic wine opens slowly in the glass to show black fruits, cigar tobacco, tar, and earthy aromas and flavors. Still firm and muscular, but finally showing signs of opening. Drink now–2008. Score 89. K

MES'CHA, CABERNET SAUVIGNON-MERLOT, 2001: A full-bodied blend of 80% Cabernet Sauvignon and 20% Merlot, the wine was made from grapes harvested in Malkiya in the Upper Galilee and aged partly in new oak and partly in one-year-old barrels for 14 months. Young and tight, with excellent focus and tempting flavors of currants, spices and cedar flavors along with a leathery note that runs throughout. As rich on its near-sweet nose as on its fully dry palate, and with a long fruity finish, this is the best wine made by the winery to date. Drink now–2008. Score 91. K

MESCHA, CHARDONNAY, 2004: Deep gold in color, medium to full-bodied, with appealing pear, citrus flavors and a hint of mango on a background of spicy oak along with a round buttery texture. Good balance between wood, acidity and fruits. Drink now–2007. Score 89. K

MES'CHA, CHARDONNAY, 2003: Golden straw in color, this medium to full-bodied white reflects its 4 months in oak with hints of smoky and spicy wood together with rich, lightly creamy layers of pear, honey and apricots. Complex and long. Drink now. Score 90. K

Adama

ADAMA, CABERNET SAUVIGNON, TERRA ROSA, 2004: Deep ruby towards garnet in color, medium to full-bodied, with good balance between yielding tannins, a light spicy wood overlay and cassis, wild berry and plum fruits. Round, satisfying and moderately long. Drink from release–2008. Tentative Score 87–89. K

ADAMA, CABERNET SAUVIGNON, TERRA ROSSA, 2003: Dark royal purple, almost inky, this medium to full-bodied red is already showing appealing currant, cherry and spice flavors and aromas. Inherent good balance between soft tannins, acidity and fruits and an appealing spicy finish. Drink now–2007. Score 87. K

ADAMA CABERNET SAUVIGNON, TERRA ROSA, 2002: Dark, tight and firm but well focused and opening nicely in the glass to reveal an array of ripe cherry, currant, spice, anise and lightly toasty oak flavors.

Supple and well focused with just the right hints of tannins that come to the fore on the long finish. Drink now. Score 88. **K**

ADAMA, MERLOT, GIR, 2004: Youthful royal purple in color, medium-bodied, with generous but soft and well-integrating tannins, the wine reflects the soil of its grapes well. Good balance between wood and blackberry, currant and light spicy and earth overtones. Drink from release–2008. Tentative Score 88–90. **K**

ADAMA, MERLOT, GIR, 2003: Dark garnet in color, medium-bodied, and somewhat internationalized in style, with soft tannins, hints of sweet cedar wood and forward plum and currant fruits. Turns a bit more complex on the lightly herbal finish. Drink now. Score 88. **K**

ADAMA, MERLOT, GIR, 2002: Dark cherry red toward garnet, this medium-bodied, lightly oaked wine has a somewhat muted nose but shows very well on the palate, opening to reveal dark plums, currants, smooth tannins and a rich lingering finish. Drink now. Score 87. **K**

ADAMA, MERLOT, BAZELET, 2003: Opening beautifully now, reflecting its 12 months in oak with appealing smoky and vanilla overlays and showing tempting blackcurrant, purple plum and berry fruits. A distinctly French-style wine, well balanced and generous. Drink now–2007. Score 89. **K**

ADAMA, MERLOT, BAZELET, 2001: Deep garnet in color and reflecting its aging in French and American oak with hints of vanilla and smoke, this medium to full-bodied red is aromatic, round and mouth-filling. Features currant, spice and black cherry flavors, smooth and polished tannins, and a rich finish with fruits that fan out beautifully on the palate. Drink now. Score 89. **K**

ADAMA, CABERNET FRANC, ROSÉ, CHARSIT, 2004: Bright cherry red in color, this medium-bodied crisply dry wine shows good balancing acidity and appealing berry, cherry and plum aromas and flavors. A well made round rose. Drink up. Score 87. **K**

ADAMA, SHIRAZ, CHARSIT, 2004: Full-bodied, with soft tannins, good hints of smoky oak and sweet cedar, and generous black plums, berries and currants. Still in its infancy but showing promise to be a simultaneously complex and easy-to-drink wine. Drink from release–2008. Tentative Score 89–91. **K**

ADAMA, SHIRAZ, CHARSIT, 2003: Deep garnet, medium to full-bodied, with firm tannins but those well integrated with spicy oak, vanilla and generous red plum and currant fruits. On the long finish, appealing light meaty and herbal overtones. Drink now–2009. Score 89. **K**

ADAMA, CHARDONNAY, GIR, 2004: Crisp, clean and with abundant minerals on the nose and palate, those matched well by citrus and melon fruits. Calls to mind a Petit Chablis. Drink now. Score 87. **K**

ADAMA, CHARDONNAY, GIR, 2003: Reflecting three months in new French and American oak, this light to medium-bodied straw colored wine shows an appealing touch of spicy-vanilla laden wood together with green apple and citrus fruits. Not long or complex, with a hint of bitterness now creeping in but still quite pleasing. Drink now. Score 86. **K**

ADAMA, CHARDONNAY, BAZELET, 2004: Light gold, medium-bodied, with citrus and tropical fruits on a lightly earthy background. Good balancing acidity keeps the wine lively and hints of earthiness and herbaceousness add complexity. Drink now–2007. Score 88. **K**

ADAMA, CHARDONNAY, BAZELET, 2003: Golden straw in color, with green reflections, this supple wine has a pleasing earthy accent to its citrus, hazelnut and pineapple notes. Appealing ripe pear flavors on the finish make this a deep, complex and satisfying wine. Drink now. Score 89. **K**

ADAMA, CHARDONNAY, 2002: Deep golden toward bronze in color, almost as if it had aged prematurely, and with aromas and flavors far too reminiscent of stewed quinces and baked apples, this medium-bodied wine lacks liveliness. Drink up. Score 74. **K**

ADAMA, SAUVIGNON BLANC, CHARSIT, 2004: Lightly oaked (2 months in *barriques*), light gold in color, medium-bodied and with lively grassy, citrus and citrus peel aromas and flavors, calling to mind the wines of France's Loire Valley. Refreshing, complex and with a long finish. Drink now–2007. Score 88. **K**

ADAMA, SAUVIGNON BLANC, GIR, 2004: Unoaked, crisply dry with light herbal and earthy hints on a background of grapefruit, orange peel and minerals. Fresh, refreshing and generous. Drink now. Score 88. **K**

Tabor

TABOR, CABERNET SAUVI- GNON, 2003: Deep royal purple, showing herbal and black olive flavors backed up nicely by currants and wild berries. Soft tannins and good balance make the wine drinkable now–2007. Score 86. **K**

TABOR, MERLOT, 2003: Medium-bodied, with soft tannins and generous berry and black cherry fruits. Not complex but pleasant. Drink now. Score 85. **K**

TABOR, SHIRAZ, 2003: Dark purple in color, with true Shiraz characteristics, and at this stage still brooding and very firm, the wine opens in the glass to reveal hints of licorice and game together with firm tannins and deep raspberry, floral accents. Clean and long, a fine Mediterranean version of Shiraz. Drink now–2007. Score 88. **K**

TABOR, GEWURZTRAMINER, 2004: Light to medium-bodied, neither crisp nor fresh with its fruits hidden by aromas and flavors of damp earth and mushrooms. Drink up. Score 74. **K**

Tanya *

Located in the town of Ofra at the foot of the Hebron Mountains, this kosher winery established by Yoram Cohen released its first wines in 2002. Drawing on Cabernet Sauvignon and Merlot grapes from Gush Etzion and the Golan Heights, production in 2002 was 2,000 bottles, in 2003, 4,800 bottles and production for 2004 was about 6,500 bottles.

TANYA, CABERNET SAUVIGNON, SPECIAL RESERVE, 2003: Dark cherry red, medium to full-bodied, with firm but already well-integrating tannins and a light influence of oak. Aromas and flavors of currants, plums, Mediterranean herbs and a hint of tobacco. Drink from release–2008. Tentative Score 82–84. K

TANYA, CABERNET SAUVIGNON, SPECIAL RESERVE, 2002: Medium-bodied and deep garnet in color, with firm but well-integrated tannins and a nice hint of wood after 4 months in small barrels. Barnyard aromas are present when first poured, but those fade away to reveal aromas and flavors of black fruits and herbs. Drink now. Score 84. K

TANYA, MERLOT, SPECIAL RESERVE, 2003: Medium-bodied, with chunky tannins and a too generous smoky-spicy influence of the oak, this holding back whatever black fruits are here. Drink from release. Tentative Score 80–82. K

TANYA, MERLOT, SPECIAL RESERVE, 2002: Dark cherry-red in color, this wine reflects its 7 months in oak with surprisingly firm tannins and very generous toasted oak aromas and flavors, both of which come together to hide the plum and berry flavors that struggle to make themselves felt. Drink now. Score 83. K

Tekoa *

Located in the village of Tekoa near Bethlehem, this small winery produces 2,000–3,000 bottles annually of organic kosher wines made entirely from Berlinka grapes. This South African varietal, usually thought of as a table grape, was brought to Israel by owner-winemaker Dov Levy Neumand.

TEKOA, BERLINKA, 2000: Lacking depth, breadth or length, and following the pattern set with the 1997, 1998 and 1999 editions, this wine had almost liquor-like cherry, berry and herbal flavors in its youth and began to oxidize and caramelize within months of release. Score 50. K

TEKOA, BERLINKA, 1997, 1998 AND 1999: Produced organically from grapes usually thought of as appropriate for table use and not for making wine. Neither smooth nor satisfying in their youth, whatever vague charms they may have had in the past are now lost as the wines have oxidized and caramelized and no longer scoreable.

Tishbi ✳✳✳

Following the initiatives of Baron Edmond de Rothschild, the Tishbi family started to plant vineyards in 1882 on the slopes of Mount Carmel near the town of Zichron Ya'akov and continued to cultivate vines throughout the next hundred years. In 1985, Jonathan Tishbi, a fourth generation member of the family, launched this family-owned winery in the nearby town of Binyamina, initially named Habaron as homage to Baron Rothschild, and later renamed Tishbi.

Working with Australian-trained winemaker Yael Saltman, the winery has just made the leap from 650,000–870,000 bottles to an output of nearly 1,000,000 annually. Drawing on grapes from their own vineyards as well as from vineyards in the Jerusalem region and the Upper Galilee, the winery produces several series, the top-of-the-line being the age-worthy Cabernet Sauvignon, Merlot and Chardonnay wines in the Jonathan Tishbi Special Reserve series. These are followed by varietal wines in the Estate and Vineyards series, and by the more popularly priced wines in the Tishbi and Baron series. The winery also produces a sparkling wine and a Port-style wine.

Special Reserve

SPECIAL RESERVE, CABERNET SAUVIGNON, BEN ZIMRA, 2003:
Still in its infancy, this deep purple, full-bodied wine already shows soft

tannins that promise to integrate nicely with spicy wood, vanilla and an array of aromas and flavors including cassis, ripe berries and plums on a light herbaceous background. Well balanced and moderately-long. Best 2007–2010. Tentative Score 87–89. **K**

SPECIAL RESERVE, CABERNET SAUVIGNON, BEN ZIMRA, 2002: Deep purple in color, ripe, bold and concentrated, the wine has solid and still firm tannins, those well balanced by oak and fruits. The chewy tannins, deep currant, oak and spicy aromas and flavors make the wine one that will profit from bottle time. Drink now–2008. Score 90. **K**

SPECIAL RESERVE, CABERNET SAUVIGNON, GUSH ETZION, 2002: Medium to full-bodied with surprisingly soft tannins and aromas and flavors of currant, cherry, plum and wild berry fruits, just the right hint of wood, and a hint of anise on the medium finish. A well-balanced wine that promises to develop with further aging. Drink now–2007. Score 88. **K**

SPECIAL RESERVE, CABERNET SAUVIGNON, BEN ZIMRA, 1999: Ripe and harmonious, this well balanced wine offers up fresh cherry, spice and plum flavors along with supple tannins, all overlaid by appealing hints of earthiness and herbs. Drink now. Score 90. **K**

SPECIAL RESERVE, CABERNET SAUVIGNON, SDE BOKER, 1999: Perhaps reflecting the origin of the grapes in the Negev Desert, the wine is not so much earthy or herbal but instead is marked by distinct flavors of green olives and spices. Full-bodied, with tannins that integrate nicely now, it also shows ripe and well focused black cherry and currant flavors along with an appealing long finish. Drink now. Score 89. **K**

SPECIAL RESERVE, CABERNET SAUVIGNON, KFAR YUVAL, 1999: With earthy currant and cherry flavors emerging through firm tannins, this rich and concentrated wine is now showing the smooth and supple texture promised in its youth. Drink now. Score 88. **K**

SPECIAL RESERVE, CABERNET SAUVIGNON, 1998: As it was during its extreme youth, this is a well-balanced, well-proportioned wine with generous cassis, plum, berry and spicy overtones. Full-bodied, with now soft and integrated tannins and a generous toasty oak overlay, and hints of anise and chocolate on the finish. Drink now. Score 90. **K**

SPECIAL RESERVE, MERLOT, KEREM KFAR YUVAL-GUSH ETZION, 2002: Graceful, with a deep, almost inky garnet color and generous but smooth tannins, this supple and well-balanced medium to full-bodied wine shows plums, ripe cherry, chocolate and gentle cedar-oak aromas and flavors along with a sweet and spicy herbal finish. Drink now–2007. Score 90. **K**

SPECIAL RESERVE, MERLOT, 1999: This deep garnet, full-bodied wine, with far more tannins than one usually anticipates in a Merlot, is nevertheless rich and flavorful, and has good balance between tannins, the oak in which it was aged, and fruits, those including spicy black cherry, plum, currant and mineral flavors. Drink now. Score 89. K

SPECIAL RESERVE, MERLOT, 1998: Smooth and generous, well balanced and harmonious, with lots of berry, currant and cherry flavors, this well made wine shows intensity and elegance. Drink up. Score 90. K

SPECIAL RESERVE, CHARDONNAY, 2004: Aged in 300 liter French barrels, this deep golden, full-bodied and buttery-creamy white shows appealing pear and vanilla aromas and flavors. At this stage somewhat dominated by the wood. Drink now–2007. Score 86. K

SPECIAL RESERVE, CHARDONNAY, 2003: Aging 4 months in new French oak barrels, this light golden colored, medium-bodied wine shows gentle touches of vanilla, spicy oak, pineapple and citrus aromas and flavors. Drink now. Score 87. K

SPECIAL RESERVE, CHARDONNAY, 2000: Medium to full-bodied Chardonnay, distinctly new world in its style and thus marked by an abundance of oak (perhaps even too much) and plenty of vanilla, but with good supporting pineapple and green apple fruits. Somewhat past its peak. Drink up. Score 85. K

Estate

ESTATE, CABERNET SAUVIGNON, 2004: Medium to full-bodied, with silky smooth tannins and layers of currant, berry and plum fruits, those matched nicely by hints of spicy wood and a light herbal overlay. Drink now–2008. Score 87. K

ESTATE, CABERNET SAUVIGNON, 2003: Deep garnet, medium to full-bodied, with an appealing earthy overtone to currant and berry fruits. Overall good balance and structure bodes well for the future. Drink now–2007. Score 87. K

ESTATE, CABERNET SAUVIGNON, 2002: Oak-aged for 12 months in small casks, this dark garnet medium to full-bodied wine offers up generous but soft and already nicely integrating tannins, appealing currant, plum and wild berry fruits, and hints of vanilla and smoky oak. Drink now. Score 87. K

ESTATE, CABERNET SAUVIGNON, 2001: Surprisingly light in color, this medium-bodied, moderately tannic wine shows fresh currant, berry and plum notes, and nicely reflects its 18 months in oak with a finish of spicy oak. Drink now. Score 86. K

ESTATE, CABERNET SAUVIGNON, 2000: Medium-bodied, with soft tannins that are already well integrated and traditional blackcurrant and spicy aromas and flavors. Drink up. Score 85. K

ESTATE, MERLOT, 2004: Made from grapes from Sde Boker in the Negev, this soft, medium-bodied wine offers a few berry and spice flavors but seems badly out of balance and even at this early stage is showing signs of browning. Drink up. Tentative Score 80–82. K

ESTATE, MERLOT, 2003: Deep garnet red, medium-bodied, with firm tannins that yield in the glass. Good balance between lightly smoky wood and plum and currant fruits all leading to a moderately long finish. Drink now. Score 86. K

ESTATE, MERLOT, 2002: A blend of 92% Merlot and 8% Cabernet Sauvignon, this dark, medium to full-bodied wine is somewhat closed on the nose but shows tempting berry, black cherry and currant flavors, those coming together with good hints of the oak and a medium-long finish. Drink now. Score 87. K

ESTATE, MERLOT, 2001: After 18 months in oak this medium to dark royal purple, medium-bodied blend of 85% Merlot and 15% Cabernet Sauvignon shows soft tannins and generous hints of vanilla from the oak as well as good plum and berry fruits, all on a lightly spicy background. Drink now. Score 86. K

ESTATE, MERLOT, 2000: An oak-aged blend of 85% Merlot and 15% Cabernet Sauvignon, this medium-bodied wine shows appealing berry and black cherry fruits along with smooth tannins and overlays of vanilla and spices. Drink now. Score 85. K

ESTATE, MERLOT, 1999: Deep in color, this lean wine has a nice vanilla edge that overlays berry, currant and herbal flavors. Drink up. Score 85. **K**

TISHBI ESTATE

2003

PINOT NOIR
DRY RED WINE

¶ IN 1882, MY GRANDFATHER, MICHAEL CHAMILETZKI, SET FOOT UPON THE LAND OF ZICHRON YAAKOV. HE MADE HIS FIRST HOME IN NEARBY SHEFEYA AND WAS CHOSEN BY BARON EDMUND DE ROTHSCHILD TO PLANT AND DEVELOP VINEYARDS ON THIS LAND. IN 1925, THE FAMOUS POET CHAIM NACHMAN BIALIK VISITED AND GAVE MICHAEL A NEW HEBREW FAMILY NAME, "TISHBI" AN ABBREVIATION MEANING "A RESIDENT OF SHEFEYA IN ISRAEL." ¶ FOUR GENERATIONS HAVE PASSED AND I STILL REMEMBER HARVESTING BY HAND IN MY FAMILY'S VINEYARDS AND BRINGING THE WAGONS OF GRAPES TO BE PRESSED IN THE NEARBY WINERY. WE STILL FOLLOW THE TRADITIONAL GROWING METHODS PASSED ON TO ME BY FATHER AND GRANDFATHER. *Jonathan Tishbi* PROPRIETOR

ESTATE, PINOT NOIR 2004: Light wood influences, soft tannins, medium-bodied, with berry, plum and light earthy-mineral hints leading to a medium-long finish. A good quaffer. Drink now. Score 85. **K**

ESTATE, PINOT NOIR, 2003: Aged in new and old oak, this attractive medium to full-bodied wine offers up light earthy, mineral and herbal overtones on a background of wild berries and red plums. Drink now. Score 87. **K**

ESTATE, CHARDONNAY, 2004: Made from organically raised grapes from the Gush Etzion region, this unoaked wine shows some melon and pear fruits but is lacking in acidity and somewhat flat on the palate. Drink now. Score 82. **K**

ESTATE, CHARDONNAY, 2002: Fermented partly in oak barrels and partly in stainless steel, this medium-bodied wine is tight and firm, with crisp citrus, pineapple and pear aromas and flavors that tend to fade in the glass. Drink up. Score 84. **K**

ESTATE, CHARDONNAY, 2000: Pleasant, crisp and with good citrus and mineral overtones, the wine is already showing age. Score 84. **K**

ESTATE, SAUVIGNON BLANC, 2004: Light straw in color, medium-bodied and aromatic, with summer fruit and green apples on the palate. Good balance between natural acidity and fruits. Drink now. Score 87. **K**

ESTATE, SAUVIGNON BLANC, 2003: Light gold in color, with orange and green tinges, this medium-bodied white offers up appealing aromas and flavors of citrus, green apples and melon fruits on a crisply fresh background. Drink now. Score 86. **K**

ESTATE, SAUVIGNON BLANC, 2002: Spicy and round, this well-balanced, generous wine shows aromas and flavors of melon, grapefruit and lemon rind along with a nice herbal touch and a floral finish. Drink up. Score 87. K

ESTATE, SAUVIGNON BLANC, 2000: Light and fruity, with apple and spice flavors, the wine is already showing age. Score 82. K

ESTATE, LATE HARVEST RIESLING, 2003: Made from Emerald Riesling grapes, this light to medium-bodied wine offers up simple but lively aromas and flavors of summer fruits and vanilla. Drink now. Score 83. K

ESTATE, WHITE RIESLING, 2004: Light straw colored, medium-bodied, with tropical and citrus fruits along with a hint of litchis. Not complex but lively and pleasant. Drink now. Score 85. K

ESTATE, WHITE RIESLING, 2003: Golden straw colored, medium-bodied, with citrus-litchi and traditional and rather marked petrol aromas that often typify Riesling. Dry, well balanced and with a lingering finish. Drink now. Score 87. K

Vineyards

VINEYARDS, CABERNET SAUVIGNON, 2004: Dark cherry red in color, medium-bodied with soft, almost unfelt tannins, and cassis, blueberry and plum flavors all on a somewhat sweet finish. Drink now. Score 84. K

VINEYARDS, CABERNET SAUVIGNON, 2003: Medium-bodied, with moderate tannins integrating nicely and appealing currant and berry fruits. Not complex but pleasant. Drink up. Score 85. K

VINEYARDS, CABERNET SAUVIGNON, 2002: Reflecting the problematic 2002 vintage, this medium-bodied blend of 85% Cabernet Sauvignon and 15% Merlot shows soft tannins and hints of wood but only modest fruits and a fairly short finish. Drink up. Score 85. K

VINEYARDS, CABERNET SAUVIGNON, 2001: This medium-bodied simple blend of 85% Cabernet Sauvignon and 15% Merlot aged 3 months in French oak is a good entry-level Cabernet, smooth, soft and fruity. Drink now. Score 84. K

VINEYARDS, MERLOT, 2004: Dark cherry red to purple in color, medium-bodied, with soft tannins and forward plum and black cherry fruits. Look as well for hints of smoky oak and Mediterranean herbs. Drink now. Score 85. K

VINEYARDS, MERLOT, 2003: Garnet red in color, this medium-bodied blend of 85% Merlot and 15% Cabernet Sauvignon offers up spicy plum and currant fruits and light hints of smoky, spicy oak. Perhaps a bit astringent. Drink now. Score 86. K

VINEYARDS, MERLOT, 2002: Ruby toward purple, medium-bodied, with soft, almost unfelt tannins and berry and currant fruits. A pleasant little wine. Drink up. Score 85. K

VINEYARDS, MERLOT, 2000: With just a bare hint of vanilla to let us know that it was aged for a few months in oak, this light to medium-bodied Merlot-Cabernet blend offers plenty of fruitiness but not enough depth or complexity. Somewhat past its peak. Drink up. Score 84. K

VINEYARDS, CARIGNAN, 2004: A wine made especially for Ikea, labeled as 85% Carignan and 15% Cabernet Sauvignon but with a remarkable resemblance to the Tishby Cabernet-Petite Sirah blend of the same year. A pleasant quaffer. Drink now. Score 84. K.

VINEYARDS, CARIGNAN, 2002: Blended with about 10% of Cabernet Sauvignon to add depth and "bite", this medium-bodied wine offers up tempting currant, berry and black cherry fruits along with a generous overlay of chocolate. Somewhat acidic. Drink up. Score 86. K

VINEYARDS, CARIGNAN, 2001: Even though this blend of 85% Carignan and 15% Cabernet Sauvignon was aged for 3–4 months in oak, it is sharp, acidic, coarse and with flavors of stewed plums and berries that are disjointed and hard. Drink up. Score 75. K

VINEYARDS, SAUVIGNON BLANC, 2004: Pale golden straw in color, unoaked and crisply dry with some grapefruit and pineapple fruits. Drink now. Score 84.K

VINEYARDS, SAUVIGNON BLANC, 2003: Light straw colored, this light to medium-bodied wine offers up appealing light herbal flavors to go with summer fruits and a bare hint of grassiness. Drink now. Score 85. K

VINEYARDS, SAUVIGNON BLANC, 2001: Pale gold in color and light to medium-bodied, this well made wine had in its youth appealing citrus and green apple aromas and flavors along with overtones of spring flowers and damp hay but is now showing age. Score 84. K

VINEYARDS, SAUVIGNON BLANC, 2000: Bright straw in color with light green reflections, and with flavors of citrus, green apples and spring flowers, this light to medium-bodied white was pleasant in its youth but is now showing age. Score 82. K

VINEYARDS, EMERALD RIESLING, 2004: Semi-dry, with grapefruit and green apple and a reasonable level of sweetness. An acceptable entry-level wine. Drink now. Score 84. K

VINEYARDS, EMERALD RIESLING, 2003: More off-dry than semi-sweet, with appealing tropical fruits, pineapple and grapefruit aromas and flavors. Medium-bodied, clean and refreshing. Drink up. Score 85. K

VINEYARDS, EMERALD RIESLING, 2002: Light, off-dry, with tropical and citrus fruit aromas and flavors and good acidity to balance out the sweetness. Drink up. Score 84. K

VINEYARDS, FRENCH-RIESLING, 2003: Surprisingly good considering the blend (about 70% French Colombard and the remainder Emerald Riesling) this lively semi-dry wine has good balancing acidity to offset moderate sweetness and appealing citrus and pineapple aromas and flavors. Drink up. Score 85. K

VINEYARDS, DRY MUSCAT, 2003: Made from Muscat of Alexandria grapes but lacking the usual flowery and sweet aroma, this crisply dry wine offers up simple fruity and minty pleasures. Not complex but pleasant. Drink up. Score 84. K

Tishbi

TISHBI, CABERNET SAUVIGNON-PETITE SIRAH 2004: Cherry red, fresh, lively and with soft tannins and berry-cherry fruits. Drink now. Score 84. **K**

TISHBI, CABERNET-PETITE SIRAH, 2003: Light to medium-bodied, this dark cherry-colored blend of 70% Cabernet Sauvignon and 30% Petite Sirah has fresh and fruity aromas and flavors of black cherries and berries. Light and pleasant on the palate. Drink now. Score 84. **K**

TISHBI, CABERNET-PETITE SIRAH, 2002: Medium-bodied and low in tannins, this deep ruby-colored wine shows berry and currant flavors. Drink up. Score 83. **K**

TISHBI, CABERNET SAUVIGNON-PETITE SIRAH, 2001: Medium-bodied with just enough tannins to give it a "bite" and good currant and berry fruits. Showing age. Score 85. **K**

TISHBI, JUNIOR, 2003: Made entirely from Carignan grapes that underwent carbonic maceration as do Beaujolais Nouveau wines, but lacking freshness and liveliness. Meant to be drunk very young. Score 79. **K**

TISHBI, SAUVIGNON BLANC, 2003: Light straw in color, with generous citrus, tropical fruit aromas and flavors. Not much similarity to Sauvignon Blanc, but an appealing quaffing wine. Drink now. Score 84. **K**

TISHBI, SAUVIGNON BLANC, 2002: Medium-bodied, with appealing grapefruit, kiwi and peach aromas and flavors along with a nice touch of spices, the wine has little resemblance to a typical Sauvignon Blanc. Drink up. Score 82. **K**

TISHBI, EMERALD RIESLING, 2004: Perhaps a bit too sweet for a semi-dry wine, but with clean, appealing citrus and floral aromas and flavors. Drink now. Score 81. **K**

TISHBI, FRENCH COLOMBARD-EMERALD RIESLING, 2004: Off-dry, with simple citrus, apple and floral aromas and flavors. Drink now. Score 82. **K**

TISHBI, FRENCH COLOMBARD-EMERALD RIESLING, 2003: Off dry, with appealing grapefruit and green apple aromas and flavors. A simple but pleasant quaffing wine. Drink up. Score 83. **K**

TISHBI, FRENCH COLOMBARD-EMERALD RIESLING, 2002: Semi dry, with generous acidity but perhaps a bit too reminiscent of grapefruit juice. Drink up. Score 82. **K**

TISHBI, MUSCAT OF ALEXANDRIA, 2002: Light to medium-bodied, with a floral nose and abundant tropical fruits, this semi-dry white is pleasant enough but lacks depth, length or balancing acidity. Drink up. Score 78. **K**

TISHBI, FRENCH-RIESLING, 2002: Semi dry, this light to medium-bodied blend of French Colombard and Emerald Riesling offers up a generously sweet and floral nose, good balancing acidity and flavors of kiwi and citrus. Drink up. Score 80. **K**

TISHBI SPARKLING WINE, 2003: Made entirely from French Colombard grapes the wine shows flavors that are somewhere between off-dry and sour, with no mousse to speak of and bubbles that fade far too quickly. This is a wine with little to recommend it. Tentative Score 68–70. **K**

TISHBI, BRUT, 2000: Made from French Colombard grapes, traditionally used to make Cognac and Armagnac brandies, this vintage Brut is fruity but lacks depth or body, and is overly acidic. The bubbles are far too large for a wine made in the traditional Champagne method. Drink up. Score 78. **K**

TISHBI BRUT, N.V.: In its youth, like the vintage version, the wine had strong but attractive overtones of yeast as well as pleasant apple, pear and citrus flavors, but lately some bottles have been corked and others disclosed as lifeless. At its best, the wine earned a Score of 87. **K**

Baron

BARON CABERNET 2000

ברון קברנה

יין אדום יבש

ALCOHOL 12.4% VOLUME 750 ML

מיוצר וממולא ע״י יקבי תשבי | יקבי הבארון בע״מ | בינימינה

BARON, CABERNET SAUVIGNON, 2004: Deep ruby towards garnet, light to medium-bodied, with black fruits and spices, an acceptable entry-level wine. Drink now. Score 83. K

BARON, CABERNET SAUVIGNON, 2003: Deep purple in color, medium-bodied and with appealing black fruits and just enough spices to hold our interest. Drink now. Score 84. K

BARON, CABERNET SAUVIGNON, 2002: Dark cherry red toward purple in color, medium-bodied, with soft tannins and appealing currant and berry flavors. Not complex or deep but pleasant enough. Drink up. Score 82. K

BARON, CABERNET SAUVIGNON, 2001: Light to medium-bodied, with tannins almost absent and with spicy and somewhat acidic berry, cherry flavors. Past its peak. Drink up. Score 80. K

BARON, CABERNET SAUVIGNON, 2000: Why this blend of Cabernet Sauvignon and Petite Sirah is said by the winery to be in the Rhone style eludes me. During its youth it was a pleasant wine, with a lean core of currant, berry and earthy flavors. Somewhat past its peak. Drink up. Score 76. K

Tulip ✶✶✶

Located near the town of Kiryat Tivon, not far from Haifa, this winery is an effort of the Itzhaki family, with Doron Itzhaki serving as the winemaker. Drawing largely on Cabernet Sauvignon, Merlot, Syrah, Sauvignon Blanc and Chardonnay grapes from Kerem Ben Zimra, other locations in the Upper Galilee and Karmei Yosef, the winery released 10,000 bottles from the 2003 vintage and produced about 27,000 from the 2004 vintage. Target production is 50,000–80,000 bottles annually by 2012.

The winery is currently releasing wines in three series: varietal Grand Reserve and Reserve; Mostly (blended wines); and Just (single vineyard wines). The winery also releases a Port-style reinforced red wine.

Grand Reserve

GRAND RESERVE, CABERNET SAUVIGNON, 2003: Made entirely from Cabernet Sauvignon grapes and destined for about 18 months of oak aging, this full bodied, deep garnet colored and still firmly tannic wine already shows the promise of elegance. Aromas and flavors of black fruits, citrus peel, chocolate and Mediterranean herbs here. Best starting in 2007. Tentative Score 88–90.

GRAND RESERVE, 1999: Medium to full-bodied and with surprisingly moderate tannins and wood influence considering that it was aged in a combination of new and old oak *barriques* for an extraordinarily long 32 months. Showing somewhat better than at an earlier tasting, now revealing currant, raspberry and black cherry fruits. Lacking complexity. Drink now. Score 86.

Reserve

RESERVE, CABERNET SAUVIGNON, 2004: Dense royal-purple towards black, full-bodied, deeply tannic and with generous wood influence but with balance and structure that bodes well for the future. As the wine develops look for spicy blackcurrant, cassis, chocolate and a light overlay of cigar tobacco. Best 2007–2009. Tentative Score 88–90.

RESERVE, CABERNET SAUVIGNON, 2003: Deep garnet towards black, medium to full-bodied and reflecting 14 months in small oak barrels with vanilla, spicy wood and appealing black fruits. Firm tannins here but good balance bodes well for the future. Drink now–2008. Score 89.

RESERVE, CABERNET SAUVIGNON, 2000: Dark garnet red, medium-bodied and reflecting its 24 months in oak with now soft, well integrated tannins and appealing currant and blackberry flavors. Perhaps a bit too acidic. Drink now. Score 86.

RESERVE, SYRAH, 2004: Full-bodied, with generous dusty, smoky oak and firm tannins but those well balanced with black fruits, chocolate and earthy-animal aromas and flavors. Needs time to settle down but bodes well for the future. Best 2007–2010. Tentative Score 87–89.

Mostly

MOSTLY, SAUVIGNON BLANC, 2004: Dark straw in color, portions of this medium-bodied blend of Sauvignon Blanc and Chardonnay (75% and 25% respectively) were oak fermented and aged *sur lie* before the final blend was made. Generous melon, pear and citrus fruits backed up nicely by light herbaceousness. Drink now. Score 87.

MOSTLY, SHIRAZ, 2004: Dark ruby towards garnet in color, this blend of Shiraz, Merlot and Cabernet Sauvignon (65%, 15% and 20% respectively) was aged primarily in new barrels. Medium to full bodied, with plum, currant and berry fruits backed up by appealing hints of earthiness and freshly tanned leather. Drink from release–2009. Tentative Score 87–89.

MOSTLY, MERLOT, 2004: Garnet towards royal purple in color, this medium-bodied blend of 77% Merlot and 23% Cabernet Sauvignon shows soft tannins integrating nicely, a judicious hand with oak and appealing red currant and wild berry fruits. Soft, round, generous and moderately long. Drink from release–2008. Tentative Score 86–88.

Just

JUST, CABERNET SAUVIGNON, 2004: Dark royal purple, developed in French and American oak for 8–9 months. Already showing good balance between spicy wood, soft, well integrating tannins and wild berry and currant fruits. Look for hints of vanilla and Mediterranean herbs on the finish. Drink from release–2009. Tentative Score 86–88.

JUST, SAUVIGNON BLANC, 2004: Light straw colored, light to medium bodied, clean, crisp and refreshing, with pineapple, green melon and citrus fruits on a generously acidic and spicy background. Drink now. Score 86.

Tzora ★★★★

Set on Kibbutz Tzora at the foothills of the Jerusalem Mountains and overlooking the Soreq Valley, this *kibbutz*-owned winery released its first wines in 1993. Initial production was about 1,500 bottles and current production is somewhat over 50,000 bottles annually.

Ronnie James, who has been the winemaker since the winery's inception, releases varietal wines as well as blends based on Cabernet Sauvignon, Merlot, Sauvignon Blanc, Chardonnay, Johannisberg Riesling and Muscat of Alexandria, many of those as single-vineyard wines. James has succeeded as very few winemakers do to consistently represent a specific Mediterranean terroir. As to the winery's labels, it is difficult to divide the wines into specific series or to know from year to year precisely which wines will be released in which series. Starting with the releases of the 2002 vintage the wines of Tzora have been kosher.

TZORA, CABERNET SAUVIGNON, NEVE ILAN, 2003: Dark garnet towards purple, medium to full-bodied, with still firm tannins but those starting to integrate and already revealing smoky oak and a pleasing earthiness on a background of currants and plums. Drink from release–2010. Tentative Score 86–88. K

TZORA, CABERNET SAUVIGNON, GIVAT HACHALUKIM, 2003: Dark garnet in color, medium to full-bodied, with appealing aromas and flavors of plums and currants and a light earthiness that come together nicely. Well balanced and long. Best 2007–2010. Score 89. K

TZORA, CABERNET SAUVIGNON, ILAN, 2001: Medium to full-bodied, this ruby toward purple wine has still firm tannins, those matched nicely by generous currant, berry and plum fruits, and herbal, mocha and leather overlays that open in the glass. Well balanced, this finely tuned wine has a long and generous finish. Drink now–2008. Score 92.

TZORA, CABERNET SAUVIGNON, GIVAT HACHALUKIM, RESERVE, 2001: Dark garnet in color, the once searing tannins of this oak-aged blend of 90% Cabernet Sauvignon and 10% Merlot have finally receded and now show excellent balance with wood, black fruits and herbaceousness, all on a light peppery background. Drink now. Score 89.

TZORA, CABERNET SAUVIGNON, GIVAT HACHALUKIM, 2001: This dark ruby toward purple, medium-bodied single vineyard wine has moderate, well-integrated tannins, generous fruits that include red currants and black cherries, and light touches of herbaceousness and white pepper. Not overly complex but a wine that makes for easy drinking. Drink now. Score 87.

TZORA, CABERNET SAUVIGNON, 2000: Aged for 20 months in *barriques*, this intense wine is living up to its promise and shows a dark ruby toward purple color and a complex interplay on the palate between blackcurrants, blackberries, pepper, sage and spicy cedar aromas and flavors. Look as well for hints of dark chocolate, eucalyptus and leather on the long finish. Drink now–2008. Score 92.

TZORA, CABERNET SAUVIGNON, TZORA VINEYARDS, 2000: This medium to full-bodied wine has firm tannins and needs time to open in the glass to reveal its wild berry, plum, violet, vanilla and chocolate aromas and flavors. Drink now. Score 89.

TZORA, CABERNET SAUVIGNON, BIN 64, SPECIAL SELECTION, 1999: A blend of 85% Cabernet Sauvignon and 15% Merlot, this complex, concentrated and full-bodied wine spent 20 months in oak before bottling. It has a garnet toward purple color, abundant but now well-integrated tannins, and aromas and flavors of currant and blackberry fruits, those nicely matched by vanilla and a tantalizing hint of spicy cedar wood on the finish. Drink now–2007. Score 89.

TZORA, CABERNET SAUVIGNON, BIN 72, SPECIAL SELECTION, 1999: Even though this wine was made from the same grapes and received the same treatment as the wine reviewed above, the grapes came from different rows in the same vineyard. The two wines are far from identical, this one being darker in color and having more of an earthy-herbal than a fruit personality and with tannins firm enough to hide whatever spices, vanilla and cedar wood present here. Drink now–2008. Score 90.

TZORA, CABERNET SAUVIGNON, MISTY HILLS, 1999: Firm and chewy, with firm tannins and delicious black cherry, currant and wild berry flavors, all overlaid by spices, vanilla and cedar wood flavor. Drink now. Score 90.

TZORA, CABERNET SAUVIGNON, SPECIAL SELECTION, NEVE ILAN, 1999: Dark purple toward black, with brownish overtones and now coming into its own, this medium to full-bodied wine offers up generous blackcurrant, wild berry, spice and vanilla flavors along with just the right touch of the oak in which it developed. Drink now. Score 87.

TZORA, CABERNET SAUVIGNON, TZORA VINEYARD, 1999: Deep royal purple in color, this medium-bodied wine has now integrated nicely and shows good balance between tannins, oak and fruits. Black cherries, forest fruits and vanilla dominate, but there is also a nice touch of spiciness that comes in on the finish. Drink up. Score 86.

TZORA, CABERNET SAUVIGNON, 1998: Firm and tight, with plenty of tannins and an attractive core of currant, plum and black cherry flavors during its youth, but now past its peak. Drink up. Score 86.

TZORA, CABERNET SAUVIGNON, SPECIAL SELECTION, 1997: When young, this wine was smooth, ripe and harmonious, with layers of plums, cherries, currants and just enough cedary oak and tobacco aromas and flavors, but it is now past its peak. Drink up. Score 85.

TZORA, MERLOT, NEVE ILAN, 2003: Full-bodied, deep garnet in color, with soft tannins. Round and soft with rich plum and black cherry fruits and just the right hint of spicy oak. Drink now–2008. Score 88. **K**

TZORA, MERLOT, SHORESH, 2003: A simple Merlot, medium-bodied with soft tannins, plenty of acidity, perhaps too much, and appealing plum and berry fruits. Drink now–2007. Score 86. **K**

TZORA, MERLOT, ESTATE WINE, 2003: Rustic in style, rough and chewy with a range of flavors that include herbs, tea, spices and leather but lacking the rich Merlot flavors that should have been there. Drink up. Score 79. **K**

TZORA, MERLOT, ILAN, 2001: This medium to full-bodied blend of 90% Merlot and 10% Cabernet Sauvignon reflects the two years it spent in new and old oak with generous but soft tannins and tempting red currant and berry flavors, those on a background of Mediterranean herbs and vanilla. Just enough spiciness here to add interest along with a medium-long finish. Drink now. Score 89.

TZORA, MERLOT, TZORA VALLEY, 1998: With its tannins now well integrated, this deep royal purple medium-bodied wine shows deep currant, cherry and spicy aromas and flavors, along with a moderately long finish highlighted by generous hints of mint, vanilla and smoky oak. Somewhat past its peak. Drink up. Score 89.

TZORA, MERLOT, 1997: Smooth and harmonious, with black cherry, currant and wild berry flavors, a hint of anise and sweet toasted oak flavors that linger on the palate, this is a wine that is simultaneously elegant and easy to drink. Past its peak. Drink up. Score 84.

TZORA, CABERNET SAUVIGNON-MERLOT, NEVE ILAN, SPECIAL SELECTION, 2003: Dark royal purple in color, with soft, already well-integrating tannins, this blend of 50% each Cabernet Sauvignon and Merlot offers generous currant and berry fruits on a long smoky finish. Drink now–2009. Score 87. K

TZORA, CABERNET SAUVIGNON-MERLOT, MISTY HILLS, 2000: Full-bodied, with cedary oak overlaying rich levels of currants, black cherries, berries and plums, the wine has a long mouth-filling finish. Drink now–2008. Score 89.

TZORA, MERLOT-CABERNET SAUVIGNON, ILAN, MISTY HILLS 2003: This blend of 60% Merlot and 40% Cabernet Sauvignon has deep ruby towards purple color, medium to full-body chunky, country style tannins, and generous oak on a rich spicy black fruit background. Mouthfilling and long. Drink now–2010. Score 87.

TZORA, CABERNET SAUVIGNON-ZINFANDEL, 2003: Aged in casks for 8 months, this medium-bodied blend of 67% Cabernet gnon and 33% Zinfandel is a bit stingy on the nose but offers g flavors of berries, black cherries and spices. An appealing entry-level wine. Drink up. Score 85. **K**

TZORA, SHORESH, JERUSALEM HILLS, 2003: A medium-bodied blend of Cabernet Sauvignon and Merlot grapes from a variety of vineyards. Appealing, somewhat sharp berry and plum flavors, somewhat coarse tannins and a good deal of heat give the wine a distinct rustic style. Drink now. Score 85. **K**

TZORA, STONE RIDGE, 2002: A medium-bodied blend of 60% Cabernet Sauvignon and 40% Merlot, this garnet red wine spent eight months in new oak barrels. With currant, plum and berry fruits that make themselves apparent on the first attack, on a lightly spicy background and matched by soft tannins, this is not a wine for long-term cellaring. Drink now. Score 87. **K**

TZORA, SAUVIGNON BLANC, SPECIAL SELECTION, 2000: Medium-bodied with tempting light grassy, orange peel and pineapple aromas and flavors along with an appealing touch of bitterness that comes in at the end. Drink up. Score 88.

TZORA, SAUVIGNON BLANC, 1999: Crisply dry and refreshing, with aromas and flavors of passion fruit, flowers, grass and hints of nectarines that creep in at the end, this well-made wine calls to mind a New Zealand Sauvignon Blanc. Somewhat past its peak. Drink up. Score 86.

TZORA, CHARDONNAY, SPECIAL SELECTION, 1998: Medium to full-bodied, this ripe, rich wine spent 8 months in oak and has a ripe core of pear, melon and apple flavors with just the right buttery texture. Past its peak. Drink up. Score 86.

TZORA, JOHANNISBERG RIESLING, 2000: Light golden in color, medium-bodied, with appealing aromas and flavors of summer fruits, green apples and spring flowers. Equally good as an aperitif. Drink. Score 87.

TZORA, JOHANNISBERG RIESLING, 1999: Bright and lively, with peach, apricot and apple fruits, the wine also shows nice hints of spices and a generous natural acidity to keep it lively. Drink up. Score 86.

TZORA, JOHANNISBERG RIESLING, 1998: Soft, generous and bright, with apple, peach, and spicy floral flavors that linger nicely on the palate. Showing age. Drink up. Score 85.

Vitkin ✳✳✳

Established by Doron and Sharona Belogolovsky on Moshav Kfar Vitkin on the central Coastal Plain, this winery released its first wines from the 2002 vintage. Winemaker Assaf Paz relies on Cabernet Sauvignon, Merlot, Zinfandel, Carignan, Cabernet Franc, Syrah, Tempranillo, Petit Verdot, Petite Sirah, Viognier, French Colombard, Johannisberg Riesling, Gewuztraminer and Muscat grapes from vintners in the Jerusalem hills as well as several other parts of the country. Production from the 2002 vintage was 2,000 bottles, from 2003 about 8,500 bottles and from 2004, 15,000 bottles.

VITKIN, CABERNET SAUVIGNON, 2002: Medium-bodied, with soft, well-integrating tannins, this moderately oaked wine offers up a generous berry-black cherry personality, the fruits complemented nicely by overlays of spices and vanilla. Drink now. Score 85.

VITKIN, CARIGNAN, 2003: Oak-aged with 10% of Petit Verdot added. Dark garnet red, the wine reflects its year in French oak barrels with generous smoke and vanilla, those matched nicely by soft tannins and generous plum and wild berry fruits. Drink now–2007. Score 87.

VITKIN, CARIGNAN, 2002: Deep royal purple in color, medium-bodied and with generous black fruits and spices. Closed now because the still massive tannins need time to integrate. Drink now. Score 86.

VITKIN, CABERNET FRANC, 2003: Dark garnet towards royal purple in color, this oak-aged, medium to full-bodied blend of 90% Cabernet Franc, 6% Petit Verdot and 4% Cabernet Sauvignon offers generous dark plum, black cherry and spice flavors, all complemented nicely by chocolate notes. On the clean, long finish look for hints of kirsch liqueur. Drink now–2007. Score 87.

VITKIN, CABERNET FRANC, 2002: Spicy and fruity, with plum and currant flavors, this soft, medium-bodied wine yields an appealing hint of cloves on the finish. Drink now. Score 84.

VITKIN, PINOT NOIR, 2003: A blend of Pinot Noir, Petit Verdot and Cabernet Sauvignon (90%, 6% and 4% respectively) that was aged in used oak for about 12 months. This deep cherry towards garnet, medium-bodied, very softly tannic wine offers up appealing berry, cherry and currant fruits on a background of vanilla and mocha. Drink now–2008. Score 87.

VITKIN, PETITE SIRAH, 2003: Dark ruby towards garnet, this medium to full-bodied and moderately tannic blend of 90% Petite Sirah and 10% Cabernet Franc developed for 14 months in oak. Aromas and flavors of blackberries and purple plums and a long spicy finish. Drink now–2007. Score 86.

VITKIN, CLASSIC, 2003: An unlikely blend of 40% Cabernet Sauvignon, 35% Syrah and 25% Carignan each vinified separately and aged in oak for six months before blending and another six months afterwards. Medium-bodied, with soft, somewhat flabby tannins, and with berry-cherry and currant flavors that fail to come together. Drink now. Score 85.

VITKIN, ROSÉ, 2004: A blend of Tempranillo, Syrah and Carignan (50%, 30% and 20% respectively), not so much pink as bright cherry red, light, dry and lively, the wine shows aromas and flavors of strawberry, cassis and orange peel. Drink now. Score 85.

VITKIN, RIESLING, 2003: Made from Johannisberg Riesling grapes, this deep golden straw colored, medium-bodied wine shows aromas and lightly spicy flavors of citrus, green gage plums and spring flowers. Drink now. Score 86.

VITKIN, GEWURZTRMAINER, 2003: Made entirely from Gewurztraminer grapes and developed *sur lie* in stainless steel, this medium-bodied dry white is generous with its traditional Gewurztraminer flavors and aromas of litchis, and spicy summer fruits. Drink now–2007. Score 86.

VITKIN, BLANC, 2003: Light to medium-bodied, this lively unoaked blend of 60% Viognier and 40% French Colombard offers pleasant notes of lime and orange peel. Clean and refreshing, a good quaffer. Drink now. Score 85.

VITKIN, LATE HARVEST RIESLING, 2003: Medium-bodied, thick in texture and unabashedly sweet, this dessert wine offers aromas and flavors of dried peaches, orange peel and wild flowers. Good balancing acidity adds liveliness. Drink now–2007. Score 85.

Yaffo ***

Founded in Jaffa in 1998 by Moshe and Anne Celniker and today located in the basement of their home in the Tel Aviv suburb of Ramat Hachayal, this small winery is currently producing about 6,000 bottles annually. Grapes, primarily Cabernet Sauvignon and Merlot, come from *kibbutz* Netiv Halamed Hey in the Jerusalem Hills and from the the Golan Heights. The winery also produces a Port-style wine.

YAFFO, CABERNET SAUVIGNON, 2003: Deep garnet towards royal purple, this still firmly tannic, medium to full-bodied and generously oaked wine shows structure and balance that bode well for its future. Already showing aromas and flavors of spicy black fruits, freshly picked herbs and an appealing earthy undercurrent that lingers nicely on the palate. Drink from release–2008. Tentative Score 86–88.

YAFFO, CABERNET SAUVIGNON, 2002: Dark in color, this medium to full-bodied oak-aged wine shows soft tannins along with blackcurrant, cherry and berry aromas and flavors. Light spices and herbs come together on a round, moderately long finish. Drink now. Score 87.

YAFFO, CABERNET SAUVIGNON, 2001: Deep garnet red, this medium-bodied wine was aged in French and American oak barrels and now shows generous currant and black cherry aromas and flavors, those coming together nicely with a light spiciness and Mediterranean herbs. Look for an appealing light earthiness and a green olive finish. Drink up. Score 87.

YAFFO, CABERNET SAUVIGNON, 2000: Made entirely from Cabernet Sauvignon grapes grown in a single vineyard in the Upper Galilee, the wine spent 12 months in French and American oak barrels. During its youth this medium-bodied and supple wine was fresh and fruity, with ripe aromas and flavors of prunes and black cherries as well as a hint of green olives. Showing age. Score 82.

YAFFO, MERLOT, 2002: Medium-bodied, with generous soft tannins and berry, black cherry, and appealing vanilla-spicy hints that come in from mid-palate. Good touches of sweet wood and a light herbaceousness. Drink now. Score 86.

YAFFO, MERLOT, 2001: Medium-bodied, with moderate tannins, plenty of black fruits and hints of vanilla and toasty oak all coming together on a moderately long finish. Drink up. Score 86.

YAFFO, MERLOT, 2000: When first released, this medium-bodied, smooth wine showed plum, raspberry and vanilla flavors but then quickly went downhill and is now well past its peak and no longer scoreable.

YAFFO, ROUGE, 2003: Deep garnet in color, medium-bodied and with soft tannins, this blend of Cabernet Sauvignon and Merlot shows generous ripe plum, currant and berry aromas and flavors. Moderately long. Drink now. Score 86.

YAFFO, ROUGE, 2002: A blend of 45% each of Cabernet Sauvignon and Merlot and 10% of Shiraz, this soft and round red offers up appealing berry, cherry and currant fruits together with well-integrated tannins and good acidity. Not complex but a pleasant quaffer. Drink up. Score 86.

Yatir ★★★★

Set in a state-of the-art winery at the foot of the Judean Hills, and under the supervision of Australian-trained winemaker Eran Goldwasser, this boutique winery is a joint venture between Carmel and the vintners of the Yatir region. The first wines released, from the 2001 vintage, include a first label age-worthy wine, Ya'ar Yatir, as well as several more approachable second label wines. Drawing its name from the Yatir Forest, located in the Judean Hills, the winery is cultivating its own vineyards with Cabernet Sauvignon, Merlot, Shiraz, Sauvignon Blanc, Chardonnay and Shiraz grapes. Current production is about 50,000 bottles and target output is 200,000 bottles annually.

Ya'ar Yatir (Yatir Forest)

YA'AR YATIR, 2002: Made from 100% Cabernet Sauvignon grapes, this dark garnet toward purple, full-bodied wine is now showing still firm tannins and gentle and well-integrated smoky oak and sweet cedar aromas, those coming together very nicely with aromas and flavors of ripe currant and purple plum fruits as well as generous hints of chocolate and mint. Drink now–2010. Score 90. **K**

YA'AR YATIR, 2001: As youthful on the nose and palate as it is in its dark ruby toward purple color, this medium to full-bodied blend of 85% Cabernet Sauvignon and 15% Merlot is already showing good integration between soft tannins and oak, and rich, still quite forward aromas and flavors of currants, wild berries and cherries. The spicy oak and generous minerals are integrating nicely and yielding a luxurious and elegant wine. Drink now–2009. Score 91. **K**

Yatir

YATIR, CABERNET SAUVIGNON, BEIT YATIR, 2002: Young and tight but well focused, with deep, firm tannins and ripe flavors of cherries, currants, anise and nice touches of earth and minerals. Distinctly

Mediterranean, the wine is drinking nicely now but will cellar well. Drink now–2009. Score 91. **K**

YATIR, CABERNET SAUVIGNON, MA'OR, 2002: Dark, ripe and intense, this well-oaked red has juicy plum and cherry flavors, and vanilla and toasty oak notes, as well as appealing overlays of herbs and spices. Needs time to show its harmony. Drink now–2010. Score 89. **K**

YATIR, MERLOT, RAMAT ARAD, 2002: Full-bodied, tannic and muscular for a Merlot, but with balance between wood, fruits and acidity that gives the wine grace and elegance. Black plums, wild berries and currants here, together with freshly picked Mediterranean herbs and a hint of granite that comes in on the long finish. Drink now–2009. Score 91. **K**

YATIR, MERLOT, 2001: Deep garnet toward royal purple in color, full-bodied, and with generous tannins well balanced by plum, currant and blackberry fruits as well as generous hints of minerals and herbs. Drink now–2007. Score 91. **K**

YATIR, CABERNET SAUVIGNON-MERLOT, 2001: A blend of 60% Cabernet Sauvignon and 40% Merlot, this medium to full-bodied wine shows a dark royal purple color, soft, already well-integrated tannins and generous blackcurrant, plum, berry, and earthy-mineral aromas and flavors. Look as well for hints of spicy oak that develop from mid-palate. Drink now. Score 89. **K**

YATIR, CABERNET SAUVIGNON-MERLOT-SHIRAZ, 2002: A blend of primarily Cabernet Sauvignon and Merlot with 10% of Shiraz added, this deep purple towards black, medium to full-bodied wine shows good balance between smoky wood, generous but soft tannins, plum and currant fruits, and a very appealing overlay of near-sweet herbaceousness. Drink now–2008. Score 88. **K**

YATIR, SAUVIGNON BLANC, 2004: Oaked for a short time, this bright straw-colored wine maintains remarkable freshness together with well enunciated aromas of citrus, tropical fruits and light herbaceousness. Medium-bodied, with crisp acidity and a long and complex finish. Drink now–2007. Score 90. **K**

YATIR, SAUVIGNON BLANC, 2003: Light gold in color, with orange and green tints, this well balanced white was aged *sur lie*. Full bodied, with traditional Sauvignon Blanc aromas and flavors of fresh-mown grass and herbs matched nicely by quince and pear fruits as well as hints of pepper, walnut and vanilla, all leading up to a long mouth-filling finish. Somewhat oaky but graceful and harmonious. Drink now–2007. Score 89. K

Ye'arim **

Located in the village of Givat Ye'arim near Jerusalem, this small winery is owned by Sasson Ben-Aharon who is also the senior winemaker for Binyamina Wineries. With vineyards in the Judean Mountains, the winery produced 1,000 bottles from the 2000 vintage, 2,000 from the 2003 vintage and 3000 from 2004.

YE'ARIM, CABERNET SAUVIGNON, SASSON'S WINE, 2002: Ruby towards garnet in color, medium to full-bodied, with soft, well-integrated tannins and spicy cedar from its 18 months in oak. Aromas and flavors of ripe berries, sweet herbs and vanilla. Drink now–2008. Score 86.

YE'ARIM, CABERNET SAUVIGNON, SASSON'S WINE, 2000: Garnet colored, this medium-bodied unfiltered blend of 95% Cabernet Sauvignon and 5% Merlot was aged in French oak *barriques* for 14 months and shows soft tannins and some spicy oak but somewhat stingy berry, currant and black cherry flavors. Drink now. Score 83.

YE'ARIM, MERLOT, SASSON'S WINE, 2003: Made entirely from Merlot grapes, this garnet towards purple, well-balanced, medium-bodied wine shows soft tannins and reflects its 15 months in French oak with a gentle touch of spicy wood. Aromas and flavors of cherries, wild berries and tobacco as well as an appealing hint of minty-chocolate on the finish. Drink now–2008. Score 86.

YE'ARIM, MERLOT, SASSON'S WINE, 2001: A blend of 92% Merlot and 8% Cabernet Sauvignon, this light, somewhat diluted red shows minimal aromas and flavors. Drink now. Score 80.

YE'ARIM, MERLOT, SASSON'S WINE, 2000: Medium to full-bodied and deep ruby toward garnet in color, with soft tannins and generous but not overwhelming wood, this unfiltered blend of 92% Merlot and 8% Cabernet Sauvignon was aged for 14 months in oak. Smooth, rich and mouth-filling. Drink now. Score 86.

Yehuda *

Located on Moshav Neve Ilan in the Jerusalem Mountains, this winery was founded by Avi Yehuda in 1998. Cabernet Sauvignon, Merlot and Sauvignon Blanc grapes come from the winery's own nearby vineyards as well as from Moshav Shoresh. Current production is 2,000–3,000 bottles annually.

YEHUDA, CABERNET SAUVIGNON, 2002: Dark ruby towards garnet in color, medium-bodied, with firm tannins that fail to integrate with the wood, both of those holding back whatever fruits may be here. A country-style wine showing too earthy barnyard sensations. Drink now. Score 77.

YEHUDA, CABERNET SAUVIGNON, 2001: Deep cherry red in color and medium-bodied, with chunky tannins and generous blackberry and cassis aromas and flavors overlaid by sweet herbs, this is a simple and distinctly country-style wine. Drink up. Score 79.

YEHUDA, CABERNET SAUVIGNON, 2000: This medium-bodied, simple country-style wine has a somewhat herbal weediness to its black fruit flavors, and chunky tannins. Drink up. Score 79.

YEHUDA, MERLOT, 2002: Light garnet with a bit of browning showing early aging. Soft tannins and stingy with its plum and wild berry fruits. Drink up. Score 77.

YEHUDA, MERLOT, 2001: With soft tannins and offering up a modest range of plum and cherry flavors, this soft, simple, vaguely oaky wine finishes with rather coarse tannins. Drink up. Score 78.

YEHUDA, MERLOT-CABERNET SAUVIGNON, 2001: A successful medium-bodied and moderately tannic blend of 40% Merlot and 60% Cabernet Sauvignon. The wine was aged in oak for several months and shows hints of vanilla and anise, with a pleasing core of cherries and wild berries. Drink up. Score 86.

YEHUDA, MERLOT-CABERNET SAUVIGNON, 1999: This simple country-style wine based on 90% Merlot and 10% Cabernet Sauvignon has a deep garnet red color, warm flavors of wild berries, cherries and currants, and just a hint of vanilla from the oak barrels in which it aged for 6 months. Somewhat one-dimensional, and with only the barest hint of tannins. Showing age and no longer scoreable.

YEHUDA, CABERNET SAUVIGNON-MERLOT, 1999: A blend of 60% Cabernet and 40% Merlot aged in oak for 6 months, this pleasant little red has appealing aromas and flavors of blackcurrants and plums, with gentle herbal and spicy overtones. Drink up. Score 82.

YEKEV YEHUDA, SAUVIGNON BLANC, 2001: This medium-bodied organic wine, a blend of 75% Sauvignon Blanc and 25% Chardonnay, offers up appealing citrus, pineapple and floral aromas that linger nicely. Past its peak and no longer scoreable.

Yiftah'el ✳

Founded in 1999 in the community of Alon Hagalil in the Upper Galilee, owner-vintners Tzvika Ofir and Avner Sofer rely on Cabernet Sauvignon, Merlot, Petite Sirah and Sangiovese grapes from their own vineyards. Production from the 2001 vintage was about 1,500 bottles, about 3,000 in 2002 and 5,000 each in 2003 and 2004.

YIFTAH'EL, MERLOT, 2003: Reflecting its 12 months in oak with generous tannins and vanilla, the wine shows as well some berry-black cherry fruits. One dimensional and short. Drink up. Score 82.

YIFTAH'EL, SANGIOVESE, 2003: Light cherry red in color, with only scarce tannins and berry, strawberry and banana aromas and flavors. Drink up. Score 80.

YIFTAH'EL, PETITE SIRAH, 2004: Cherry red towards garnet, with chunky, country-style tannins and with primary aromas and flavors of very ripe plums turning somewhat bitter on the finish. Drink up. Score 83.

YIFTAH'EL, CABERNET-MERLOT, 2002: A medium-bodied, lightly tannic oak-aged blend of 60% Cabernet Sauvignon and 40% Merlot. Not complex but pleasant. Drink up. Score 83.

Yuval Ben-Shoshan **

Established by agronomist Yuval Ben-Shoshan on Kibbutz Bror Hail in the Negev Desert, this winery released its first wine from the vintage of 1998. Grapes, including Cabernet Sauvignon and Merlot, are currently drawn from the area of Kerem Ben Zimra in the Galilee. The winery's first release was of 2,000 bottles and production is currently about 4,000 bottles annually.

YUVAL BEN-SHOSHAN, CABERNET SAUVIGNON, 2003: Dark ruby towards garnet, medium to full-bodied, with well integrating soft tannins balanced by spicy oak and aromas and flavors of currants and plums. On the moderately long finish look for hints of espresso coffee and anise. Drink from release–2008. Tentative Score 86–88.

YUVAL BEN-SHOSHAN, CABERNET SAUVIGNON, AVDAT, 2002: Deep garnet red, medium to full-bodied, with generous tannins well balanced by hints of spicy oak, and blackcurrant and anise aromas and flavors. Drink now–2007. Score 87.

YUVAL BEN-SHOSHAN, CABERNET SAUVIGNON, 1999: Firm and compact, but opening to reveal black cherry, currant, cedar and spice flavors that turn smooth and supple. Firm tannins, but good concentration and richness come together nicely. Drink up. Score 88.

YUVAL BEN-SHOSHAN, CABERNET SAUVIGNON, 1998: There are two versions of this wine, one labeled "Gold" and the other "Silver", each made from grapes from a separate vineyard. Both wines are medium to full-bodied, have smooth tannins and show inherent good balance but the Gold has a deeper color, is more aromatic and tends to be dominated by not entirely pleasing flavors and aromas of plums. Drink up. Score for both wines 85.

YUVAL BEN-SHOSHAN, MERLOT, AVDAT, 2003: Medium-bodied, with firm but well-integrating tannins and appealing plum, black cherry and smoky wood aromas and flavors. Well balanced and appealing. Drink now. Score 86.

YUVAL BEN-SHOSHAN, CABERNET SAUVIGNON-MERLOT, 2001: Harmonious and smooth, with soft ripe tannins and an attractive core of currant, cherry and wild berry flavors and aromas. Well focused and with flavors that linger nicely. Drink now. Score 88.

YUVAL BEN-SHOSHAN, CABERNET SAUVIGNON-MERLOT, 2000:
Medium to full-bodied, this garnet red, unfiltered blend of 70% Cabernet Sauvignon and 30% Merlot shows good black fruits, hints of spices and a light vanilla overlay. Pleasant, but somewhat one-dimensional. Drink up. Score 85.

Zauberman ✶✶✶✶

Founded in 1999 by Itzik Zauberman and located in the town of Gedera in the Southern Plains, this small winery draws on organically raised grapes from its own vineyards nearby as well as using grapes from Karmei Yosef. First release was 1,500 bottles and current production is about 3,000 bottles annually.

ZAUBERMAN, CABERNET SAUVIGNON, LIMITED EDITION, 2001: Dark royal purple toward black in color, full-bodied, concentrated and tannic, with aromas and flavors that include dried plums and cherries, red berries, chocolate, honey and spices, This powerful, near-massive and complex wine, made by drying the grapes before pressing them much in the way that Italian Amarone is made, is approachable now if given at least 30 minutes in the glass to open. Drink now–2012. Score 93.

ZAUBERMAN, CABERNET SAUVIGNON, 2000: Well balanced, dark and rich, this concentrated wine shows good currant, plum, vanilla and herbal aromas and flavors well balanced by tannins and wood. Rich bitter-sweet overtones call to mind wines made in Italy by the *ripasso* method. Long and mouth-filling. Drink now–2009. Score 90.

ZAUBERMAN, MERLOT, 2002: Deep garnet toward royal purple in color, this medium to full-bodied unfiltered wine shows good balance between smoky oak, soft tannins and fruits. The wine has aromas and flavors of berries, currants and anise along with a generous earthiness on a moderately long finish. Drink now. Score 91.

ZAUBERMAN, MERLOT, 2001: The best Merlot ever from this winery, and one of the best ever made in Israel. Remarkably rich and full-bodied, this deep garnet toward purple wine shows delicious plum, cherry and currant fruits along with anise, vanilla and spicy oak and a complex and long finish. Still young and tight, but already well focused and harmonious. Drink now–2008. Score 93.

ZAUBERMAN, MERLOT, 2000: Medium to full-bodied, and firmer in texture than most local Merlot wines, the wine shows good balance between wood, acidity and fruits and abundant blackberry, cherry, anise and vanilla flavors. Supple, spicy and generous, with a long finish. Drink now. Score 89.

ZAUBERMAN, MERLOT, 1999: This blend of 94% Merlot and 6% Cabernet Sauvignon was aged in new French oak barrels for 8 months and has smooth tannins and attractive cherry, herbal and wood flavors, as well as intrinsically good balance. Drink up. Score 86.

Zemora ***

Set in a newly constructed facility in Moshav Beit Zayit in the Jerusalem Mountains, winemaker Baruch Yosef, formerly owner-winemaker of the Nachal Prat winery, released his first wines from the 2000 vintage. Grapes are drawn largely from the Jerusalem Mountain area and include Cabernet Sauvignon, Merlot, Cabernet Franc, Sangiovese and Chardonnay. Production for 2003 was 7,000 bottles and for 2004 approximately 50,000 bottles. Plans are to continue to grow and to provide private label wines for various sources. Starting with the 2004 vintage, the wines are kosher.

ZEMORA, CABERNET SAUVIGNON, 2003: Blended with 15% of Merlot, this oak-aged wine already shows overall good balance, medium to full-body and soft tannins that promise to integrate nicely. Look for an array of plum, blackcurrant, orange peel and light herbal aromas and flavors. Drink from release–2009. Tentative Score 86–88.

ZEMORA, CABERNET SAUVIGNON, 2002: Garnet toward deep purple in color, this medium to full-bodied, softly tannic wine shows appealing currants, wild berries and spices, along with a generous hint of sweet cedar on the finish. Has a somewhat heavy hand with the oak. Drink now–2007. Score 86.

ZEMORA, CABERNET SAUVIGNON, 2001: Royal purple in color, this ripe and smooth wine has a supple texture, a generous core of currant, cherry and berry flavors, and soft tannins that make themselves felt primarily on the finish. Drink now. Score 86.

ZEMORA, MERLOT, 2002: Medium-bodied, with gentle tannins and appealing berry, black cherry, anise and black pepper aromas and flavors, together with very generous wood that will not be to everyone's taste. Drink now–2007. Score 86.

ZEMORA, MERLOT, 2001: Dark cherry red toward garnet, with firm but well-integrated tannins and tempting blueberry, blackberry and currant aromas and flavors, this medium to full-bodied wine shows good balance between fruits, tannins and a gentle wood. Drink now. Score 87.

ZEMORA, MERLOT, 2000: Medium to full-bodied with generous oak, but that well balanced by tannins and fruits. Look for plum, currant and raspberry aromas and flavors, those on a lightly spicy and herbal background. Moderately long and mouth filling. Drink now. Score 87.

ZEMORA, CABERNET FRANC, 2003: Made from grapes from the Meron vineyards, this medium-bodied red shows chunky, country-style tannins, a generous hand with the oak reflecting a good deal of smoke and vanilla, those overshadowing somewhat the plum and berry flavors. Drink from release–2007. Tentative Score 84–86.

ZEMORA, SANGIOVESE, 2003: Blended with 15% of Cabernet Sauvignon but still lacking backbone and showing rather flabby tannins. Light to medium-bodied, perhaps even a bit diluted on the palate, with skimpy berry-black cherry fruits. One dimensional and short. Drink now. Score 84.

ZEMORA, CABERNET SAUVIGNON-MERLOT, 2003: Medium bodied, with chunky, country-style tannins but showing nicely on the nose and palate with currant, wild berry and spicy aromas and flavors. A good entry-level wine. Drink now. Score 85.

ZEMORA, RED, 2004: A blend of Cabernet Sauvignon, Merlot and Shiraz (70%, 24% and 6% respectively), the grapes blended before oak aging. Medium to full-bodied, with firm tannins, generous spicy-smoky oak and appealing plum, berry and cassis fruits. Round and mouthfilling but not long. Drink now. Score 84. K

ZEMORA, RED, 2001: A blend of 70% Cabernet Sauvignon and 30% Merlot that reflects its 24 months in *barriques* with a rather heavy hand of smoky oak. Low in tannins, round and with uncomplicated black fruits. Drink up. Score 84.

ZEMORA, CHARDONNAY, 2004: Dark golden-straw in color, medium to full-bodied, with pineapple, guava and citrus fruits on a generously oaked but creamy background. Drink now. Score 86. K

ZEMORA, CHARDONNAY, 2001: Deep gold, reflecting generous wood and upfront citrus, melon and spicy pear flavors, those on a medium-bodied background. Still somewhat unripe, but complex and smooth, with an appealing creamy finish. Somewhat past its peak. Drink up. Score 84.

Afterword

Sparkling wines

For many hundreds of years, the wine most often associated with the superior way of life has been Champagne. Attributed a soul, temperament and wit, many Frenchmen are convinced that Champagne can do them no harm, no matter how much of it they consume. Madame de Pompadour declared that "it is the only wine that makes a woman more beautiful after drinking" and Josephine Beauharnais, the not-always faithful wife of Napoleon, wrote to her sister that "the thought of making love without a bottle of Champagne alongside my bed is merely silly." This delightful beverage is so much a cultural phenomenon in France that a person who dislikes Champagne is pitied, or regarded as sick, disabled or depraved.

In 1688, when the Benedictine monk Dom Perignon was placed in charge of the wine cellars of the Abbey of Hautvilliers near Epernay, his odd ideas about making wine had his colleagues wondering whether he was a clairvoyant, a saint or something of a madman. If one accepts the popular mythology, this untutored chemist had the brilliant idea of adding small amounts of yeast and sugar to bottles of wine. This led to a secondary fermentation which in turn released gas under pressure into the wine. Dom Perignon had discovered a way to make wine sparkle, and since then sparkling Champagne has become the source for an entire mythology. It goes without saying that only wines that come from the Champagne region of France are entitled to be called "Champagne." All other wines, even those made by what has come to be known as the *methode champenoise,* are properly referred to as "sparkling wines."

Making Champagne is a lengthy process. Fermented grape juices, the produce of many different vineyards, are blended and then bottled with a mixture of sugar and yeast to induce a second fermentation. This produces carbon dioxide which, since it is sealed in, dissolves in the wine and creates the fizz. Since the yeast forms an ugly deposit, the bottles are stored with their heads down and are turned occasionally, thereby forcing this deposit to flow downwards towards the corks. This process is known as *riddling*. Towards the end of the process, which takes anywhere from six months to two years, the necks of the bottles are placed in an icy-cold brine solution. This freezes the sediment which can then be expelled.

Because the fermentation process has eaten up all of the sugar, the wine is now completely dry, verging on sourness and therefore it is next given a dose of a bit more sugar. Finally it is corked with special corks that seal it hermetically. The neck of the bottle is then encircled with wire-mesh so that the pressure of the gas in the bottle does not blow the cork out. The tops of the bottles are wrapped in gold or silver foil and the wine is finally ready to start working its magic.

There are four major levels of sweetness for Champagne and sparkling wines—*brut*, which is very dry; *sec*, which is dry; *demi-sec* which is really quite sweet; and the sweet *riche*, which is essentially a dessert wine. Three Israeli wineries are currently producing sparkling wine. The Golan Heights Winery produces Brut (a blend of Pinot Noir and Chardonnay) and Blanc de Blancs (made entirely from Chardonnay), both in its top of the line Yarden Series; Tishbi produces Tishbi Brut, and Carmel makes The President's Wine. The wines are reviewed in the appropriate section of each winery.

How to open a bottle of sparkling wine

Champagne and other sparkling wines require special handling because their corks are under a great deal of pressure. If not treated with care, these corks can become dangerous missiles propelled through the air with surprising force. Although the popping of Champagne corks creates a festive atmosphere, it is the wrong way to open a sparkling wine because in addition to being dangerous, it harms the wine. One of the reasons that Champagne is special is the bubbles, and popping the cork without care reduces the amount of bubbles.

To avoid this, start by peeling off the foil surrounding the cork and neck of the bottle. While applying pressure to hold the cork in, carefully loosen the metal straps holding the cork. After the straps are removed, grasp the cork firmly, continuing to press and gently twist the bottle, not the cork. When you hear the gas begin to escape around the edges of the cork, do not let the cork escape your grip. The gentle hissing sound will be followed by a barely audible pop, this indicating that you have done the job properly. In this way the wine will not form a foam that will suddenly gush out of the bottle and the bubbles will be preserved.

A Guide to Tasting Wines

Wine tasting is not a complex or difficult task. All that is required is the use of one's senses of sight, smell and taste. Before setting out to taste wines, try to eliminate as many distractions as possible. During the actual tasting, for example, extraneous aromas (e.g. food, perfume and aftershave lotion) should be avoided as they interfere with the ability to appreciate the aromas and bouquet of the wine. Also, during a tasting, try as hard as possible to ignore the comments by others in order not to be influenced by their opinions. Be sure to use high quality glasses (ideally of thin crystal) as this enhances the flavors and aromas of wines. A separate glass should be provided for each wine, this allowing the taster to return to earlier tasted wines in order to make comparisons. The glasses should be, of course, perfectly clean, without any aroma of soap or detergent. Glasses should be filled to no more than 20% of their capacity as this will give ample room for swirling the wine, that process serving to aerate and release the more subtle aromas and flavors of the wine being tasted.

Basic Rules for tasting wines

- Professionals can sample fifty or more wines at a single sitting, but it is widely agreed that in a private tasting, alone at home or at a friendly gathering, the number of wines for tasting should not exceed eight.

- White wines should be tasted before reds, and within each group wines that are light in body should be tasted before fuller-bodied wines. When tasting wines of the same variety, such as Cabernet Sauvignon or Merlot, always start with the youngest wines and end with the most mature.

- Wines should be served at their proper temperatures. Young reds should be opened about fifteen or twenty minutes before the tasting, and more mature reds about half an hour before they are poured.

- You can either place the bottles on the table with the labels exposed or place each bottle in a paper bag, each bag identified only by a number, for a blind tasting. I prefer blind tastings, for the power of suggestion is strong and it is difficult to be entirely objective vis à vis a label of a prestigious Chateau.

- Wines should be arranged on the table in the order they are to be tasted. I suggest using a felt-tipped pen to put a number on each bottle and then to mark the corresponding number on the base of each glass in order to avoid any confusion.

- Professional wine tasters spit the wine in order to avoid intoxication, but there is no need to spit at a home tasting where much of the pleasure comes from drinking the wine. For those that choose to spit, prepare adequate receptacles (clay jugs, low vases and Champagne buckets are ideal).

- Allow half a bottle per person. That is to say, for eight people you will need four bottles. When pouring during the tasting, remember that the average sampling should be small enough to allow room for swirling the wine in the glass. Whatever wines are left over after the actual tasting can be served with the meal or snacks afterward.

- Use a tasting form such as that illustrated in the following section or record your impressions on a piece of paper. Making notes helps people to make up their minds before they commit themselves.

- Food should be served after a wine tasting and never before or during because food changes the taste of wine. If you must have something on the table, use unsalted and sugar-free white bread.

Wine Appreciation

1. VISUAL APPEARANCE

In order to best see the color and clarity of a wine, hold your glass against a white background (a white tablecloth or even a blank sheet of white paper will do) and tilt the glass away from yourself slightly so that the exposed surface is larger. Red wines can be anywhere from bright cherry red in color to dark and opaque, in fact almost black. Although most white wines will have a light golden-straw color, they can range from almost colorless to deep golden, and rosé or blush wines are only rarely true pink and can vary from purple-pink to orange or even bright ruby red. Whatever the color, the wine should be perfectly clear. Wines that have thrown a sediment will become clear as the sediment settles.

Consider whether the color is deep or pale and whether it is vivid and youthful or browning and perhaps showing age. While the glass is tilted look as well at the rim (that point where the wine meets the glass), for it is not generally a positive sign if the color at the rim fades to an almost watery consistency. After noting the qualities of the color, swirl the wine in the glass gently and then hold it up to see the legs or tears—these are the threads of wine that appear and linger on the inside of the glass. These are an accurate indicator of the alcohol level in the wine; the broader and more viscous the legs, the greater the alcohol content and, according to many, a good indicator of the wine's ability to age. At the same time, note whether the wine is *frizzante*, that is to say, whether it has tiny little bubbles in it. Although this is acceptable in some white wines (e.g. Muscadet de Sevres et Maine *sur lie*, Vinho Verde, Moscato d'Asti), and occurs in many white wines when they have been overly chilled, such bubbles indicate a fault in nearly all red wines.

When evaluating Champagnes or other sparkling wines, the bubbles should be sharp, small and long lasting, rising from a central point in the glass.

A hint: Never taste wines under fluorescent light as this makes all red wines appear brown.

2. SMELL

It surprises many to realize that people with a normal sense of smell can identify more than 1,000 different aromas. That should not be daunting, however, as the process of identifying aromas is a largely automatic one and although we may sometimes "struggle" to distinguish between the aroma of a blackberry or raspberry, our associations with aromas are quite strong. In order to best evaluate and appreciate the aromas of a wine, swirl the glass rapidly for a few seconds, place your nose well into the glass and inhale deeply through your nostrils.

One of the first sensations to be evaluated is the alcohol content of the wine. If the wine appears to be highly alcoholic, ask yourself whether it is a fortified wine (e.g. Sherry, Port, Madeira) or whether the strong alcoholic aromas reflect a fault. After that, consider whether the wine smells as youthful or as mature as it appears to the eye, whether the aromas are smooth and harmonious, whether they are distinctive, bland or reticent and whether they are simple or complex. Consider as well whether there is a creamy, spicy or vanilla note to the aromas as this may give a hint about whether the wine was aged in oak. Also consider whether the wine has any "off" aromas that may indicate a fault. With a bit of practice it becomes possible for many to identify from aroma alone the variety of the grape used and even the region in which the wine was made.

A hint: a slight musky aroma can add great charm but when exaggerated almost always reveals a fault in the wine.

3. TASTE

When actually setting out to taste the wine, take a good mouthful, close the lips firmly and swirl the wine vigorously in order to coat the entire mouth. This is important because different taste sensations are perceived by different parts of the mouth (sweetness on the tip of the tongue, sourness on the sides, bitterness on the back and the roof of the mouth, saltiness on the fronts and side of the tongue). Some tasters also draw a bit of air into the mouth believing this will accentuate the flavors.

The first thing to be noted is whether the flavors are in accord with the aromas of the wines. Then, with the wine lingering in the mouth, identify the various taste sensations imparted. Ask yourself: are the flavors pronounced and easily identifiable or somewhat confused; is the wine clean or muddy; are the tannins, acidity, wood and fruits in balance; are the tannins and wood in good proportion to the fruits; is the level of sweetness appropriate for the wine?

Keep in mind that the major goal of tasting is not only to evaluate a wine but to determine whether it is to your taste. Wine tasting is not a guessing game but with increased practice and repeated tastings, many come to the point where they can identify and discuss the grape variety, area of origin and age and quality of the wines they are tasting.

A hint: A wine dominated by a single flavor is one-dimensional and thus lacking excitement.

Among the fruit aromas and flavors to be sought in white wines: citrus (especially lemon, grapefruit, lime and citrus peel), apple, melon, pear, peach, apricot, grapes, figs and, especially in sweet dessert wines, dried fruits. Also in white wines look for hints of grassiness, herbaceousness, honey, and a creamy sensation. Fruits to be found in red wines include, among others, black and red currants (sometimes referred to as cassis), plums and a variety of berries. Other taste sensations that may be imparted by red wines are chocolate, coffee and tobacco. In both reds and whites look for aromas and flavors imparted by oak aging, those including spicy or smoky oak, sweet cedar, asphalt and vanilla. Be aware that some of the aromas and flavors traditionally found in a red may appear in a white and vice versa.

TASTING FORMS

Because few of us have perfect memories, one of the very best aids in tasting wines is to use an organized sheet for keeping notes. Such sheets, used by professional wine tasters as well as amateurs, help to organize our thoughts and to leave a permanent record for future reference with which to compare the same wine or similar wines. The act of writing our reactions down also serves to implant our thoughts in long-term memory.

The tasting form that is illustrated on the opposite page (and is in larger format on the inside of the dust jacket of this book) is meant for those purposes. Readers may feel free to reproduce this form for their own use or for the use of friends, and should the original be lost, a downloadable and printable copy can be found at: www.tobypress.com/rogov/tasting.pdf.

How I Do My Wine Tastings

In general, I partake of three kinds of tastings—those I hold in my own home on an almost daily basis; trade and professional tastings that are held by importers or at wine exhibitions; and friendly tastings held at wineries, wine shops, restaurants, or at the homes of people kind enough to invite me to share their wines.

Under ideal circumstances tastings are done blind, the taster knowing only the broad category of wines being tasted but not being allowed to see the label. This eliminates biases that might arise from previous experience. This is not difficult to arrange; one person opens and pours the wines into numbered glasses and the taster sees the bottles only after having made notes and assigned scores. The peak time for tastings is during the morning hours, long enough after a first coffee but before one has developed a true sense of hunger. The tasting session actually starts the day before, when a list is compiled of the wines that must be tasted. The next morning, about an hour before the actual tasting, an assistant opens the bottles, adding several wines that are not on the list but which fall into the same category. The

ROGOV'S GUIDE TO ISRAELI WINES
RATING CHART

Toby

Name of Wine:	Date of Tasting:
Vintage Year:	Date Obtained:
Country of Origin:	Price:
Wine Region:	

	COMMENTS
VISUAL APPEARANCE: (0–5 POINTS)	
Clarity: (*cloudy, dull, clear, brilliant*)	
Depth and Intensity of Color (*watery, pale, medium, deep, dark*)	
Color: White Wines—green tinge, pale yellow, yellow, gold, brown	
Red Wines—purple, garnet, red, brown	
Viscosity: Light sparkle, watery, normal, heavy, oily	
Champagnes Only:	
Length of mousse	
Finesse and Sharpness of bubbles	
Duration of bubbles	Points: _____
AROMAS AND BOUQUET: (0–15 POINTS)	
Attractiveness (*neutral, clean, attractive, outstanding, off*)	
Aroma and Bouquet (*fruits and others*) (*none, light, positive, identifiable*)	
Intensity (*pleasant, complex, powerful, overpowering*)	Points: _____
FLAVORS AND PALATE IMPRESSIONS (0–15 POINTS)	
Sweetness (*bone dry, dry, medium-dry, medium-sweet, very sweet*)	
Acidity (*flat, refreshing, marked, tart*)	
Body (*very light and thin, light, medium, full-bodied, heavy*)	
Tannin—(*Red wines only*) (*astringent, hard, dry, soft*)	
Tactile impression (*slight sparkle, watery, normal, heavy, oily*)	
Flavor (*stingy, medium, generous, exaggerated*)	
Taste Sensations (*fruits, oak, vanilla, spices, herbs, etc*)	
Alcohol (*low, medium, ideal, high*)	
Finish (*Length*) (*short, medium, long, very long*)	
Balance (*unbalanced, well balanced, very well balanced*)	Points: _____
OVERALL IMPRESSION (0–15 POINTS)	
Coarse, poor, acceptable, fine, outstanding	Points: _____
To arrive at a final score, add up the points in each of the boxes and add 50.	Score: _____

purpose of this is to eliminate the possibility of "guessing" at what wines have been set in front of the taster. The wines are then poured in groups of six to eight, each glass being given the same number as is placed on the bottle. Those "flights" are then set on the table. The taster tastes the first flight, makes notes and assigns scores, and then shifts those glasses to the back of the table so that another flight can be set, and this continues until the tasting has been completed. Leaving the glasses on the tables allows the taster to return to the various wines for a retasting to see how the wine has opened over time.

The room in which I do my tasting is well lit and as odor-free as possible; the only things on the table are my notepad, sugar-free and salt-free bread, mineral water, a large sheet of blank white paper, and a bucket for spitting. By the end of the tasting, my notepad contains all of my impressions of the wines and the scores I have awarded them, and only then do I compare the glasses to the bottles, inserting the names of the wines I have tasted.

Many critics instruct their assistants to "double-up" occasional wines—that is to say, to serve the same wine at least twice during a tasting, in glasses with different numbers. This is an excellent check on the taster's judgment, for if during the course of the tasting the same score or a score of plus or minus one point is awarded, it shows that one was truly focused on the task at hand. On the other hand, scores of the same wine that differ by two or more points indicate that either the taster's palate or sense of concentration was not well enough honed that morning. In such cases, most critics will simply discard all of the tasting notes from that session and return to those wines on a future occasion.

Several Words about Scores

A great many people walk into wine stores and order this or that wine entirely on the basis of its high score. This is a mistake. A score is nothing more than a critic's attempt to sum up in digits the overall quality of a wine. Scores can provide a valid tool, especially when awarded by experienced critics, but they should not be separated from the tasting notes that precede them; for although a score may be a convenient summary, it says nothing about the style, personality or other important traits of the wine in question and therefore cannot give the consumer a valid basis for choice.

There are, however, three major advantages to scores. First of all, scores can serve as initial guides for the overall impression of the wine in question. Second, scores also give an immediate basis for comparison of that wine to others in its category and to the same wine of the same winery from earlier years. Finally, such scores give valuable hints as to whether the wine in question is available at a reasonable value for one's money.

The scores awarded in this book should be taken as merely one part of the overall evaluation of the wine, the most important parts of which are the tasting notes that give details about the body, color, aromas, flavors, length and overall style of the wine. It is also important to keep in mind that scores are not absolute. The score earned by a light and hyper-fruity wine made from Gamay grapes, a wine meant to be consumed in its youth, cannot be compared to that given to a deep, full-bodied wine made from a blend of Cabernet Sauvignon, Merlot and Cabernet Franc, the peak of drinking for which may come only five, ten or even thirty years later on. Numerical comparisons between the wines of the great Chateaux of Bordeaux and those meant to be consumed within weeks or months of the harvest is akin to comparing, by means of a single number, the qualities of a 1998 Rolls Royce and a 1965 Volkswagen Beetle.

Even if there was a perfect system for rating wines (and I do not believe such a system exists), no two critics, no matter how professional or well intentioned they may be, can be expected to use precisely the same criteria for every facet of every wine they evaluate. Even when similar scoring systems are used by different critics, readers should expect to find a certain variation between them. The trick is not in finding the critics with whom you always agree, but those whose tasting notes and scores give you direction in finding the wines that you most enjoy.

My own scoring system is based on a maximum of 100 points interpreted as follows:

95–100   Truly great wines
90–94   Exceptional in every way

86–89	Very good to excellent and highly recommended
81–85	Recommended but without enthusiasm
70–79	Average but at least somewhat faulted
Under 70	Not recommended

Glossary of Wine Terminology

ACIDITY: An important component of wine. A modicum of acidity adds liveliness to wine, too little makes it flat and dull, and too much imparts a sour taste. The acids most often present in wines are tartaric, malic and lactic acids.

AFTERTASTE: The flavors and aromas left in the mouth after the wine has been swallowed.

ALCOHOL CONTENT: Percent by volume of alcohol in a wine. Table wines have usually between 11.5–13.5% in alcohol content but there is an increasing demand for wines as high as 15–16%.

ALCOHOLIC: A negative term, referring to wines that have too much alcohol and are thus hot and out of balance.

AROMA: Technically this term applies to the smells that come directly from the grapes, whereas bouquet applies to the smells that come from the winemaking process. In practice the two terms are used interchangeably.

ATTACK: The first sensations imparted by a wine.

AUSTERE: A wine that lacks fruits or is overly tannic or acidic.

BALANCED: The term used to describe a wine in which the acids, alcohol, fruits, tannins and influence of the wood in which the wine was aged are in harmony.

BARNYARD: Aromas and flavors that call to mind the barnyard, and when present in excess impart dirty sensations, but when in moderation can be pleasant.

BARREL: The wood containers used to ferment and hold wine. The wood used in such barrels is most often French or American oak but other woods can be used as well.

BARREL AGING: The process in which wines mature in barrels after fermentation.

BARRIQUE: French for "barrel" but specifically referring to oak barrels of 225 liter capacity in which many wines are fermented and/or aged.

BLANC DE BLANCS: White wines made entirely from white grapes.

BLEND: A wine made from more than one grape variety or from grapes from different vintages. Some of the best wines in the world, including most of the Bordeaux wines, are blends of different grapes selected to complement each other.

BLUSH WINE: A wine that has a pale pink color imparted by very short contact with the skins of red grapes.

BODY: The impression of weight or fullness on the palate. Results from a combination of fruits and alcohol. Wines range from light to full-bodied.

BOTTLE AGING: The process of allowing wine to mature in its bottle.

BOTRYTIS CINEREA: Sometimes known as "noble rot", this is one of the few fungi that is welcomed by winemakers, for as it attacks the grapes it shrivels them, drains the water and concentrates the sugar, thus allowing for the making of many of the world's greatest sweet wines.

BOUQUET: Technically, the aromas that result from the winemaking process, but the term is used interchangeably with aroma.

BRUT: Bone dry. A term used almost exclusively to describe sparkling wines.

BUTTERY: A positive term for rich white wines, especially those that have undergone malolactic fermentation.

CARBONIC MACERATION: Method of fermenting red wine without crushing the grapes first. Whole clusters of grapes are put in a closed vat together with carbon dioxide, and the fermentation takes place within the grape berries, which then burst.

CARAMELIZED: A wine that has taken on a brown color, and sweet and sour aromas and flavors, often due to exposure to oxygen as the wine ages.

CLONE: A vine derived by vegetative propagation from cuttings, or buds from a single vine called the mother vine.

CLOYING: A wine that has sticky, heavy or unclean aromas or flavors.

COARSE: A wine that is rough or overly alcoholic. Appropriate in some country-style wines but not in fine wines.

CORKED: A wine that has been tainted by TCA (2,4,6 Tricholoraniole), increasingly caused by faulty corks. TCA imparts aromas of damp, moldy and decomposing cardboard to a wine. Sometimes only barely detectable, at other times making a wine unapproachable.

COUNTRY-STYLE: A simple wine that is somewhat coarse but not necessarily unpleasant.

CREAMY: A soft, silky texture.

CRISP: A clean wine with good acidity.

DENSE: Full in flavor and body.

DESSERT WINE: A sweet wine. Often served as an accompaniment to goose-liver dishes at the start of a meal.

DIRTY: A wine typified by off aromas or flavors resulting from either poor vinification practices or a faulty bottling process.

DRINKING WINDOW: The predicted period during which a wine will be at its best.

EARTHY: Sensations of freshly turned soil, minerals, damp leaves and mushrooms.

ELEGANT: A wine showing finesse or style.

EVERYDAY WINES: Inexpensive, readily available and easy to drink wines, lacking sophistication but at their best pleasant accompaniments to food.

FERMENTATION: A process by which yeast reacts with sugar in the must, resulting in the creation of alcohol.

FILTRATION. Usually done just prior to bottling, the process of filtering of the wine in order to remove large particles of sediment and other impurities. Over-filtration tends to rob wines of their aromas and flavors.

FINISH: The aromas and flavors that linger on the palate after the wine has been swallowed.

FIRMNESS: The grip of a wine, determined by its tannins and acidity.

FLABBY: The opposite of crisp, often a trait of wines that lack acidity and are thus dull and weak.

FLAT: Synonymous to flabby.

FORTIFIED WINE: A wine whose alcoholic strength has been intensified by the addition of spirits.

FRIZZANTE: Lightly sparkling.

GRASSY: A term often used to describe white wines made from Sauvignon Blanc and Gewurztraminer grapes.

GREEN: In the positive sense, wines that are tart and youthful but have the potential to develop. In the negative sense, a wine that is unripe and sour.

HARSH: Always a negative term, even more derogatory than "coarse".

HERBACEOUS: Implies aromas and flavors of grass, hay, herbs, leather and tobacco.

HOT: The unpleasant, sometimes burning sensation left on the palate by an overly alcoholic wine.

ICE WINE: A dessert wine made by a special method in which the grapes are left on the vine until frozen and then pressed while still frozen. Only the water in the grape freezes and this can be removed, leaving the must concentrated and very sweet. In warm weather areas the freezing process may be done in the winery.

INTERNATIONALIZED WINES: Reds or whites that are blended to please any palate. At their best such wines are pleasant, at their worst simply boring.

LATE HARVEST: In such a harvest grapes are left on the vines until very late in the harvest season, the purpose being to obtain sweeter grapes that will be used to make dessert wines.

LEES: Sediments that accumulate in the bottom of the barrel or vat as a wine ferments.

LENGTH: The period of time in which the flavors and aromas of a wine linger after it has been swallowed.

LIGHT: Low in alcohol or body. Also used to describe a wine low in flavor.

LIVELY: Clean and refreshing.

LONG: A wine that offers aromas and flavors that linger for a long time after it has been swallowed.

LONGEVITY: The aging potential of a wine, dependent on balance and structure.

MALOLACTIC FERMENTATION: A second fermentation that can occur naturally or be induced, the purpose of which is to convert harsh malic acid to softer lactic acid.

MATURE: A wine that has reached its peak after developing in the bottle.

MELLOW: A wine that is at or very close to its peak.

METHODE CHAMPENOISE: The classic method for making Champagne by inducing a second fermentation in the bottle.

MID-PALATE: Those aroma and taste sensations felt after the first attack.

MOUSSE: The foam and bubbles of sparkling wines. A good mousse will show long-lasting foam and sharp, small, concentrated bubbles.

MOUTH FILLING: A wine that fills the mouth with satisfying flavors.

MUST: The pre-fermentation mixture of grape juice, stem fragments, skins, seeds and pulp, that results from the grape crushing process.

NOUVEAU: Term that originated in Beaujolais to describe very young, fruity and light red wines, often made from Gamay grapes and by the method of carbonic maceration. Such wines are always meant to be consumed very young.

NOSE: Synonymous with bouquet.

OAK: The wood most often used to make the barrels in which wines are fermented or aged. The impact of such barrels is reflected in the level of tannins and in its contribution to flavors of smoke, spices and vanilla to the wines

OAKED: A wine that has been fermented and/or aged in oak barrels.

OXIDIZED: A wine that has gone off because it has been exposed to oxygen or to high temperatures.

PEAK: The optimal point of maturity of a given wine.

PERSONALITY: The overall impression made by an individual wine.

RESIDUAL SUGAR: The sugar that remains in a wine after fermentation has been completed.

RIPASSO: A second fermentation that is induced on the lees of a wine made earlier.

ROUND: A wine that has become smooth as its tannins, acids and wood have integrated.

RUSTIC: Synonymous with country-style.

SHARP: Overly acidic.

SHORT: A wine whose aromas and flavors fail to linger or to make an impression after the wine has been swallowed.

SMOKY: A flavor imparted to a wine from oak casks, most often found in unfiltered wines.

SMOOTH: A wine that sits comfortably on the palate.

STEWED: The sensation of cooked, overripe or soggy fruit.

STINGY: A wine that holds back on its aromas or flavors.

SULFITES: Usually sulfur dioxide that is added to wine to prevent oxidation.

SUR LIE: French for "on the lees". A term used to describe the process in which a wine is left in contact with its lees during fermentation and barrel aging.

TANNINS: Phenolic substances that exist naturally in wines and extracted from the skins, pips and stalks of the grapes, as well as from development in new oak barrels. Tannins are vital for the longevity of red wines. In young wines, tannins can sometimes be harsh, but if the wine is well balanced they will blend with other substances in the wine over time, making the wine smoother and more approachable as it ages.

TANNIC: A wine still marked by firm tannins. In their youth, many red wines tend to be tannic and need time for the tannins to integrate.

TCA: 2,4,6-Tricholoraniole. See "corked".

TERROIR: The reflection of a vineyard's soil, altitude, microclimate, prevailing winds, and other natural factors that impact on the quality of the grapes, and consequently on the wines produced from them.

THIN: Lacking in body or fruit.

TOASTING: Searing the inside of barrels with an open flame when making the barrels. Heavy toasting can impart caramel-like flavors to a wine; medium toasting and light toasting can add vanilla, spices or smokiness to the wine, all positive attributes when present in moderation.

VANILLA: Aroma and flavor imparted to wines from the oak barrels in which they age.

VARIETAL WINE: A wine that contains at least 85% of the grape named on the label.

VARIETAL TRAITS: The specific colors, aromas and flavors traditionally imparted by a specific grape variety.

VEGETAL: An often positive term used for a bouquet of rounded wines, in particular those made from Pinot Noir and Chardonnay grapes whose aromas and flavors call to mind vegetables rather than fruits.

VINTAGE: (a) Synonymous with harvest; (b) A wine made from grapes of a single harvest. In accordance with EU standards, a vintage wine must contain at least 85% grapes from the noted year.

WATERY: A wine so thin that it feels diluted.

WOOD: Refers either to the wood barrels in which the wine ages or to a specific aroma and flavor imparted by the barrels.

YEAST: A kind of fungus, vital to the process of fermentation.

Contacting the Wineries

Agur Winery
Moshav Agur 99840
Tel: 054 7599672 Fax: 02 9910483
yashuv@netvision.net.il

Alexander Winery
Meshek 112, Moshav Beit Yitzhak 42970
Tel: 09 8822956 Fax: 09 8872076
a_wine@netvision.net.il

Aligote Winery
Moshav Gan Yoshiya 38850
Tel/Fax: 04 6258492
aligote@aviv-flowers.co.il

Alon Wineries
Moshav Alonei Aba 36005
Tel 04 9535251 Fax: 04 9800727
alonwine@netvision.net.il

Amiad Winery
Kibbutz Amiad 12335
Tel: 04 6909850

Amphorae Vineyard
POB 12672 Herzliya 46733
Tel 04 9840702
gil@amphorae-v.com
www.amphorae-v.com

Amram's Winery
Moshav Ramot Naftali 13830
Tel/Fax: 04 6960039
amramswine@hotmail.co.il

The wineries' addresses, numbers etc were correct at time of going to press; we can take no responsibility for changes in contact details after that point.

Anatot Winery
POB 3390 Givat Ze'ev 90917
Tel/Fax: 02 5362565
info@anatotwinery.co.il
www.anatotwinery.co.il

Avidan Winery
253 Weizmann Street, Ra'anana 43721
Tel: 09 7719382 Fax: 09 771 2679
avidanwine@walla.com

Bar Winery
22 Ha'avoda Street, Binyamina 30500
Tel: 04 6388545
alanbar@zahav.net.il

Barkai Vineyards
Moshav Roglit 99865
Tel/Fax: 02 9993281
ettai@walla.co.il

Barkan Wine Cellars
POB 146 Kibbutz Hulda 76842
Tel: 08 9355858 Fax: 08 9355859
Martha-export@barkan-winery.co.il
www.barkan-winery.co.il/daf1.html

Bazelet Hagolan Winery
Moshav Kidmat Tsvi, POB 64, Katzrin 12900
Tel: 04 6827223 Fax: 04 6820084
shuly@feldman.co.il
www.bazelet-hagolan.co.il

Beit-El Winery
Beit-El 90628
Tel/Fax: 02 9971158
hmanne@netvision.net.il

Benhaim Winery
34 Sderot Ben-Zvi, Ramat-Gan 52247
Tel: 03 6762656
benhaim@benhaim.co.il
www.benhaim.co.il

Ben Hannah Winery
POB 115 Shilat 73188
Tel: 050 6434253
benhanna-winery@softhome.net

Binyamina Wine Cellars
POB 34, Binyamina 30550
Tel: 04 6388643 Fax: 04 6389021
info@binyaminawines.co.il
www.binyaminawines.com

Birya Winery
Birya, 13805
Tel: 050 6405221 Fax: 04 6923815
drporat@zehav.net.il

Bustan Winery
POB 55 Moshav Sharei Tikva, 44860
Tel: 052 3942700
bustanwinery@yahoo.com

Bustan Hameshusheem Winery
Moshav Had Ness 12950
Tel: 052 4358407

Carmel Winery
Rishon Letzion, Zichron Ya'akov
Tel: Rishon Letzion 03 9488888
Tel: Zichron Ya'akov 04 6390105
www.carmelwines.co.il

Domaine du Castel
Moshav Ramat Raziel 90974
Tel: 02 5342249 Fax: 02 5700995
castel@castel.co.il
www.castel.co.il

The Cave
c/o Binyamina Winery, POB 34, Binyamina 30550
Tel: 04 6388643 Fax: 04 6389021
thecave@zahav.net.il

Chateau Golan
Moshav Eliad 12927
Tel: 04 6600026 Fax: 04 6600274
shatoltd@netvision.net.il
www.chateaugolan.com

Chillag Wine
39 Leonardo da Vinci Street, Tel Aviv 64955
Tel: 054 4562057 Fax: 03 69121903
chillag@netvision.net.il

Clos de Gat
Kibbutz Har'el 99740
Tel: 02 9993505 Fax; 02 9993350
harelca@netvision.net.il
www.closdegat.com/intro.html

Dahlia Winery
Kibbutz Dahlia 19239
Tel: 04 9897325
rozanna_b@dalia.org.il

Dalton Winery
Dalton Industrial Park, Merom Hagalil 13815
Tel: 04 6987683 Fax: 04 6987684
info@dalton-winery.com
www.dalton-winery.com

Deux Paysans Winery
Moshav Kochav Ya'ir 98123
Tel: 09–7495141
levenbah@netvision.net.il

Dicos Winery
Meshek 37, Moshav Ginaton 73110
Tel: 08–9243135

Efrat Wine Cellars
1 Steinberg Street, Motza, Jerusalem 90822
Tel: 02 5346022 Fax: 02 5340760
office@efratwine.co.il
www.efratwine.co.il

Ella Valley Vineyards
Kibbutz Netiv Halamed Hey 99855
Tel: 02 9994885 Fax: 02 9994876
ella@ellavalley.com

Essence Winery
Ma'aleh Tsvi'a 20129
Tel: 04 6619058 Fax 04 6619054
essencewines@zvia.org.il

Flam Winery
9 Avshalom Street, Rishon Le Zion 75285
Tel: 08 9247420 Fax: 08 9283838
golanfla@netvision.net.il

Gadot Winery
Kibbutz Gadot 12325
Tel: 050 5278733
shalman@gadot.org.il

Galai Winery
Moshav Nir Akiva 85365
Tel: 08 9933713 Fax: 08 9931287
galai-winery@bezeqint.net

Galil Mountain Winery
Kibbutz Yiron 13855
Tel: 04 6868740 Fax: 04 6868506
winery@galilmountain.co.il
ww.galilmountain.co.il

Gat Shomron Winery
Karnei Shomron 44855
Tel: 050 7264855
na_lior@walla.co.il

Gefen Adderet Winery
4 Elazar Street, POB 4125, Gan Yavne 70800
Tel: 08 8570354 Fax: 08 8673708
winery@yossef.com
www.winery.yossef.com

Gesher Damia Winery
2 Hatavor Street, Pardess Hannah-Karkur 37011
Tel/Fax: 04 6388451
damiya@walla.co.il

Ginaton Winery
Meshek 19, Moshav Ginaton 73110
Tel: 052 3932403
tdouk@zahav.net

Givon Winery
POB 140, Givon Hachadasha 90901
Tel: 02 5362966
segal@telrancom.com

Golan Heights Winery
POB 183, Industrial Zone, Katzrin 12900
Tel: 04 6968420 Fax: 04 6962220
ghwinery@golanwines.co.il
www.golanwines.co.il

Goshen Winery
Tel: 1 800 232200

Greenberg Winery
51 Hameginim Street, Herzliya 46686
Tel: 052 3237689
elegant@netvision.net.il

Gush Etzion Winery
POB 1415, Efrat 90435
Tel: 02 9934592
winery@actcom.co.il

Gustavo & Jo Winery
19 Marvah Street, Kfar Vradim
Tel: 04 9972190
boia@netvision.net.il

Hakerem Winery
Qiryat Arba 90100
Tel: 02 9961120

Hamasrek Winery
Moshav Beit Meir 90865
Tel: 02 5701759 Fax: 02 5336592
hamasrek@netvision.net.il
www.hamasrek.com

Hans Sternbach Winery
Meshek 83, Moshav Givat Yeshayahu 99825
Tel: 02 9990162 Fax: 02 9911703
sk-Gadi@zahav.net.il

Har-Noy Winery
Moshav Karmei Yosef 99797
Tel: 08 9287615
fharnoy@hotmail.com

Hatabor Winery
POB 22, Kfar Tavor 15241
Tel: 04 6767889
ssiecodo@zahav.net.il

Hevron Heights Winery
Moshav Geulim 42820
Tel: 09 8943711 Fax: 09 8943006
mm@churchill.fr

Israel Wine Institute
4 Haraz Street, Rehovot 76120
Tel: 08 9475693 Fax: 08 9469017

Kadesh Barnea Winery
Meshek 43, Moshav Kadesh Barnea 85513
052 2672552
practice@netvision.net.il

Kadita Winery
Bikta Bekadita
POB 1052, Safed
Tel: 050 6933219
winery@kadita.co.il
www.kadita.co.il/winery/intro.html

Karmei Yosef Winery
Karmei Yosef 99797
Tel: 08 9286098
hadar_z@bravdo.co.il
www.bravdo.com

Katlav Winery
Meshek 8, Moshav Nes Harim 99885
Tel/Fax: 02 5701404
yosss@bezeqint.net

Kella David Winery
Moshav Givat Yeshayahu 99825
Tel: 02 9994848 Fax: 02 9992734

La Terra Promessa Winery
Meshek 44, Moshav Shachar 79335
Tel: 08 6849093 Fax: 08 6848878
laterrapromessa@bezeqint.net

Lachish Winery
Moshav Lachish 79360
Tel: 054 7920151
galiam@bezeqint.net

Domaine de Latroun
Latroun Monastery 99762
Tel: 08 9255180

Maccabim Winery
Maccabim-Re'ut 71908
Tel: 050 8503362
info@maccabimwinery.com

Maor Winery
Moshav Ramot, Ramat Hagolan 12948
Tel: 052 8515079
danny@maorwinery.com
www.maorwinery.com

Margalit Winery
POB 4055 Caesaria 38900
Tel: 050 5334433 Fax 04 6262058
a_m_n_l@netvision.net.il
www.margalit-winery.com

Meishar Winery
41 Meishar 76850
Tel: 08 8594759
zosh_s@netvision.net.il
www.meishar.co.il

Meister Winery
33 Schoonat Hashalom, Rosh Pina 12000
Tel: 054 4976940
meister@bezeqint.net
www.ruth-meister.co.il

Miles Winery
Moshav Kerem Ben Zimra 13815
Tel: 04 6980623
mils014@013.net.il

Mony Winery
Dir Rafat Monastery, POB 275, Beit Shemesh 99000
Tel: 02 9916629 Fax: 02 9910366
monywines@walla.co.il
www.ymp.co.il/moni/

Nachal Amud
Meshek 17, Moshav Kfar Shamai 20125
Tel: 04 6989825

Nachshon Winery
Kibbutz Nachson 99760
Tel: 08 9278641 Fax: 08 9278607
mata_n@nachshon.co.il
http://winery.nachshon.org.il/~ido/iski/Iski_yekev.htm

Nashashibi Winery
Kfar A'ablin 30012
Tel: 054 6387191

Natuf Winery
Meshek 45, Kfar Truman 73150
Tel: 052 2608199
natuf@012.net.il

Neot Smadar Winery
Kibbutz Neot Smadar 88860
Tel: 08 6358111

Odem Mountain Winery
Moshav Odem 12473
Tel: 050 55220248 Fax: 04 6817551
megolan@012.net.il

Pelter Winery
Moshav Tsofit 44925
Tel: 052 8666384

Ra'anan Winery
Moshav Ganei Yochanan 76922
Tel: 08 9350668
orsss@zahav.net.il

Ramim Winery
Meshek 64, Moshav Shachar 79335
Tel: 054 4608080 Fax: 08 6849122
enrad@multinet.net.il

Recanati Winery
POB 12050, Industrial Zone, Emek Hefer
Tel: 04 6222288 Fax: 04 6222882
info@recanati-winery.com
www.recanati-winery.com

Red Poetry
Havat Tal, Karmei Yosef 99797
Tel: 08 9210352
talfarm@bezeqint.net

Rosh Pina Winery
Rosh Pina 12000
Tel: 050 5271073

Rota Winery
Havat Rota, DN Halutza 85515
Tel: 054 4968703 Fax: 02 9910714

Rozenbaum Winery
Kibbutz Malkiya 13845
Tel/Fax: 04 6943388

Ruth Winery
Kfar Ruth 73196
Tel: 050 6980098
maortal@012.net.il

Salomon Winery
Moshav Amikam 37830
Tel: 04 6380475

Saslove Winery
POB 10581 Tel Aviv 69085
Tel: 09 7492697 Fax: 03 6492712
winery@saslove.com
www.saslove.com

Sassy Winery
24 Sderot Ha'atzmaut, Bat Yam 59378
Tel: 052 2552012

Sataf Winery
Moshav Aminadav 90885
Tel: 050 6223182
yosik@molsa.gov.il

Savion Winery
Mevaseret Zion 90805
Tel: 02 5336162

Sde Boker Winery
Kibbutz Sde Boker 84993
Tel: 050 7579212 Fax 08 6560118
winery@sde-boker.org.il

Sea Horse Winery
Moshav Bar Giora 99880
Tel: 050 7283216 Fax: 02 5709834
info@seahorsewines.com
www.seahorsewines.com

Segal Wines
Kibbutz Hulda 76842
Tel: 08 9358860 Fax: 08 9241222
segal@segalwines.co.il

Smadar Winery
31 Hameyasdim Street, Zichron-Ya'akov 30900
Tel: 04 6390777

Sode Hayain Winery
Moshav Tirat Yehuda 73175
Tel: 03 9712048
reuven_co@bezeqint.net
www.wine4u.co.il

Soreq Winery
Moshav Tal Shachar 78805
Tel: 08 9340542 Fax: 08 9348916
soreq_w@zahav.net.il

Srigim Winery
POB 174 Moshav Srigim 99835
Tel: 050 6991398 Fax: 02 9991512
motim@mahkteshim.co.il

Tabor Winery
POB 422, Kfar Tavor 15241
Tel 04 6760444, Fax 04 6772061
twc@twc.co.il
www.taborwinery.co.il

Tanya Winery
Ofra 90627
Tel: 054 4354034
Yoram5733@walla.co.il

Tekoa Winery
Tekoa 90908
Tel: 02 9964903

Tishbi Estate Winery
33 Hameyasdim Street, Zichron Ya'akov 30900
Tel: 04 6380435 Fax 04: 6280223
Tisbhi_g@netvision.net.il
www.preker.co.il/israelwines/tishbi/index2.html

Tulip Winery
24 Hacarmel Street, Kiryat Tivon 36081
Tel/Fax: 04 9830573
tulip@tulip-winery.co.il

Tzora Vineyards
Kibbutz Tzora 99803
Tel: 02 9908261 Fax: 02 9915479
info@tzorawines.com
www.tzorawines.com

Vitkin Winery
POB 267 Kfar Vitkin 40200
Tel: 09 8663505 Fax: 03 7256258
vtrknwine@netvision.net.il

Yaffo Winery
15 Rozov Street, Tel Aviv 69716
Tel: 03 6474834
yaffowine@zahav.net.il
www.yaffowinery.com

Yatir Winery
POB 5210, Arad
Tel: 08 9959090 Fax: 08 9959050
y_yatir@zahav.net.il
www.yatir.net

Ye'arim Winery
Moshav Givat Ye'arim 90970
Tel: 052 5791080
sassons_wine@hotmail.co.il

Yehuda Winery
Neve Ilan 90850
Tel: 02 5348175 Fax: 02 5348100
yekev_yehuda98@hotmail.co.il

Yiftah'el Winery
Alon Hagalil 17920
Tel: 04 9861466
hadassr@bezeqint.net

Yuval Ben-Shoshan Winery
Kibbutz Bror-Hail 79152
Tel: 08 6803321 Fax: 08 6803667
niva_yuval@walla.com

Zauberman Winery
50 Piness Street, Gedera 70700
Tel: 08 8594680
www.zaubermanwines.com

Zemora Winery
POB 451 Mevaseret Tzion 90805
Tel: 052 2636850 Fax: 02 5346166
zvika@agam-ins.com

Index

Agur 31
Alexander 33
Aligote 38
Alon 40
Amiad 42
Amphorae 43
Amram's 48
Anatot 49
Avidan 51

Bar 53
Barkai 54
Barkan 55
Bazelet Hagolan 65
Beit-El 68
Ben-Hannah 73
Benhaim 69
Binyamina 75
Birya 83
Bravdo *see* Karmei Yosef
Bustan 84
Bustan Hameshusheem 87

Carmel 88
Castel 102
Chateau Golan 109
Chillag 114
Clos de Gat 117

Dahlia 119
Dalton 120
Deux Paysans 128
Dico's 130
Domaine de Latroun *see* Latroun

Domaine du Castel *see* Castel

Efrat 131
Ella Valley 137
Essence 141

Flam 142

Gadot 147
Galai 148
Galil Mountain 150
Gamla *see* Golan Heights Winery
Gat Shomron 155
Gefen Adderet 156
Gesher Damia 157
Ginaton 158
Givon 160
Golan *see* Golan Heights Winery
Golan Heights Winery 161
Goshen 185
Greenberg 186
Gush Etzion 187
Gustavo & Jo 189

Hakerem 191
Hamasrek 192
Hans Sternbach 194
Har'el *see* Clos de Gat
Har-Noy 196
Har Odem *see* Odem Mountain
Hatabor 197
Hevron Heights 198

Israel Wine Institute 201

Kadesh Barnea 203
Kadita 205
Karmei Yosef 207
Katlav 209
Katzrin *see* Golan Heights
    Winery
Kella David 210
Kfira 211

Lachish 216
La Terra Promessa 213
Latroun 217
Lavie 219

Maccabim 220
Maor 221
Margalit 222
Meishar 229
Meister 232
Meron 233
Miles 235
Mony 237

Nachal Amud 239
Nachshon 240
Nashashibi 245
Natuf 246
Neot Smadar 247
Noach *see* Hevron Heights

Odem Mountain 249
Orna Chillag *see* Chillag

Pelter 252

Ra'anan 253
Ramim 255
Recanati 260
Red Poetry 266
Rosh Pina 267

Rota 268
Rozenbaum 269
Ruth 271

Salomon 272
Saslove 273
Sasson's *see* Ye'arim
Sassy 279
Sataf 280
Savion 281
Sde Boker 282
Sea Horse 284
Segal 288
Smadar 295
Sode Hayain 296
Soreq 297
Srigim 300

Tabor 301
Tanya 306
Tekoa 307
Terra Promessa *see* La
    Terra Promessa
The Cave 108
Tishbi 308
Tulip 319
Tzora 322

Vitkin 328

Yaffo 331
Yarden *see* Golan Heights
    Winery
Yatir 333
Ye'arim 336
Yehuda 337
Yiftah'el 339
Yuval Ben-Shoshan 340

Zauberman 342
Zemora 344

About the Author

Daniel Rogov is Israel's most influential and preeminent wine critic. He writes weekly wine and restaurant columns in the respected newspaper *Haaretz*, and contributes regularly to two prestigious international wine books—Hugh Johnson's *Pocket Wine Book* and Tom Stevenson's *Wine Report*.

The fonts used in the book are from the Chaparral family